D0036858

THE CREATION HYPOTHESIS

Scientific Evidence for an Intelligent Designer

J. P. Moreland, editor

FOREWORD BY
PHILLIP E. JOHNSON

INTERVARSITY PRESS
DOWNERS GROVE, ILLINOIS 60515

InterVarsity Press® is the book-publishing division of InterVarsity Christian Fellowship®, a student movement active on campus at hundreds of universities, colleges and schools of nursing in the United States of America, and a member movement of the International Fellowship of Evangelical Students. For information about local and regional activities, write Public Relations Dept., InterVarsity Christian Fellowship, 6400 Schroeder Rd., P.O. Box 7895, Madison, WI 53707-7895.

All Scripture quotations, unless otherwise indicated, are taken from the HOLY BIBLE, NEW INTERNATIONAL VERSION®. NIV®. Copyright © 1973, 1978, 1984 by International Bible Society. Used by permission of Zondervan Publishing House. All rights reserved.

Portions of chapter 4 have been adapted from Hugh Ross's books The Fingerprint of God, second edition (Promise Publishing, 1991), and The Creator and the Cosmos (NavPress, 1993).

Figure 5.3 is from Irving Geis and R. E. Dickerson, The Structure and Action of Proteins (Benjamin, 1969). Permission has been requested from the author.

Stephen C. Meyer, "The Methodological Equivalence of Design & Descent," and William A. Dembski, "On the Very Possibility of Intelligent Design," ©1994 by the Pascal Centre, Ancaster, Ontario, Canada. Used by permission. The Pascal Centre, established in 1988 by Redeemer College, specializes in studies of the relationship between faith and science from a biblical perspective. The opinions expressed in The Creation Hypothesis are strictly those of the authors and do not necessarily represent the Pascal Centre or Redeemer College.

Cover photographs: background, Tony Stone Images; inset, ©1994 Micheal Simpson/FPG International Corp.

ISBN 0-8308-1698-4

Printed in the United States of America ∞

Library of Congress Cataloging-in-Publication Data

The Creation hypothesis: scientific evidence for an intelligent
   designer/edited by J. P. Moreland; foreword by Phillip E. Johnson.
        p.   cm.
   Includes bibliographical references.
   ISBN 0-8308-1698-4
   1. Creationism.   2. God—Proof, Cosmological.   3. Naturalism.
   4. Religion and science.   I. Moreland, James Porter, 1948-
   BS651.C6926   1993
   231.7'65—dc20   93-42724
                                                          CIP

17	16	15	14	13	12	11	10	9	8	7	6	5	4
08	07	06	05	04	03	02	01	00	99	98	97	96	

Foreword

There is no more interesting intellectual subject than what this book calls "the creation hypothesis." Are we *created* beings who exist because a supernatural intelligence brought about our existence for a purpose? Or are we accidental products of some purposeless material mechanism that cares nothing about us or what we do?

It is practically impossible to discuss this important question in any of our great secular universities, let alone in the public high schools. The reason is that modernist culture is ruled by a philosophy called *scientific naturalism*, which insists that the entire history of the cosmos belongs to the subject matter of natural science. Science, by the same philosophy, is inherently committed to *naturalism*. Naturalism is the doctrine that the cosmos has always been a closed system of material causes and effects that can never be influenced by anything from "outside"—like God. It follows from such philosophical premises that "God" is an aspect of human subjectivity or a fantasy. Evolution in naturalistic philosophy is a "fact" that is real for everyone, whereas God is merely an entity in the minds of those who believe.

Naturalism rules the secular academic world absolutely, which is bad enough. What is far worse is that it rules much of the Christian world as well. As Stephen Meyer's essay in this volume points out, it is common for philosophers even at conservative Christian institutions to accept the rules of scientific naturalism, and to accept them for no better reason than that the secular world wills it to be so. It is no wonder that the best students from these institutions so often emerge with a naturalistic outlook; that is how they have been taught to think.

The domination of naturalistic philosophy in our intellectual institutions has had disastrous consequences for Christian faith. It has also led science itself astray. Some of the best examples of how naturalism makes bad science are in the essay "Information and the Origin of Life" by Walter L. Bradley and Charles Thaxton. Scientific naturalists have had to pretend that the "mystery of life's origins" is well on the way to a solution, and to further that illusion they have deceived themselves and filled their textbooks with misleading information. In the stereotyped view of the evolution-creation controversy it is the believers in creation who are supposed to pit "faith" against "reason." Yet anyone who reads Bradley and Thaxton with an open mind can see that it is the chemical evolutionists who are blinded by their faith in naturalistic solutions and who cannot see the meaning of the fact that is staring them in the face.

The creation hypothesis is a metaphysical starting point for inquiry, not a detailed doctrinal position that limits the possibilities that may be considered. A creationist is simply a person who believes that God creates, or is at least willing to consider that as a possibility. Whether God took a short or a long time to create and to what extent he employed secondary causes as a mechanism are subjects on which lively debates among creationists should be expected. Disagreements are particularly to be expected because we all have to work with data that have been provided by metaphysical naturalists, and we have to decide how to remove the layers of naturalistic interpretation to uncover the facts that could have been interpreted differently.

So read the essays in this volume not with the expectation that you will find the finished truth, but with the hope that you will find the beginnings of a great project to discover the truth, a project that I think will command the attention of the best thinkers of the twenty-first century. The time when scientific naturalism could not be challenged is already finished. The challenge has begun, and it will grow more powerful every year. This volume is an important contribution toward that search for truth.

Phillip E. Johnson

Preface

We wish to give special thanks to John Ankerberg and John Weldon for their role in the production of this book. It was a series of programs on *The John Ankerberg Show,* as well as their interest in the topic, that prompted the book's writing.

There are eleven contributors to this work, and we are all in agreement with the vast majority of what is contained in the following pages. Nevertheless, each person is solely responsible for the material bearing his name, though we are grateful to each other for input and advice at various stages in the development of the book.

We hope the present work will be a source of stimulation to others to see that the issues we discuss are far from being settled in favor of macroevolutionary theory or, more generally, metaphysical or methodological naturalism. You should bear in mind that in a volume like this one, where an attempt is made to survey a number of related fields, it is impossible to cover everything thoroughly. Thus there are occasions when we can only suggest that a Designer-hypothesis is consistent with certain data or a better explanation of those data than evolutionary naturalism is. On other occasions space allows us to develop these points in some detail. Such are the limitations of a single work of this type, but we trust that this work is substantial enough to be taken seriously even when some of the ideas we advance are not very popular.

INTRODUCTION

J. P. Moreland

Ideas matter. In fact, what we believe and the way we see things largely determine the type of people we will become and the behavior we will exhibit. Because ideas matter, Christians and non-Christians alike should desire to know truth wherever it can be found. Moreover, Christians have a special intellectual and moral obligation to follow Augustine's advice: we have a duty, he said, to show that our Scriptures do not contradict what we have reason to believe from reliable sources outside them. In short, Christians have the obligation and privilege of developing and propagating an integrated Christian worldview.

The modern era has been called the era of science. Whether or not this is true, one thing seems clear—scientific ideas have had an impact on what people believe and how they see the world, as well as on the methods of investigation they think ought to be employed in our search for knowledge. If Christians are going to develop and propagate an integrated worldview, they must work together to integrate their theological beliefs and the assertions of science that seem reasonable. Currently there are several models of science-theology integration, among which are these:

1. Science and theology are concerned with two distinct realms of reality (natural-supernatural, spatiotemporal-eternal), and science and theology are subservient to very different objects (e.g., the material universe and God) and

can be defined only in relation to them.

2. Science and theology are noninteracting, complementary approaches to the same reality; as such, they adopt very different standpoints, ask and answer very different kinds of questions, involve different levels of description, employ very different cognitive attitudes (e.g., objectivity and logical neutrality in science, personal involvement and commitment in theology), and are constituted by very different language games. These different, authentic perspectives are partial and incomplete and therefore must be integrated into a coherent whole. However, each level of description is complete at its own level, with no gaps at that level for the other perspective to fill and with no possibility of direct competition and conflict.

3. Science generates a metaphysic in terms of which theology is then formulated.

4. Theology provides a context wherein the presuppositions of science (understood in a realistic way—i.e., with science seen as a rational, progressive intellectual activity that secures truer and truer theories about the external, theory-independent world) are most easily justified.

5. Science can fill out details and help to apply theological principles, and vice versa.

6. Science and theology are interacting approaches to the same reality that can be in conflict in various ways (e.g., mutually exclusive, or logically consistent but not mutually reinforcing) or can be in concord in various ways.

It is possible to hold one or more of these simultaneously in different areas of science-theology integration. However, position 6 alone allows for direct interaction, conflict and mutual reinforcement. Currently most intellectuals who focus on these issues reject position 6 and embrace the popular, but in our view mistaken, notion that theological beliefs—such as the notion of a direct, miraculous act of God—should play no role within the scientific enterprise.

This book is an attempt to defend, use and illustrate position 6, though this should not be taken to imply that we reject positions 1-5 as appropriate aspects of a total strategy for science-theology integration. We will develop position 6 by defining and defending what we will call *theistic science,* and we will focus our attention on issues in the creation-evolution controversy.

Theistic science is defined and illustrated at some length in chapter one. But to explain it briefly, theistic science is rooted in the idea that Christians ought to consult all they know or have reason to believe in forming and testing hypotheses, explaining things in science and evaluating the plausibility of various scientific hypotheses, and among the things they should consult are propositions of theology (and philosophy). The theistic science can be considered a research program (a series of theories that are continuous in some sense—for example, various theories of atomism in the history of science have been part of the same research program) that, among other things, is based on two propositions:

1. God, conceived of as a personal, transcendent agent of great power and intelligence, has through direct, primary agent causation and indirect, secondary causation created and designed the world for a purpose and has directly intervened in the course of its development at various times (including prehistory, history prior to the arrival of human beings).

2. The commitment expressed in proposition 1 can appropriately enter into the very fabric of the practice of science and the utilization of scientific methodology.

The distinction between primary and secondary causation, while capable of much more subtle clarification than I can give here, is nevertheless fairly straightforward. Roughly, what God did in parting the Red Sea was a primary causal act of God; what he did in guiding and sustaining the sea before and after that miracle involved a secondary cause. Primary causes are God's unusual way of operating; they involve his direct, discontinuous, miraculous actions. Secondary causes are God's normal way of operating, by which he sustains natural entities and processes in existence and employs them mediately to accomplish some purpose through them. Either way God is constantly active in the world, but his activity takes on different forms.

Proposition 1 is the more important of the two, for unless one embraces some form of scientism (to be discussed below), it could be true and rational to believe irrespective of proposition 2. However, the two propositions taken together are an important part of theistic science as that term is used in this book. As mentioned earlier, theistic science is a research program. Thus it is consistent with a number of different theories that specify it—e.g., progressive creationist models, young-earth creation science and other models.

Some Christians object to theistic science on theological grounds, especially when theistic science is applied to the evolution-creation controversy. For many of them, the integration of science and theology should eschew position 6 above, focus on 1-5, especially on view 2, and avoid theistic science. Moreover, these brothers and sisters are convinced that a proper interpretation of the biblical text renders most reasonable some form of theistic evolution.

We do not have space in this book to respond to this position, but two points should be kept in mind. First, many Christian intellectuals, including Old Testament scholars, do not believe that Genesis is consistent with theistic evolution as it is usually presented. Instead they opt for some form of special creationism. We side with these scholars, and in our view neither we nor they are guilty of a simplistic "folk" exegesis of the biblical text. Second, even if you, the reader, agree with the theistic evolutionary view, we hope that you will keep an open mind as you read further. At the very least, what follows should help you understand why some of us do not agree with the theistic evolutionary position or with the complementary model of integration in this area of investigation.

Before we look at specific aspects of theistic science as they are presented throughout this book, it is important to look at some preliminary issues. The remainder of this introduction will focus on certain theistic arguments for God's existence, along with associated philosophical and theological distinctions that relate directly to theistic science; it closes with an overview of the chapters to follow. Before we proceed, however, there is an ideology, currently quite popular, that if true would render pointless the project of this book. It is the view known as *scientism.*

Scientism

Scientism is the view that science is the very paradigm of truth and rationality. If something does not square with currently well-established scientific beliefs, if it is not within the domain of entities appropriate for scientific investigation, or if it is not amenable to scientific methodology, then it is not true or rational. Everything outside of science is a matter of mere belief and subjective opinion, of which rational assessment is impossible. Science, exclusively and ideally, is our model of intellectual excellence.

Actually, there are two forms of scientism: *strong scientism* and *weak scientism.* Strong scientism is the view that some proposition or theory is true or rational to believe if and only if it is a scientific proposition or theory—that is, if and only if it is a well-established scientific proposition or theory, which in turn depends upon its having been successfully formed, tested and used according to appropriate scientific methodology. There are no truths apart from scientific truths, and even if there were, there would be no reason whatever to believe them.

Advocates of weak scientism allow for the existence of truths apart from science and are even willing to grant that they can have some minimal, positive rationality status without the support of science. But advocates of weak scientism still hold that science is the most valuable, most serious and most authoritative sector of human learning. Every other intellectual activity is inferior to science. Further, there are virtually no limits to science. There is no field into which scientific research cannot shed light. To the degree that some issue or belief outside science can be given scientific support or can be reduced to science, to that degree the issue or belief becomes rationally acceptable. Thus we have an intellectual and perhaps even a moral obligation to try to use science to solve problems in other fields that heretofore had been untouched by scientific methodology. For example, problems having to do with the mind should be addressed by the methods of neurophysiology and computer science.

Note that advocates of weak scientism are not merely claiming that, for example, a belief that the universe had a beginning, supported by good philosophical and theological arguments, gains *extra* support if that belief also has good scientific arguments for it. This claim is relatively uncontroversial, because usually if some belief has a few good supporting arguments and later gains more good supporting arguments, this will increase the rationality of the belief in question. In fact, this line of argumentation will be used throughout this book. In our view, various theological beliefs (e.g., God created and designed the world) are rational without the support of science. Nevertheless, scientific discoveries can tend to count in favor of or against such beliefs, and we will argue that many of these discoveries have offered strong support for certain theological propositions. But this is not what weak scientism implies, because this point cuts both ways. For it will equally be the case that good philosophical and theological arguments for a beginning will increase the rationality of such a belief initially supported only by scientific arguments. Advocates of weak scientism are claiming that fields outside science gain if they are given scientific support, but not vice versa.

If either strong or weak scientism is true, this would have drastic implications for the integration of science and theology. If strong scientism is true, then theology is not a cognitive enterprise at all and there is no such thing as theological knowledge. If weak scientism is true, then the conversation between theology and science will be a monologue, with theology listening to science and waiting for science to give it support. For thinking Christians, either of these alternatives is unacceptable. What then should we say about scientism?

Note first that strong scientism is self-refuting. A proposition (or sentence) is self-refuting if it refers to and falsifies itself. For example, "There are no

English sentences" and "There are no truths" are self-refuting. Strong scientism is not itself a proposition *of* science, but a second-order proposition *of* philosophy *about* science to the effect that only scientific propositions are true or rational to believe. And strong scientism is itself offered as a true, rationally justified position to believe. Now, propositions that are self-refuting are not ones that could have been true but just happen to be false. Self-refuting propositions are necessarily false—that is, it is not possible for them to be true. What this means, among other things, is that no amount of scientific progress in the future will have the slightest effect on making strong scientism more acceptable.

There are two more problems that count equally against strong and weak scientism. First, scientism (in both forms) does not adequately allow for the task of stating and defending the necessary presuppositions for science itself to be practiced (assuming scientific realism). Thus scientism shows itself to be a foe and not a friend of science.

Science cannot be practiced in thin air. In fact, science itself presupposes a number of substantive philosophical theses that must be assumed if science is even going to get off the runway. Each of these assumptions has been challenged, and the task of stating and defending these assumptions is one of the tasks of philosophy. The conclusions of science cannot be more certain than the presuppositions it rests on and uses to reach those conclusions.

Strong scientism rules out these presuppositions altogether, because neither the presuppositions themselves nor their defense is a scientific matter. Weak scientism misconstrues their strength in its view that scientific propositions have greater cognitive authority than those of other fields like philosophy. This would mean that the conclusions of science are more certain than the philosophical presuppositions used to justify and reach those conclusions, and that is absurd. In this regard, the following statement by John Kekes strikes at the heart of weak scientism:

> A successful argument for science being the paradigm of rationality must be based on the demonstration that the presuppositions of science are preferable to other presuppositions. That demonstration requires showing that science, relying on these presuppositions, is better at solving some problems and achieving some ideals than its competitors. But showing that cannot be the task of science. It is, in fact, one task of philosophy. Thus the enterprise of justifying the presuppositions of science by showing that with their help science is the best way of solving certain problems and achieving some ideals is a necessary precondition of the justification of

science. Hence philosophy, and not science, is a stronger candidate for being the very paradigm of rationality.[1]

Here is a list of some of the philosophical presuppositions of science:

1. the existence of a theory-independent, external world
2. the orderly nature of the external world
3. the knowability of the external world
4. the existence of truth
5. the laws of logic
6. the reliability of our cognitive and sensory faculties to serve as truth-gatherers and as a source of justified beliefs in our intellectual environment
7. the adequacy of language to describe the world
8. the existence of values used in science (e.g., "test theories fairly and report test results honestly")
9. the uniformity of nature and induction
10. the existence of numbers

There is a second problem that counts equally against strong and weak scientism: the existence of true and rationally justified beliefs outside of science. The simple fact is that true, rationally justified beliefs exist in a host of fields outside of science. Strong scientism does not allow for this fact, and it is therefore to be rejected as an inadequate account of our intellectual enterprise.

Moreover, some propositions believed outside science (e.g., "Red is a color," "Torturing babies for fun is wrong," "I am now thinking about science") are better justified than some believed within science (e.g., "Evolution takes place through a series of very small steps"). It is not hard to believe that many of our currently held scientific beliefs will and should be revised or abandoned in one hundred years, but it would be hard to see how the same could be said of the extrascientific propositions just cited. Weak scientism does not account for this fact. Furthermore, when advocates of weak scientism attempt to reduce all issues to scientific ones, this often has a distorting effect on an intellectual issue. Arguably, this is the case in current attempts to make the existence and nature of mind a scientific problem.[2]

In sum, scientism in both forms is inadequate. There are domains of knowledge outside and independent of science, and while we have not shown this here, theology is one of those domains. In fact, since theology, philosophy and science are all domains that contain items of knowledge and rational belief, an integrated worldview will be one that gives appropriate attention to all three. Theistic science is an attempt to do just that. Scientism notwithstanding, theology and philosophy are fields that give us knowledge and rationally justified beliefs. In the next section we will look at two major attempts in natural theology (that branch of theology that gives us knowledge of the existence and nature of God from the study of the natural world) to provide evidence for the existence of God.[3]

Important Features of Arguments for God's Existence

Philosophical arguments for God's existence have had a long and distinguished history. And while these arguments are philosophical in nature, nevertheless, they often gain support or are criticized from findings in science. As later chapters will show, recent scientific discoveries have provided strong support to two main arguments for God's existence: the kalam cosmological argument and different types of design arguments. Since the scientific data relevant to these claims will be covered later, my purpose here is to clarify certain background issues involved in these two kinds of arguments for God.

The kalam cosmological argument can be diagrammed as a series of exhaustive dilemmas in the following way:[4]

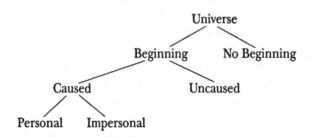

The defender of the argument tries to establish one horn of each dilemma and thus to argue for these three premises:
1. The universe had a beginning.
2. The beginning of the universe was caused.
3. The cause of the beginning of the universe was personal.

Let us look briefly at each premise, starting with the first. The fact that the universe had a beginning can be given both philosophical and scientific support. One important philosophical argument for premise 1 involves the impossibility of crossing or traversing an actual infinite number of events one at a time. It is impossible to cross an actual infinite ($\aleph_0$). For example, if a person started counting 1, 2, 3, . . . , then one could count forever and never reach a time when an actual infinite amount of numbers had been counted.

The series of numbers counted could increase forever without limit, but it would always be finite. Now, suppose we represent the events in the history of the universe as follows:

Past _____ $-\aleph_0$ . . . -3   -2   -1   0 _____ Present

The present moment is marked zero, and each moment in the past (e.g., yesterday, 1500 B.C.) is a point on the line. Now if the universe never had a beginning, then there is no end on the left side of the line. Rather, it extends infinitely far into the past. If the universe had no beginning, then the number of events crossed to reach the present moment would be actually infinite. It would be like counting to zero from negative infinity. But since one cannot cross an actual infinite (regardless of whether you count to positive infinity from zero or to zero from negative infinity), then the present moment could never have arrived if the universe were beginningless. This means that since the present is real, it was only preceded by a finite past, and there was a beginning or first event!

One important objection has been raised against this argument.[5] According to some critics, the argument assumes what it is trying to prove—namely, a beginning. They claim that the argument pictures a beginningless universe as a universe with a beginning time, T, infinitely far away, from which the present moment must be reached. But, they claim, a beginningless universe has *no* beginning, not one infinitely far away. These critics go on to assert that if one begins with the present and runs through the past one event at a time (yesterday, day before yesterday, etc.), then one will never come to an event from which the present is unreachable.

Unfortunately, this criticism represents a gross misunderstanding of the argument. The kalam argument does not assume a beginning time infinitely far from the present.[6] It is precisely the lack of such a beginning that causes most of the problems. If there were no beginning, then coming to the present moment would require crossing an actual infinite number of events—analogous to counting to zero from negative infinity—and such a cross is impossible, as was pointed out above.

Further, coming to the present moment by crossing an infinite past would be a journey that could not even get started. Counting to positive infinity from zero can at least begin, even if it cannot be completed. Counting to zero from negative infinity cannot be completed *or* started. Such a task is like trying to jump out of an infinitely tall bottomless pit. The whole idea of getting a foothold in the series in order to make progress is unintelligible. Take any specifiable event in the past. In order to reach that event, one would already have to traverse an actual infinite, and the problem is perfectly iterative—it applies to each point in the past.

Critics of the argument go wrong in picturing a beginningless universe as an indefinite past, not an infinite one. They invite us to start at the present, work through the past mentally by forming a growing series of events as we work backward, and try to specify a point we could reach that is unreachable from the present! But that is not the correct picture. If we count backward a day at a time, the problem will not be in trying to reach the present from the day we have counted (say we count back fifty million years, stop momentarily and ask if the present is reachable from that moment). The problem will be in the fact that for each point (e.g., the moment that was realized fifty million years ago) we count, that point is no better off than the present moment—it could not have happened either if the universe was beginningless, because it would require crossing an actual infinite to reach it, just as the present moment requires.

There is, then, a good philosophical argument for the fact that the universe had a beginning (premise 1). But premise 1 can be given scientific support from at least two sources: the big bang theory and the second law of thermodynamics. Since the details of these arguments are covered in chapter four, little needs to be said here. Regarding the big bang theory, Christians are divided about its worth. Now while it may be true that a full-blown acceptance of every detail of the theory may not harmonize with certain respectable ways of understanding Genesis 1, one thing seems clear: in spite of certain scientific problems with the big bang theory, it is currently the most reasonable and widely respected view, and it does confirm the fact that the space-time physical universe had a beginning.

Regarding the second law of thermodynamics and its applicability to the question of a beginning of the universe, an argument can be developed along the following lines: The universe is irreversibly running out of energy available to do work, and since it hasn't reached an equilibrium state yet, it must have had a finite past. Why? If the universe had already existed throughout an actually infinite past, then it would have reached an equilibrium state an infinite number of days ago, but it obviously has not done so.

Some critics of this argument have claimed that the universe is not a thing and that the second law cannot be applied to the universe as a whole but only to different space-time regions of the universe.[7] Three things can be said in response to this objection.

First, the universe *is* a thing in the sense that it is a whole with parts, and as a whole it has certain unique properties (mean density, temperature, pressure, radius, deceleration, age), as do other entities we would classify as things.[8]

Second, if the universe is a whole that is equal to the sum of all its spatiotemporal parts, then the second law clearly applies to the universe, because the second law applies to each and every region of the universe and the whole universe *just is* the collection of each and every region. The critic cannot cite any place at all in the space-time universe where the second law does not apply.

Third, if the universe is a whole that is greater than its parts, then it could be argued that the second law only applies to each and every part of the universe but not to the universe as a whole. But now the "universe as a whole" becomes a separate, metaphysical entity standing over and above each spatiotemporal region of it, and the "universe as a whole" takes on some of the classical attributes of God—it is nonphysical (the basic law governing the physical universe, the second law, does not apply to it), immutable, invisible, spaceless and timeless (and, according to the kalam argument, capable of spontaneously willing a first event into being).

Such an entity is hardly at home in a worldview that is trying to treat all entities as parts of physical reality open to scientific investigation. Naturalism can be defined as the view that reality is exhausted by the spatiotemporal world of physical entities embraced by our best scientific theories.[9] Given this widely accepted view of naturalism, the "universe as a whole" would not be a natural entity. At the very least it looks like the God of Spinoza, and it takes on some of the classical attributes of the God of Christian theism, as already mentioned. Either way, naturalism is dead.

Regarding premise 2 of the kalam cosmological argument (the beginning of the universe was caused), it can be understood as being justified by the principle that every event has a cause. It would seem that this principle is quite reasonable. While we may not always know the cause for some event, it seems reasonable to always believe that a given event has a cause. In favor of this principle is, arguably, our entire, uniform experience. We simply find the world to be such that events don't pop into existence without causes.

Some argue that certain quantum events do not have causes. But in light of the reasonableness of the causal principle, it seems best to say that we do not know what the causes are for some of these events, rather than to conclude that there are no causes. Both of these positions—there are causes for quantum events currently unknown to us versus there are no causes for quantum events—are equally compatible with observations (try to think of an observation consistent with one view and not with the other), and the former harmonizes with and preserves a principle for which there is overwhelming empirical evidence.

Some may also object that if we hold that all events need causes, then what caused God? But we can consistently hold that all events need causes and that God does not need a cause because God is not an event. Furthermore, the question "What or who made God?" is a pointless category fallacy, like the question "What color is the note C?" The question "What made X?" can only be asked of Xs that are by definition makeable. But God, if he exists at all, is a necessary being, the uncreated Creator of all else. This definition is what theists mean by "God," even if it turns out that no God exists. Now, if that is what "God" means, that the question "What made God?" turns out to be "What made an entity, God, who is by definition unmakeable?"

However, even if we grant that some events do not need causes, we can still embrace premise 2 (the beginning of the universe was caused) if we ground this premise not in the idea that all events have causes, but in the claim that whatever begins to exist has a cause. Here we could grant, for the sake of argument, that quantum objects *change* without a cause. But this still does not show that quantum entities *come into existence* without a cause.

It would seem then that all events, or at least all beginnings of existence, need causes, including the beginning of the universe. What about premise 3 (the cause of the beginning of the universe was personal)? Whatever created the universe's beginning existed in a timeless, changeless, immutable, space-less state of affairs (all time and space resulted *from* the first event). How can an effect (the first event) be produced by such a state of affairs as its cause?

The world gives us examples of two basic types of efficient causes (the means that produces an effect). The first kind is the one that governs the behavior of physical or natural causal relationships and is the primary focus of science. It is called state-state or event-event causation.[10] In general, state-state causation can be characterized in this way: an event of kind K in circumstances of kind C occurring to an entity of kind E causes an event of kind Q to occur. An example is a brick breaking a glass or a ball hitting and moving another one.

Consider the brick and glass. Here an event of kind K (the moving of the brick and its touching of the surface of the glass) in circumstances of kind

C (the glass being in a solid and not liquid state) occurring to an entity of kind *E* (the glass object itself, say a window) causes an event of kind *Q* (the breaking of the glass) to occur. The cause is not the brick, but rather a state or event realized in the brick—namely, the moving-of-the-brick. The effect is the breaking-of-the-glass. The following are true of all examples of state-state causation: the cause is an event, the cause exists earlier than and simultaneous with the effect, and the transfer of power from the cause to the effect is a change requiring time.

It should be clear that the first event could not be produced by such a causal mechanism, because the first event must be caused by something timeless, changeless, and which can spontaneously and immediately produce the first event. State-state causal sequences presuppose temporal succession; thus such a causal relation cannot itself account for the beginning of time and the coming-to-be of the first event itself.

There is a second type of efficient cause called agent causation. This type of causation occurs when a person acts, say when I raise my arm or speak. The cause is a substance or thing (a self), not a temporally prior event or state inside a thing, and the effect (the raising of the arm) is produced immediately, directly and spontaneously as the self simply exercises and actualizes its causal powers to raise its arm. This type of causal relationship does not require an earlier temporal event to be the cause of an effect that exists a moment later, and thus it is a good model for how a first event could have been generated.

In sum, the kalam cosmological argument is an attempt to argue that the universe began to exist as a result of the causal activity of a person. The preceding discussion has been brief, and further details of the scientific aspects of the argument follow in chapter four. My purpose here has been to overview the argument and discuss some of the basic objections that have been raised against it.

There is a second argument for God's existence that surfaces throughout this book—the design argument. Let us turn to a consideration of it.

The design argument's most fundamental point can be put in this way. Science cannot explain away all examples of order (or other design-bearing features—e.g., beauty, information) as being the result of merely natural processes, because scientific explanations presuppose and must start with ordered entities and laws. For example, a scientific explanation may explain the order in a water molecule as something produced by purely natural processes when hydrogen and oxygen come together in certain ways. But clearly such an explanation, while giving a natural explanation of the order of a water molecule, must nevertheless appeal to highly ordered entities (the hydrogen and oxygen) and highly ordered laws of nature (various laws governing chemical reactions). Scientific explanations cannot get off the ground without starting with ordered entities and laws. Thus there will always be ordered entities and laws that will be brute, unexplainable givens for science.

Now our experience teaches us that, regularly, order (and, even more clearly, information—see chapter five) is originated and introduced into the world as the direct result of intelligent persons who intentionally act. Thus the ultimate ordered entities and laws that exist in the universe must either be taken as brute, unexplainable realities (remember, science cannot explain them even in principle) or explained with the resources we use every day to explain other examples of order—as the result of an intelligent mind. There is no good reason to leave these examples of order as brute, unexplained realities, and there *is* good precedent to explain them as the result of a mind; the design argument capitalizes on this insight.

A number of issues need clarification before the force of the design argument can be properly appreciated.[11] The first of these is the different kinds of design utilized by the argument. Throughout history and currently, a number of very different kinds of design have been appropriated by advocates of the argument:

☐ the intricacy of the laws of nature and their orderly, regular application to phenomena in the natural world

☐ the order present in various aspects of reality (e.g., the orbit of the planets, various biological structures like the eye)

☐ the delicate concurrence of a number of factors (e.g., cosmic constants, conditions on earth, the properties of water) that serve as necessary conditions for life to appear

☐ the presence of aspects of the world beneficial to life

☐ the simplicity of the world and the laws describing it, along with the complexity of the world (e.g., the complex interaction of various parts in living organisms that cooperate with one another for certain ends such as allowing the organism to see)

☐ the information content in DNA

☐ the trustworthiness of the senses and intellect as truth-gatherers from the world around us, as well as the aptness of that world to be known by those senses and intellect

☐ the beauty and elegance of the various aspects of the world and of the equations used to describe the world

Three things should be said about these various kinds of design. First, their staggering force and power can be appreciated only through a detailed presentation of each one. It may be easy to dismiss the abstract statement "Living organisms have an order that points to a designer." It is another thing altogether to look at the details of the cell, a DNA molecule, the eye or the development of a monarch butterfly, and to dismiss them as irrelevant as evidence for theism. In other words, the design argument does not merely appeal to the fact of different kinds of design to make its case. The real case comes from the degree, intensity, delicacy and texture of the details of those examples of design.

Second, the fact that there are so many different kinds of design gives the argument greater strength by providing a broader range of data for the argument to utilize. For example, there are biological and nonbiological instances of design. Thus, even if evolutionary theory completely neutralized the former (and later chapters will show that this is not the case), the design argument could still utilize the latter.

Finally, these different kinds of design suggest at least five different models of God as Designer:

□ God as engineer (e.g., in the order, efficiency and complexity of the world)

□ God as speaker and author (e.g., in the information content in DNA)

□ God as playful artist (e.g., in the aesthetic aspects of the world)

□ God as mathematician (e.g., in the mathematical character of the world and the different laws that describe it, as well as in the usefulness of mathematics as means for discovering new laws describing reality)

□ God as provider (e.g., in the beneficial aspects of reality, in the suitability of the senses and intellect for gaining knowledge of the world)

There is no reason to limit God as Designer to any one of these. All of them capture different aspects of what Christian theists mean when they claim God as Designer.

A second issue helpful in understanding the design argument is the different forms the argument takes. First, the argument can be understood as an argument from analogy. An argument from analogy takes the following form:

A has properties $F, G, H, I.$
B has properties $F, G, H.$
Therefore (probably) B has $I.$

Let A be an apple and F, G, H, I be the properties of being red, round, firm and sweet. Now let B be a second apple. The argument from analogy says that if B is red, round and firm, then the analogy between it and A is quite strong. Therefore, it is probable that B is sweet as well.

In the design argument, A is a human artifact, F, G and H are the various types of design (order, information, beauty), and I is the property of being designed by an intelligent mind. B is the universe or some entity in it (e.g., DNA, the eye, the presence of various cosmic constants). Understood in this way, the design argument builds on an analogy between human artifacts and the universe or some aspect of it (e.g., both a watch and the eye are complex wholes with mutually interacting and coadapted parts that work together for an end—telling time and seeing), and since the former are the result of intelligence, then (probably) the latter is as well.

The strength of an argument from analogy turns on the adequacy and appropriateness of the comparison between the two entities (A and B above) in the argument. Any two things will be alike and unlike; the analogy form of the design argument claims that the degree and relevance of the similarities between human artifacts and the universe or various aspects within it outweigh dissimilarities.

In addition to an argument from analogy, the design argument can be understood as an example of what philosophers call an "inference to the best explanation." In an argument of this sort, a range of phenomena present themselves as a problem to be solved. After we ponder the phenomena, a hypothesis may suggest itself as one that adequately explains the data and removes our puzzlement and surprise regarding those data. The data point to that hypothesis and tend to confirm it.

An example may help. Suppose I get a terrible stomachache. Then it dawns on me that I just ate a gallon and a half of ice cream, two bags of popcorn and a lot of candy on an empty stomach. A hypothesis suggests itself as the best explanation of the stomachache—it arose because of what I had just eaten. Other hypotheses may also suggest themselves, but I should adopt the explanation that best solves the problems for which it was postulated.

In general, an inference to the best explanation starts with a range of phenomena to be solved and postulates a hypothesis that removes our puzzlement and surprise about those phenomena by providing an explanation of them, and those phenomena tend to confirm that hypothesis.

Regarding the design argument, the various features of design present themselves as puzzles that strike us as odd, surprising, and in need of an explanation. If we postulate a designing intelligence behind them, then they have an explanation and our puzzlement regarding them is removed. Advocates of this form of the design argument claim that on a naturalistic hypothesis, these phenomena are surprising and without adequate explanation compared to the designer hypothesis.

A third form of the design argument is worth mentioning. This is called the Bayesian approach to the design argument, because it utilizes an approach to evidence evaluation known as Bayes's theorem:

$$P(T/E) = \frac{P(E/T) \times P(T)}{P(E)}$$

$P(T/E)$ = the posterior probability of T given evidence E.

$P(E/T)$ = the likelihood of E given T (i.e., how strong is the connection between T and E? if we accept T, does that make E 100 percent likely, or does it just make the occurrence of E merely plausible?).

$P(T)$ = the prior probability that T is true apart from evidence E. This is the prior probability of T.

$P(E)$ = the probability that E will obtain apart from acceptance of T, called the expectedness of E.

A term like $P(T/E)$ means "the probability that theory T is true given the fact of evidence E." Bayes's theorem gives a way of determining the conditional probability of T (conditional because the probability T is conditioned on the fact that evidence E is assumed) as a function of the three probability factors to the right of the equals sign. Bayes's theorem says that the probability of T being true given evidence E is equal to the prior probability of T being true apart from evidence E obtaining, multiplied by the likelihood that E will occur given that T is true, divided by the prior probability that E is expected to occur without T being true.

If the probability that T is true given E is greater than the probability that T is true without E, that is, if $P(T/E)$ is greater than $P(T)$, then the evidence E offers positive support for T. In the design argument, T is the hypothesis of a theistic Designer and E is the evidence provided by design. The Bayesian form of the design argument says that the probability that a theistic Designer exists given the design in the universe is equal to the probability that design would occur in the universe given that it was designed by God—$P(E/T) = 1$ on Christian theism because the Christian conception of God implies that if such a God exists, he would make a world of design—times the probability that a theistic Designer exists apart from the evidence from design (say, based on other arguments for God), divided by the likelihood that the universe would bear the type of design it has even if God did not exist.

Advocates of the Baysian form of the design argument claim that (1) the probability of theism's being true apart from the evidence of design, i.e., $P(T)$, is not insignificant because of other arguments (religious experience, miracles, the moral argument, the kalam argument, etc.); (2) the likelihood that the type of design we find in the world would occur if God did not exist, i.e., $P(E)$, is quite low.

Point 2 is important for the rest of this book. We claim that when one actually examines the scientific evidence for the real design in the world, it becomes much less plausible to believe that the design in this world is the result of chance or some other factor apart from God.

What do we mean by *chance*? A. R. Peacocke has distinguished two senses relevant to this context.[12] First, there is the epistemological usage of *chance*. Peacocke points out that when we toss a coin, we say that the chances of heads or tails are even. But we know that if we knew the precise values of the relevant parameters, we could predict which side the coin would fall on in any given toss. So the use of *chance* in this context refers to our partial ignorance of what is going on; this use of *chance* does not entail that there is no causality in the sequences of events under discussion. This sense of *chance* is not the one creationists often use.

Peacocke highlights a second sense of *chance* which means "accidental, random, indifferent." Here chance describes the intersection of two otherwise unrelated causal chains. For example, if you are walking down a sidewalk and are struck by a dropping from a bird flying overhead, then the intersection of these two causal chains is accidental, random and purely by chance. The fact that these two sequences of events intersected was not necessary; it was accidental and by chance. This is the basic sense of *chance* used by creationists.

So far we have looked at different kinds of design used in design arguments, and we have examined three different forms that a design argument can take. A final issue that needs to be addressed has to do with criticisms of the design argument. We cannot undertake an exhaustive treatment of these criticisms, but a few brief points may be helpful as an introduction to later chapters.

One of the most important discussions of the design argument is David Hume's *Dialogues Concerning Natural Religion,* written during the 1750s. Among Hume's criticisms of the argument, one is of special importance for later chapters of our book.[13] Advocates of the design argument sometimes cite as evidence for a Designer the occurrence of various factors necessary for the existence of life (various cosmic constants, the properties of water, etc.). Critics from Hume to the present have responded by pointing out that we should not be surprised by these data. If the world had been one in which intelligent life could not have arisen, then we should not be here to discuss the matter. The factors are necessary for people to be around to puzzle over them, and thus we should not be surprised at their occurrence.

To see what is wrong with this objection, let us suppose that an advocate of the design argument cites a number of factors, *a-g,* that are part of the world and are necessary preconditions for the emergence of life. Hume and his followers interpret the design argument as follows. Theists are supposedly saying, "Isn't it amazing that the factors necessary for life preceded us instead of some other factors that make life impossible preceding us!" In other words, theists are comparing these two different world courses:

World Course 1: *a* through *g* obtain, and human beings appear

World Course 2: alternate factors (say *h* through *n*) obtain, and human beings appear

Note that worlds 1 and 2 differ in the factors that obtain in them, but the presence of human beings is held constant. This is indeed a bad argument, because it is hard to see how humans could emerge in any world other than one in which the factors necessary for their emergence are actualized!

But this is not the correct interpretation of the design argument. Advocates of the design argument are offering the following comparison:

World Course 1: *a* through *g* obtain, and human beings appear

World Course 2: alternate factors (say *h* through *n*) obtain, and no human life appears

Advocates of the design argument are claiming that the emergence of any life, including human life, was incredibly unlikely and required the actualization of a delicately balanced set of preconditions, and the realization of these preconditions require explanation provided by the existence of a Designer.

Even the atheist J. L. Mackie saw the flaw in Hume's criticism:

> There is only one actual universe, with a unique set of basic materials and physical constants, and it is therefore surprising that the elements of this unique set-up are just right for life when they might easily have been wrong. This is not made less surprising by the fact that if it had not been so, no one would have been here to be surprised. We can properly envisage and consider alternative possibilities which do not include our being there to experience them.[14]

Before we leave the topic of the use of cosmic constants in the design argument, we should consider one more criticism.[15] This view, called the "multiple worlds ensemble" view, asserts that in addition to the actual world in which we live, there exists an infinite number of parallel universes. All physically possible universes exist parallel to one another, each world is inaccessible to each other world, and the world we live in is just one of an infinite number of worlds that exist. Some of those worlds are highly ordered, some not, and the reason we are in an ordered one is that we could not exist in the disordered worlds. Thus no Designer is needed to explain the fact that we are in a delicately balanced world.

However, the multiple worlds ensemble theory is not convincing. The view appears to be contrived, made up largely to avoid theistic conclusions. Furthermore, if one is going to embrace a view of reality that allows for bizarre entities like alternative parallel worlds, then one should not have intellectual difficulties with the notion of a Designer or Creator God. For example, one can no longer reject the existence of God because God is not detectable by sensory experience, since multiple worlds are not sense-detectable either. Finally, there is little or no additional evidence for these parallel universes, but there is additional evidence for God apart from the existence of the delicately balanced preconditions for life in our world. So if one compares the relative merits of theism and the multiple worlds ensemble view, the former wins hands down.

A third objection to the design argument is the general theory of macroevolution. Since issues surrounding macroevolution are addressed at length in this book, there is little need to cover this objection in detail. The objection states that evolutionary theory makes the design argument implausible because (1) evolution shows that what appears to be cases of purposeful design and planning is really just apparent design, and (2) the eerie designlike features of the living world are the result of a mindless process of chance and necessity, and thus the God hypothesis is unnecessary.

Theists have taken three broad strategies in response to this objection. First, advocates of the design argument can grant, for the sake of argument, that evolutionary theory neutralizes biological examples of design, but go on to build a design argument on nonbiological examples of design (e.g., beauty, the necessary preconditions for life, etc.). Since evolutionary theory is defined only for biological objects and processes, evolution cannot touch this type of design argument.

Second, theists can grant, for the sake of argument, that the general theory of evolution is true, and go on and build a design argument based on broader features of order and purpose, even on the existence of the mechanisms of evolution. It can be claimed that evolution merely explains how God designed the living world; it does not remove the need for a Designer. This response grows stronger the more we discover that living things are even more complicated than was believed to be the case during the time of Darwin. As the intricacy of organisms becomes more apparent, it becomes less plausible to believe that the processes of evolution could mindlessly produce life, and it becomes more plausible to believe that they were guided by an Intelligence in such a way as to overcome the improbabilities of life arising in the first place.

The main problems with this response are that it is hard to square with the early chapters of Genesis and with the empirical facts of science itself. So while this response could be adopted merely for the sake of argument, the authors of this book do not utilize it. The third strategy is to criticize evolutionary theory and present a creationist alternative to it. Throughout this book this third strategy, along with strategy one listed above, constitutes the main response to evolutionary critiques of design.

One final criticism of the design argument should be mentioned. Some claim that living organisms and their parts, as well as the process by which they came to be, are inefficient. Certain features of some organisms (e.g., homologous structures) are not as efficient as they could be; this is easy to explain if those features resulted from a random, mindless process of evolution, but it is not easy to explain if those features came from an omniscient, omnipotent God who was an optimally efficient Designer.

Four things can be said in response to this problem. First, as Kurt Wise points out in chapter six, there is reason to doubt that such features really exist, given our limited knowledge of the complexity of living organisms and given the fact that the features in question seem to work quite nicely (see Wise's discussion for details). Second, the whole concept of "efficiency" may be the wrong one when applied to God and design in these cases. When God is conceived as Designer, the engineering model—which values efficiency and is a relatively late, Western value—is not the only or even best one. Other models discussed earlier (e.g., God as playful artist) may be more accurate descriptions of God as Designer and Creator of life. Beauty may have been more important to him than efficiency of design. Furthermore, the whole concept of efficiency becomes a value only if one presupposes limited resources. And while such a presupposition may make sense for finite designers, it is hardly applicable to God.[16]

Finally, as Paul Nelson has pointed out, evolutionary arguments of this sort show quite clearly that a model of God as Designer can have empirically testable implications. We do not think arguments of this sort make their case for the reasons just cited. But the structure of reasoning they employ exhibits the interplay between a theological model (in this case, of God as optimal engineer) and empirical, scientific data (homologous structures). These kinds of arguments have frequented the writings of evolutionary scientists from Darwin himself to the present. And they illustrate the fact that theistic science is, in fact, science. If scientific data can be used negatively to undercut a certain theological model of God as Designer (even if that model is inadequate), then scientific data can also be used positively; in any case, the negative and positive arguments both illustrate the use of theological beliefs within the practice of science. What is sauce for the goose is sauce for the gander.

Is Naturalism Necessary?

Before we turn from our discussion of the kalam and design arguments, it is crucial to emphasize one important thing. The kalam argument gives us reason to believe that an immaterial, transcendent agent underlies the origin of the material universe and that this agent is more fundamental in being than the material universe.

With the kalam argument as a first step, we turn to the design argument to see if we can learn more about the nature and existence of this agent. When we recall that science itself cannot, even in principle, explain all examples of order naturally, and that order can and ought to be explained by the action of an intelligent Agent, the combined lessons from the kalam and design arguments give us an important conclusion. Before we even begin to investigate the scientific details of the universe in which we live, we already have reason to reject philosophical naturalism (the view that the space-time material universe is all there is). We also have reason to reject methodological naturalism. This will be discussed in more detail in chapter one. Roughly, methodological naturalism is the claim that within science we must adopt a naturalist standpoint in explaining things in science. But unless there is some strong reason for accepting this claim (and chapter one will argue that no such reason exists), then we have every right—indeed, we have a duty—to bring to our study of the details of the natural world a prior belief in a transcendent, powerful Agent who began and designed the universe.

A major theme of this book is that certain scientific factors (such as the origin and fine-tuning of the universe, the origin of life and information systems, the origin of major taxonomic groups, and the origin of human language and linguistic abilities) help to confirm the kalam cosmological argument and the design argument for God's existence.[17] We have looked at some background issues that are involved in assessing this claim.

But this book is not merely about the claim that certain factors justify the assertion that a Creator and Designer God exists. This book also claims that these factors and the inference to God justified by them can legitimately be seen as, in part, *scientific* matters. True, the most important issue is whether the inference to God is a rational one, not whether it is an issue of science. Theology does not need the support of science to be rational. But given the general respect of science in our culture, it is still interesting to consider the relative merits of theistic science (with its employment of a Creator and De-signer) and evolutionary theory as rival *scientific* hypotheses.

Looking Ahead

With this in mind, the chapters to follow are arranged in two parts. Part one focuses on issues in the philosophy of science. The purpose here is to look at the nature of science, the relationship between science and theology, the relative merits of theistic science and methodological naturalism, and prob-lems with inferring a Designer from data obtained through the natural scien-ces. Part two looks directly at four different areas of science: the origin of the universe and its fine-tuning, the origin of life and the information it contains, the origin of major taxonomic groups of organisms, and the origin of human language and linguistic capacities. In each area the argument will be advanced that certain phenomena in that area of science cannot be adequately explained within naturalistic evolutionary categories and that those phenomena are best explained by the actions of a Creator and intelligent Designer.

In chapter one I look directly at the assertion that science must presuppose methodological naturalism. If this thesis is true, then theistic science, along with inferences to a Designer from scientific phenomena, would be inappropriate to the very nature of science. I break the doctrine of methodological naturalism down into four distinct theses and criticize each one. I then offer a brief sketch of theistic science by showing several different ways that theological beliefs can enter into the very fabric of scientific practice. The chapter closes with a response to three objections frequently raised against theistic science.

Chapter two, by Stephen Meyer, takes up where chapter one leaves off and further develops the idea that the notion of an intelligent Designer can be part of scientific practice. Meyer evaluates the claim that there cannot be a scientific theory of creation/design since the notion of a Creator/Designer is outside the bounds of scientific methodology. Meyer centers his attention on various attempts to draw a line of demarcation between science and nonscience or pseudoscience and judges them a failure. More specifically, he shows that each alleged condition of science (e.g., science must explain by natural law) will count equally for and against the evolutionary notion of descent with modification versus the thesis of intelligent design. These two explanatory paradigms, claims Meyer, are equivalent in their scientific and methodological status. The main reason the demarcationist arguments fail is that they do not take into account the general characteristics of the historical sciences. When these characteristics are taken into account, the case for the scientific and methodological legitimacy of an intelligent Designer hypothesis is greatly strengthened.

If the ideas developed in the first two chapters are correct, then there is nothing in principle wrong with using theological notions like that of an intelligent Designer within science. Still, most secular thinkers regard this world as the kind of place where it is impossible for an intelligent Designer—usually conceived of as God—to become perfectly evident on rational and empirical grounds. Thus even if the notion of an intelligent Designer did not violate the nature of science, one would never be justified in inferring such a Designer instead of holding out for a naturalistic explanation of the phenomenon in question. The purpose of chapter three, by Bill Dembski, is to refute this widely held view. Dembski argues that the world is the kind of place where supernatural design can indeed become perfectly evident on rational and empirical grounds. To make his case Dembski looks not to miracles but to the intractable problems of computer science. What makes his argument work is the existence of computational problems for which finding a solution is beyond the computational resources of the universe, but for which checking a solution, once it is available, is easy.

Given that the notion of an intelligent Designer can be a legitimate concept within science, and given that such a notion can, in fact, be inferred on rational and empirical grounds, the question can be asked, Do the findings of science justify such an inference? Can theological beliefs about certain scientific phenomena be confirmed by and used to explain those phenomena? These are the problems that occupy part two.

In chapter four Hugh Ross examines evidence in astronomy for the existence of a personal God. Ross gives a detailed investigation of the evidence for a beginning to the universe and criticizes models that seek to avoid that conclusion. Next Ross turns his attention to several design parameters in the universe by looking at the nature and degree of fine-tuning of various features of the cosmos. He also criticizes alternatives to theism as ways of explaining this fine-tuning.

In chapter five Walter Bradley and Charles Thaxton develop a detailed analysis of various origin of life theories, and along the way they offer a fascinating argument for an intelligent Designer for life's origin. They review and critique the paradigm of the origin of life originally suggested by Oparin, often called "soup theory." The minimum functions associated with living systems, including processing energy, storing information and replicating, appear to require an amazing amount of molecular complexity. This complexity is seen to be analogous to information. Possible naturalistic origins for such a large amount of biological information are reviewed and found wanting. An intelligent cause is posited as the most reasonable explanation for the origin of biological information.

In chapter six Kurt Wise takes up the topic of the origin of life's major groups. He points out that macroevolutionary theory has cited several lines of evidence as support for its claims, including homologous structures, vestigial organs, biogeographical distribution and suboptimal improvisations. Wise points out that these phenomena can be explained by an intelligent Designer hypothesis as well. Moreover, claims Wise, there are further phenomena that an intelligent Designer hypothesis explains better than current versions of macroevolutionary theory: the incredible degree and nature of the complexity of life, the integration of the different levels of complexity one finds in living systems, and the aesthetic nature of living things.

In chapter seven John Oller (a linguist) and John Omdahl (a biochemist) explore human beings' undeniable capacity to express themselves through various representational systems, of which language is the most abstract and versatile. Other representational systems include our senses and our abilities to move, touch, point to and otherwise reveal to ourselves and others our reactions to the happenings of our experience.

Oller and Omdahl show how language capacity is unique to human beings and how it reveals a supremely articulated special design. The human language capacity is rivaled only by another cascading network of representational systems, the unfolding complexities of life specified in DNA. One of the most interesting unsolved mysteries of all, argue Oller and Omdahl, is how the human language capacity is specified in the human genome. This chapter begins with Charles Darwin and follows key elements of the discussion of this mystery up to the present. Oller and Omdahl examine the close relationship between language and intelligence and also explore the remarkable analogy between linguistic and biological texts. In the final analysis, they argue, the human language capacity is utterly unlike the "languages" taught to apes, and a number of critical defining properties of human languages are completely absent from the communicative behaviors of other species.

Each chapter in this book is followed by a bibliography. To facilitate your further reading, items in the bibliographies are coded: B for beginner-level, I for intermediate or A for advanced.

In our view, the evidence in this book is strong. However, there is still much resistance to this type of argumentation. There are many reasons for the resistance. But it can be explained, at least in part, by the dominance of naturalism both within science and outside science in academic culture generally, as well as by the religious function that evolutionary naturalism plays for many people. Darwin, it has been said, made the world safe for atheists. In our view that world is not as safe as atheists may think. In fact, many scientists have said, in various contexts, that evolutionary theory is in a period of crisis. To show this, we have included an appendix by John Ankerberg and John Weldon. They have compiled a list of statements, taken in context, to show that a number of scientists, sometimes in unguarded moments and usually without the intent of abandoning evolutionary theory, have frankly expressed their own intellectual doubts about various aspects of evolutionary naturalism.

Over twenty years ago Thomas Kuhn wrote a groundbreaking book called *The Structure of Scientific Revolutions*. While some of Kuhn's points are outdated and others must be judged unacceptable—especially the conceptual relativism found in a strong reading of his book—much of his thinking is still valuable. In particular, Kuhn made the point that many scientific discoveries come from people outside the mainstream of the dominant theory (he called it a paradigm) currently embraced by the scientific community. This is because, as outsiders, they have not been trained merely to see the data in a certain way; their perceptual grid or theoretical orientation is not so unquestioned and accepted as to have embedded itself in the subconscious level so that the data *must* be made to fit that orientation.

Kuhn went on to say that advocates of a theory that challenges the dominant paradigm often experience various kinds of sociological pressure to conform with that paradigm. They may be called pseudoscientists, they may have difficulty getting published in standard professional journals, and in general they may be ostracized by the scientific community. Nevertheless, Kuhn points out that these small rebel groups have been extremely valuable to the progress of science, because they challenge major paradigms and urge that anomalies be taken seriously.

We believe Kuhn's general point applies with real force to the current rise of theistic science. We hope that our readers will suspend judgment about theistic science and try to give a fair hearing to the evidence. Emotional reactions and labels such as "pseudoscience" do nothing to facilitate growth and understanding. Even if you decide that the writers of this book do not make their case, they are nevertheless qualified scholars who are attempting to do respectable work. We ask you to judge that work fairly and openly. Such an approach can only lead to mutual understanding and progress.

PART I

CREATION, DESIGN & PHILOSOPHY OF SCIENCE

1
THEISTIC SCIENCE & METHODOLOGICAL NATURALISM

J. P. Moreland

Recently a growing body of literature has focused on the debate about how science and theology ought to be integrated. One aspect of this debate is the dialogue between those who advocate what is called "theistic science" and those who claim that science by its very nature presupposes methodological naturalism. The purpose of this chapter is to join this dialogue by offering a critique of methodological naturalism and a limited defense of theistic science.

It is beyond the scope of this chapter to focus on attempts to define *theistic science* to everyone's satisfaction, even if such a thing were possible. In its broadest sense, theistic science is rooted in the idea that Christians ought to consult all they know or have reason to believe in forming and testing hypotheses, in explaining things in science, and in evaluating the plausibility of various scientific hypotheses, and among the things they should consult are propositions of theology. Theistic science can be considered a research program (a series of theories that are continuous in some sense—for example, various theories of atomism in the history of science have been part of the same research program) that, among other things, is based on two propositions:

1. God, conceived of as a personal, transcendent agent of great power and intelligence, has through direct, primary agent causation and indirect, secondary causation created and designed the world for a purpose and has directly intervened in the course of its development at various times (includ-

ing prehistory, history prior to the arrival of human beings).

2. The commitment expressed in proposition 1 can appropriately enter into the very fabric of the practice of science and the utilization of scientific methodology.

Proposition 1 is the most important of the two, for unless one embraces some form of scientism, it could be true and rational to believe irrespective of proposition 2. However, the two propositions taken together are an important part of theistic science, and I will be offering a limited defense of the controversial thesis that theistic science, including propositions 1 and 2, is a legitimate and important part of a more general Christian understanding of the integration of science and theology, and that theistic science does not violate the nature of science.

Since theistic science is a research program, it is consistent with a number of different theories that specify it—for example, progressive creationist models, young-earth creation science and other models. Michael Ruse addresses one version of theistic science, but his comments apply to other versions as well: "Even if Scientific Creationism were totally successful in making its case as science, it would not yield a *scientific* explanation of origins. Rather, at most, it could prove that science shows that there can be *no* scientific explanation of origins."[1] Elsewhere Ruse says, "The Creationists believe the world started miraculously. But miracles lie outside of science, which by definition deals with the natural, the repeatable, that which is governed by law."[2]

Interestingly, a significant number of Christian scholars have made similar claims.[3] For example, philosopher Paul de Vries and scientist Howard J. Van Till have argued that natural science, by its very nature, presupposes and is constituted by *methodological naturalism* (hereafter MN), and that concepts like God and direct acts of God are not properly part of it. By *natural science* (hereafter NS; defined ostensively to keep from begging the question) is meant the scientific endeavors called physics, chemistry, geology, astronomy, biology and related fields.[4] Thus theistic science is fundamentally misguided, because it has a faulty philosophy of science and an improper view of how science and theology should be integrated.

It is not clear whether advocates of MN like de Vries and Van Till are claiming that in principle the very nature of NS entails the impropriety of theistic science or that theistic science may be science but is nevertheless not an empirically fruitful research program and should be abandoned. I believe a straightforward reading of their writings suggests the former, and this is the claim that I will examine first. I will take up the latter interpretation toward the end of this chapter.

De Vries's and Van Till's statements are strong assertions with serious implications for the nature of the integration of science and theology. In what follows I will first discuss some important preliminary considerations that set the context for further deliberation about these matters, then state and criticize the positions of de Vries and Van Till as representatives of the view under scrutiny, and finally suggest how theistic science can or perhaps ought to enter into NS; I will look at three main criticisms of this position.

Preliminary Considerations

Certain issues must be clarified before we can proceed. For one thing, consider the following propositions:

1. By its very nature, NS must adopt MN.

2. Theistic science is religion and not science.

It is important to remember that these claims are not first-order claims *of* science about some scientific phenomenon. Rather, they are second-order philosophical claims *about* science. They are metaclaims that take a vantage point outside science and have science itself as their subject of reference. Thus the field of philosophy, especially philosophy of science, will be the proper domain from which to assess these claims, not science. Scientists are not experts in these second-order questions, and when they comment on them, they do so qua philosophers, not qua scientists.

Second, we need to distinguish three different types of theory changes that can happen as science develops. Part of the history of science involves theory replacement—episodes of theory-change in which latter theories replace earlier ones that are abandoned. The first type of theory replacement includes standard examples of a new theory replacing an old one and the old one, while still considered a scientific theory, being for some reason no longer considered adequate. These types of changes are entirely first-order changes. Let us call them TC_1. An example would be the change from phlogiston chemistry to oxygen chemistry.

Further, there are replacements in which not only is an old theory replaced with a new one, but there is a rearrangement in epistemic virtues valued by the scientific community or a subcommunity within it. Roughly, in this context an epistemic virtue is a normative property that, if possessed by a theory, confers some degree of rational justification on that theory. An epistemic virtue is a feature that increases a theory's rationality. A theory's epistemic virtues might include the following:

☐ simplicity
☐ empirical accuracy
☐ success in prediction
☐ fruitfulness for guiding new research
☐ capacity for solving its internal and external conceptual problems
☐ use of certain types of explanations or certain methodological rules and not others (e.g., "appeal to efficient and not final causes")

Now, sometimes a theory change occurs in such a way that the abandoned theory, while still considered scientific, is not merely judged no longer acceptable. If the new theory embodies a different epistemic virtue than does the old one, then the theory change can be an occasion for claiming that the old epistemic virtue is no longer a good one, or at least not as good as was previously thought. For example, the shift from vital force theories of organisms to more mechanistic or physicalist views of organism involved an abandonment of the old theories as well as the elevation of an epistemic virtue: "views organisms in light of a machine model and eschews explanations of living processes in terms of vital forces, fluids or final causes." Here the abandoned theory is still considered to have been a scientific one, but the theory change is the occasion for a rearrangement of epistemic virtues. These types of theory changes are both first- and second-order changes, since part of the analysis of the relative merits of epistemic virtues is philosophical in nature. Let us call these types of theory changes TC_2.

Finally, there are theory changes in which the replaced theory is not merely considered an abandoned theory; instead, it is no longer thought to have been a scientific theory in the first place. Here the discarded theory does not pass from being a good scientific theory to being an unacceptable scientific theory. Rather, the theory passes from being an apparently good scientific theory to never having been a scientific theory in the first place, or at least to no longer being regarded as scientific. Let us call these episodes TC_3. It is sometimes thought that the shift from creationist theories to Darwinism is an example of this type of theory change.[5]

As one goes from TC_1 to TC_3, there is an increased burden of proof on the one claiming that the episode of theory replacement is an example of that type of shift. This is true because more is claimed for a TC_2 shift than for a TC_1 shift, and more still for a TC_3 shift. It is one thing to claim that an old theory is not as good as a new theory. It is a stronger claim to assert that an epistemic virtue embodied by the old theory is no longer as good as one embodied by a new theory. Even if that claim is true in regard to this specific theory replacement—and even here the new theory may be better than the old one by virtue of other or cumulative factors, and not merely by virtue of a particular epistemic factor—it requires justification before one can generalize the relative merits of two epistemic virtues to other areas of science or to other theories in the same area of science. It is an even stronger claim to assert that the abandoned theory was never science to begin with, or that in light of the new theory it should no longer be regarded as such. It is a radical position to claim that practitioners of an abandoned theory that they and advocates of rival scientific theories took to be a scientific theory (how else could they take themselves to be advocates of *rival* scientific theories?) were not even practicing science. Surely the burden of proof is on anyone making such a strong claim.

It is important to keep these insights about theory change in mind for the following reason. Most advocates of MN with whom I am familiar seem to claim that in principle the very nature of science rules out the very possibility of theistic science. Apparently in their reading of the history of science, enough TC_3 changes have occurred to justify in principle ruling out theistic science as a scientific research program at all.

However, as I mentioned earlier, it may be that advocates of MN really mean something else. Perhaps they believe that scientific claims must in some sense be empirically accessible, that when theistic science has been used to generate and solve various empirical problems it has repeatedly been a failure. Thus theistic science has been an extremely weak research program in terms of its empirical problem-solving effectiveness; while it is science, it is bad science. If this is what advocates of MN really mean, then they must say so more clearly. Moreover, this understanding of their views may involve, among other things, a way of understanding parts of the history of science as a series of TC_2 changes that justify the epistemic virtue "solves empirical problems" above other virtues, especially the one requiring that a research program solve *conceptual* problems. I will return to this point toward the end of the chapter.

There is a third preliminary consideration worth mentioning. If someone is going to state that given the intellectual equipment that humans do in fact have, some feature is part of the very essence of NS or is a necessary condition for NS, then it becomes impossible for NS to be practiced if that feature is not present. That is, there is no possible world where humans have our current intellectual equipment, NS is exemplified as a practice, and the feature in question is not present. This will be important to remember when it comes time to assess the claims of Van Till and de Vries.

A Clarification of Methodological Naturalism

Two representative advocates of MN have been Paul de Vries and Howard J. Van Till.[6] MN, as it is presented by de Vries and Van Till, has four central defining features.

1. The goal of NS. According to de Vries, the goal of NS is to explain contingent natural phenomena strictly in terms of other contingent natural phenomena, that is, "to place events in the explanatory context of physical principles, laws, fields" (p. 388). Explanations refer only to natural objects and events and not to the personal choices and actions of human or divine agents.

According to Van Till, "The 'epistemic' goal of the natural sciences is to gain knowledge of the intrinsic intelligibility discernible in the physical properties, behavior, and formative history of the physical world in which we live. The principal forms of this knowledge are the results of empirical investigation and the product of scientific theorizing about the composition, structure, behavior, and history of the physical systems we observe" (p. 136).

2. Methodological naturalism versus metaphysical naturalism. De Vries claims that "the natural sciences are committed to the systematic analysis of matter and energy within the context of methodological naturalism" (p. 389). Within NS answers are sought to questions within nature, within the nonpersonal and contingent created order. For example, in describing how two charged electrodes separate hydrogen and oxygen gas when placed in water, the "God hypothesis" is both unnecessary and out of place. Science is irrelevant to the question of the existence of God, because the God question is totally outside the domain of NS and its adoption of MN. By contrast, metaphysical naturalism is a philosophical perspective that denies the existence of God. MN and metaphysical naturalism are totally separate things, and the former has no bearing at all on the latter.

Van Till's views are similar to those of de Vries. According to Van Till, the object of natural scientific study is "the physical universe—no more, no less. It is the world of atoms and of the subatomic particles constituting them. It is the world of things made of atoms" (pp. 127-28). "The object of scientific investigation must be empirically accessible: there must be some way to interact with it physically" (p. 128).

But while the entire physical universe is the object of study, not all of its qualities or aspects are within the domain of scientific inquiry. The natural sciences study the physical universe with its constituent parts, but they only focus on the physical properties of physical objects, the physical behavior of a physical system or the formative history of the universe and its inhabitants—that is, of physical systems. "Only those qualities that are *intrinsic* (i.e., wholly resident within the empirically accessible physical universe) are included within the domain of scientific inquiry" (p. 131). Questions about transcendent issues (e.g., ultimate origins, any consideration of beings or agents that transcend the physical universe, the governance of the universe) lie completely outside the domain of NS.

It is important to remember that these statements by de Vries and Van Till (e.g., that the world of atoms is the object of study for NS) are not just illustrations of what scientists do. If that were the case, then these points, as illustrations, could not be used to argue that theological beliefs cannot be part of NS. And de Vries and Van Till clearly argue this point. For them to justify this view about theological beliefs, these and other aspects of MN must be taken as necessary conditions for NS.

3. Natural scientific explanation. So far as I can tell, neither de Vries nor Van Till offers a full-blown, explicit statement of his views regarding scientific explanation in the natural sciences. However, an implicit model of explanation emerges from what we have already seen. For de Vries, "science does not merely describe events" (p. 388); more important, the main (perhaps only) goal of science is to seek explanations of natural phenomena by answering how-questions. An answer to a how-question will describe regular, empirically observable patterns in the natural world (such as the relationship between pressure, temperature and volume of a gas) and explain them by describing a natural mechanism that provides such an explanation. These explanations must be understood in realist ways—as referring to real entities or processes in the natural world and giving true, or approximately true, descriptions of these entities/processes.

Van Till's views are similar to de Vries's; however, he has a slight but important difference in emphasis. He seems to agree that scientific laws and theories must be understood in realist ways, and he insists that a large, perhaps major, focus of science is to answer explanatory how-questions by describing mechanisms and processes that tell us how physical behaviors and formative histories are generated. But in contrast to de Vries, Van Till also emphasizes the fact that a major part of science is not merely explaining how phenomena take place but also establishing the existence of the phenomena themselves and describing what they, in fact, are. NS answers what-questions as well as how-questions, and for Van Till the former do not appear to be mere means or occasions for doing the latter.

4. A complementarian view of integration and agency. Finally, de Vries and Van Till both hold to a complementarian view of integrating NS and theology. In particular, de Vries, and perhaps Van Till also, applies a complementarian view to agency and action theory—human and divine. For example, de Vries analyzes an activity of raising one's hand to vote at a club meeting (pp. 389-90). At a NS level, a complete account at that level could be given of such an act in terms of brain states, neurons and the like. Such an account would be true and complete at that level of explanation. But a complete noninteracting description of that event could be given at another level by appealing to my purposes and reasons for voting the way I did.

Van Till's views are somewhat unclear on this point, especially when it comes to human action. He maintains that at least some human actions (e.g., choices and options that we select on the basis of considerations beyond the material world) cannot be defined fully by their physical aspects alone, but require the use of categories involving the relationship between the material world and nonmaterial entities.[7] But this relationship is unclear. Van Till may mean that certain human actions merely have mental and physical aspects that are categorically complementary to each other. Or he may mean that the physical aspects of some human behaviors have mental components that are part of the necessary causal conditions that produce those behaviors, so that the physical will need to be combined with the mental in a supplementary way. I am inclined to take the former interpretation of his view, because it fits better into the overall pattern of his thought, but I leave the matter open.

When we turn to divine activity, however, things are clearer. According to Van Till, God has created the world with *functional integrity:* "By this term I mean to denote a created world that has no functional deficiencies, no gaps in its economy of the sort that would require God to act immediately, temporarily assuming the role of creature to perform functions within the economy of the created world that other creatures have not been equipped to perform."[8]

It would seem to follow from this that apart from miracles in human history like the resurrection of Jesus, the acts of God in the created order are carried out by means of secondary causation, and theological descriptions are complementary to natural science descriptions of those acts.

A Critique of Methodological Naturalism

It is important to keep in mind what de Vries and Van Till are asserting. They are attempting to show that theological concepts are outside the boundaries of NS. To show this, they must present their characterization of NS as describing the very essence of NS, or at least necessary conditions of NS. This is a strong claim, and in my view an implausible one.

Consider first the goal of science as stated in MN. De Vries and Van Till both assume scientific realism in characterizing the goal of science. Now scientific realism may in fact be true. But if the goal of NS is stated in realist terms, and if the stated goal of NS is presented as a necessary condition for NS, then antirealist statements of the goal of science (e.g., to merely save the phenomena) become impossible. They are logically inconsistent with NS. But this is simply false. Antirealist treatments of the goals of NS are philosophies of *science*. And they may be true. If NS is consistent with antirealist statements of the goals of NS, then a realist interpretation of those goals cannot be offered as a necessary condition for NS.

Furthermore, it is implausible to claim that there is only one goal of NS, or even a most important goal. The fact is that a number of goals have been offered as possible epistemic ends for scientific theory formation, use and testing: theories should be simple (which, in turn, is capable of various interpretations), empirically accurate, predictively successful, internally clear and consistent, useful in solving external conceptual problems (rational problems raised against a theory from other disciplines, such as theology, metaphysics or logic), fruitful in guiding new research, and avoid certain kinds of explanatory devices (e.g., action at a distance, final causes), but use other devices (e.g., prefer particles to fields).[9] In addition, these goals are capable of both realist and antirealist interpretations. For the realist, the presence of one or more of these epistemic virtues signals that a theory is true or approximately true and/or that its central terms are referring terms. For the antirealist, the presence of these virtues merely shows that the theory is rational, solves problems, saves the phenomena and so forth. I conclude, then, that the MN statement of *the* goal of science is inadequate.

My point here is not that MN must be formulated in realist terms, for it is certainly possible that one could advance an antirealist version of MN. Rather, the point is that attempts to discredit theistic science that rely on demarcationist criteria have not been successful, and I am arguing that the same conclusion should be drawn regarding MN as stated by de Vries and Van Till. In light of the poor track record of demarcationist arguments, I suspect that other attempts to appropriate this strategy against theistic science, such as antirealist versions of MN, would be similarly unsuccessful, but I shall not pursue that here.

In a similar fashion, the MN statement of methodological naturalism must be judged inadequate. For one thing, de Vries identifies naturalism with physicalism (p. 388). But this is incorrect. Roughly, in this context naturalism is the denial of the existence of God and the assertion that the totality of existing things that make up reality exclude superhuman personal agents. But one could be a naturalist without being a physicalist, say by embracing Platonic forms, possibilia or abstract objects like sets, and one could be a physicalist and not a naturalist (e.g., if one held that God is a physical object). Second, and more important, the MN characterization of science's naturalistic methodology itself suffers from the fact that since it is a necessary condition for NS, it renders alternative characterizations logically impossible. For example, it is at least possible, and surely consistent with science, that a phenomenalistic understanding of science, in the spirit of Berkeley, Mach and certain logical positivists, is true. But some of these approaches to science deny the existence of a material universe and reduce physical object statements to statements about actual or possible sense data which turn out to be private mental entities. If such views are even possible philosophies of science, then one cannot make the existence or study of matter a necessary condition for natural science.

Furthermore, if antirealist philosophies of science, such as those of Larry Laudan and Bas van Fraassen, are true, then there most likely *is* no world of atoms or subatomic particles.[10] These are useful fictions. Thus one cannot make the study of atoms and their subatomic parts a necessary condition for NS. And even if we grant the existence of atoms, surely ontologies that take events or fieldlike entities to be real and atoms or other thinglike entities to be fictions or logical constructs are consistent with natural science.[11] MN fails to allow for this possibility. Moreover, to which atoms is Van Till referring—Dalton's, Thomson's, Newton's, Bohr's, the atoms of quantum theory or some future model?

More could be said, but perhaps enough has been offered to cause us to pause and observe an important lesson derived from our treatment of the goal and method of science according to MN.[12] Laudan has shown that attempts to draw a line of demarcation between science and nonscience or pseudoscience are rooted in a desire to identify beliefs that are " 'sound' and 'unsound,' 'respectable' and 'cranky,' or 'reasonable' and 'unreasonable.' "[13] Such attempts are rooted in polemical battles that for one reason or another try to show that some cognitive practice is not really science at all.

Now this is clearly the explicit cognitive goal in the MN of de Vries and

Van Till, however laudable their motives and intentions are on other grounds. But demarcationist arguments have failed, including those of de Vries and Van Till. Theistic science has been recognized as science by philosophers and scientists throughout much of the history of science.[14] Thus the burden of proof is on anyone who would revise this tradition, and demarcationist arguments in general, and those of de Vries and Van Till in particular, have not met that burden of proof. Moreover, regarding the creation-evolution controversy, this burden of proof is increased when we recognize that the Darwinian revolution was only a TC_1 shift, or at most perhaps a TC_2 shift. Advocates of MN seem to imply that it was a TC_3 shift; however, they have not made their case for this stronger claim. In my view, Laudan's advice applies to MN: "If we would stand up and be counted on the side of reason, we ought to drop terms like 'pseudo-science' and 'unscientific' from our vocabulary; they are just hollow phrases which do only emotive work for us. As such, they are more suited to the rhetoric of politicians and Scottish sociologists of knowledge than of empirical researchers."[15]

But the matter need not be left here. Two other features of MN, natural scientific explanation and a complementarian view of integration and agency, should be considered. It seems most helpful not to focus directly on these aspects of MN but to address them in the context of a brief presentation of how theological beliefs have been and can continue to be appropriate parts of NS. Therefore, in what follows I will try to give, in Saul Kripke's sense,[16] a "better picture" of how theological notions figure into the practice of science than the one offered by MN, though I readily admit that the "picture" to follow needs more details and refinements.

Theological Beliefs and the Fabric of Natural Science

Theology can provide metaphysical pictures of what was and was not going on in the formation of some entity (the universe, first life, the basic kinds of life, humankind or, for some, the geological column).[17] These pictures can serve as guides for new research (e.g., by postulating that a purpose will be found for vestigial organs), they can yield predictions that certain theories (e.g., theories of naturalistic mechanisms like natural selection working at the level of macroevolution, theories entailing a beginningless universe) will be falsified, and they can yield predictions that certain discoveries will be made (e.g., the Cambrian explosion, gaps in the fossil record, fixity of created "kinds").[18] In this way theology can serve as a resource for a negative heuristic (paths of research to avoid—e.g., for Cartesian mechanics, avoid working on action at a distance) and a positive heuristic (paths of research to pursue).[19]

Part of scientific methodology involves the psychology of discovery. While there is no algorithm (no step-by-step procedure) for scientific discovery, scientists often generate conceptual gestalts by adduction from tacit knowledge of a domain of scientific study. However, some conceptual gestalts are derived from "the top down"—that is, from a prior commitment to a broader metaphysical view of reality (which can in turn come from theology)—and these can be used to guide research and yield positive and negative predictions. In cases like this a philosophical or theological theory can provide answers to "what-questions": (1) what an entity is (e.g., living organisms are substances irreducible to property-things or physical entities), (2) what caused an event (e.g., first life was directly created by a primary causal act of God) or (3) what historical sequence actually took place (e.g., human beings arose in the Mideast). These answers can, in turn, be used as part of our background knowledge for evaluating things (including rival hypotheses), and they can be supported or falsified by scientific attempts to discover the truth about those what-questions even if there is no further how-question to be answered (e.g., that God directly caused the big bang through an act of primary causation).

Further, theology can provide and help to solve external and internal conceptual problems. Scientific laws and theories typically involve observational concepts and their associated observational terms (e.g., "is red," "sinks,"), as well as theoretical concepts and their associated terms (e.g., "is an electron," "has zero rest mass"). Often scientists try to solve both empirical and conceptual problems.[20] Roughly, an empirical problem is one of the observational aspects of some range of scientific data that strikes us as odd and in need of an explanation. For example, what is the precise movement of the tides, and why do they move as they do?

Frequently scientists will try to solve conceptual problems, which come in two types: internal and external. Internal conceptual problems arise when the theoretical concepts within a theory are defective in some way—perhaps they are vague, unclear, contradictory or circularly defined. External conceptual problems arise for some scientific theory, T, when T conflicts with some doctrine of another theory, T', and that doctrine of T' is rationally well founded, regardless of the discipline with which T' is associated. NS has always interacted with other fields of study in complicated, multifaceted ways that defy a simple characterization.

An external conceptual problem can arise in philosophy or theology, but enters into the very fabric of science because it interfaces with and tends to count against a given scientific theory. Part of the practice of science is to make sure that a scientific theory solves its problems, external conceptual problems included. Thus external conceptual problems provide counterexamples to the complementarian model of science-theology integration, because they are cases where science and another discipline like philosophy or theology directly interact at the same level in an epistemically positive or negative way.

For example, Darwin and many of his followers up to the present have advocated a physicalist understanding of living organisms, including human beings.[21] Paul Churchland's remark is typical:

> The important point about the standard evolutionary story is that the human species and all of its features are the wholly physical outcome of a purely physical process. . . . If this is the correct account of our origins, then there is neither need, nor room, to fit any nonphysical substances or properties into our theoretical account of ourselves. We are creatures of matter. And we should learn to live with that fact.[22]

If someone had good philosophical or theological reasons to reject physicalism, then these reasons would provide external conceptual problems for any version of naturalistic evolutionary theory (and most modern versions *are* naturalistic, because as Churchland correctly notes, they include the view that the only mechanism responsible for our appearance is a physical process).

Here is another example. According to David Hull,

> The implications of moving species from the metaphysical category that can appropriately be characterized in terms of "natures" to a category for which such characterizations are inappropriate are extensive and fundamental. If species evolve in anything like the way that Darwin thought they did, then they cannot possibly have the sort of natures that traditional philosophers claimed they did. If species in general lack natures, then so does *Homo sapiens* as a biological species. If *Homo sapiens* lacks a nature, then no reference to biology can be made to support one's claims about "human nature." Perhaps all people are "persons," share the same "personhood," etc., but such claims must be explicated and defended *with no reference to biology*. Because so many moral, ethical, and political theories depend on some notion or other of human nature, Darwin's theory brought into question all these theories. The implications are not entailments. One can always dissociate *"Homo sapiens"* from "human being," but the result is a much less plausible position.[23]

Again, if someone has good philosophical or theological reasons to believe in the existence of human nature or the moral or political theories grounded in human nature, these would provide external conceptual problems for naturalistic versions of evolutionary theory.

Note carefully: Hull acknowledges that the relationship between, say, evolution and the philosophical or theological notion of "human nature" is not an entailment relation. It is logically possible to hold the two in a complementary way. But Hull correctly points out that epistemically speaking, two propositions or conceptual issues can relate to one another in important ways other than logical consistency. And it is this epistemic point that is captured in the two examples of external conceptual problems—nonphysicalist views of living organisms (including humans) and the existence of human nature, along with moral/political theories grounded in human nature.

Science has never exhausted the rational, nor has science ever been a discipline or set of disciplines intellectually isolated from direct interaction, mutual reinforcement or competition from other fields of study, especially philosophy and theology. External conceptual problems provide a way for intellectual issues from other fields of study to enter into the very fabric of science when it comes time to assess a scientific theory for its problem-solving effectiveness, because part of that assessment will be evaluating for external conceptual problems. MN does not leave room for external conceptual problems, and thus it is a revisionary account of the way science has been practiced and an inadequate model for how science ought to be practiced.

Theology can also provide solutions to certain internal conceptual problems that are difficulties for naturalistic theories (e.g., illegitimate spectator interference at certain crucial points in prebiotic soup experiments to isolate reactant products or guide reactions down nonrandom pathways, providing a divine Designer to overcome probability considerations that are obstacles to a chance origination of life).

Theology can provide predictions (or retrodictions) of empirical data (e.g., that humans arose in the Mideast, various inferences from models of a universal flood, young-earth predictions about the age of the earth, gaps in the fossil record) and explanations for empirical problems that arise in the practice of science (e.g., the origin of life, information in DNA). The fact that some theological predictions may have been falsified is evidence of this (as some have argued, erroneously in my view, regarding homologous structures and their congruence with certain models of God as Designer). These predictions (or retrodictions) arise because the theological propositions that generate them can be used in scientific explanations of the things they predict.

It is simply false to assert that scientists explain things merely by using natural laws, say by invoking a covering law model of scientific explanation. Scientists also explain by citing causal entities, processes, events or actions. For example, cosmologists explain certain aspects of the universe not only by using natural laws but also by citing the big bang as a single causal event.[24]

Now, some branches of science, including SETI, archaeology, forensic science, psychology and sociology, use personal agency and various internal states of agents (desires, willings, intentions, awarenesses, thoughts, beliefs) as part of their description of the causal entities, processes, events or actions cited as explanations for certain phenomena.[25] For example, Richard De-Charms claims that "a scientific concept of self that does not encompass personal causation is inadequate."[26] Thus there is nothing nonscientific about appealing to personal agency and the like in a scientific explanation, and it is this insight that creationists express in their view of theistic science.

It may be objected that such appeals are permissible in the human sciences but not in the so-called natural sciences like biology and paleontology. But this response is clearly question-begging in that it is an attempt to define and classify examples of "natural science" by smuggling MN into the definition, rather than by using neutral ostensive definitions of natural science. If in fact certain phenomena are best explained by the intelligent Creator/Designer hypothesis, or even if such explanations are merely logically possible, then biology, paleontology and other fields will not be "natural" sciences except in the ostensive sense. And clearly, classification of a science as "natural" in the methodological sense should *follow after* arguments about the data rather than being a question-begging Procrustean legislation used to eliminate other views by definition.

In fact, such question-begging legislations can and have hurt science, not helped it, by ruling out of court the consideration of important options in explaining data. This is clearly the case in cognitive psychology and artificial-intelligence models of consciousness. Recently John Searle has argued that fifty years of philosophy of mind, artificial intelligence and cognitive psychological models of consciousness have been a waste of time in a number of ways. Says Searle,

> How is it that so many philosophers and cognitive scientists can say so many things that, to me at least, seem obviously false? . . . I believe one of the unstated assumptions behind the current batch of views is that they represent the only scientifically acceptable alternatives to the antiscientism

that went with traditional dualism, the belief in the immortality of the soul, spiritualism, and so on. Acceptance of the current views is motivated not so much by an independent conviction of their truth as by a terror of what are apparently the only alternatives. That is, the choice we are tacitly presented with is between a "scientific" approach, as represented by one or another of the current versions of "materialism," and an "unscientific" approach, as represented by Cartesianism or some other traditional religious conception of the mind.[27]

In my view, it is this methodological naturalist straitjacket that would deny to, say, biology, paleontology and the study of origins the same freedom of movement.

Theistic science does not limit the role of theology in science to cases of God's primary causal activity. Nevertheless, Christians need to ask themselves this question: If God did certain things through primary causal actions, then what methodology should we adopt to allow for the testing and use of a belief in these actions? Surely any view of science that disallows primary causes in principle could be seriously confining and distorting, just like the materialist assumptions noted by Searle in the study of consciousness.

Theology can shed light on various issues in the confirmation of scientific hypotheses in at least five ways: (1) by providing rationally justified background beliefs against which rational assessment of a specific scientific theory can be made (e.g., given the belief that humankind was created by a primary causal act of God, then various evidences for prehuman ancestral forms would carry less weight than they would without this background belief), (2) by yielding positive and negative results that can be tested (see above), (3) by recommending certain methodological rules over others (e.g., preferring explanations of living organisms on a substance model over those that treat them as machines and property-things when the two types of explanations come into conflict), (4) by specifying a certain ranking of epistemic virtues in certain cases (e.g., in origin of life research, preferring theories that solve external and internal conceptual problems to those that claim to offer fruitful avenues in guiding research for naturalistic mechanisms for how life arose) and (5) by providing extrinsic goals for science (to glorify God, to show that our Scriptures are not in conflict with what it is reasonable to believe from sources outside them) and helping to justify intrinsic goals for science (for example, some Christian theists use their theism to justify scientific realism and thus the goal of truth for scientific progress).

We are now in a position to evaluate the MN model of naturalistic scientific explanation, which seems to limit scientific methodology to answering how-questions with naturalistic mechanisms (de Vries) or to overemphasize this aspect of scientific methodology (which may be implicit in Van Till). As we have seen, science answers what-questions even when it cannot in practice or in principle answer how-questions. That is, it is a legitimate part of the business of NS to establish a phenomenon even if, for some reason, a naturalistic mechanism to explain *how* that phenomenon came or comes about cannot be given or has not yet been given.

For example, scientists established certain facts about the extinction of the dinosaurs, even though for some time there was no universal agreement as to what mechanism was responsible for their death. Furthermore, science postulates ultimates or brute givens viewed as causal entities, processes, events or actions and for which no mechanism or how-question is even possible. The initial conditions of the big bang, the values of the ultimate constants of nature (e.g., the universal gravitational constant) and the existence and properties of ultimate particles (if there are any) could be taken as things that would be ultimates for science. According to some, all science can do is establish these phenomena. Because they are ultimates, there can be no mechanism more basic than they which could serve as an answer to a how-question explaining them. In science, ultimates explain other things, but they themselves, qua ultimates, are givens without explanation.

If theology implies that there is a gap between *A* and *B*, that *A* is a result of a primary agent-causal activity of God and that *B* is the result of intelligent design, then establishing scientific implications and predictions from these postulates and marshaling scientific evidence, both negative and positive, can be genuine parts of NS, even if no natural mechanism exists to serve as an answer to a how-question. Some of these predictions are examples of what are called *proscriptive generalizations*. Proscriptive generalizations make strong assertions about what will not be the case if a certain theory is true. They describe phenomena that the theory proscribes and thus are in principle falsifiable.[28]

To be sure, the phenomenon in question (e.g., the origin of life) would not be entirely open to natural scientific investigation (some of the issues would be strictly theological—e.g., why God acted to create in the first place), but this does not imply that the phenomenon would not fall within the domain of science in any sense. Advocates of MN seem preoccupied with how-questions and regularly recurring phenomena (e.g., electrolysis experiments) for which there are natural mechanisms that are complementary to theological concerns and to God's secondary causal activity. But this partial picture does not exhaust NS, as we have seen.[29]

The same may be said of the complementarian view of integration and divine agency. When God acts via secondary causes, when regularly recurring phenomena generated by natural mechanisms are in view, then theology may legitimately be seen as complementary to science. But such a picture only allows for state-state causation of phenomena, in which a state of affairs serves as a cause for another state of affairs (the effect)—for example, the moving of one billiard ball causes the moving of a second billiard ball on contact.

But when God acts as a primary cause, God acts as an agent cause.[30] I cannot attempt a detailed sketch of agent causation here. But the important thing about agent causation is this. The cause of an action (whether raising my arm, voting in an election or directly creating first life) is a substance— the agent itself—and not a state of affairs in the agent. There is no sufficient set of prior conditions inside or outside the agent, mental or physical, that guarantee the effect. The agent must exercise his or her causal powers as a substance and simply act for a reason.

This means that when it comes to states of affairs produced by agent causes (the hand being raised, life being created), there will be a gap between the state of affairs that existed prior to that effect and the state of affairs which is (or is correlated with) the effect.[31]

When I raise my arm, the state of affairs in me at the physical level just prior to my raising of my arm—say in my brain and central nervous system— will not be sufficient to cause my arm to rise, and the physical state of affairs correlated with my arm's being raised will not be smoothly continuous with that prior state of affairs. Rather, there will be a discontinuous "gap" at the physical level from one state of affairs to the other due to my own causal role. The presence of such a gap has been widely recognized by philosophers as part of agent causation. In fact, it has even been used to argue that substance dualism and agent causation are false because they violate the principle of the conservation of energy.[32] Similar gaps would exist in cases of God's primary causal agency, and these gaps (e.g., between inorganic materials and first life) could, at least in principle, be scientifically detectable.[33]

In sum, the complementarian view of de Vries (and perhaps Van Till) has an inadequate understanding of substance, agency and agent causation. As a result, complementarity advocates fail to see that the effects of God's primary agent-causal activity could leave gaps that could be scientifically detectable, or they simply deny such activities altogether, appealing to the "functional integrity" of the creation.

This, then, is a brief sketch of how theological beliefs can be integrated within NS. It may be helpful at this point to offer a short response to three objections that are frequently raised against the type of picture I am advocating as a contrast to MN.

Criticisms of the Model

Objection 1. The theistic science model utilizes an epistemically inappropriate "God-of-the-gaps" strategy in which God only acts when there are gaps in nature; one appeals to God merely to fill gaps in our scientific knowledge of naturalistic mechanisms. These gaps are used in apologetic, natural-theology arguments to support Christian theism. Scientific progress is making these gaps increasingly rare, and thus this strategy is not a good one.

Reply. First, the model does not limit God's causal activity to gaps. God is constantly active in sustaining and governing the universe. Nature is not autonomous. Moreover, theistic science need not have any apologetical aim at all. A Christian theist may simply believe that he or she should consult all we know or have reason to believe is true—including theological beliefs—in forming, evaluating and testing scientific hypotheses and in solving scientific problems. And even if someone uses theistic science with apologetical intentions, that person would not need to limit his or her apologetical case to gaps. Among other things, the model merely recognizes a distinction between primary and secondary causes (however much this needs further refinement) and goes on to assert that (at least) the former could have scientifically testable implications, irrespective of the apologetic intentions of such a recognition.

Second, the model does not appeal to or attempt to explain in light of God and his activities to cover our ignorance, but only when good theological or philosophical reasons are present, such as when certain theological or philosophical reasons would cause us to expect a discontinuity in nature where God acted via primary causation (e.g., the origin of the universe, first life, basic "kinds" of life).

Third, even if the gaps in naturalistic scientific explanations are getting smaller, this does not prove that there are no gaps at all. It begs the question to argue that just because most alleged gaps turn out to be explainable in naturalistic terms without gaps at that level of explanation, all alleged gaps will turn out this way. After all, it is to be expected that gaps will be few. Gaps due to primary divine agency are miracles, and they are in the minority for two reasons: (1) God's usual way of operating (though I acknowledge the need for further clarity regarding this notion) is through secondary causes. Primary causal gaps are God's extraordinary, unusual way of operating; by definition, these will be few and far between. (2) The evidential or sign value of a miraculous gap arises most naturally against a backdrop where the gaps are rare, unexpected and have a religious context (there are positive theological reasons to expect their presence).

Finally, scientists—creationists and noncreationists alike—have made a distinction between "empirical" and "historical" science, and this distinction is helpful for answering the God-of-the-gaps problem (see chapter two). Roughly, empirical science is a nonhistorical, empirical approach to the world that focuses on repeatable, regularly recurring events or patterns in nature (e.g., the relationship between pressure, temperature and volume in a gas). By contrast, historical science is historical in nature and focuses on past singularities that are not repeatable (including the origin of the universe, first life, various kinds of life).

Advocates of this distinction claim that appealing to God is legitimate in historical science even if illegitimate in empirical science, because the former deals with cases where, theologically speaking, God's primary causal activity is to be found, while the latter deals with God's secondary causal activity.[34] Now, it could be argued that most cases of where God was appealed to as a cover for our ignorance of a gap were cases having to do with empirical science, not historical science. Thus when those gaps are filled by naturalistic mechanisms, the conclusion to draw is not that God should never be appealed to in an explanation of some scientifically discoverable phenomenon but that the notion of a primary causal act of God should be limited to cases in historical science precisely because of the differences between primary and secondary causation that is captured in the distinction between historical and empirical science.

Objection 2. The notion of God directly creating life is not something directly observable. And in any case, the claim that God did something by a primary causal action would always be empirically equivalent with an alternative explanation—namely that there is an undiscovered natural mechanism that accounts for the phenomenon in question. Thus such a claim is not empirically testable and is therefore outside the bounds of NS. Something like this may be behind Van Till's assertion that "the object of scientific investigation must be empirically accessible; there must be some way to interact with it physically."[35]

Reply. The role of observation and empirical testability in natural science is extremely complicated, and an adequate treatment of these issues would require discussion of the observation-theory distinction, the meaning and reference of theoretical terms, the nature of seeing, and many other matters. For our present purposes, however, three brief points can be made.

First, it is generally agreed by advocates of the hypothetico-deductive view of science and by others that in NS, individual propositions are not brought to the bar of experience piecemeal, but rather, entire sets of propositions or groups of theories are tested for an empirical implication. A hypothesis is generated, implications are drawn from the hypothesis (along with auxiliary assumptions), and various parts of the hypothesis (especially those that describe unobservable entities) are indirectly "verified" by further experiment or observation. A specific proposition (this magnetic field has such and such properties) may be empirically untestable, even in principle. But if it is embedded in a theory or set of theories with testable results, then the proposition can be an appropriate part of a natural scientific theory. Similarly, the statement "God directly created first life" may not be empirically testable by itself, but it could have empirical implications when embedded in a network of other propositions.

Second, a number of philosophers, such as Bas C. van Fraassen, have shown that a given set of empirical data will be empirically equivalent with a potentially infinite number of different scientific theories that provide metaphysical models of what is going on at the theoretical level.

In the days of logical positivism, some philosophers tried to reduce all scientific statements to statements about sets of actual or potential private sense data. The point is not that they were correct. The point is that their reductions were empirically equivalent with alternative theories that utilized material object language and more metaphysical claims about occult entities, natures and unobservables thought to be causally responsible for observational phenomena. These different accounts were underdetermined by observational data. The fact that two theories are empirically equivalent and the fact that one theory utilizes metaphysical entities that are not empirically observable in themselves are not sufficient to keep that theory from being a scientific theory. The concept of God or an act of God may be inappropriate for some other reason, but the objection we are currently considering does not capture that impropriety.

Third, if two theories, *A* and *B*, are empirically equivalent, and if *A* solves internal or external conceptual problems better than *B*, then, all things being equal, A is to be preferred to B. If A involves an appeal to God and primary causes to explain, say, the origin of life, and B is the claim that there is an undiscovered natural mechanism, then A would be preferable to B, all things being equal, if A solves theological and philosophical problems unsolved by B.

Objection 3. Theistic science is not a fruitful research program for solving empirical problems or for guiding new research and yielding new empirically testable constructs in other areas of investigation. Because of this, theistic science, while still science in principle, should be abandoned.

Reply. This may be what is actually behind MN. De Vries and Van Till may read the history of science as a series of TC_2 shifts that justify abandoning theistic science as an empirically fruitless (or even falsified) research program. If so, they have put their views rather badly, and a number of Christians have been led to believe that the history of science is one of TC_3 shifts such that theistic science is not a science in principle.

First, while I am not a historian of science, I am somewhat suspicious of this charge. I think it could be argued that much of the acceptance of Darwinism (which was the major contributor to the abandonment of theistic science) was sociological, philosophical and spiritual (it made the world safe for atheists, as Richard Dawkins has said), much like what Searle has shown to be the case in the current acceptance of materialist research programs in the mind-body problem. We need more Christians in the history of science to help us honestly evaluate the track record of theistic science.

Moreover, even if we grant that, say, theistic scientists' utilizations of theological concepts have not fruitfully suggested new lines of empirical research (and this need not be granted), all that follows from this is that theistic scientists need to do more work developing the infrastructure of their models, not that their models are not part of natural science or that they cannot be empirically fruitful where appropriate.[36] Some of this development is already taking place, but work here is woefully inadequate. I suggest that more research money be directed here.

Furthermore, an appeal to empirical fruitfulness in the cases we are considering may be question-begging and can represent a naive understanding of the intricacies of fruitfulness as a criterion for assessing the relative merits of rival research programs.

Two rivals may solve a problem differently depending on the way each theory depicts the phenomenon to be solved. Copernicus solved the motion of the planets by placing the sun in the center of the universe. Ptolemy had solved that motion by a complicated set of orbitals with smaller orbitals (epicycles) contained within larger ones. The two solutions were different (and not necessarily of equal effectiveness). Thus the standards for measuring one research program may differ substantially from those relevant to its rival.

I am not saying that rivals are incommensurable. I am simply pointing out that it is often more complicated to compare rivals than is usually thought to be the case. If one rival is the dominant paradigm, the less acceptable research program (and theistic science would fit this category) can easily be judged a failure by standards set by its rival. And this can be Procrustean.

For example, it is possible for two rivals to rank the relative merits of epistemic virtues in different ways or even give the same virtue different meanings or applications. Rivals can differ radically about the nature, application and relative importance of a particular epistemic virtue.

Creationists and evolutionists do not need to attempt to solve a problem, say a gap in the fossil record, in precisely the same way, nor do they need to employ the same types of solutions or rank various epistemic virtues identically in their solutions. Creationists may elevate the virtue "solves theological or philosophical internal and external conceptual problems" above the virtue "offers solutions yielding empirically fruitful lines of new research." There is nothing unscientific about this at all, and it is question-begging to claim that a criterion of empirical fruitfulness set by one research program (say, the search for evolutionary mechanisms) should be most important for a rival program and that if it is not, the rival is not even science (or not as rationally acceptable as its more empirically fruitful competitor).

Theistic science may be more fruitful in solving *conceptual* problems than a rival research program, and this may be more important to theistic science than *empirical* fruitfulness. More work needs to be done here. But even if I am only partially correct, then given the current preference for the empirical over the conceptual, and given the general lack of appreciation of the role of conceptual problems in the history of science, an epistemic assessment of theistic science is likely to be more negative than it deserves.

Finally, sometimes one rival will consider a phenomenon basic and not in need of a solution, empirical or otherwise. It may therefore disallow questions about how or why that phenomenon occurs and thus can hardly be faulted for not suggesting fruitful lines of empirical research for mechanisms whose existence is not postulated by the theory. As Nicholas Rescher has pointed out: "One way in which a body of knowledge S can deal with a question is, of course, by *answering* it. Yet another, importantly different, way in which S can deal with a question is by disallowing it. S *disallows* [Q] when there is some presupposition of Q that S does not countenance: given S, we are simply not in a position to raise Q."[37]

For example, motion was not natural in Aristotle's picture of the universe, so examples of motion posed problems in need of explanation. But in Newton's picture of the universe, uniform, linear motion is natural, and only changes in motion pose problems in need of solution. Suppose a Newtonian and an Aristotelian are trying to solve the observational problem of how and why a particular body is moving in uniform linear motion. The Aristotelian must tell how or why the body is moving to solve the problem. But the Newtonian can disallow the need for a solution by labeling the phenomenon a basic given for which no solution, no how-question utilizing a more basic mechanism, is possible.

Similarly, certain phenomena like the origin of life and gaps in the fossil record are not problems in need of solution for creationism, beyond an appeal to the primary causal agency of God. But they are problems for evolutionary theory, and fruitful lines of research for new mechanisms must be sought. It is naive and question-begging to fault creationists for not developing fruitful problem-solving strategies for such gaps; these phenomena are basic for creationists. In this case, it is enough for creationists to use theological notions to guide them in the quest for scientific tests to establish the phenomena predicted by their theological constructs. Once the what-question is answered, there is no further material or mechanistic how-question that arises.[38]

Finally, in certain cases advocates of theistic science can be more open than their MN counterparts to allowing the empirical data to speak for themselves. This is especially true in areas where God could have acted through primary or secondary causation, even if, theologically speaking, the former is more likely. As an example of this, consider the research by Kok, Taylor and Bradley (see chapter five for more details).[39] In their view, the functional specificity in the amino acid sequences in the proteins of living organisms is due to the primary causal activity of a Designer.[40] Based on this assumption, they predicted and "verified" the fact that different forms of self-ordering tendencies in matter, especially steric interference—which allegedly gives rise to nonrandom, preferential amino acid sequencing in proteins—are absent. If such interference had been found, the researchers would have seen God's activities in designing these sequences as secondary causes. However, advocates of MN would seem to be in a position of *requiring* such interference, or something of the sort, due to their commitment to MN and secondary causation.

Alvin Plantinga has challenged Christian scholars to develop a "theistic science" that stands in sharp contrast with a science that adopts methodological naturalism.[41] This chapter—indeed this whole book—is an attempt to underscore that challenge. Advocates of MN have not succeeded in showing that this challenge is fundamentally misguided or that science in principle must adopt methodological naturalism. However, because the problem of methodological naturalism is of such crucial importance for the issues developed in part two of this book, we need to look at further matters in the philosophy of science relevant to questions about design, the nature of science and methodological naturalism. In chapter two Stephen Meyer will develop two further aspects of this dialogue: (1) the methodological equivalence of the thesis of design and descent in conjunction with an analysis of attempts to draw a line of demarcation between science and nonscience or pseudoscience and (2) important features of the historical sciences.

Bibliography
General Books in the Philosophy of Science
Harre, Rom. *The Philosophies of Science.* Oxford, U.K.: Oxford University Press, 1972. [I]

Kourany, Janet A. *Scientific Knowledge: Basic Issues in the Philosophy of Science.* Belmont, Calif.: Wadsworth, 1987. [A]

Ratzsch, Del. *Philosophy of Science.* Downers Grove, Ill.: InterVarsity Press, 1986. [B]

The Integration of Science and Theology
Bauman, Michael, ed. *Man and Creation: Perspectives on Science and Religion.* Hillsdale, Mich.: Hillsdale College Press, 1993. [I]

Hasker, William, ed. *Creation/Evolution and Faith. Christian Scholar's Review* (special issue) 21 (September 1991). [I]

Jaki, Stanley. *The Road of Science and the Ways to God.* Chicago: University of Chicago Press, 1978. [I]

Moreland, J. P. *Christianity and the Nature of Science.* Grand Rapids, Mich.: Baker Book House, 1989. [I]

Moreland, J. P., and David Ciocchi. *Christian Perspetives on Being Human.* Grand Rapids, Mich.: Baker Book House, 1993. [B]

Peacocke, Arthur R. *Creation and the World of Science.* Oxford, U.K.: Oxford University Press, 1979. [A]

Polkinghorne, John C. *One World: The Interaction of Science and Theology.*

Princeton, N.J.: Princeton University Press, 1987. [I]

Van Till, Howard J., Robert E. Snow, John H. Stek and Davis A. Young. *Portraits of Creation*. Grand Rapids, Mich.: Eerdmans, 1990. [I]

Van Till, Howard J., Davis A. Young and Clarence Menninga. *Science Held Hostage*. Downers Grove, Ill.: InterVarsity Press, 1988. [B]

Issues in Reductionism

Connell, Richard J. *Substance and Modern Science*. Notre Dame, Ind.: University of Notre Dame Press, 1988. [I]

2
THE METHODOLOGICAL EQUIVALENCE OF DESIGN & DESCENT: CAN THERE BE A SCIENTIFIC "THEORY OF CREATION"?

Stephen C. Meyer

During the last thirty years the idea of design has undergone a renaissance in some scientific and philosophical circles. Developments in physics and cosmology, in particular, have placed the word *design* back in the scientific vocabulary as physicists have unveiled a universe apparently fine-tuned for the possibility of human life (see discussion in chapter four). The speed of light, the strength of gravitational attraction, the properties of the water molecule and many other features of the cosmic architecture appear to have been fortuitously arranged and balanced for human benefit.

While many have postulated so-called anthropic principles or "many worlds scenarios" to explain (or explain away) this apparent design without recourse to God,[1] some have eschewed these secular notions and posited the activity of a preexistent intelligence—a Creator—as the simplest explanation for the "coincidences" upon which life seems to depend. As Sir Fred Hoyle has suggested, a commonsense interpretation suggests that "a superintellect has monkeyed with physics"[2] in order to make life possible. Similarly, astronomer George Greenstein wrote in a recent book provocatively subtitled *Life and Mind in the Cosmos:* "The thought insistently arises that some supernatural agency—or rather Agency—must be involved. Is it possible that suddenly, without intending to, we have stumbled upon scientific proof of the existence of a Supreme Being? Was it God who stepped in and so providentially crafted the cosmos for our benefit?"[3]

Despite this renewal of interest in the (intelligent) design hypothesis among physicists and cosmologists, biologists have remained reluctant to consider such notions. As historian of science Timothy Lenior has observed, "Teleological thinking has been steadfastly resisted by modern biology. And yet, in nearly every area of research biologists are hard pressed to find language that does not impute purposiveness to living forms."[4]

The tendency Lenior has observed among biologists seems both puzzling and ironic. At first glance, the complexity of living systems far exceeds any encountered in the physical sciences. Information-storage and transfer systems, regulatory and feedback mechanisms, structures for manufacturing and repairing precisely coded and sequenced strings of chemical "symbols"—all on a miniaturized scale—characterize even the simplest cells. Ernst Haeckel's nineteenth-century vision of simple "homogeneous globules of plasm"[5] has yielded to the modern molecular image of a complex cellular factory.

Moreover, the growing awareness of biological complexity has created something of an impasse in contemporary origins theory (see the chapter by Bradley and Thaxton in this volume). Various contradictory conjectures[6] have appeared as scientists have attempted to explain how purely natural processes could have given rise to the unlikely and yet functionally specified systems found in biology—systems that comprise, among other things, massive amounts of coded genetic information. The origin of such information, whether in the first protocell or at those discrete points in the fossil record that attest to the emergence of structural novelty, remains essentially mysterious on any current naturalistic evolutionary account.

Not surprisingly, critical scientific analyses of both chemical and neo-Darwinian evolutionary theory have proliferated in recent years.[7] Some observers have gone so far as to characterize origin-of-life studies and neo-Darwinism as paradigms in crisis or degenerate research programs.[8] As biophysicist Dean Kenyon, a once-prominent origin-of-life researcher, said concerning his own discipline several years ago: "The more . . . we have learned in recent two or three decades about the chemical details of life, from molecular biology and origin-of-life studies . . . the less likely does a strictly naturalistic explanation of origins become."[9]

Similarly, Francis Crick has written, "An honest man, armed with all the knowledge available to us now, could only state that in some sense, the origin of life appears at the moment to be almost a miracle, so many are the conditions which would have been satisfied to get it going."[10]

While Kenyon has since embraced the design hypothesis (thus explaining his fall from prominence), Crick and most others in the biological community have remained firmly committed to the view that naturalistic processes will eventually suffice to explain the origin of new biological information and structure. Thus, despite the current impasse and a growing body of at least highly suggestive evidence for intelligent design, discussion of the design hypothesis has remained almost entirely out of bounds in biology. Why?

At least part of the reason for this reticence may not be hard to discern. Biologists, and scientists generally, assume the rules of science prohibit any deviation from a strictly materialistic mode of analysis. Even most physicists sympathetic to design would quickly label their intuitions "religious" or "philosophical" rather than "scientific." Science, it is assumed, must look for exclusively natural causes. Since the postulation of an intelligent Designer or Creator clearly violates this methodological norm, such a postulation cannot qualify as a part of a scientific theory. Thus Stephen J. Gould refers to "scientific creationism" not just as factually mistaken but as "self-contradictory nonsense."[11] As Basil Willey put it, "Science must be provisionally atheistic, or cease to be itself."[12]

Most scientists who are theists also accept this same conception of science. As Raymond Grizzle wrote in a prominent evangelical scientific journal recently, "God cannot be part of a scientific description. . . . [Further], any description that *implies* a creator will probably also be looked at as improper by most scientists."[13] Nancey Murphy, a philosopher and Fuller Seminary professor, agrees. She wrote recently in the same journal: "Science qua science seeks naturalistic explanations for all natural processes. Christians and atheists alike must pursue scientific questions in our era without invoking a Creator. . . . Anyone who attributes the characteristics of living things to creative intelligence has by definition stepped into the arena of either metaphysics or theology."[14]

Yet on what basis is this definition of science asserted? For Murphy and Grizzle the answer seems clear. A respect for the rules and practices of science as they have come down to us dictates that Christians should avoid invoking creative intelligence in their theories. In Murphy's words, *"For better or worse, we have inherited a view of science as methodologically atheistic"*[15] (emphasis added). Grizzle, too, appeals to convention to justify methodological naturalism:

All modern science, not just biological evolutionary theory, by definition

excludes God. . . . There is no rule book that spells this out, and indeed
it has been argued that it is an arbitrary restriction. Furthermore, this has
become the case only in the last 100 years or so. Nonetheless, this is one
of the restrictions almost universally put upon science by those who practice it, and it seems to me quite desirable and likely that science will retain
this restriction in the foreseeable future.[16]
Of course, it does not follow that just because science is or has been wholly
naturalistic, it should remain so. The indicative does not, after all, imply the
imperative. Therefore, Murphy and Grizzle's appeal to convention and current practice invites scrutiny of the grounds on which the scientific community has asserted naturalism as normative to its practice. Indeed, if the cus-
tomary definition of science is exposed as *just* an arbitrary convention, some
practicing scientists may wish to repudiate it, especially if they now judge
empirical evidence sufficient to motivate a consideration of some nonnaturalistic theory of origins. In any case, beyond a fallacious appeal to power,
it would be difficult to see why those disinclined to accept methodological
naturalism should not be free to operate under a less restrictive definition of
science.

However Christian intellectuals might go about defending methodological
naturalism, secular defenders of the principle assure us that the prohibition
against invoking God or creative intelligence is anything but arbitrary. Instead, they assert that good independent reasons exist for the conventional
exclusion of such notions from all scientific theories.[17] Theories of design or
creation do not, they say, meet objective standards of scientific method and
practice. Such theories do not explain by reference to natural law, nor do they
manifest a host of other features of true scientific theories such as testability,
observability and falsifiability. Thus, unlike naturalistic evolutionary theories,
creationist or design theories are methodologically deficient. Creationist theories may or may not be true, but they can never—that is, in principle—be
considered scientific.[18]

The use of what philosophers of science call "demarcation arguments"—
arguments that purport to distinguish science from pseudoscience, metaphysics or religion—in defense of a favored theory has a long history. Darwin
himself employed such arguments to defend his theory from idealist and
creationist challenges.[19] While philosophical arguments about what does or
does not constitute science have generally been discredited within philosophy
of science, they nevertheless continue to play a vital role in persuading biologists that alternative scientific explanations do not, and in the case of

nonnaturalistic theories *cannot,* exist for biological origins. Indeed, various demarcation criteria are often cited by scientists as reasons for rejecting the very possibility of intelligent design.[20]

The purpose of this chapter is to examine the case against the possibility of a scientific theory of intelligent design or creation. Several of the criteria said to distinguish the scientific status of naturalistic evolutionary theories (hereafter "descent") from admittedly nonnaturalistic theories of creation or design (hereafter "design") will be examined. It will be argued that a priori attempts to make distinctions of scientific status on methodological grounds inevitably fail and, instead, that a general equivalence of method exists between these two competing approaches to origins. In short, I will argue that intelligent design and naturalistic descent are methodologically equivalent—that is, that design and descent prove equally scientific or equally unscientific depending upon the criteria used to adjudicate their scientific status and provided metaphysically neutral criteria are selected to make such assessments. In the process of making this argument, I will also discuss whether a scientific theory of creation or design could be formulated or whether methodological objections, forever and in principle, make the assertion of a scientific theory of creation an "oxymoron" or "self-contradictory nonsense," as Ruse,[21] Stent,[22] Gould[23] and others[24] have claimed.

Throughout this paper, the alliterative terms *design* and *descent* will be used as a convenient shorthand to distinguish two types of theories: (1) those that invoke the causal action of an *intelligent* agent (whether divine or otherwise) as part of the explanation for the origin of biological form or complexity and (2) those (such as Darwin's "descent with modification") that rely solely on *naturalistic* processes to explain the origin of form or complexity.

By way of qualification, it should be noted that by defending the methodological and scientific legitimacy of design, this chapter is not seeking to rehabilitate the empirically inadequate biology of many nineteenth-century creationists or their belief in the absolute fixity of species; nor is it attempting to endorse modern young-earth geology. The following analysis concerns the methodological legitimacy of design in principle as defined above, not the empirical adequacy of specific theories that might invoke intelligent design in the process of making other empirical claims.

The methodological equivalence of intelligent design and naturalistic descent will be suggested in three stages by three lines of argument. First, the reasons for the failure of demarcation arguments within philosophy of science generally will be examined and recapitulated. This analysis will suggest that attempts to distinguish the scientific status of design and descent a priori may well be suspect from the outset on philosophical grounds. Second, an examination of specific demarcation arguments that have been employed against design will follow. It will be argued that not only do these arguments fail, but they do so in such a way as to suggest an equivalence between design and descent with respect to several features of allegedly proper scientific practice—that is, intelligent design and naturalistic descent will be shown equally capable or incapable of meeting different demarcation standards, provided such standards are applied disinterestedly. Third, design and descent will be compared in light of recent work on the logical and methodological character of historical inquiry. This analysis will show that the mode of inquiry utilized by advocates of both design and descent conforms closely to that evident in many other characteristically historical disciplines. Thus a more fundamental methodological equivalence between design and descent will emerge as a result of methodological analysis of the historical sciences.

Part 1: The General Failure of Demarcation Arguments

To show that design "can never be considered a scientific pursuit,"[25] biologists and others have asserted that design does not meet certain objective criteria of scientific method or practice. In short, biologists have employed so-called demarcation arguments to separate a scientific approach to origins (descent) from an allegedly nonscientific approach (design). While an examination of the particular criteria employed in such arguments will not concern us in the first part of this chapter, the general practice of demarcation will.

From the standpoint of the philosophy of science, the use of demarcation arguments is generally problematic. Historically, attempts to find methodological "invariants" that provide a set of necessary and sufficient conditions for distinguishing true science from pseudoscience have failed.[26] Moreover, most current demarcation arguments presuppose an understanding of how science operates that reflects the influence of a philosophy of science known as logical positivism. Yet since the 1950s philosophers of science have decisively rejected positivism for a number of very good reasons (see below). As a result, the enterprise of demarcation has generally fallen into disrepute among philosophers of science.

In his essay "The Demise of the Demarcation Problem," philosopher of science Larry Laudan gives a brief but thorough sketch of the different grounds that have been advanced during the history of science for distinguishing science from nonscience.[27] He notes that the first such grounds concerned the degree of certainty associated with scientific knowledge. Science, it was thought, could be distinguished from nonscience because science produced certainty whereas other types of inquiry such as philosophy produced opinion. Yet this approach to demarcation ran into difficulties as scientists and philosophers gradually realized the fallible nature of scientific disciplines and theories. Unlike mathematicians, scientists rarely provide strict logical demonstrations (deductive proofs) to justify their theories. Instead, scientific arguments often utilize inductive inference and predictive testing, neither of which produces certainty. As Owen Gingerich has argued, much of the reason for Galileo's conflict with the Vatican stemmed from Galileo's inability to meet scholastic standards of deductive certainty—a standard that he regarded as neither relevant to nor attainable by scientific reasoning.[28] Similar episodes subsequently made it clear that science does not necessarily possess a superior epistemic status; scientific knowledge, like other knowledge, is subject to uncertainty.

By the nineteenth century, attempts to distinguish science from nonscience had changed. No longer did demarcationists attempt to characterize science on the basis of the superior epistemic status of scientific theories; rather, they attempted to do so on the basis of the superior methods science employed to produce theories. Thus science came to be defined by reference to its method, not its content. Demarcation criteria became methodological rather than epistemological.[29]

Nevertheless, this approach also encountered difficulties, not the least of which was a widespread disagreement about what the method of science really is. If scientists and philosophers cannot agree about what *the* scientific method is, how can they disqualify disciplines that fail to use it? Moreover, as the discussion of the historical sciences in part three of this chapter will make clear, there may well be more than one scientific method. If that is so, then attempts to mark off science from nonscience using a single set of methodological criteria will most likely fail. The existence of a variety of scientific methods raises the possibility that no single methodological characterization of science may suffice to capture the diversity of scientific practice. Using a single set of methodological criteria to assess scientific status could therefore result in the disqualification of some disciplines already considered to be scientific.[30]

As problems with using methodological considerations grew, demarcationists shifted their focus again. Beginning in the 1920s, philosophy of science took a linguistic or semantic turn. The logical positivist tradition held that scientific theories could be distinguished from nonscientific theories not because scientific theories had been produced via unique or superior methods, but because such theories were more meaningful. Logical positivists asserted that all meaningful statements are either empirically verifiable or logically undeniable. According to this "verificationist criterion of meaning," scientific theories are more meaningful than philosophical or religious ideas, for example, because scientific theories refer to observable entities such as planets, minerals and birds, whereas philosophy and religion refer to such unobservable entities as God, truth and morality.

Yet as is now well known, positivism soon self-destructed. Philosophers came to realize that positivism's verificationist criterion of meaning did not achieve its own standard. That is, the assumptions of positivism turn out to be neither empirically verifiable nor logically undeniable. Furthermore, positivism's verificationist ideal misrepresented much actual scientific practice. Many scientific theories refer to unverifiable and unobservable entities such as forces, fields, molecules, quarks and universal laws. Meanwhile, many disreputable theories (e.g., the flat-earth theory) appeal explicitly to "common-sense" observations. Clearly, positivism's verifiability criterion would not achieve the demarcation desired.

With the death of positivism in the 1950s, demarcationists took a different tack. Other semantic criteria emerged, such as Sir Karl Popper's falsifiability. According to Popper, scientific theories were more meaningful than non-scientific ideas because they referred only to empirically falsifiable entities.[51] Yet this, too, proved to be a problematic criterion. First, falsification turns out to be difficult to achieve. Rarely are the core commitments of theories directly tested via prediction. Instead, predictions occur when core theoretical commitments are conjoined with auxiliary hypotheses, thus always leaving open the possibility that auxiliary hypotheses, not core commitments, are responsible for failed predictions.

Newtonian mechanics, for example, assumed as its core three laws of motion and the theory of universal gravitation. On the basis of these, Newton made a number of predictions about the positions of planets in the solar system. When observations failed to corroborate some of his predictions, he did not reject his core assumptions. Instead, he scrutinized some of his auxiliary hypotheses to explain the discrepancies between theory and observation. For example, he examined his working assumption that planets were perfectly spherical and influenced only by gravitational force. As Imre Lakatos has shown, Newton's refusal to repudiate his core in the face of anomalies enabled him to refine his theory and eventually led to its tremendous success.[32] Newton's refusal to accept putatively falsifying results certainly did not call into question the scientific status of his gravitational theory or his three laws.

The function of auxiliary hypotheses in scientific testing suggests that many scientific theories, including those in so-called hard sciences, may be very difficult, if not impossible, to falsify conclusively. Yet many theories that have been falsified in practice via the consensus judgment of the scientific community must qualify as scientific according to the falsifiability criterion. Since they have been falsified, they are obviously falsifiable, and since they are falsifiable, they would seem to be scientific.[33]

And so it has gone generally with demarcation criteria. Many theories that have been repudiated on evidential grounds express the very epistemic and methodological virtues (testability, falsifiability, observability, etc.) that have been alleged to characterize true science. Many theories that are held in high esteem lack some of the allegedly necessary and sufficient features of proper science. As a result,[34] with few exceptions[35] most contemporary philosophers of science regard the question "What methods distinguish science from non-science?" as both intractable and uninteresting. What, after all, is in a name? Certainly not automatic epistemic warrant or authority. Thus philosophers of science have increasingly realized that the real issue is not whether a theory is scientific but whether it is true or warranted by the evidence. Thus, as Martin Eger has summarized, "demarcation arguments have collapsed. Philosophers of science don't hold them anymore. They may still enjoy acceptance in the popular world, but that's a different world."[36]

The "demise of the demarcation problem," as Laudan calls it, implies that the use of positivistic demarcationist arguments by evolutionists is, at least prima facie, on very slippery ground. Laudan's analysis suggests that such arguments are not likely to succeed in distinguishing the scientific status of descent vis-à-vis design or anything else for that matter. As Laudan puts it, "If we could stand up on the side of reason, we ought to drop terms like 'pseudo-science.'. . . They do only emotive work for us."[37]

If philosophers of science such as Laudan are correct, a stalemate exists in our analysis of design and descent. Neither can automatically qualify as science; neither can be necessarily disqualified either. The a priori methodological merit of design and descent are indistinguishable if no agreed criteria exist by which to judge their merits.

Yet lacking any definite metric, one cannot yet say that design and descent are methodologically equivalent in any nontrivial sense. In order to make this claim we must compare design and descent against some specific standards. Let's now consider the specific demarcation arguments that have been erected against design. For though demarcation arguments have been discredited by philosophers of science generally, they still enjoy wide currency in the scientific and "popular world,"[38] as the following section will make abundantly clear.

Part 2: Specific Demarcation Arguments Against Design

Despite the consensus among philosophers of science that the demarcation problem is both intractable and ill-conceived, many scientists continue to invoke demarcation criteria to discredit quacks, cranks and those otherwise perceived as intellectual opponents. Yet to the average working scientist Laudan's arguments against demarcation may seem counterintuitive at best. On the surface it may appear that there ought to be some unambiguous criteria for distinguishing such dubious pursuits as parapsychology, astrology and phrenology from established sciences such as physics, chemistry and astronomy. That most philosophers of science say that there are not such criteria only confirms the suspicions many scientists have about philosophers of science. After all, don't some philosophers of science say that scientific truth is determined by social and cultural context? Don't some even deny that science describes an objective reality?

Well, as it turns out, one does not need to adopt a relativistic or antirealist view of science to accept what Laudan and others say about the demarcation problem. Indeed, the two positions are logically unrelated. Laudan is not arguing that all scientific theories have equal warrant (quite the reverse) or that scientific theories never refer to real entities. Instead, he simply says that one cannot define science in such a way as to confer automatic epistemic authority on favored theories simply because they happen to manifest features alleged to characterize all "true science." When evaluating the warrant or truth claims of theories, we cannot substitute abstractions about the nature of science for empirical evaluation.

Nevertheless, establishing Laudan's general thesis is not the main purpose of this chapter. This chapter is not seeking to establish the impossibility of demarcation in general, but the methodological equivalence of intelligent design and naturalistic descent. Since some may yet doubt that demarcation *always* fails, the following section will examine some of the specific demarcation arguments that have been deployed against design by proponents of descent.[39] It will suggest that these arguments fail to provide any grounds for distinguishing the methodological merit of one over the other and, instead, that careful analysis of these arguments actually exposes reasons for regarding design and descent as methodologically equivalent. Indeed, the following analysis will suggest that metaphysically neutral criteria do not exist that can define science narrowly enough to disqualify theories of design *tout court* without also disqualifying theories of descent on identical grounds.

Unfortunately, to establish this conclusively would require an examination of all the demarcation arguments that have been used against design. And indeed, an examination of evolutionary polemic reveals many such arguments. Design or creationist theories have been alleged to be necessarily unscientific because they (a) do not explain by reference to natural law,[40] (b) invoke unobservables,[41] (c) are not testable,[42] (d) do not make predictions,[43] (e) are not falsifiable,[44] (f) provide no mechanisms,[45] (g) are not tentative,[46] and (h) have no problem-solving capability.[47]

Due to space constraints, a detailed analysis of only the first three arguments will be possible. Nevertheless, an extensive analysis of (a), (b) and (c) will follow. These three have been chosen because each can be found in one form or another all the way back to the *Origin of Species*. The first one, (a), is especially important because the others derive from it—a point emphasized by Michael Ruse,[48] perhaps the world's most ardent evolutionary demarcationist. Consequently an analysis of assertion (a) will occupy the largest portion of this section.[49] There will also be a short discussion of arguments (d), (e) and (f) and references to literature refuting (g) and (h). Thus while an exhaustive analysis of all demarcationist arguments will not be possible here, enough will be said to allow us to conclude that the principal arguments employed against design do not succeed in impugning its scientific status without either begging the question or undermining the status of descent as well.

Explanation via natural law. Now let us examine the first, and according to Michael Ruse[50] most fundamental, of the arguments against the possibility of a scientific theory of design. This argument states: "Scientific theories must explain by natural law. Because design or creationist theories do not do so, they are necessarily unscientific."

This argument invokes one of the principal criteria of science adopted by Judge William Overton after hearing the testimony of philosopher of science Michael Ruse in the Arkansas creation-science trial of 1981-82.[51] As recently as March 1992, Ruse has continued to assert "must explain via natural law" as a demarcation criterion, despite criticism from other philosophers of science such Philip Quinn and Larry Laudan.[52] Ruse has argued that to adopt the scientific outlook, one must accept that the universe is subject to natural law, and further, that one must never appeal to an intervening agency as an explanation for events. Instead, one must always look to what he calls "unbroken law" if one wishes to explain things in a scientific manner.

There are several problems with this assertion and the conception of science that Ruse assumes.[53] In particular, Ruse seems to assume a view of science that equates scientific laws with explanations. There are two problems with this view and correspondingly two main reasons that "explains via natural law" will not do as a demarcation criterion.

First, many laws are descriptive and not explanatory. Many laws describe regularities but do not explain why the regular events they describe occur. A good example of this drawn from the history of science is the universal law of gravitation, which Newton himself freely admitted did not explain but instead merely described gravitational motion. As he put it in the "General Scholium" of the second edition of the *Principia*, "I do not feign hypotheses"—in other words, "I offer no explanations."[54] Insisting that science must explain by reference to "natural law" would eliminate from the domain of the properly scientific all fundamental laws of physics that describe mathematically, but do not explain, the phenomena they "cover."[55] For the demarcationist this is a highly paradoxical and undesirable result, since much of the motivation for the demarcationist program derives from a desire to ensure that disciplines claiming to be scientific match the methodological rigor of the physical sciences. While this result might alleviate the "physics envy" of many a sociologist, it does nothing for demarcationists except defeat the very purpose of their enterprise.

There is a second reason that laws cannot be equated with explanations or causes. This, in turn, gives rise to another reason that science cannot be identified only with those disciplines that explain via natural law. Laws cannot be equated with explanations, not just because many laws do not explain but also because many explanations of particular events, especially in applied or historical science, may not utilize laws.[56] While scientists may often use laws to assess or enhance the plausibility of explanations of particular events, analysis of the logical requirements of explanation has made clear that the citation of laws is not necessary to many such explanations.[57] Instead, many explanations of particular events or facts, especially in the historical sciences, depend primarily, even exclusively, upon the specification of past causal conditions and events rather than laws to do what might be called the "explanatory work." That is, citing past causal events often explains a particular event better than, and sometimes without reference to, a law or regularity in nature.[58]

One reason laws play little or no role in many historical explanations is that many particular events come into existence via a series of events that will not regularly reoccur. In such cases laws are not relevant to explaining the contrast between the event that has occurred and what could have or might have ordinarily been expected to occur. For example, a historical geologist seeking to explain the unusual height of the Himalayas will cite particular antecedent factors that were present in the case of the Himalayan orogeny but were absent in other mountain-building episodes. Knowing the laws of geophysics relevant to mountain-building generally will aid the geologist very little in accounting for the contrast between the Himalayan and other orogenies, since such laws would presumably apply to all mountain-building episodes. What the geologist needs in the search for an explanation in this case is not knowledge of a general law but evidence of a unique or distinctive set of past conditions.[59] Thus geologists have typically explained the unique height of the Himalayas by reference to the past position of the Indian and Asian land masses (and plates) and the subsequent collision that occurred between them.

The geologist's situation is very similar to that faced by historians generally. Consider the following factors that might help explain why World War I began: the ambition of Kaiser Wilhelm's generals, the Franco-Russian defense pact and the assassination of Archduke Ferdinand. Note that such possible explanatory factors invariably involve the citation of past events, conditions or actions rather than laws. Invoking past events as causes in order to explain subsequent events or present evidences is common both in history and in natural scientific disciplines such as historical geology. As Michael Scriven has shown, one can often know what caused something even when one cannot relate causes and effects to each other in formal statements of law.[60] Similarly, William Alston has shown that laws alone often do not explain particular events even when we have them.[61] The law "Oxygen is necessary to combustion" does not explain why a particular building burned down at a particular place and time.[62] To explain such a particular fact requires knowing something about the situation just before the fire occurred. It does little good to know scientific laws; what one requires is information concerning, for example, the presence of an arsonist or the lack of security at the building or the absence of a sprinkler system. Thus Alston concludes that to equate a law with an explanation or cause "is to commit a 'category mistake' of the most flagrant sort."[63]

Perhaps another example will help. If one wishes to explain why astronauts were able to fly to the moon when apples usually fall to the earth, one will not primarily cite the law of gravity. Such a law is far too general to be primarily relevant to explanation in this context, because the law allows for a vast array of possible outcomes depending on initial and boundary conditions. The law stating that all matter gravitates according to an inverse square law is consistent with both an apple falling to the earth and with an astronaut flying to the moon. Explaining why the astronaut flew when apples routinely fall, therefore, requires more than citing the law, since the law is presumed operative in both situations. Accounting for the differing outcomes—the falling apple and the flying astronaut—will require references to the antecedent conditions and events that differed in the two situations. Indeed, explanation in this case involves an accounting of the way engineers have used technology to alter the *conditions* affecting the astronauts to allow them to overcome the constraints that gravity ordinarily imposes on earthbound objects.

Such examples suggest that many explanations of particular events—explanations that occur frequently in fields already regarded as scientific—such as cosmology, archaeology, historical geology, applied physics and chemistry, origin-of-life studies and evolutionary biology—would lose their scientific status if Ruse's criterion of "explains via natural law" were accepted as normative to all scientific practice.

Consider an example from evolutionary biology that impinges directly on our discussion. Stephen Jay Gould, Mark Ridley and Michael Ruse argue that the "fact of evolution"[64] is secure even if an adequate theory has not yet been formulated to describe or explain how large-scale biological change generally occurs. Like Darwin, modern evolutionary theorists insist that the question whether evolution[65] did occur can be separated logically from the question of the means by which nature generally achieves biological transformations. Evolution in one sense—historical continuity or common descent—is asserted to be a well-established scientific theory[66] because it alone explains a diverse class of present data (fossil progression, homology, biogeographical distribution, etc.), even if biologists cannot yet explain how evolution in another sense—a general process or mechanism of change—occurs. Some have likened the logical independence of common descent and natural selection to the logical independence of continental drift and plate tectonics. In both the geological situation and the biological there exist theories about *what happened* that explain why we observe many present facts, and separate theories that explain *how* things *could have* happened as they apparently did. Yet the former purely historical explanations do not require the latter nomological[67] or mechanistic explanations to legitimate themselves. Common descent explains some facts well, even if nothing yet explains how the transformations it requires could have occurred.

This example again illustrates why historical explanations do not require laws.[68] More important, it also demonstrates why Ruse's demarcation criterion proves fatal to the very Darwinism he is seeking to protect. Common descent, arguably the central thesis of the *Origin of Species*, does not explain by natural law. Common descent explains by postulating a hypothetical pattern of historical events which, if actual, would account for a variety of presently observed data. Darwin himself refers to common descent as the *vera causa* (that is, the actual cause or explanation) for a diverse set of biological observations.[69] In Darwin's historical argument for descent, as with historical explanations generally, postulated past causal events (or patterns thereof) do the primary explanatory work. Laws do not.[70]

At this point the evolutionary demarcationist might grant the explanatory function of antecedent events but deny that scientific explanations can invoke *supernatural* events. To postulate naturally occurring past events is one thing, but to postulate supernatural events is another. The first leaves the laws of nature intact; the second does not and thus lies beyond the bounds of science. As Ruse and Richard Lewontin have argued, miraculous events are unscientific because they violate or contradict the laws of nature, thus making science impossible.[71]

Many contemporary philosophers disagree with Ruse and Lewontin about this, as have a number of good scientists over the years—Isaac Newton and Robert Boyle, for example. The action of agency (whether divine or human) need not violate the laws of nature; in most cases it merely changes the initial and boundary conditions on which the laws of nature operate.[72] But this issue must be set aside for the moment. For now it will suffice merely to note that the criterion of demarcation has subtly shifted. No longer does the demarcationist repudiate design as unscientific because it does not "explain via natural law"; now the demarcationist rejects intelligent design because it does not "explain naturalistically." To be scientific a theory must be naturalistic.

But why is this the case? Surely the point at issue is whether there are independent and metaphysically neutral grounds for disqualifying theories that invoke nonnaturalistic events—such as instances of agency or intelligent design. To assert that such theories are not scientific because they are not naturalistic simply assumes the point at issue. Of course intelligent design is not wholly naturalistic, but why does that make it unscientific? What noncircular reason can be given for this assertion? What independent criterion of method demonstrates the inferior scientific status of a nonnaturalistic explanation? We have seen that "must explain via law" does not. What does?

Unobservables and testability. At this point evolutionary demarcationists must offer other demarcation criteria. One that appears frequently both in conversation and in print finds expression as follows: "Miracles are unscientific because they can not be studied empirically.[73] Design invokes miraculous events; therefore design is unscientific. Moreover, since miraculous events can't be studied empirically, they can't be tested.[74] Since scientific theories must be testable, design is, again, not scientific." Molecular biologist Fred Grinnell has argued, for example, that intelligent design can't be a scientific concept because if something "can't be measured, or counted, or photographed, it can't be science."[75] Gerald Skoog amplifies this concern: "The claim that life is the result of a design created by an intelligent cause can not be tested and is not within the realm of science."[76] This reasoning was recently invoked at San Francisco State University as a justification for removing Professor Dean Kenyon from his classroom. Kenyon is a biophysicist who has embraced intelligent design after years of work on chemical evolution. Some of his critics at SFSU argued that his theory fails to qualify as scientific because it refers to an unseen Designer that cannot be tested.[77]

The essence of these arguments seems to be that the unobservable character of a designing agent renders it inaccessible to empirical investigation and thus precludes the possibility of testing any theory of design. Thus the criterion of demarcation employed here conjoins "observability and testability." Both are asserted as necessary to scientific status, and the converse of one (unobservability) is asserted to preclude the possibility of the other (testability).

It turns out, however, that both parts of this formula fail. First, observability and testability are not both necessary to scientific status, because observability at least is not necessary to scientific status, as theoretical physics has abundantly demonstrated. Many entities and events cannot be directly observed or studied—in practice or in principle. The postulation of such entities is no less the product of scientific inquiry for that. Many sciences are in fact directly charged with the job of inferring the unobservable from the observable. Forces, fields, atoms, quarks, past events, mental states, subsurface geological features, molecular biological structures—all are unobservables inferred from observable phenomena. Nevertheless, most are unambiguously the result of scientific inquiry.

Second, unobservability does not preclude testability: claims about unobservables are routinely tested in science indirectly against observable phenomena. That is, the existence of unobservable entities is established by testing the explanatory power that would result if a given hypothetical entity (i.e., an unobservable) were accepted as actual. This process usually involves some assessment of the established or theoretically plausible causal powers of a given unobservable entity. In any case, many scientific theories must be evaluated indirectly by comparing their explanatory power against competing hypotheses.

During the race to elucidate the structure of the genetic molecule, both a double helix and a triple helix were considered, since both could explain the photographic images produced via x-ray crystallography.[78] While neither structure could be observed (even indirectly through a microscope), the double helix of Watson and Crick eventually won out because it could explain other observations that the triple helix could not. The inference to one unobservable structure—the double helix—was accepted because it was judged to possess a greater explanatory power than its competitors with respect to a variety of relevant observations. Such attempts to infer to the best explanation, where the explanation presupposes the reality of an unobservable entity, occur frequently in many fields already regarded as scientific, including physics, geology, geophysics, molecular biology, genetics, physical chemistry, cosmology, psychology and, of course, evolutionary biology.

The prevalence of unobservables in such fields raises difficulties for defenders of descent who would use observability criteria to disqualify design. Darwinists have long defended the apparently unfalsifiable nature of their theoretical claims by reminding critics that many of the creative processes to which they refer occur at rates too slow to observe. Further, the core historical commitment of evolutionary theory—that present species are related by common ancestry—has an epistemological character that is very similar to many present design theories. The transitional life forms that ostensibly occupy the nodes on Darwin's branching tree of life are unobservable, just as the postulated past activity of a Designer is unobservable.[79] Transitional life forms are theoretical postulations that make possible evolutionary accounts of present biological data. An unobservable designing agent is, similarly, postulated to explain features of life such as its information content and functional integration. Darwinian transitional, neo-Darwinian mutational events, punctuationalism's "rapid branching" events, the past action of a designing agent—none of these are directly observable. With respect to direct observability, each of these theoretical entities is equivalent.

Each is roughly equivalent with respect to testability as well. Origins theories generally must make assertions about what happened in the past to cause present features of the universe (or the universe itself) to arise. They must reconstruct unobservable causal events from present clues or evidences. Positivistic methods of testing, therefore, that depend upon direct verification or repeated observation of cause-effect relationships have little relevance to origins theories, as Darwin himself understood. Though he complained repeatedly about the creationist failure to meet the *vera causa* criterion—a nineteenth-century methodological principle that favored theories postulating observed causes—he chafed at the application of rigid positivistic standards to his own theory. As he complained to Joseph Hooker: "I am actually weary of telling people that I do not pretend to adduce *direct* evidence of one species changing into another, but that I believe that this view in the main is correct because so many phenomena can be thus grouped and *explained*"[80] (emphasis added).

Indeed, Darwin insisted that direct modes of testing were wholly irrelevant to evaluating theories of origins. Nevertheless, he did believe that critical tests could be achieved via indirect means. As he stated elsewhere: "This hypothesis [common descent] must be tested . . . by trying to see whether it explains several large and independent classes of facts; such as the geological succession of organic beings, their distribution in past and present times, and their mutual affinities and homologies."[81] For Darwin the unobservability of past events and processes did not mean that origins theories are untestable. Instead, such theories may be evaluated and tested indirectly by the assessment of their explanatory power with respect to a variety of relevant data or "classes of facts."

Nevertheless, if this is so it is difficult to see why the unobservability of a Designer would necessarily preclude the testability of such a postulation. Though Darwin would not have agreed, the basis of his methodological defense of descent seems to imply the possibility of a testable theory of design, since the past action of an unobservable agent could have empirical consequences in the present just as an unobservable genealogical connection between organisms does. Indeed, Darwin himself tacitly acknowledged the testability of design by his own attempts to expose the empirical inadequacy of competing creationist theories. Though Darwin rejected many creationist explanations as unscientific in principle, he attempted to show that others were incapable of explaining certain facts of biology.[82] Thus sometimes he treated creationism as a serious scientific competitor lacking explanatory power; at other times he dismissed it as unscientific by definition.

Recent evolutionary demarcationists have contradicted themselves in the same way. The quotation cited earlier from Gerald Skoog ("The claim that life is the result of a design created by an intelligent cause can not be tested and is not within the realm of science") was followed in the same paragraph by the statement "Observations of the natural world also make these dicta [concerning the theory of intelligent design] suspect."[83] Yet clearly something cannot be both untestable in principle and subject to refutation by empirical observations.

The preceding considerations suggest that neither evolutionary descent with modification nor intelligent design is ultimately untestable. Instead, both theories seem testable indirectly, as Darwin explained of descent, by a comparison of their explanatory power with that of their competitors. As Philip Kitcher—no friend of creationism—has acknowledged, the presence of unobservable elements in theories, even ones involving an unobservable Designer, does not mean that such theories cannot be evaluated empirically. He writes, "Even postulating an unobserved Creator need be no more unscientific than postulating unobserved particles. What matters is the character of the proposals and the ways in which they are articulated and defended."[84]

Thus an unexpected equivalence emerges when design and descent are evaluated against their ability to meet specific demarcation criteria. The demand that the theoretical entities necessary to origins theories must be directly observable if they are to be considered testable and scientific would, if applied universally and disinterestedly, require the exclusion not only of design but also of descent. Those who insist on the joint criteria of observability and testability, conceived in a positivistic sense, promulgate a definition of correct science that evolutionary theory manifestly cannot meet. If, however, a less severe standard of testability is allowed, the original reason for excluding design evaporates. Here an analysis of specific attempts to apply demarcation criteria against design actually demonstrates a methodological equivalence between design and descent.

Other demarcation criteria. I claim that a similar equivalence between design and descent will emerge from an analysis of each of the other criteria—(d) through (h)—listed above.[85] Falsification, for example, in addition to the problems mentioned in part one, seems an especially problematic standard to apply to origins theories. So does prediction. Origins theories must necessarily offer ex post facto reconstructions. They therefore do not make predictions in any strong sense. The somewhat artificial "predictions" that origins theories do make about, for example, what evidence one ought to find if a given theory is true are singularly difficult to falsify since, as evolutionary paleontologists often explain, "the absence of evidence is no evidence of absence."[86]

Similarly, the requirement that a scientific theory must provide a causal mechanism fails to provide a metaphysically neutral standard of demarcation for several reasons. First, as we have already noted, many theories in science are not mechanistic theories. Many theories that explicate what regularly happens in nature either do not or need not explain why those phenomena occur mechanically. Newton's universal law of gravitation was no less a scientific theory because Newton failed—indeed refused—to postulate a mechanistic cause for the regular pattern of attraction his law described. Also, as noted earlier, many historical theories about *what* happened in the past may stand on their own without any mechanistic theory about *how* the events to which such theories attest could have occurred. The theory of common descent is generally regarded as a scientific theory even though scientists have not agreed on a completely adequate mechanism to explain how transmutation between lines of descent can be achieved. In the same way, there seems little justification for asserting that the theory of continental drift became scientific only after the advent of plate tectonics. While the mechanism provided by plate tectonics certainly helped render continental drift a more persuasive theory,[87] it was nevertheless not strictly necessary to know the mechanism by which continental drift *occurs* (1) to know or theorize that drift *had occurred* or (2) to regard the continental drift theory as scientific.

Yet one might concede that causal mechanisms are not required in all scientific contexts, but deny that origins research is such a context. One might argue that since origins theories necessarily attempt to offer causal explanations, and since design admittedly attempts to explain the origin of life or major taxonomic groups, its failure to offer a mechanism disqualifies it as an adequate theory of origins.

But this argument has difficulties as well. First, an advocate of design could concede that his theory does not provide a complete causal explanation of how life originated without forfeiting scientific status for the theory. Present clues and evidences might convince some scientists *that* intelligence played a causal role in the design of life, without those same scientists' knowing exactly *how* mind exerts its influence over matter. All that would follow in such a case is that design is an incomplete theory, not that it is an unscientific one (or even an unwarranted one). And such incompleteness is not unique to design theories. Both biological (as just discussed) and chemical evolutionary theories have often provided less than completely adequate causal scenarios. Indeed, most scientific theories of origin are causally incomplete or inadequate in some way.

In any case, asserting mechanism as necessary to the scientific status of origins theories begs the question. In particular, it assumes without justification that all scientifically acceptable causes are *mechanistic* causes. To insist that all causal explanations in science must be mechanistic is to insist that all causal theories must refer only to material entities (or their energetic equivalents). Yet this requirement is merely another expression of the very naturalism whose methodological necessity has been asserted because of ostensibly compelling demarcation arguments. Insofar as the statement "All scientific theories must be mechanistic" *is* a demarcation argument, this requirement is evidently circular. Science, the demarcationist claims, must be mechanistic because it must be naturalistic; it must be naturalistic because otherwise it would violate demarcation standards—in particular, the standard that all scientific theories must be mechanistic.

This argument clearly assumes the point at issue, which is whether or not there are independent—that is, metaphysically neutral—reasons for preferring exclusively materialistic causal explanations of origins over explanations that invoke putatively immaterial entities such as creative intelligence, mind, mental action, divine action or intelligent design. While philosophical naturalists may not regard the foregoing as real or (if real) immaterial, they certainly cannot deny that such entities could function as causal antecedents if they were.

Thus we return to the central question: What noncircular reason can be offered for prohibiting the postulation of nonmechanistic (e.g., mental or intelligent) causes in scientific origins theories? Simply asserting that such entities may not be considered, whatever the empirical justification for their postulation, clearly does not constitute a justification for an exclusively naturalistic definition of science. Theoretically there are at least two possible types of causes: mechanistic and intelligent. The demarcationist has yet to offer a noncircular reason for excluding the latter type.[88]

Part 3: The Methodological Character of Historical Science

Let us now turn to a more fundamental reason for the methodological equivalence of design and descent. As stated earlier, the equivalence of design and descent follows from an understanding of the distinctive logical and methodological character of the historical sciences. An examination of scientific disciplines concerned with past events and causes, such as evolutionary biology, historical geology and archaeology, reveals a distinctive pattern of inquiry that contrasts markedly with nonhistorical sciences such as branches of chemistry, physics or biology that are concerned primarily with the discovery and explication of general phenomena. This section will show that both design and descent do, or could, instantiate this distinctive historical pattern of scientific investigation. In other words, a fundamental methodological equivalence between design and descent derives from a common concern with history—that is, with historical questions, historical inferences and historical explanations.

We can see this historical concern first by looking at why the demarcation arguments analyzed earlier fail. Consider, for example, the assertion that to be scientific one must explain by reference to natural law. To insist that "science must explain by natural law" betrays much confusion—about the alleged universality of explanation in science, about the necessary role of laws in explanations and about the distinction between laws and causes. But fundamentally this demarcation criterion fails to do the work required of it by evolutionary writers because it ignores that some scientific disciplines ("historical" according to my lexicon) seek to explain events or data not primarily by reference to laws but by reference to past causal events or sequences of events—what might be called "causal histories." Since natural laws are not necessary to such activity, the demarcation criterion "must explain by natural law" can't be used to distinguish between two competing programs of historical scientific research, whether evolutionary or otherwise.

Next consider the idea that scientific theories must not postulate unverifiable or unobservable entities. Certainly this criterion is untenable in light of many fields, not the least of which is modern physics. Yet it is completely irrelevant to historical study almost in principle. All historical theories depend on what C. S. Peirce called "abductive inferences."[89] Such inferences frequently posit unobservable past events in order to explain present phenomena, facts or clues. Making a claim about history nearly always involves postulating, invoking, or inferring an unobservable event or entity that cannot be studied directly. The attempt to distinguish the methodological merit of competing origins theories on the basis of unobservables therefore seems quite misguided and futile.

Finally, consider the claim that to be scientific a theory must be testable. As we saw above, neither design nor descent can meet standards of testability that require strict verifiability. I have also emphasized that neither can meet standards of testability that depend on notions of repeatability. Yet both can meet alternate standards of testability, such as inference to the best explanation or "consilience," that involve notions of comparative explanatory power. This equivalence was suggested again from the historical nature of the claims that design and evolutionary theorists make. Like other historical theorists, both make claims about events they believe occurred in the past that cannot be directly verified and may never recur. Yet like other historical theories, these theories can be tested after the fact by reference to their comparative explanatory power. To impose stricter standards ignores the limitations inherent in all historical inquiry and thus again fails to provide grounds for distinguishing the status of competing historical or origins theories.

So the evolutionary demarcation arguments above seem to fail in part because they attempt to impose (as normative) criteria of method that ignore the historical character of origins research. Indeed, each one of the demarcationist arguments listed above fails because it overlooks a specific characteristic of the historical sciences. But what are these characteristics? And could *they* provide grounds for distinguishing the scientific, or at least methodological, status of design and descent?

The nature of historical science. Answering these questions will require briefly summarizing the results of my doctoral research on the logical and methodological features of the historical sciences.[90] Through that research I have identified three general features of historical scientific disciplines. These features derive from a concern to reconstruct the past and to explain the present by reference to the past. They distinguish disciplines motivated by historical concerns from disciplines motivated by a concern to discover, classify or explain unchanging laws and properties of nature. These latter disciplines may be called "inductive" or "nomological" (from the Greek word *nomos*, for law); the former type may be called "historical."[91] I contend that historical sciences generally can be distinguished from nonhistorical scientific disciplines by virtue of the three following features.

1. The historical interest or questions motivating their practitioners: Those in the historical sciences generally seek to answer questions of the form "What happened?" or "What caused this event or that natural feature to arise?" On the other hand, those in the nomological or inductive sciences generally address questions of the form "How does nature normally operate or function?"

2. The distinctively historical types of inference used: The historical sciences use inferences with a distinctive logical form. Unlike many nonhistorical disciplines, which typically attempt to infer generalizations or laws from particular facts, historical sciences make what C. S. Peirce has called "abductive inferences" in order to infer a past event from a present fact or clue. These inferences have also been called "retrodictive" because they are temporally asymmetric—that is, they seek to reconstruct past conditions or causes from present facts or clues. For example, detectives[92] use abductive or retrodictive inferences to reconstruct the circumstances of a crime after the fact. In so doing they function as historical scientists. As Gould has put it, the historical scientist proceeds by "inferring history from its results."[93]

3. The distinctively historical types of explanations used: In the historical sciences one finds causal explanations of particular events, not nomological descriptions or theories of general phenomena. In historical explanations, past causal events, not laws, do the primary explanatory work. The explanations cited earlier of the Himalayan orogeny and the beginning of World War I exemplify such historical explanations.[94]

In addition, the historical sciences share with many other types of science a fourth feature.

4. Indirect methods of testing such as inference to the best explanation: As discussed earlier, many disciplines cannot test theories by direct observation, prediction or repeated experiment. Instead, testing must be done indirectly through comparison of the explanatory power of competing theories.

Descent as historical science. Enough has been said previously—about the function of common descent as an explanatory causal history, the retrodictive character of Darwin's inference of common descent and his use of indirect methods of theory evaluation—to suggest that evolutionary research programs conform closely to the general methodological pattern of the historical sciences. But a few additional observations may make this connection more explicit.

With respect to the first characteristic of historical science enumerated above (historical motive or purpose), Darwin clearly was motivated by such a purpose. One of Darwin's primary goals in the *Origin of Species* was to establish a historical point[95]—namely, that species had not originated independently but had derived via transmutation from one or very few common ancestors. Indeed, Darwin sought to show that the history of life resembled a single, continuous branching tree, with the first and simplest living forms represented by the base of a tree and the great diversity of more complex forms, both past and present, represented by the connecting branches. This picture of biological history contrasted markedly with that of his creationist opponents, who envisioned the history of life as an array of parallel (nonconvergent) lines of descent. Darwin's (perhaps primary) purpose in the *Origin of Species* was to argue for this continuous view of life's history as opposed to the discontinuous view favored by his creationist opponents.

Thus he would repeatedly explicate his priorities in such a way as to show the primacy of his concern to demonstrate the historical thesis of common descent, even over his concern to establish the efficacy of his proposed mechanism, natural selection. He himself tells us what he had in mind: "I had two distinct objects in view; *firstly* to shew that species had not been separately created [i.e., that they had evolved from common ancestors], and *second,* that natural selection had been the chief agent of change"[96] (emphasis added).

Similarly, at the close of his chapter 13 Darwin states the priorities of his argument by concluding: "The several classes of facts which have been considered . . . proclaim so plainly that the innumerable species, genera, and families with which the world is peopled are all *descended* . . . from common parents and have been modified in the course of descent, that I should without hesitation adopt this view, *even if* it were unsupported by other facts or arguments"[97] (emphasis added).

Not only was Darwin motivated by a historical purpose, but he also used (concerning feature 2 above) a characteristically historical mode of reasoning. As Gould has argued so persuasively, Darwin used historical inferences. Beginning in the middle of his chapter on the "Geological Succession of Organic Beings" and continuing through his next three chapters, Darwin offered a series of arguments to support his historical claim of common descent.[98] These arguments are instances of retrodictive or abductive reasoning. In each case, extant evidence from the fossil record, comparative anatomy, embryology and biogeography were used as clues from which to infer a pattern of past biohistorical events. Notice, for example, the language Darwin uses in his argument from vestigial structures: "Rudimentary organs may be compared with the letters in a word, still retained in the spelling but become useless in the pronunciation, but *which serve as a clue in seeking for its derivation.*"[99]

Notice, too, the temporally asymmetric character of each of the inferences he employs: "The several *classes of facts* which have been considered . . . proclaim so plainly that the innumerable species, genera, and families with which the world is peopled are all *descended,* each within its own class or group, *from common parents.*"[100] As Gould has written, Darwin used a method of "inferring history from its results."[101]

Darwin not only inferred an historical past, but (with respect to feature 3 above) he also formulated historical explanations. Indeed, a reciprocal relationship exists between historical inferences and explanations. Historical scientists will often seek to infer causal antecedents that, if true, would explain the widest class of relevant data. The causal past inferred on the basis of its potential to explain will often serve, when accepted, as an explanation. Darwin repeatedly argued that the supposition that all organisms descended from common parents should be accepted because it "explains several large and independent classes of facts."[102] Moreover, common descent (and the past events implied by it) served as a *causal* explanation for Darwin. He refers to "propinquity of descent" as *"the only known cause* of the similarity of organic beings."[103] Elsewhere he refers to common descent or "propinquity of descent" as the *vera causa* (or true cause) of organic similarity.[104] By inferring descent as a past cause, Darwin constructed a historical explanation in which a pattern of past events did the primary explanatory work in relation to the facts of biogeography, fossil progression, homology and so on. As Gould has put it, the *Origin of Species* makes "the claim that *history* stands as the coordinating reason for relationships among organisms."[105]

The explanatory function of antecedent events and causal histories is perhaps even more readily apparent in the work of many chemical evolutionary theorists. Alexander Oparin, Russian scientist and father of modern origin-of-life research, formulated detailed causal histories involving a sequence of hypothetical past events to explain how life emerged in its present form.[106] The formulation of these "scenarios," as they are called in origin-of-life biology, has remained an important part of origin-of-life studies to the present.[107] Thus evolutionary biologists employ not only historical inferences but also historical explanations in which past causal events, or patterns thereof, serve to explain the origin of present facts.

As already discussed, Darwin also (with respect to feature 4 above) employed a method of indirect testing of his theory by assessing its relative explanatory power. Recall his statement that "this hypothesis [i.e., common descent] must be tested . . . by trying to see whether it explains several large and independent classes of facts"[108] He makes this indirect and comparative method of testing even more explicit in a letter to Asa Gray:

> I . . . test this hypothesis [common descent] by comparison with as many general and pretty well-established propositions as I can find—in geographical distribution, geological history, affinities &c., &c. And it seems to me that, *supposing* that such a hypothesis were to explain such general propositions, we ought, in accordance with the common way of following all sciences, to admit it till some *better* hypothesis be found out.[109] (emphasis added)

Design as historical science. The foregoing suggests that evolutionary biology, or at least Darwin's version of it, does conform to the pattern of inquiry described above as historically scientific. To show that design and descent are methodologically equivalent with respect to the historical mode of inquiry outlined above, it now remains to show that a design argument or theory could exemplify this same historical pattern of inquiry.

In the case of feature 1 this equivalence is quite obvious. As just noted, a clear logical distinction exists between questions of the form "How does nature normally operate or function?" and those of the form "How did this or that natural feature arise?" or "What caused this or that event to occur?" Those who postulate the past activity of an intelligent Designer do so as an answer, or partial answer, to questions of the latter historical type. Whatever the evidential merits or liabilities of design theories, such theories undoubtedly represent attempts to answer questions about what caused certain features in the natural world to come into existence. With respect to an interest in origins questions, design and descent are clearly equivalent.

Design and descent are also equivalent with respect to feature 2. Inferences to intelligent design are clearly abductive and retrodictive. They seek to infer a past unobservable cause (an instance of creative mental action or agency) from present facts or clues in the natural world such as the information content of DNA, the functional coadaptation of biomolecules, the sudden appearance of a new form in the fossil record, the uniqueness of human language and the hierarchical organization of biological systems.[110] Moreover, just as Darwin sought to strengthen the retrodictive inferences that he made by showing that many facts or classes of facts could be explained on the supposition of descent, so too may proponents of design seek to muster a wide variety of clues to demonstrate the explanatory power of their theory. In the second half of this volume, for example, evidence from at least four distinct domains of the natural world will be cited to demonstrate the explanatory power (or "consilience") of the design inference.

With respect to feature 3, design inferences, once made, may also serve as causal explanations. The same reciprocal relationship between inference and explanation that exists in arguments for descent can exist in arguments for design. Thus, as noted, an inference to intelligent design may gain support because it could, if accepted, explain many diverse classes of facts. Clearly, once adopted it will provide corresponding explanatory resources. Moreover, theories of design involving the special creative act of an agent conceptualize that act as a causal event,[111] albeit involving mental rather than purely physical antecedents. Indeed, design theories—whether posited by young-earth Genesis literalists, old-earth progressive creationists, theistic macromutationalists or religiously agnostic biologists—refer to antecedent causal events or express some kind of causal scenario just as, for example, chemical evolutionary theories do. As a matter of method, advocates of design and descent alike seek to postulate antecedent causal events or event scenarios in order to explain the origin of present phenomena. With respect to feature 3, design and descent again appear methodologically equivalent.

Much has already been said to suggest that with respect to feature 4 design may be tested indirectly in the same way as descent. Certainly, advocates of design may seek to test their ideas as Darwin did—against a wide class of relevant facts and by comparing the explanatory power of their hypotheses against competitors'. Indeed, many biologists who favor design now make their case for it on the basis of its ability to explain the same evidences that descent can as well as some that descent allegedly cannot (such as the presence of sequentially encoded information in DNA).[112]

Thus design and descent again seem methodologically equivalent. Both seek to answer characteristically historical questions, both rely upon abductive inferences, both postulate antecedent causal events or scenarios as explanations of present data, and both are tested indirectly by comparing their explanatory power against that of competing theories.

A theory of everything? Yet before one is willing to concede this methodological equivalence, one might demand to know that design can really function as a valid explanation without trivializing scientific inquiry. The perennial worry about allowing theories of design, of course, concerns not their explanatory power but the inability to constrain that power. This concern lies behind

some secular scientists' worry that a theory of design would leave them nothing to do, since presumably the phrase "God did it" could be invoked as the
answer to every scientific question. As David Hull wrote recently, "Scientists
have no choice [but to define science as totally naturalistic]. Once they allow
reference to God or miraculous forces to explain the first origin of life or the
evolution of the human species, they have no way of limiting this sort of
explanation."[113] This worry also finds expression in the familiar theistic worry
about embarrassing "God-of-the-gaps" arguments, as J. P. Moreland pointed
out in chapter one. So both theists and secularists may worry: "If design is
allowed as a (historically) scientific theory, couldn't it be invoked at every turn
as a theoretical panacea, stultifying inquiry as it goes? Might not design become a refuge for the intellectually lazy who have refused to study what
nature actually does?"

Well, of course it might. But so might the incantation "Evolution accomplished X." Nevertheless, design need not stultify inquiry, nor can it be offered appropriately in every context as a theoretical panacea. The distinction
between the historical sciences and the nomological or inductive sciences
helps to explain why. Indeed, it helps to show how design can be both
legitimated (as a possible historical explanation) and at the same time constrained or even prohibited, depending on the context of inquiry. In other
words, the distinction between the historical and the nomological helps to
show why the past action of an intelligent agent may serve as a legitimate
explanation in the historical sciences, whereas it would not in many nonhistorical scientific contexts.

When a research program concentrates on questions of how nature normally (unassisted by the special activity of agency) operates, any reference to
agency (whether divine or human) becomes inappropriate because it fails to
address the question motivating the inquiry. A geologist who inquires about
the stress-strain relationship of a particular type of rock at various temperatures will rightly regard the postulation of God's creative activity (or, for that
matter, a corresponding evolutionary scenario) as irrelevant to her inquiry.
As noted above, nomological or inductive scientific endeavor typically seeks
to infer or explain general nomological relations (i.e., scientific laws), whereas
historical sciences typically infer past causal events. To propose the action of
agency (as an event in space and time) when a law is required simply misses
the context and character of nomological inquiry. Neither divine nor human
action qualifies as a law. To offer either when a law is sought is syntactically
inappropriate. To offer "God did it" as an answer to a question such as "How

does weightlessness generally affect crystal growth?" clearly misses the point of the question. The answer does not so much violate the rules of science as the rules of grammar. Such an answer not only stultifies inquiry but misses the point of such inquiry altogether.

It does not follow, however, that references to agency are necessarily inappropriate when we are reconstructing a causal history—that is, when we are attempting to answer questions about how a particular feature in the natural world (or the universe itself) arose. In the first place, classical examples of inappropriate postulations of divine activity (God-of-the-gaps arguments) occur almost exclusively in the inductive or nomological sciences, as Newton's ill-fated use of agency to provide a more accurate description of planetary motion suggests.[114] Second, many fields of inquiry routinely invoke the action of agents to account for the origin of features or events within the natural world. Forensic science, history and archaeology, for example, all sometimes postulate the past activity of human agents to account for the emergence of particular objects or events. Several such fields suggest a clear precedent for inferring the past causal activity of intelligent agents within the historical sciences. Imagine the absurdity of someone's claiming that scientific method had been violated by the archaeologist who first inferred that French cave paintings had been produced by human beings rather than by natural forces such as wind and erosion.

There is another, more fundamental reason that postulating the past action of agency can be appropriate in the historical sciences. That again has to do with the nature of historical explanations. As already noted, historical explanations require the postulation of antecedent causal events; they do not seek to infer laws.[115] To offer past agency as part of a historical explanation is therefore logically and syntactically appropriate. The type of theoretical entity provided—a past causal event—corresponds to the type required by historical explanations. Simply put, past agency is a causal event. Agency, therefore, whether seen or unseen, may serve as a logically and syntactically appropriate theoretical entity in a historical explanation, even if it could not do so in a nomological or inductive theory. Mental action may be a cause, even if it is certainly not a law.

In any case, postulations of design are constrained by background knowledge about the causal powers and proclivities of both nature and agency. In addition to the features of historical explanation mentioned already, successful historical explanations (as I have discussed elsewhere)[116] must usually meet independent criteria of causal adequacy. This criterion, which seems to function normatively in much historical scientific practice, expresses the idea that postulated causal antecedents should generally be known to be capable of producing the relevant *explanandum*—that is, the event or object requiring explanation. In other words, before a cause can be postulated to have been present in the past, one should know that some causal precedent (which is not the same thing as knowing a law) exists for believing the cause capable of producing the effect of interest. Intelligent design can be offered, therefore, as a necessary or best causal explanation only when naturalistic processes seem incapable of producing the *explanandum* effect, and when intelligence is known to be capable of producing it and thought to be more likely to have produced it. Thus modern scientific advocates of design such as Charles Thaxton or Walter Bradley (see their chapter in this present volume) insist that they postulate antecedent intelligent activity not because of what we do not know but because of what we *do* know about what is and is not capable of producing coded information.[117] Conversely, there are many effects that do not, based on our present background knowledge of causal powers, suggest design as a necessary, best or most likely historical explanation.

Postulations of design are constrained in yet another way. There are many particular events, even in history, for which design could not be considered the best or most likely explanation. The reason for this is that postulations of intelligent design are constrained by background assumptions about the proclivities of potential designing agents, both human and divine. Most biblical theists, for example, assume that God acts in at least two ways: (1) through the natural regularities or laws that he upholds and sustains through his invisible power and (2) through more dramatic, discernible and discrete actions at particular points in time. Because theists assume that the second mode of divine action is by far the rarer and usually associated with the accomplishment of some particular divine purpose on behalf of human beings (e.g., creation or redemption), they assume that divine action of the second variety will be unlikely as an explanation of most particular events. In philosophical terms, theists generally approach their study of nature with a set of background assumptions that would lead them to regard most hypotheses of divine action as unlikely, though not completely impossible. Theism itself constrains design inferences. Thus theistic background assumptions would generally allow consideration of special divine action as the best or most likely explanation for a particular event only when it seemed empirically warranted *and theologically plausible*. Nevertheless, given a biblical (though not necessarily literalist) understanding of creation and sufficient empirical justification, there is no reason to believe that both these conditions could not be met in some cases, as with, for example, explanations of the origin of life, human consciousness and the universe.

The above considerations suggest that allowing the design hypothesis as the best explanation for some events in the history of the cosmos will not cause science to grind to a halt. While design does have the required logical and syntactic features of some scientific (i.e., historical) explanations, it cannot be invoked appropriately in all scientific contexts. Furthermore, because effective postulations of design are constrained by empirical considerations of causal precedence and adequacy and by extraevidential considerations such as simplicity[118] and theological plausibility,[119] concerns about design theory functioning as a "theory of everything" or "providing cover for ignorance" or "putting scientists out of work" can be shown to be largely unfounded. Many important scientific questions would remain to be answered if one adopted a theory of design. Indeed, *all* questions about how nature normally operates without the special assistance[120] of agency remain unaffected by whatever view of origins one adopts. And that, perhaps, is yet another equivalence between design and descent.

Conclusion: Toward a Scientific Theory of Creation

So what should we make of these methodological equivalencies? Can there be a scientific theory of intelligent design?

At the very least it seems we can conclude that we have not yet encountered any good in principle reason to *exclude* design from science. Design seems to be just as scientific (or unscientific) as its evolutionary competitors when judged according to the methodological criteria examined above. Moreover, if the antidemarcationists are correct, our lack of universal demarcation criteria implies there cannot be a negative a priori case against the scientific status of design—precisely because there is not an agreed standard as to what constitutes the properly scientific. To say that some discipline or activity qualifies as scientific is to imply the existence of a standard by which the scientific status of an activity or discipline can be assessed or adjudicated. If no such standard presently exists, then nothing positive (or negative) can be said about the scientific status of intelligent design (or any other theory for that matter).

But there is another approach that can be taken to the question. If (1) there exists a distinctively historical pattern of inquiry, and (2) a program of origins research committed to design theory could or does instantiate that pattern, and (3) many other fields such as evolutionary biology also instantiate that pattern, and (4) these other fields are already regarded by convention as science, there can be a very legitimate if convention-dependent sense in which design may be considered scientific. In other words, the conjunction of the methodological equivalence of design and descent and the existence of a convention that regards descent as scientific implies that design should—by that same convention—be regarded as scientific too. Thus, one might quite legitimately say that both design and descent are historically scientific research programs, since they instantiate the same pattern of inquiry.

Perhaps, however, one just really does not want to call intelligent design a scientific theory. Perhaps one prefers the designation "quasi-scientific historical speculation with strong metaphysical overtones." Fine. Call it what you will, provided the same appellation is applied to other forms of inquiry that have the same methodological and logical character and limitations. In particular, make sure both design and descent are called "quasi-scientific historical speculation with strong metaphysical overtones."

This may seem all very pointless, but that in a way is just the point. As Laudan has argued, the question whether a theory is scientific is really a red herring. What we want to know is not whether a theory is scientific but whether a theory is true or false, well confirmed or not, worthy of our belief or not. One can not decide the truth of a theory or the warrant for believing a theory to be true by applying a set of abstract criteria that purport to tell in advance how all good scientific theories are constructed or what they will in general look like.

Against method? Now none of the above should be construed to imply that methodology does not matter. The purpose of this essay is not to argue, as Paul Feyerabend does, against method.[121] Methodological standards in science can be important for guiding future inquiry along paths that have been successful in the past. The uniformitarian and/or actualistic method in the historical sciences, for example, has proved a very helpful guide to reconstructing the past, even if it can't be used as demarcation between science and pseudoscience, and even if some theories constructed according to its guidelines turn out to be false.

Standards of method may also express some minimal logical and epistemic conditions of success—for example, the conditions related to causal explanation.[122] Successful causal explanations must as a condition of logical sufficiency cite more than just a necessary condition of a given outcome.[123] To explain why a given explosion occurred, it will not suffice to note that oxygen was present in the atmosphere; nor can the death of a patient be explained simply by citing the patient's birth, though clearly birth is necessary to death. These cases illustrate how methodological guidelines (whether tacit or explicit) can help eliminate certain (in this case logically) inadequate hypotheses, even if such guidelines cannot be used to define science exhaustively. Methodological anarchism need not result from a rejection of methodological demarcation arguments.

Nevertheless, following methodological criteria and recipes (of any of the preceding types) does not guarantee theoretical success; nor, again, can such recipes be used to define science exhaustively, if for no other reason than the variety of scientific methods that exist. Moreover, methodological recipes can sometimes become fatal to the success of inquiry if they so dictate the content of acceptable theorizing that they automatically eliminate empirically and logically possible explanations or theories.

And this, I believe, has occurred within origins research. The deployment of flawed or metaphysically tendentious demarcation arguments against legitimate theoretical contenders has produced an unjustified confidence in the epistemic standing of much evolutionary dogma, including "the fact of evolution" defined as common descent. If competing hypotheses are eliminated before they are evaluated, remaining theories may acquire an undeserved dominance.

So the question isn't whether there can be a scientific theory of design or creation. The question is whether design should be considered as a competing hypothesis alongside descent in serious origins research (call it what you will). Once issues of demarcation are firmly behind us, understood as the red herrings they are, the answer to this question *must* clearly be yes—that is, if origins biology is to have standing as a fully rational enterprise, rather than just a game played according to rules convenient to philosophical materialists.

Naturalism: the only game in town? G. K. Chesterton once said that "behind every double standard lies a single hidden agenda."[124] Advocates of descent have used demarcation arguments to erect double standards against design, suggesting that the real methodological criterion they have in mind is naturalism. Of course for many the equation of science with the strictly materialistic or naturalistic is not at all a hidden agenda. Scientists generally treat "naturalistic" as perhaps the most important feature of their enterprise.[125] Clearly, if naturalism is regarded as a necessary feature of all scientific hypotheses, then design will not be considered a scientific hypothesis.

But must all scientific hypotheses be entirely naturalistic? Must scientific origins theories, in particular, limit themselves to materialistic causes? Thus far none of the arguments advanced in support of a naturalistic definition of science has provided a noncircular justification for such a limitation. Nevertheless, perhaps such arguments are irrelevant. Perhaps scientists should just accept the definition of science that has come down to them. After all, the search for natural causes has served science well. What harm can come from continuing with the status quo? What compelling reasons can be offered for overturning the prohibition against nonnaturalistic explanation in science?

In fact, there are several. First, with respect to origins, defining science as a strictly naturalistic enterprise is metaphysically gratuitous. Consider: It is at least logically possible that a personal agent existed before the appearance of the first life on earth. Further, as Bill Dembski argues in the next chapter,[126] we do live in the sort of world where knowledge of such an agent could possibly be known or inferred from empirical data. This suggests that it is logically and empirically possible that such an agent (whether divine or otherwise) designed or influenced the origin of life on earth. To insist that postulations of past agency are inherently unscientific in the historical sciences (where the express purpose of such inquiry is to determine what happened in the past) suggests we know that no personal agent could have existed prior to humans. Not only is such an assumption intrinsically unverifiable, it seems entirely gratuitous in the absence of some noncircular account of why science should presuppose metaphysical naturalism.

Second, to exclude by assumption a logically and empirically possible answer to the question motivating historical science seems intellectually and theoretically limiting, especially since no equivalent prohibition exists on the possible nomological relationships that scientists may postulate in nonhistorical sciences. The (historical) question that must be asked about biological origins is not "Which materialistic scenario will prove most adequate?" but "How did life as we know it actually arise on earth?" Since one of the logically and syntactically appropriate answers to this later question is "Life was designed by an intelligent agent that existed before the advent of humans," it seems rationally stultifying to exclude the design hypothesis without a consideration of all the evidence, including the most current evidence, that might support it.

The a priori exclusion of design diminishes the rationality or origins research in another way. Recent nonpositivistic accounts of scientific rationality suggest that scientific theory evaluation is an inherently comparative enterprise. Notions such as consilience[127] and Peter Lipton's inference to the best explanation[128] discussed above imply the need to compare the explanatory power of competing hypotheses or theories. If this process is subverted by philosophical gerrymandering, the rationality of scientific practise is vitiated. Theories that gain acceptance in artificially constrained competitions can claim to be neither "most probably true" nor "most empirically adequate." Instead such theories can only be considered "most probable or adequate among an artificially limited set of options."

Moreover, where origins are concerned only a limited number of basic research programs are logically possible.[129] (Either brute matter has the capability to arrange itself into higher levels of complexity or it does not. If it does not, then either some external agency has assisted the arrangement of matter or matter has always possessed its present arrangement.) The exclusion of one of the logically possible programs of origins research by assumption, therefore, seriously diminishes the significance of any claim to theoretical superiority by advocates of a remaining program. As Phillip Johnson has argued,[130] the use of "methodological rules" to protect Darwinism from theoretical challenge has produced a situation in which Darwinist claims must be regarded as little more than tautologies expressing the deductive consequences of methodological naturalism.

An openness to empirical arguments for design is therefore a necessary condition of a fully rational historical biology. A rational historical biology must not only address the question "Which materialistic or naturalistic evolutionary scenario provides the most adequate explanation of biological complexity?" but also the question "Does a strictly materialistic evolutionary scenario or one involving intelligent agency or some other theory best explain the origin of biological complexity, given all relevant evidence?" To insist otherwise is to insist that materialism holds a metaphysically privileged position. Since there seems no reason to concede that assumption, I see no reason to concede that origins theories must be strictly naturalistic.

Acknowledgments
For helpful comments and criticisms I would like to thank Ed Olson, Forrest Baird, Dale Bruner, Bill Dembski, Norman Krebbs, J. P. Moreland, Paul Nelson and Jitse van der Meer. For assistance with typing references I would like to thank Lorrie Nelson. For generous research support I thank the Pascal Centre in Ontario, Canada, and C. Davis Weyerhaeuser.

Bibliography

Books

Ambrose, E. J. *The Nature and Origin of the Biological World.* New York: Halstead, 1982. [A]

Augros, R., and G. Stanciu. *The New Biology.* Boston: Shambhala, 1987. [B]

Barrow, John D., and Frank J. Tipler. *The Anthropic Principle and the Structure of the Physical World.* New York: Oxford University Press, 1986. [A]

Brooks, Daniel R., and E. O. Wiley. *Entropy and Evolution.* Chicago: University of Chicago Press, 1985. [A]

Cairns-Smith, A. G. *Genetic Takeover and the Mineral Origins of Life.* Cambridge, U.K.: Cambridge University Press, 1982. [I]

————. *Seven Clues to the Origin of Life.* Cambridge, U.K.: Cambridge University Press, 1986. [B]

Chesterton, G. K. *Orthodoxy.* London: John Lane, 1909. [I]

Crick, F. *Life Itself.* New York: Simon and Schuster, 1981. [B]

Darwin, Charles. *The Descent of Man.* 2nd ed. New York: A. L. Burt, 1874. [I]

————. *The Origin of Species by Means of Natural Selection.* 1859; rpt. Harmondsworth, U.K.: Penguin, 1984. [I]

Darwin, F., ed. *Life and Letters of Charles Darwin.* 2 vols. London: D. Appleton, 1896. [I]

————. *More Letters of Charles Darwin.* 2 vols. London: Murray, 1903. [I]

De Beer, G. *Homology: An Unsolved Problem.* London: Oxford University Press, 1971. [A]

Denton, Michael. *Evolution: A Theory in Crisis.* London: Adler and Adler, 1986. [I]

Ebert, James, et al. *Science and Creationism: A View from the National Academy of Science.* Washington, D.C.: National Academy Press, 1987. [B]

Eldredge, Niles. *Time Frames: The Evolution of Punctuated Equilibria.* Princeton, N.J.: Princeton University Press, 1985. [A]

Fann, K. T. *Peirce's Theory of Abduction.* The Hague: Martinus Nijhoff, 1970. [A]

Feyerabend, Paul. *Against Method.* London: Verso, 1978. [A]

Fox, S. W., and K. Dose. *Molecular Evolution and the Origin of Life.* San Francisco: W. H. Freeman, 1972. [A]

Futuyma, Douglas J. *Science on Trial.* New York: Pantheon Books, 1983. [I]

Gillespie, N. C. *Charles Darwin and the Problem with Creation.* Chicago: University of Chicago Press, 1979. [A]

Graham, G. *Historical Explanation Reconsidered.* Aberdeen: Aberdeen University Press, 1983. [A]

Grasse, P. P. *Evolution of Living Organisms.* New York: Academic, 1977. [A]

Greenstein, George. *The Symbiotic Universe: Life and Mind in the Cosmos.* New York: Morrow, 1988. [I]

Gribbin, J., and M. Rees. *Cosmic Coincidences.* London: Black Swan, 1991. [I]

Haeckel, Ernst. *The Wonders of Life.* London: Watts, 1905. [I]

Ho, Wing Meng. "Methodological Issues in Evolutionary Theory." D.Phil. thesis, Oxford University, 1965. [A]

Hoyle, F., and S. Wickramasinghe. *Evolution from Space.* London: J. M. Dent, 1981. [I]

Hull, David L. *Darwin and His Critics.* Chicago: University of Chicago Press, 1973. [A]

Johnson, Phillip E. *Darwin on Trial.* 2nd ed. Downers Grove, Ill.: InterVarsity Press, 1993. [I]

Judson, H. *The Eighth Day of Creation.* New York: Simon and Schuster, 1979. [A]

Kauffman, S. *The Origins of Order.* Oxford, U.K.: Oxford University Press, 1992. [A]

Kavalovski, V. "The *Vera Causa* Principle: A Historico-Philosophical Study of a Meta-theoretical Concept from Newton Through Darwin." Ph.D. dissertation, University of Chicago, 1974. [A]

Kenyon, D., and P. W. Davis. *Of Pandas and People: The Central Question of Biological Origins.* Dallas: Haughton, 1993. [I]

Kitcher, Philip. *Abusing Science.* Cambridge, Mass.: MIT Press, 1982. [I]

Kuppers, B. *Information and the Origin of Life.* Cambridge, Mass.: MIT Press, 1990. [A]

Lenior, Timothy. *The Strategy of Life.* Chicago: University of Chicago Press, 1982. [A]

Lewis, C. S. *God in the Dock.* London: Collins, 1979. [B]

Lipton, Peter. *Inference to the Best Explanation.* London: Routledge, 1991. [I]

Lovtrup, Søren. *Darwinism: The Refutation of Myth.* Beckingham, Kent, U.K.: Croom Helm, 1987. [I]

Meyer, Stephen C. "Of Clues and Causes: A Methodological Interpretation of Origin of Life Studies." Ph.D. thesis, Cambridge University, 1990. [A]

Morowitz, H. J. *Energy Flow in Biology.* New York: Academic, 1968. [A]

Newton, Isaac. *Isaac Newton's Papers and Letters on Natural Philosophy.* Edited by I. Bernard Cohen. Cambridge, Mass.: Harvard University Press, 1958. [A]

Oparin, A. I. *The Origin of Life.* Translated by S. Morgulis. New York: Macmillan, 1938. [I]

Peirce, C. S. *Collected Papers.* Edited by C. Hartshorne and P. Weiss. 6 vols. Cambridge, Mass.: Harvard University Press, 1931. [A]

Prigogine, I., and G. Nicolis. *Self Organization in Nonequilibrium Systems.* New York: Wiley, 1977. [A]

Ridley, Mark. *The Problems of Evolution.* Oxford, U.K.: Oxford University Press, 1985. [B]

Ruse, Michael. *Darwinism Defended: A Guide to the Evolution Controversies.* London: Addison-Wesley, 1982. [I]

————. *The Philosophy of Biology.* London: Hutchinson's University Library, 1973. [B]

Shapiro, R. *Origins.* London: Heinemann, 1986. [B]

Sober, E. *Reconstructing the Past.* Cambridge, Mass.: MIT Press, 1988. [A]

Swinburne, Richard. *The Concept of a Miracle.* London: Macmillan, 1970. [A]

Tetry, Andree. *A General History of the Sciences,* vol. 4. London: Thames and Hudson, 1966. [I]

Thaxton, Charles, Walter L. Bradley and Roger Olsen. *The Mystery of Life's Origin.* New York: Philosophical Library, 1984. [A]

Whewell, William. *The Philosophy of the Inductive Sciences.* 2 vols. London: Parker, 1840. [A]

Wicken, J. *Evolution, Thermodynamics and Information.* Oxford, U.K.: Oxford University Press, 1987. [A]

Yockey, H. P. *Information Theory and Molecular Biology.* Cambridge, U.K.: Cambridge University Press, 1992. [A]

Articles in Journals

Alston, W. P. "The Place of the Explanation of Particular Facts in Science." *Philosophy of Science* 38 (1971): 13-34. [A]

Beade, Pedro. "Falsification and Falsifiability in Historical Linguistics." *Philosophy of the Social Sciences* 19 (1989): 173-81. [A]

Bradley, Walter L. "Thermodynamics and the Origin of Life." *Perspectives on Science and Christian Faith* 40, no. 2 (1988): 72-83. [I]

Brady, R. H. "Dogma and Doubt." *Biological Journal of the Linnean Society* 17 (1982): 79-96. [I]

Cairns-Smith, A. G. "The First Organisms." *Scientific American,* June 1985, pp. 90-100. [I]

Carr, B. J., and M. J. Rees. "The Anthropic Principle and the Structure of the Physical World." *Nature* 278 (1979): 610. [A]

Cech, Thomas R. "Ribozyme Self-Replication?" *Nature* 339 (1989): 507-8. [A]

Collingridge, D., and M. Earthy. "Science Under Stress: Crisis in Neo-Darwinism." *History and Philosophy of the Life Sciences* 12 (1990): 3-26. [I]

Colwell, Gary. "On Defining Away the Miraculous." *Philosophy* 57 (1982): 327-37. [A]

Crick, F. "The Origin of the Genetic Code." *Journal of Molecular Biology* 38 (1968): 367-79. [A]

Crick, F., and L. Orgel. "Directed Panspermia." *Icarus* 19 (1973): 341-46. [I]

Dickerson, R. E. "Chemical Evolution and the Origin of Life." *Scientific American* 239 (1978): 70-85. [I]

Dose, K. "The Origin of Life: More Questions Than Answers." *Interdisciplinary Science Review* 13 (1988): 348-56. [I]

Eger, Martin. "A Tale of Two Controversies: Dissonance in the Theory and Practice of Rationality." *Zygon* 23 (1988): 291-326. [A]

Eigen, M., W. Gardner, P. Schuster and R. Winkler-Oswaititich. "The Origin of Genetic Information." *Scientific American* 244 (1981): 88-118. [I]

Gingerich, Owen. "The Galileo Affair." *Scientific American,* August 1982, pp. 133-43. [I]

Gould, Stephen Jay. "Darwinism Defined: The Difference Between Theory and Fact." *Discovery,* January 1987, pp. 64-70. [B]

_____. "Evolution and the Triumph of Homology: Or, Why History Matters." *American Scientist* 74 (1986): 60-69. [B]

_____. "Is a New Theory of Evolution Emerging?" *Paleobiology* 6 (1980): 119-30. [A]

Grizzle, Raymond. "Some Comments on the 'Godless' Nature of Darwinian Evolution, and a Plea to the Philosophers Among Us." *Perspectives on Science and Christian Faith* 44 (1993): 175-77. [B]

Hempel, C. "The Function of General Laws in History." *Journal of Philosophy* 39 (1942): 35-48. [I]

Hoyle, Fred. "The Universe: Past and Present Reflections." *Annual Review of Astronomy and Astrophysics* 20 (1982): 16. [I]

Hull, David. "God of the Galápagos." *Nature* 352 (1991): 485-86. [B]

Huxley, T. H. "Biogenesis and Abiogenesis" (presidential address to the British Association of the Advancement of Science for 1870). *Discourses: Biological and Geological* 8 (1896): 229-71. [I]

_____. "On the Physical Basis of Life." *The Fortnightly Review* 5 (1869): 129-45. [I]

Kenyon, D. "The Creationist View of Biological Origins." *NEXA Journal,* Spring 1984, pp. 28-35. [I]

————. "Going Beyond the Naturalistic Mindset in Origin-of-Life Research." Paper presented to Conference on Christainity and the University, Dallas, February 9-10, 1985. [I]

Kenyon, D., and A. Nissenbaum. "On the Possible Role of Organic Melanoidin Polymers as Matrices for Prebiotic Activity." *Journal of Molecular Evolution* 7 (1976): 245-51. [A]

Kok, R. A., J. A. Taylor and Walter L. Bradley. "A Statistical Examination of Self-Ordering of Amino Acids in Proteins." *Origins of Life and Evolution of the Biosphere* 18 (1988): 135-42. [A]

Laudan, Larry. "William Whewell on the Consilience of Inductions." *The Monist* 55 (1971): 368-91. [A]

Lewin, Roger. "Evolutionary Theory Under Fire." *Science* 210 (1980): 883. [B]

Liben, Paul. "Science Within the Limits of Truth." *First Things,* December 1991, pp. 29-32. [I]

Macnab, R. "Bacterial Mobility and Chemotaxis: The Molecular Biology of a Behavioral System." *CRC Critical Reviews in Biochemistry* 5 (1978): 291-341. [A]

Maher, K., and D. Stevenson. "Impact Frustration of the Origin of Life." *Nature* 331 (1988): 612-14. [A]

Mandelbaum, M. "Historical Explanation: The Problem of Covering Laws." *History Theory* 1 (1961): 229-42. [A]

Margulis, L., J. C. Walker and M. Rambler. "Reassessment of Roles of Oxygen and Ultraviolet Light in Precambrian Evolution." *Nature* 264 (1976): 620-24. [A]

Martin, R. "Singular Causal Explanation." *Theory and Decision* 2 (1972): 221-37. [A]

Matthews, C. N. "Chemical Evolution: Protons to Proteins." *Proceedings of the Royal Institution* 55 (1982): 199-206. [A]

Meyer, Stephen C. "Open Debate on Life's Origin." *Insight,* February 21, 1994, pp. 27-29. [B]

————. "A Scopes Trial for the '90s." *The Wall Street Journal.* December 6, 1993, p. A14. [B]

Miller, S., and J. Bada. "Submarine Hotsprings and the Origin of Life." *Nature* 334 (1988): 609-10. [A]

Moore, J. N. "Paleontological Evidence and the Organic Evolution." *Journal of the American Scientific Affiliation* special edition, *Origins and Change,* 1978, pp. 49-55. [I]

Mora, P. T. "Urge and Molecular Biology." *Nature* 199 (1963): 212-19. [A]

Moreland, J. P. "Scientific Creationism, Science and Conceptual Problems."
    Forthcoming in *Perspectives on Science and Christian Faith.* [A]

Murphy, Nancey. "Phillip Johnson on Trial: A Critique of His Critique of
    Darwin." *Perspectives on Science and Christian Faith* 45, no. 1 (1993): 26-36. [I]

Padian, Kevin. "Gross Misrepresentation." *Bookwatch Reviews* 2 (1989): 2-3. [B]

Raup, D. "Conflicts Between Darwin and Paleontology." *Field Museum of Nat-
    ural History Bulletin* 50, no. 1 (1979): 24-25. [I]

_____ . "Evolution and the Fossil Record." *Science,* July 17, 1981, p. 289. [I]

Recker, D. "Causal Efficacy: The Structure of Darwin's Argument Strategy in
    the *Origin of Species.*" *Philosophy of Science* 54 (1987): 147-75. [A]

Ruse, Michael. "Commentary: The Academic as Expert Witness." *Science, Tech-
    nology and Human Values* 11, no. 2 (1986): 66-73. [B]

_____ . "Creation Science Is Not Science." *Science, Technology and Human
    Values* 7, no. 40 (1982): 72-78. [I]

_____ . "They're Here!" *Bookwatch Reviews* 2 (1989): 4. [B]

Saunders, P. T, and M. W. Ho. "Is Neo-Darwinism Falsifiable—and Does It
    Matter?" *Nature and System* 4 (1982): 179-96. [A]

Scott, Eugenie, et al. "Why Pandas and People?" *Bookwatch Reviews* 2 (1989):
    1. [B]

Scriven, Michael. "Causation as Explanation." *Nous* 9 (1975): 3-15. [A]

_____ . "Explanation and Prediction in Evolutionary Theory." *Science* 130
    (1959): 477-82. [I]

_____ . "The Logic of Cause." *Theory and Decision* 2 (1971): 49-66. [A]

Shapiro, R. "Prebiotic Ribose Synthesis: A Critical Analysis." *Origins of Life and
    Evolution of the Biosphere* 18 (1988): 71-85. [A]

Skoog, Gerald. "A View from the Past." *Bookwatch Reviews* 2 (1989): 1-2. [B]

Smith, J. Maynard. "Hypercycles and the Origin of Life." *Nature* 280 (1979):
    445-46. [I]

Thagard, Paul. "The Best Explanation: Criteria for Theory Choice." *Journal
    of Philosophy* 75 (1978): 77-92. [A]

Thomson, K. S. "The Meanings of Evolution." *American Scientist* 70 (1982): 529-
    31. [I]

Tipler, F. "How to Construct a Falsifiable Theory in Which the Universe
    Came into Being Several Thousand Years Ago." *Proceedings of the Biennial
    Meeting of the Philosophy of Science Association* 2 (1984): 873-902. [A]

Walton, J. C. "Organization and the Origin of Life." *Origins* 4 (1977): 16-35. [A]

Yockey, H. P. "A Calculation of the Probability of Spontaneous Biogenesis by
    Information Theory." *Journal of Theoretical Biology* 67 (1977): 377-98. [A]

_____ . "Self Organization Origin of Life Scenarios and Information Theory." *Journal of Theoretical Biology* 91 (1981): 13-31. [A]

Zaug, A. J., and T. R. Cech. "The Intervening Sequence RNA of Tetrahymena Is an Enzyme." *Science* 231 (1986): 470-75. [A]

Conference Presentations and Papers in Books

Alston, William. "God's Action in the World." In *Evolution and Creation*. Edited by Ernan McMullin. Notre Dame, Ind.: University of Notre Dame Press, 1985. [A]

Courtenay, W. "The Dialectic of Omnipotence in the High and Late Middle Ages." In *Divine Omniscience and Omnipotence in Medieval Philosophy*. Edited by T. Ruduvsky. Dordrecht, Netherlands: D. Reidel, 1985. [A]

Dembski, William A. "The Very Possibility of Intelligent Design." Paper presented at Science and Belief, First International Conference of the Pascal Centre, Ancaster, Ontario, August 11-15, 1992. [I]

Doyle, Sir A. C. "The Boscome Valley Mystery." In *The Sign of Three: Peirce, Holmes, Popper*. Edited by T. Sebeok. Bloomington: Indiana University Press, 1983. [B]

Fox, S. W. "Proteinoid Experiments and Evolutionary Theory." In *Beyond Neo-Darwinism*. Edited by M. W. Ho and P. T. Saunders. New York: Academic, 1984. [A]

Gish, Duane. "Creation, Evolution and the Historical Evidence." In *But Is It Science?* Edited by Michael Ruse. Buffalo, N.Y.: Prometheus Books, 1988. [B]

Gould, Stephen Jay. "Evolution as Fact and Theory." In *Science and Creationism*. Edited by Ashley Montagu. New York: Oxford University Press, 1984. [B]

_____ . "Genesis and Geology." In *Science and Creationism*. Edited by Ashley Montagu. New York: Oxford University Press, 1984. [I]

_____ . "The Senseless Signs of History." In *The Panda's Thumb*. New York: Norton, 1980. [B]

Grinnell, F. "Radical Intersubjectivity: Why Naturalism Is an Assumption Necessary for Doing Science." Paper presented at Darwinism: Scientific Inference or Philosophical Preference? conference, Southern Methodist University, Dallas, March 26-28, 1992. [A]

_____ . "Selforganization in Evolution." In *Selforganization*. Edited by S. W. Fox. New York: Adenine, 1986. [A]

Hempel, C. "Explanation in Science and in History." In *Frontiers of Science and Philosophy*. Edited by R. Colodny. Pittsburgh: University of Pittsburgh Press,

1962. [A]

Hull, David. "Darwin and the Nature of Science." In *Evolution from Molecules to Men.* Edited by David Bendall. Cambridge, U.K.: Cambridge University Press, 1985. [A]

Kehoe, A. "Modern Anti-evolutionism: The Scientific Creationists." In *What Darwin Began.* Edited by Laurie R. Godfrey. Boston: Allyn and Bacon, 1985. [B]

Kenyon, D. "A Comparison of Proteinoid and Aldocyanoin Microsystems as Models of the Primordial Cell." In *Molecular Evolution and Protobiology.* Edited by K. Matsuno, K. Dose, K. Harada and D. L. Rohlfing. New York: Plenum, 1984. [A]

Kline, A. David. "Theories, Facts and Gods: Philosophical Aspects of the Creation-Evolution Controversy." In *Did the Devil Make Darwin Do It?* Edited by David B. Wilson. Ames: Iowa State University Press, 1983. [I]

Lakatos, Imre. "Falsification and the Methodology of Scientific Research Programmes." In *Criticism and the Growth of Knowledge.* Edited by Imre Lakatos and Alan Musgrave. Cambridge, U.K.: Cambridge University Press, 1970. [A]

Laudan, Larry. "The Demise of the Demarcation Problem." In *But Is It Science?* Edited by Michael Ruse. Buffalo, N.Y.: Prometheus Books, 1988. [A]

———. "More on Creationism." In *But Is It Science?* Edited by Michael Ruse. Buffalo, New York: Prometheus Books, 1988. [I]

———. "Science at the Bar—Causes for Concern." In *But Is It Science?* Edited by Michael Ruse. Buffalo, New York: Prometheus Books, 1988. [I]

Leslie, John. "Modern Cosmology and the Creation of Life." In *Evolution and Creation.* Edited by Ernan McMullin. Notre Dame, Ind.: University of Notre Dame Press, 1985. [A]

Lewontin, R. Introduction to *Scientists Confront Creationism.* Edited by L. Godfrey. New York: Norton, 1983. [B]

McMullin, Ernan. "Introduction: Evolution and Creation." In *Evolution and Creation.* Edited by Ernan McMullin. Notre Dame, Ind.: University of Notre Dame Press, 1985. [I]

Moorhead, P. S., and M. M. Kaplan. *Mathematical Challenges to the Neo-Darwinian Interpretation of Evolution.* Philadelphia: Wistar Institute Press, 1967. See especially papers and comments from M. Eden, M. Shutzenberger, S. M. Ulam and P. Gavaudan. [A]

Mora, P. T. "The Folly of Probability." In *The Origins of Prebiological Systems and of Their Molecular Matrices.* Edited by S. W. Fox. New York: Academic, 1965. [I]

Overton, William R. "United States District Court Opinion: *McLean* v. *Arkansas.*" In *But Is It Science?* Edited by Michael Ruse. Buffalo, New York: Prometheus Books, 1988. [B]

Pattee, H. H. "The Problem of Biological Hierarchy." In *Towards a Theoretical Biology,* vol. 3. Edited by C. H. Waddington. Edinburgh: Edinburgh University Press, 1970. [A]

Peirce, C. S. "Abduction and Induction." In *The Philosophy of Peirce.* Edited by J. Buchler. London: Routledge, 1956. [I]

Popper, Karl. "Darwinism as a Metaphysical Research Program." In *But Is It Science?* Edited by Michael Ruse. Buffalo, New York: Prometheus Books, 1988. [I]

Quinn, Philip L. "Creationism, Methodology and Politics." In *But Is It Science?* Edited by Michael Ruse. Buffalo, New York: Prometheus Books, 1988. [A]

———. "The Philosopher of Science as Expert Witness." In *But Is It Science?* Edited by Michael Ruse. Buffalo, New York: Prometheus Books, 1988. [B]

Root-Bernstein, Robert. "On Defining a Scientific Theory: Creationism Considered." In *Science and Creationism.* Edited by Ashley Montagu. New York: Oxford University Press, 1984. [I]

Ruse, Michael. "Darwinism: Philosophical Preference, Scientific Inference and Good Research Strategy." Paper presented at Darwinism: Scientific Inference or Philosophical Preference? conference, Southern Methodist University, Dallas, March 26-28, 1992. [I]

———. "Karl Popper's Philosophy of Biology." In *But Is It Science?* Edited by Michael Ruse. Buffalo, New York: Prometheus Books, 1988. [I]

———. "Origin of Species." In *But Is It Science?* Edited by Michael Ruse. Buffalo, New York: Prometheus Books, 1988. [I]

———. "A Philosopher's Day in Court." In *But Is It Science?* Edited by Michael Ruse. Buffalo, New York: Prometheus Books, 1988. [B]

———. "The Relationship Between Science and Religion in Britain, 1830-1870." In *But Is It Science?* Edited by Michael Ruse. Buffalo, New York: Prometheus Books, 1988. [I]

———. "Scientific Creationism." In *But Is It Science?* Edited by Michael Ruse. Buffalo, New York: Prometheus Books, 1988. [I]

———. "Witness Testimony Sheet: *McLean* v. *Arkansas.*" In *But Is It Science?* Edited by Michael Ruse. Buffalo, New York: Prometheus Books, 1988. [B]

Scriven, Michael. "Causes, Connections and Conditions in History." In *Philosophical Analysis and History.* Edited by W. Dray. New York: Harper & Row, 1966. [A]

————. "New Issues in the Logic of Explanation." In *Philosophy and History*. Edited by S. Hook. New York: New York University Press, 1963. [A]

————. "Truisms as the Grounds for Historical Explanations." In *Theories of History*. Edited by P. Gardiner. Glencoe, Ill.: Free Press, 1959. [A]

Sedgwick, Adam. "Objections to Mr. Darwin's Theory of the Origin of Species." In *But Is It Science?* Edited by Michael Ruse. Buffalo, New York: Prometheus Books, 1988. [I]

Stent, Gunther S. "Scientific Creationism: Nemesis of Sociobiology." In *Science and Creationism*. Edited by Ashley Montagu. New York: Oxford University Press, 1984. [I]

Valentine, J., and D. Erwin. "Interpreting Great Developmental Experiments: The Fossil Record." In *Development as an Evolutionary Process*. Edited by Rudolf Raff and Elizabeth Raff. New York: Alan R. Liss, 1985. [I]

Webster, Gerry. "The Relations of Natural Forms." In *Beyond Darwinism*. Edited by M. W. Ho and P. T. Saunders. New York: Academic, 1984. [A]

Wicken, J. "Thermodynamics, Evolution and Emergence: Ingredients for a New Synthesis." In *Entropy, Information and Evolution*. Edited by Bruce H. Weber, David J. Depew and James D. Smith. Cambridge, Mass.: MIT Press, 1988. [A]

Wigner, E. "The Probability of the Existence of a Self-Reproducing Unit." In *The Logic of Personal Knowledge: Essays Presented to Michael Polanyi*. Edited by Edward Shils. London: Routledge and Kegan Paul, 1961. [A]

Willey, B. "Darwin's Place in the History of Thought." In *Darwinism and the Study of Society*. Edited by M. Banton. Chicago: Quadrangle Books, 1961. [I]

3
ON THE VERY POSSIBILITY OF INTELLIGENT DESIGN

William A. Dembski

Gotthold Ephraim Lessing is perhaps best remembered for the following celebrated remark: "Accidental truths of history can never become the proof of necessary truths of reason." In the history of ideas Lessing's remark is doubly significant for having appeared in a work concerned with how rational beings like us can be rationally justified in holding religious beliefs (*Über den Beweis des Geistes und der Kraft,* 1777). Lessing aimed his remark at the truths of theology, not at the necessary truths of mathematics. By stressing as he did that any religious affirmation based on historical events is a matter of faith and not reason, Lessing inserted a wedge between the eternal truths of revelation and the messy contingencies of history. The effect of Lessing's remark was therefore to decouple the events of history from the truths of revelation. The conception of history that ensued stood in contrast with that of Augustine, Aquinas or Bossuet, for whom history was always the medium by which revelation became concrete and knowable (the Incarnation of Christ serving as the primary example). Lessing therefore did much more than accept Leibniz's distinction between necessary truths of reason (e.g., that $2 + 2 = 4$) and contingent truths about the world (e.g., that Lincoln was president during the Civil War); he also endorsed Spinoza's thesis in the *Tractatus Theologico-Politicus* that the truths of history, however well confirmed, are incapable of giving us definite knowledge about God.

Two hundred years later, after multiple revolutions in science and philosophy, though Lessing's name is no longer a household word his dictum still characterizes the secular response to any inference that begins with the messy contingencies of history and ends with a nonvacuous claim about God. Of course much of what has been called natural theology has depended on just such an inference. Paul's claim that God's "eternal power and divine nature, invisible though they are, have been understood and seen through the things he has made" (Romans 1:20 NRSV) not only stands in clear opposition to Lessing's dictum but has throughout church history been seen as granting the imprimatur to natural theology.

The two pillars of Christian apologetics have traditionally been natural theology and historical evidences. Both have leaned heavily on contingent facts about the world to support theological claims about the existence, nature and purposes of God. Natural theology and evidential apologetics differ in scope and emphasis, not in the importance they attach to contingent facts. Natural theology inquires into what can be known about God through the study of nature and the exercise of reason. On this view nature becomes God's general revelation to humankind, and reason the tool for comprehending nature. Natural theology, if you will, harvests the general revelation for insights into the deity. Evidential apologetics, on the other hand, takes the special revelation of Scripture and ecclesiastical tradition and tries to validate it through such disciplines as history, archaeology, anthropology, literary criticism and philology.

It remains that both natural theology and evidential apologetics look to contingent facts about the world to settle questions about God. Against this Lessing and his modern-day successors hold that both enterprises are ill-conceived. Lessing's denial that definite knowledge about God is possible through studying the world has become commonplace. Indeed, in secular circles Lessing's dictum has become axiomatic.

Unfortunately, many Christian thinkers have conceded Lessing's point, if only to sidestep the relentless critique of secularism. Theological pessimism over the soundness of reason in the face of sin is one reason for this concession. Thus a thoroughgoing Calvinist might argue that Lessing's dictum is innocuous, since a mind blinded by sin will hardly be amenable to the persuasion of reason. Pessimism about the power of both reason and empirical investigations to obtain insights about God is therefore consistent with at least a tacit acceptance of Lessing's dictum.

Theological diffidence also plays into the concession. Science in its imperialist mode seeks to provide a total account of the world in purely naturalistic categories. Since the supernatural is by definition beyond the reach of naturalistic categories, theologians with a stake in the supernatural often find themselves intimidated, forced to relegate their religious claims to second-rate epistemological categories like the noumenal, the subjective and the mystical. For a religion like Christianity, whose chief claim had always been that in Christ the divine has invaded the natural world, to admit Lessing's dictum is to surrender the empirical content of this claim. The unfortunate consequence of severing the Incarnation from its empirical content is that it issues in a fideism that on the one hand holds little attraction to modern-day secularists and on the other hand bears little resemblance to the faith of Augustine, the Cappadocian Fathers, Aquinas, Wycliffe, Luther, Calvin and Wesley—all of whom believed not just in the Incarnation, but in an actual bodily resurrection of Christ that among other things served to validate the Incarnation.

Theological pessimism and diffidence aside, the question remains whether Lessing's dictum is true. Lessing's dictum claims that "accidental truths of history can never become the proof of necessary truths of reason." What sort of claim is this? Lessing certainly had religious sympathies. He always retained some conception of God, even if it was Spinozist. Whatever he thought of God, he certainly regarded God as having some influence over the accidental truths of history. He was therefore not seeking an ontological distinction between the accidental truths of history and the necessary truths of reason.

The key word in his dictum is *proof.* Lessing's dictum is an epistemological claim. We can't *prove* eternal things from temporal things. Lessing claims a limitation on knowledge. Now whenever someone informs me that I can't know something, I find myself recalling the words of G. K. Chesterton: "We don't know enough about the unknown to know that it is unknowable."

Certainly if Lessing means that contingent facts cannot provide strict mathematico-deductive proofs of necessary truths, I would agree. But Lessing's claim is uninteresting if this is how he construes proof. His claim becomes interesting only if proof is broadly conceived. Is the world incapable of supplying convincing evidence for theological truths? It's worth remembering that in Lessing's day deism was the rage. For deists it was anathema that God should violate nature by sporadic interventions. Miracles were taboo. As Voltaire put it, "To suppose that God will work miracles is to insult Him with impunity." This sentiment was imported to the North American continent by Ralph Waldo Emerson, who likewise believed that God's dignity would be threatened by miracles: "To aim to convert a man by miracles is a profanation of the soul.'"[1] Suffice it to say, Lessing would not have admitted miracles as a counterexample to his dictum.

What then can serve as a counterexample to his dictum? What sort of necessary theological truth can, at least in principle, be strongly supported by contingent facts about the world? The existence of a supernatural Designer, I claim, fits the bill. I look for three things in a supernatural Designer—intelligence, transcendence and power. By power I mean that the Designer can actually do things to influence the material world—perform miracles if desired. By transcendence I mean that the Designer cannot be identified with any physical process, event or entity—the latter can at best be attributed to, not equated with, the Designer. By intelligence I mean that the Designer is capable of performing actions that cannot adequately be explained by appealing to chance—the Designer can act so as to render the chance hypothesis untenable. I shall argue that contingent facts are well equipped to provide compelling evidence that these three attributes are consistently united in one being.

The Kantian Question

Even if we are skeptical about whether miracles can serve as valid counterexamples to Lessing's dictum, miracles are a good place to start looking for contingent facts that implicate noncontingent truths. The use of miracles to confirm faith goes back at least to the doubting Thomases of Scripture and extends to the Woody Allens of today. Normally the connection is stated in terms of a challenge:

If only God would give me some clear sign! Like making a large deposit in my name at a Swiss bank.[2]

In uttering this remark, Woody Allen issues a challenge (perhaps to God, perhaps to no one). Suppose for the moment that there is a God and that this God decides to take Allen seriously. Would an unexpected seven million dollars, say, in Allen's Swiss bank account rightly convince him that God is real? Suppose a thorough examination of the bank records fails to explain how the money appeared in his account. Should Allen conclude that God has given him a sign?

Since I can't answer for Woody Allen, let me answer for myself. If I were a famous personality who had uttered Allen's remark and subsequently found an additional seven million dollars in my Swiss bank account, I would certainly not attribute my unexpected good fortune to the largesse of an eccentric deity. It's not that I don't believe in God—I do. But my theology constrains me to think it unworthy of God to grant flippant requests like Allen's and then apparently ignore the urgent requests of so many suffering people in the world.

In this situation I would refuse to acknowledge a miracle for theological reasons. Barring theological reasons, however, I would still refuse to acknowledge a miracle. Why? Well, other explanations readily come to mind. If I had uttered the remark and were as famous as Allen, and if seven million dollars then appeared in my account, I would probably conclude that some eccentric billionaire with a religious agenda was trying to convert me to his cause. The strange appearance of the seven million was fiendishly designed to make me believe in God. But alas, I'm too clever for them!

There is a point to these musings. Allen's remark is clearly funny; however, if taken seriously it becomes self-defeating. If God were in fact to do what Allen requested, Allen and just about anyone else would remain unconvinced. But perhaps Allen's error was in asking for too picayune a sign from God. After all, if God is all he is cracked up to be (omniscient, omnipresent, omnipotent, infinite, perfect and so on), God can certainly do a lot more than deposit a paltry seven million dollars in a Swiss bank account. Why not ask God to do something truly flamboyant? Norwood Russell Hanson, philosopher of science extraordinaire at Yale until his premature death, did just this when he described the conditions under which he would become a theist:

> I'm not a stubborn guy. I would be a theist under some conditions. I'm open-minded. . . . Okay. Okay. The conditions are these: Suppose, next Tuesday morning, just after breakfast, all of us in this one world are knocked to our knees by a percussive and ear-shattering thunderclap. Snow swirls, leaves drop from trees, the earth heaves and buckles, buildings topple and towers tumble. The sky is ablaze with an eerie silvery light, and just then, as all of the people of this world look up, the heavens open, and the clouds pull apart, revealing an unbelievably radiant and immense Zeus-like figure towering over us like a hundred Everests. He frowns darkly as lightning plays over the features of his Michelangeloid face, and then he points down, *at me*, and explains for every man, woman and child to hear: "I've had quite enough of your too-clever logic chopping and word-watching in matters of theology. Be assured, Norwood Russell Hanson, that I do most certainly exist!"[3]

Would that do it? I suggest that a prodigy of the sort described might not elicit the faith Hanson seems to think mandatory. Flamboyance has its price. There is the theological price: no God of any respectable theology would engage in the sort of magic show that Hanson desires to see. But even if we leave theological scruples aside, there is the question about how best to explain the prodigy Hanson describes. Certainly there are other explanations besides the appeal to God. Hallucinations, dreams, smoke and mirrors, and holographic simulations are just a few of the alternative explanations that spring to mind. Flamboyant miracles, precisely because they involve a large-scale disruption of the normal course of events, instead of producing faith might actually work against faith by causing us to question our normally-taken-for-granted sensory experience. For God to do things that are too bizarre might cause us to question our own sanity and therefore our capacity to assess whether God exists.

Finally, even if we don't question our sanity, it's not clear we get a supernatural Designer in the full sense of the word. Certainly a being that could meet Hanson's challenge would be intelligent and powerful, but it's not at all clear that this being would be transcendent as well. Presumably it's possible for technologically advanced extraterrestrials to offer us a freak show that would cause us to take seriously their claims to godhood, much as we Westerners might be able to dazzle the aborigines of Borneo into believing that we are gods through the power of our technologies. Dazzle alone, however, won't buy you transcendence. A Designer who is strictly outside the physical universe has to be more than a good entertainer.

So the question remains whether God in his capacity as a supernatural Designer can do anything that would provide convincing proof that he had indeed acted. Let me put it this way: Is there anything that has, could or might happen in the world from which it would be reasonable to conclude that a supernatural Designer had acted? Are there or could there be any facts in the world for which an appeal to a supernatural Designer is the best explanation? Or to reverse the question, is supernatural design always an easy way out, a lame excuse, a prescientific device that invariably misses the best explanation?[4]

We are asking a transcendental question in the Kantian sense: What are the conditions for the possibility of knowing that an instance of supernatural design has occurred in the actual world? This question must be answered at the outset, for if this world is the type of place where anything even in principle that happens can be adequately explained apart from teleology and design, then Lessing was right. Might the world do something, however quirky, that would convince us of design?

An illustration may help. Imagine a peculiar art studio filled with 10-x-10-

inch canvases, a full range of oil paints and a robot that paints the canvases with the paints. The robot divides each canvas into a grid of one-inch squares and paints each square with precisely one color. Imagine that this robot also has visual sensors and thus can paint scenes presented to its visual field, though only crudely, given its coarse-grained approach to painting.

Imagine next that Elvis Presley and an Elvis impersonator come to have their portraits painted by this robot. Will the portraits distinguish Elvis from his impersonator? Because the representations on canvas are so crude, if the impersonator is worth his salt the two portraits will be indistinguishable. Our imaginary art studio cannot distinguish the real Elvis from the fake Elvis.

This example indicates what is at stake in determining whether design has at least the possibility of being detected and empirically grounded. Putative instances of design abound. But is it possible within this world to distinguish authentic from spurious design, should instances of authentic design even exist? Or is this world like that art studio—just as the portraits painted at the studio cannot distinguish the real from the fake Elvis, is it impossible for our empirical investigations of the world to distinguish authentic from spurious design?

Now Lessing's dictum implies just this—that the world is the kind of place where all objective phenomena, insofar as they can be explained rationally, must be explained without recourse to nonnaturalistic factors. For to transcend naturalistic factors by invoking God is to say something about God and thus to establish necessary truths from accidental truths. Nonnaturalistic factors therefore have no place in rational explanation. George Gaylord Simpson puts it this way: "There is neither need nor excuse for postulation of nonmaterial intervention in the origin of life, the rise of man, or any other part of the long history of the material cosmos."[5] Simpson claims that the world is the kind of place where no objective, empirical finding can ever legitimately lead us to postulate design (what he calls "nonmaterial intervention").

This is a bold claim. The question remains whether it is true. In the case of the art studio, it is true that the robot's portraits of Elvis and his impersonator will fail to distinguish the two. The paintings produced in the studio are simply too coarse-grained to do any better. From these paintings there is, to use Simpson's phrase, "neither need nor excuse for postulation of" two Elvises—the real and the fake. From the portraits alone we might legitimately infer only one sitter. But is the world so coarse-grained that it cannot even in principle produce events that would evidence design? This is what both

Simpson and Lessing seem to be affirming. A little reflection, however, indicates that this claim cannot be right.

Oracles

The method of science fiction has become popular within philosophy in recent years. Its analogue in the physical sciences is the thought experiment. What we do is imagine an event or circumstance that, though not in our power to produce, nevertheless might take place (perhaps only as an extremely improbable thermodynamic accident).[6] Thought experiments are supposed to stretch our thinking and give us fresh insights into well-worn areas of study. Since Lessing and his more recent counterparts like Simpson believe the actual world is incapable of producing events that clearly exhibit design, the task before us is to formulate a thought experiment that shows that the world does indeed possess this power. We are after a type of thought experiment that implicates design. I shall demonstrate that the world is sufficiently fine-grained to produce events for which design is a compelling inference.

I'll start by considering a general class of thought experiments. These are the thought experiments from theoretical computer science known as *oracles*. Oracles are thought experiments that solve intractable problems—that is, problems that currently cannot be solved by computational means. Intractable problems are those that can be programmed but require too long to run and those that are incapable of being programmed at all (e.g., the problem of determining whether the decimal expansion of π has a hundred consecutive 7s currently constitutes an intractable computational problem). On the other hand, problems that can be programmed and whose programs yield a solution after a reasonable amount of running time are known as tractable (sorting problems, as in alphabetizing lists, constitute tractable computational problems). Now computer scientists are not ready to give up on intractable problems. After all, intractable problems might become tractable if a program could be discovered that solved the problem without eating up too many computational resources. So to keep their hands on the pulse of intractable problems, computer scientists regularly employ oracles.

An oracle can be conceived as a black box that solves a certain problem or class of problems instantaneously but for which the method of solution is a matter of ignorance. The reason for calling the box "black" is that we don't know what's going on inside—the box is opaque. We don't know, nor do we care, what's happening inside the box. All that's necessary is that the oracle reliably solve the problems it is supposed to solve. How it goes about it, or even whether there is a practical way of going about it, we don't care.

Since oracles are thought experiments, oracles don't exist as programs running on real computers—if they did, the whole notion of an oracle would be redundant. Oracles are purely conceptual devices. They solve problems, often subproblems of bigger problems, without specifying a method. In computer science divide-and-conquer is generally the strategy of choice. To solve a problem, break it into smaller problems and then solve these subproblems individually. Often the solution to a big problem can be reduced to a collection of smaller problems, all of which but one is tractable. In this case it can be useful to supply an oracle that solves the one remaining intractable problem. With this oracle in hand, the original problem can be solved. In this way the oracle for the subproblem illuminates the original problem. Conversely, any solution to the original problem illuminates the oracle.

For this discussion we shall focus on one particular type of oracle. This is the type that in solving problems beyond the capacity of human or computer problem-solvers produces a solution that nevertheless is verifiable by human or computer problem-solvers. Generally in mathematics and computer science we are confident that a problem has been solved when we have carried out some well-defined procedure that is guaranteed to lead to a solution. If no such procedure exists, we are unable by our own efforts to secure a solution. Nevertheless, it may be possible to check whether a proposed solution is correct, even if we have no idea how the proposed solution was discovered. Here then is where the oracle comes in. *Checking* a solution is typically easier than *generating* a solution. The oracle will solve our problems for us. We want to be sure, however, that the oracle has solved them correctly—we don't want the oracle misleading us. We therefore need a way of checking up on the oracle to make sure it is producing correct results.

A simple example might help. Suppose your education in arithmetic was abysmal; suppose all you learned was how to do addition. Subtraction, multiplication and division are beyond you. You never figured them out, and you have no way of doing them even if your life depended on it. Suppose you are not alone. For some reason, in the years you were educated a whole generation learned nothing about arithmetic except addition. The bank where you deposit your money recognizes this deficiency. Because it wants you to maintain an active checking account, it encourages you (and its other customers like you) to learn how to subtract so that you can keep your checkbook up to date. You resist this.

Tired of encouraging remedial arithmetic for its customers, the bank manager issues to each bank customer an oracle that subtracts—a calculator. You are intrigued. Finally you can keep your checkbook up to date without having to consult your children (whose course in arithmetic included subtraction but, alas, not multiplication and division).

But because you are skeptical by nature, you wonder whether the bank gave you an oracle that subtracts accurately. After all, the bank might have an interest in supplying you with a misleading oracle that indicates you have less in your account than you actually do (say by subtracting more than it should). The bank might then try to keep the difference. But now you learn from your daughter, who knows both addition and subtraction, that you can check up on the oracle by adding what was subtracted and the difference, and then seeing whether it equals your previous total.

You know addition. You can therefore keep tabs on the oracle, even if you don't know how or why it tells you what it does. To your relief, you find that the oracle does indeed subtract correctly.[7]

Oracles that can be checked in this way are *verifiable*. Verifiable oracles provide solutions we can check to problems we cannot solve. In what follows we shall limit ourselves to verifiable oracles. These oracles enable us to address the question that has been exercising us: Is there anything that might happen in the world that would convince us a Designer has acted? Lessing refused to give design a place in rational inquiry. Simpson claimed there could never be a need to postulate "nonmaterial intervention." Together they answer this question with a resounding no. The following oracle, however, shows that the answer to this question must in fact be yes.

The Incredible Talking Pulsar

Imagine that astronomers have discovered a pulsar some three billion light-years from the earth. The pulsar is, say, a rotating neutron star that emits regular pulses of electromagnetic radiation in the radio frequency range. The astronomers who found the star are at first unimpressed by their discovery— another star to catalog. One of the astronomers, however, is a ham radio operator. Looking over the pattern of pulses one day, he finds that they are in Morse code. Still more surprisingly, he finds that the patterns of pulses signal coded English messages.[8]

Word quickly spreads within the scientific community, and from there to the world at large. Radio observatories around the globe start monitoring the "talking" pulsar. The pulsar isn't just transmitting random English messages but is instead intelligently communicating with the inhabitants of Earth. In fact, once the pulsar has gained our attention, it identifies itself. The pulsar informs us that it is the mouthpiece of Yahweh, the God of both Old and New Testaments, the Creator of the universe, the final Judge of humankind.

Pretty heady stuff, you say. But to confirm this otherwise extravagant claim, the pulsar agrees to answer any questions we might put to it. The pulsar specifies the following method of posing and answering questions. The descendants of Levi are to make an ark like the one originally constructed under Moses (see Exodus 25). This ark is to be placed on Mount Zion in Israel. Every hour on the hour, a question written in English is to be placed inside the ark. Ten minutes later the pattern of pulses reaching earth from the pulsar will answer that question with an English message in Morse code.[9]

The information transmitted through the pulsar proves to be nothing short of fantastic. Medical doctors learn how to cure AIDS, cancer and a host of other diseases. Archaeologists learn where to dig for lost civilizations and how to make sense of them. Physicists get their long sought-after unification of the forces of nature. Meteorologists are forewarned of natural disasters and weather patterns years before they occur. Ecologists learn effective methods for cleansing and preserving the earth. Mathematicians obtain proofs to many long-standing open problems—in some cases proofs they can check, but proofs they could never have produced on their own. The list of credits could be continued, but let us stop here.

What shall we make of the pulsar? Regardless of whether the pulsar is in fact the mouthpiece of Yahweh, it creates serious difficulties for any naturalistic conception of the world. Not only is there no way to square the pulsar's behavior with our current scientific understanding of the world, but it is hard to conceive how any naturalistic explanation will *ever* account for the pulsar's behavior. For instance, our current scientific understanding, based on Einsteinian special relativity, tells us that messages cannot be relayed at superluminal speeds—that is, faster than the speed of light. Since the pulsar is three billion light-years from the earth, any signal we receive from the pulsar was sent billions of years ago. Yet the pulsar is, as it were, responding to our questions within ten minutes of their being placed inside the ark. The pulsar's answers therefore seem to precede our questions by billions of years.

To get around this, physicists might wish to postulate reverse causality (in which the causes, instead of preceding their effects, actually come later than their effects) or superluminal signaling (signaling at speeds faster than the speed of light). This is perhaps more congenial than postulating "nonmaterial intervention," but reverse causality and superluminal signaling hardly begin to address the questions raised by the pulsar. It is inescapable that in dealing with the pulsar we are dealing with not just an intelligence but a superintelligence. Now by superintelligence I don't mean an intelligence that at this time surpasses human capability but that humans can hope to attain in time. Nor do I mean a superhuman intelligence that might nevertheless be realized in some finite, rational, material agent embedded in the world (say an extraterrestrial intelligence or a conscious supercomputer). By superintelligence I mean an intelligence that surpasses anything that physical processes are capable of offering. This is an intelligence that exceeds anything that humans or other finite, rational agents in the universe are capable of even in principle.

How can we see that the pulsar instantiates a superintelligence? Theoretical computer science and the notion of a computational resource help point the way. The functioning of any computer can be fully described by the switching of finitely many on-off devices, commonly known as bits. Just what physical form the bits take is unimportant (Babbage's original inference engine was purely mechanical; nowadays bits are instantiated electronically). What is important is that the bits allow exactly two states and reliably indicate which one of the two states currently obtains. Now it is intuitively obvious that according to this picture a computer becomes increasingly powerful as the number of bits increases along with the speed with which the bits can be turned on and off. The number of available bits corresponds to the computer's memory size, the maximal switching rate of the bits to the computer's clock speed. Together, memory size and clock speed determine the computer's computational resources.

Now there are problems in computer science which can be shown mathematically to require more computational resources for their solution than are available in the universe. Think of it this way: the universe can supply only so many bits for use in a computer; moreover, the laws of physics limit the speed with which any of these bits can be switched. Together these constraints limit how big and fast a computer can be, and thereby the range and complexity of the problems that can be solved on any computer. Any computer built out of the physical stuff of the universe will be limited by these constraints.

We can put some numbers to these constraints. There are estimated to be no more than 10^{80} elementary particles in the universe. The properties of matter are such that bits, whatever form they take, cannot be switched faster than 10^{45} times per second.[10] The universe itself is about a billion times younger than 10^{25} seconds (assuming the universe is around ten billion years old). Given these upper bounds, no computation exceeding $10^{80} \times 10^{45} \times 10^{25} = 10^{150}$ elementary steps is possible within the universe, where by an elementary step I mean the switching of an on-off device, conceived abstractly as the switching of a binary integer (= bit). Note that the units of this equation are as follows: 10^{80} is a pure number—an upper bound on the number of elementary particles in the universe; 10^{45} is in hertz-oscillations or bit-switches per second; 10^{25} is in seconds—an upper bound on the number of seconds that the universe endures; finally, 10^{150} is in oscillations or bit-switches—the total number of bit-switches throughout the course of the universe. For a computation of this complexity (i.e., 10^{150} bit-switches) to be carried out in the universe, then, every available elementary particle in the universe would have to serve as an elementary storage device (= memory bit) capable of switching at 10^{45} hertz over a period of a billion billion years.

Of course, 10^{150} is incredibly generous as an upper bound on the complexity of computations possible in the universe. Here are a few reasons a much smaller bound will do:

☐ Quantum mechanical considerations indicate that reliable memory storage is unworkable below the atomic level,[11] since at this level quantum indeterminacy will make not only storage but also reading and writing of information impossible. Hence each elementary storage device will have to consist of more than one elementary particle.

☐ The preceding calculation treats the universe as a giant piece of random access memory (RAM) that is controlled by a processor outside the universe operating at 10^{45} hertz with instant access to any memory location in RAM. In fact, the processor will itself have to take up part of the universe. Moreover, its access to memory locations will have in most cases to be measured in light-years and not in 10^{45}-second chunks. Even with massively parallel processing, computation speeds will fall far below the 10^{45}-hertz upper bound.

☐ Finally, the bound of 10^{25} seconds for the maximum running time of a computation is excessive, since either the heat death or the collapse of the universe will probably have occurred by then.

Suffice it to say, even with the entire universe functioning as a computer, no computation requiring 10^{150} elementary steps, much less 10^{150} floating point operations, is feasible.[12]

Now it is possible to pose problems in computer science for which the quickest solution requires well beyond this number of steps, yet for which with a solution in hand it is possible even for humans using ordinary electronic computers to check whether the solution is correct. Factoring integers into primes is thought to be one such problem. Since the factorization problem is easy to understand, let me treat it as though it were one of the "provably hard" problems. If at some time in the future a "quick" algorithm or step-by-step procedure is found for factoring numbers, we shall need to modify this example; nevertheless, my contention that there are problems whose solution is beyond the computational resources of the universe, yet verifiable by humans, will still hold.[13]

What is the factorization into primes of 1,961? Solving this requires a bit of work. But if you are given the prime numbers 37 and 53, it is a simple matter to check whether these are prime factors of 1961. In fact, $37 \times 53 = 1,961$. Factoring is hard, multiplication is easy. We can therefore go to our pulsar with numbers thousands of digits long and ask it to factor them. Factoring numbers that long is totally beyond our present capabilities and in all likelihood exceeds the computational limits inherent in the universe by many, many orders of magnitude. (When I was following the literature on factoring a few years back, numbers beyond two hundred digits in length could not be factored unless they had either small or special prime factors.) Nevertheless, it is easy enough to check whether the pulsar is getting the factorizations right, even for numbers thousands of digits in length.

The pulsar is a superintelligent verifiable oracle. As a verifiable oracle, it extends our knowledge of the world by enabling us to verify its claims. I indicated that science, history and even the future all fall within the pulsar's competence. Such knowledge is beyond human capabilities and therefore guarantees that the pulsar's knowledge is superhuman. But in such matters of contingent fact we might still wonder whether the pulsar's intelligence is similar to our own, only much more sophisticated. Such an intelligence might still derive from some physical system and be tied fundamentally into the material universe. The pulsar's solution of intractable computational problems, however, makes it tough to avoid postulating "nonmaterial intervention." Indeed, the resources simply aren't there in the material universe to account for the pulsar's solution to intractable computational problems.

Let me put it this way: If you've solved a problem and the resources for solving the problem weren't available in U, then you had to go outside U to solve the problem. In this case U is the universe. The pulsar's solving of intractable computational problems guarantees that the superintelligence communicating through the pulsar is in fact a supernatural intelligence.

Lessons from the Pulsar

What lessons can we learn from the pulsar? First, we should infer that a Designer in the full sense of the word is communicating through the pulsar—a Designer who is both intelligent and transcendent. Intelligence is certainly not a problem here. Alan Turing's famous test for intelligence (1950) pitted computer against human in a contest where a human judge was to decide which was the computer and which was the human. If the human judge could not distinguish the computer from the human, Turing wanted intelligence attributed to the computer. This operationalist approach to intelligence has since been questioned, by theists on one end and hard-core physicalists on the other. But the basic idea that there is no better test for intelligence than coherent natural language communication remains intact. If we can't legitimately attribute intelligence to the pulsar, then no attribution of intelligence should count as legitimate. Transcendence is clear as well, given our discussion of intractable computational problems. Suffice it to say, a being that solves problems beyond the computational resources of the material world is not material. When we can confirm that such problems have in fact been solved for us, we cannot avoid postulating "nonmaterial intervention."

Second, we should consider unacceptable any appeal to chance in explaining the pulsar's behavior. Confronted with our pulsar, the inveterate naturalist might want to adopt the following line: Pulsars emit electromagnetic radiation in pulses, but the precise causal factors for spacing the pulses are beyond our knowledge. Over an extended period of time, the number of sequences of pulses that the pulsar might emit is huge. Of these the number of coherent English messages in Morse code is still huge, but minute when compared to the total number of possible sequences. Hence it is possible that in observing the pulsar we are merely witnessing an extremely unlikely chance event. The chance process responsible for the event appears to be communicating with us intelligently through the pulsar, but in fact it isn't. Randomness and chance alone are at work. Perhaps there are other pulsars out there also emitting coherent English messages by chance. Naturalists might even want to refer to such pulsars as "informational singularities." Most worlds obeying our physical laws don't contain informational singularities. Ours, however, might just be one of those worlds that contains an informational singularity.

The inveterate naturalist is urging a chance hypothesis. Not only does this appeal to chance violate every conceivable canon of statistical reasoning, but it is also highly implausible. In the event of such a talking pulsar, a much more plausible hypothesis would be that the works of Shakespeare were the product of chance (cf. T. H. Huxley's simian typists[14]).

Third, we should note that many of the physical details in the pulsar example could be changed without affecting our general conclusions. I chose the pulsar because it is startling. It clashes with special relativity and turns naturalism on its head. Nevertheless, any physical system whose dynamics are unpredictable could provide convincing evidence of design. Consider, for instance, a chunk of uranium undergoing radioactive decay. Suppose that whenever a uranium atom from the chunk decays, we treat it as a pulse. Suppose moreover that the sequence of pulses so derived from the chunk of uranium can be interpreted as English messages in Morse code. The chunk of uranium becomes in this way an oracle that communicates with us much as the pulsar. Indeed, the content of its messages can be identical with that of the pulsar. Note that if the chunk of uranium is made available to public scrutiny, its empirical support becomes as secure as that of the pulsar.

Fourth, the possibility of a superintelligent verifiable oracle is independent of whatever our current scientific understanding of the world happens to be. Science always operates against a backdrop of regularities. Although these regularities restrict what is physically possible, they cannot restrict the messages that physical systems operating within those regularities are capable of transmitting. Take the physical system that makes up me. I claim that I am able to transmit any conceivable English message in Morse code. Suppose a neuroscientist wants to dispute this claim. To succeed he must produce a counterexample—a message in Morse code that I am unable to produce, say because my nervous system is constituted in a particular way. But this is absurd, for I can certainly copy the message if it is presented to me. And what is to prevent my getting the message and copying it? Perhaps now the neuroscientist wants to team up with a physicist, with the neuroscientist claiming that I shall never be able to reproduce a certain message if it is not presented to me, and the physicist guaranteeing that the message shall indeed never be presented to me (presumably because the constitution and dynamics of the physical world precludes this message from getting through to me). Let's say the neuroscientist is right. How can the physicist validate her claim? Can she guarantee that nobody will steal the message and get it into my hands? Can she guarantee that no pulsar will transmit the message to me? Can she guarantee that when I look at the random behavior of a quantum mechanical system, I won't to my surprise find the message transmitted to me? Physics has no way of barring the message from me and hence has no way of preventing me from copying the message once it is in my possession. A fortiori it has no way of limiting the messages that the physical system named Bill Dembski is capable of transmitting—save one: if the message is too long, I might expire before transmitting the whole message.

The fifth and final lesson I want to draw is this: Access to a superintelligent verifiable oracle may be limited and yet totally convincing to those who have access. The pulsar is an example of an oracle accessible to the inhabitants of earth generally. Indeed, observatories around the globe can monitor and record its transmissions. Access to an oracle can, however, be restricted. Suppose I have a magic penny. Whenever I flip the penny twice, I treat two tails in a row as a dot, two heads in a row as a dash, a tail followed by a head as a letter space and a head followed by a tail as a word space. Whenever I flip the coin an even number of times, I now interpret the sequence of coin flips as a message in Morse code. What makes my penny magic is that it communicates to me English messages in Morse code. Suppose the penny communicates profound and marvelous things about the world, much as the pulsar did. Suppose, however, that I refuse to tell anyone about my magic penny. I myself will be convinced that a Designer is communicating with me through the penny, even though I may never care to convince anyone else of this fact. If I care to share my magic penny with a group of friends, then they will become believers in the penny. Yet the public at large will remain unconvinced.[15] Suffice it to say that individuals with access to a superintelligent verifiable oracle have completely convincing evidence for design, even if they are unable to convince those without the access.

The Evidence for Design

The pulsar shows that ours is the type of world where design has at least the possibility of becoming perfectly evident—with the pulsar, empirical validation for design can be made as good as we like. Design is therefore knowable on rational and empirical grounds.

I've belabored this point because it is precisely what Lessing and his modern-day disciples would rather not grant. But once it is granted that the occurrence of certain events would constrain us to postulate design, the question arises whether any such events have actually occurred. Now it is obvious that the pulsar is an exercise in overkill. No instance of design so resoundingly obvious is known. A follow-up question therefore arises as well: How much more subtle can the evidence for design be and yet clearly implicate design? This in turn leads to still another question: Why isn't the evidence for design as resoundingly obvious as it might be? Let me list and number these questions as follows:

Q1. Have any events that would constrain us to postulate design actually occurred, and if so, what are they?

Q2. How subtle can the evidence for design be and still constrain us to postulate design? In particular, what methods of inquiry would enable us reliably to detect these more subtle instances of design?

Q3. Why isn't the evidence for design as obvious as it might be?

Since this essay is an inquiry into the possibility of design, rather than into the actual evidence for design or even the precise methodology for detecting design, I am not, strictly speaking, obligated to answer these questions. After all, I've answered the question I set out to answer—namely, whether the world we inhabit is the kind of place where a Designer can become perfectly evident. As we've seen, the answer to this question is a definite yes. Nevertheless, I have a serious interest in these other questions as well. Indeed, I've addressed Q1 and Q2 elsewhere[16] and am currently coauthoring a book on the topic.[17] What's more, in the book you are reading Moreland and Meyer respond to Q2 and Ross, Bradley and Thaxton respond to Q1. Yet because I am a practical man who regards design as a topic worth discussing only insofar as design can make a genuine difference in how we live and view the world, I'll take up these three questions here, though briefly.

Bertrand Russell, philosopher, mathematician and author of, among other works, *Why I Am Not a Christian,* was once asked how he would respond if upon dying he found himself in the presence of God and was asked why he hadn't believed in God's existence during his stay on earth. Russell's response was summed up in three words: *Not enough evidence!* Now I submit that most persons on hearing of this response would conclude that in Russell we have a careful thinker who won't let himself be swayed by bogus or equivocal evidence. In other words, most people nowadays would regard Russell's skepticism as sober and measured. Atheism is regarded as a reasonable position these days because God, if he exists, has been too lazy or secretive to furnish us with convincing proofs of his existence.

It's worth noting that this attitude is of recent vintage. In other epochs atheism has been considered perverse and unreasonable. Thus the apostle Paul could write, "What can be known about God is plain to them, because God has shown it to them. Ever since the creation of the world his eternal power and divine nature, invisible though they are, have been understood and seen through the things he has made. So they are without excuse" (Romans 1:19-20 NRSV).

Well then, what has God done to make his existence plain? If we look to nature, two things have stood out historically: the cosmos and living systems. The cosmos and living systems have historically been thought to provide excellent reasons for postulating design. Here then is the short answer to Q1. Since in their essays Hugh Ross, Walter Bradley and Charles Thaxton will take up the cosmos and living systems, showing how our scientific understanding of them, far from undermining design, makes design all the more compelling, I shall leave Q1 aside and turn to Q2, which is where the real philosophical difficulties lie.

With respect to the cosmos and living systems, Q2 might be formulated as follows: If the cosmos and living systems provide such compelling evidence for design, why aren't more people convinced? I suggest that the problem lies not with the evidence per se but with the methods of inquiry that are adopted to interpret the evidence. These methods decide whether design is even a legitimate area for inquiry in the first place. Indeed, there are methods of inquiry that do not permit design to get off the ground. The chief antagonist here is of course methodological naturalism, which excludes design from rational discourse on a priori grounds. Although methodological naturalism was the topic of chapters one and two by J. P. Moreland and Steve Meyer, I have a few thoughts to add to the matter.

The received view within scientific and academic circles generally is that science is on safest ground when it remains committed to naturalistic explanation. To invoke a Designer is seen as a serious compromise not only of scientific endeavor generally but also of scientific integrity. The worry is always that by invoking the supernatural, we give in to ignorance and superstition. A well-known Sidney Harris cartoon makes the point well. Two scientists are standing at a blackboard. A course of calculations is interrupted by the phrase "Then a miracle occurs." In the caption, one of the scientists asks the other whether he might not be more explicit on this last point.

Although what Americans call "political correctness" is a fairly recent development, scientific correctness has been with us for some time. C. A. Coulson summarizes the key tenet of scientific correctness as follows: "When we come to the scientifically unknown, our correct policy is not to rejoice because we have found God; it is to become better scientists."[18] Ian Barbour adds, "We would submit that it is scientifically stultifying to say of any puzzling phenomenon that it is 'incapable of scientific explanation,' for such an attitude would undercut the motivation for inquiry. And such an approach is also *theologically dubious,* for it leads to another form of the 'God of the gaps,' the *deus ex machina* introduced to cover ignorance of what may later be shown to have natural causes."[19]

There is something heroic in the sentiments expressed by Coulson and Barbour. Given a difficult problem, the proper attitude is not to capitulate and admit irremediable ignorance, but rather to press on and struggle for a solution. What's more, even if no solution exists, we are to follow the example of Sisyphus, forever trying to roll the rock up the hill, ever striving to obtain a naturalistic solution rather than lapsing into the easy comforts of a sybarite and gratuitously invoking divine agency. Better to attempt the impossible than take the easy way out. Above all, we are to be ever mindful of C. S. Peirce's celebrated dictum "Do not block the way of inquiry." Among naturalists, any appeal to God or the supernatural represents not just a violation of this dictum but a descent into rank superstition.

While the sentiments that drive this commitment to naturalistic explanation are no doubt heroic, even Promethean, I submit that they are also misguided and derive from a fundamental confusion. Methodological naturalism confuses appeals to God that mask our ignorance of natural causes with appeals to God that arise because we have exhausted the full range of possible natural causes. To show what is at stake, let me quote the last line of astronomer Edwin Hubble's *The Realm of the Nebulae:* "Not until the empirical resources are exhausted need we pass on to the dreamy realms of speculation." When Hubble wrote this line in the 1930s, he clearly believed that our empirical resources would not be exhausted and that our entrance into the dreamy realms of speculation could be postponed indefinitely. Indeed, Hubble did not intend his statement as a concession to dreamy speculators like me. Nevertheless, Hubble's statement is a concession. What's more, it is a nonvacuous concession, because empirical resources come in limited supplies and do get exhausted. Moreover, as soon as empirical resources are exhausted, naturalistic explanation loses its monopoly as the only legitimate explanatory strategy for science.

We've already seen how this worked with the pulsar—it exhausted our computational resources (= a type of empirical resource) and therefore required that we posit a nonmaterial intelligence. What about living systems? Now while I don't deny that some speciation occurs in the manner described by Darwin, when it comes to the origin of life there is a compelling argument to be made for design. Indeed, there are features of living systems that exhaust Hubble's empirical resources in the same way that a pulsar that solves intractable computational problems exhausts our computational resources.

Such a revived design argument begins with living systems, looks to results from probability and information theory, cybernetics, computational complexity theory, molecular biology, and chemistry, and concludes that any naturalistic alternative to design fails. Since this argument will require an entire book to develop (a book that I am currently writing), I won't expand on it further here.

Methodological naturalism suffers yet another drawback. Not only does it confuse appeals to God that result from our ignorance of natural causes with appeals to God that result from our knowledge of the essential limitations to natural causes, but it also perpetuates a prejudice whose effect, far from facilitating inquiry, positively hinders it. The prejudice is this: that naturalistic explanation is somehow intrinsically better than nonnaturalistic explanation. This is certainly a value judgment. I call it a prejudice because its effect on inquiry is limiting and destructive.

Scientific inquiry, and inquiry in general, strives as far as possible to remove ignorance about how the world is and works. On this point I shall assume there is no controversy.[20] Now suppose for the moment that God is an efficient cause in the material world, and that this God has assembled certain articles of matter with complete precision and control at the level of elementary particles. Then if the complexity and organization of such articles is sufficiently high, it may be possible to distinguish them reliably from articles produced through the regularities of nature, the effects of chance notwithstanding. But in this case any naturalistic explanation of such God-assembled articles will simply be false, since naturalistic explanation will in this case attribute the wrong cause—natural lawlike processes rather than God. If ours is a world where God exists and actually does things, naturalism, by blocking on a priori grounds explanations that appeal to God, will actually block the way of inquiry—contrary to Peirce's dictum.

Naturalism artificially limits our options. If ours is a world where God exists and actually does things that he intends us to know about, then naturalism prevents us from obtaining such knowledge. Methodological naturalism is therefore itself, to use Barbour's phrase, "scientifically stultifying."

Finally, let me say a few words about the last question, Q3. I call it the perspicuity question: Why isn't design more obvious? When posed by an unsympathetic interlocutor, this question is intended to point up how inherently disreputable the notion of design really is. Implicit in this question is the view that if a Designer existed, this Designer would spare no pains making himself evident (perhaps by giving us a pulsar). Since obviously he has not made himself perfectly evident, he must not exist, or his existence need not concern us.

In this form the argument against design parallels a standard version of the argument against God from evil. The argument from evil poses the following dilemma: If God is able but not willing to prevent evil, he is wicked. If God is willing but not able to prevent evil, he is impotent. Whence evil? In the case of design this dilemma can be recast as follows: If a Designer is able but not willing to make himself perfectly evident, he is obscurantist. If he is willing but not able to make himself perfectly evident, he is inconsequential. What need therefore to postulate a Designer?[21]

I believe it is this dilemma, often unspoken, that has been chiefly responsible for the demise of design arguments. This world is the type of place where design can become perfectly evident by any canons of scientific rigor. Moreover, instances of design more subtle than the pulsar exist and continue to convince many. The dilemma therefore has the effect of removing all subtlety from design: unless the Designer hits us with a sledgehammer, we shall remain unconvinced! No hints, no suggestions, no indications are judged sufficient to implicate design. This attitude is, I suggest, both obtuse and unscientific. Historically, science has judged the world a subtle place which our rationality succeeds in understanding only through toil and creative insight. Scientific discovery is not a matter of going to a cosmic supermarket where all the goods stare us in the face and everything is obvious from the labels. Scientific discovery is the work of a detective who with limited information reconstructs how the world is (if you're a realist about science) or formulates an empirically adequate account of how the world behaves (if you're an antirealist).

How evident must design be to be plausible? How subtle can it be and remain plausible? I believe the proper course is not to prejudge these questions but rather to consider what evidence there is for design and how best to make sense of it. I find it disingenuous for anyone to assume that if a Designer has attempted to reveal himself in the natural order, this revelation must be not only obvious but also ostentatious—not only is God supposed to sign each of his artifacts much as a painter signs a finished canvas, but God is supposed to use neon lights. Since the Designer has avoided ostentatious displays, one is supposed to conclude that no Designer is revealed in the natural order. It is a fact, however, that human reasoning and problem solving must regularly transcend the obvious.

Inferring design is an activity humans engage in all the time. People find it important to distinguish purposeful, premeditated actions from chance events. Was a hit-and-run accident really an accident, or was it a calculated assassination? Anyone who has sampled the suspense-action films that clutter the cinemas understands the difference. The distinction between design and accident is not just widely recognized—whole industries are, as it were, dedicated to demarcating the distinction. These industries include patent offices, copyright offices, insurance companies, statisticians, cryptographers and detectives, to name a few. Now these industries typically refer design to human agents. But as we saw with the pulsar, circumstances might just as well constrain us to refer design to an intelligent agent strictly outside the physical world.

I conclude this essay with an observation from Pascal. In the *Pensées* (194) Pascal offers an insight that from the perspective of Christian theology is indispensable for understanding the difficulties that come with design:

> If the Christian faith boasted of having a perfectly clear and unveiled view of God, to claim that nothing in the world demonstrates its truth with clarity would constitute an attack on the faith. But since, on the contrary, the Christian faith affirms that men are in darkness and estranged from God, that God does in fact give himself the name of *Deus absconditus* [Isaiah 45:15], . . . those who charge that nothing reveals the truth of Christianity in fact reveal how negligent they are in searching for the truth.[22]

Pascal describes the search for religious truth as neither straightforward nor futile. Because "men are in darkness and estranged from God," the search isn't straightforward. Because negligence is the primary obstacle to obtaining the truth, the search isn't futile.

Christian theology has long held that design is one of the ways God reveals himself to the world. Yet according to Pascal it is precisely because design is a way God reveals himself to the world that design will not be obvious. Design isn't transparently obvious, for people "are in darkness and estranged from God." To say this, however, is not to give theology an easy way out. Lessing offered theology an easy way out with his celebrated dictum. He regarded reason as powerless to demonstrate religious truth. Pascal, on the other hand, affirmed no such thing. For Pascal the problem was not with reason but with neglect and willful blindness. I urge Christians to ponder this point and ask themselves whether in relegating design to the garbage heap of passé theologies, as so many have done, they have not rather closed off an avenue by which people might otherwise come to know God.

* * *

In the first three chapters we have focused on philosophical issues relevant to understanding the nature of science and the role that theological concepts, such as of a Creator and intelligent Designer, can play within science. We have also looked at topics in the debate about the very possibility of inferring intelligent design from data gathered from within the natural world. In part two we turn to a more detailed look at different areas in science that bear upon the creation-evolution controversy and more generally upon the question whether there is evidence for a Creator and intelligent Designer. In chapter four Hugh Ross picks up the thread of our discussion by examining evidence in astronomy and related fields.

Acknowledgment
For research support I thank the Pascal Centre, Ancaster, Ontario.

Bibliography
Coincidence
Grim, Patrick, ed. *Philosophy of Science and the Occult.* 2nd ed. Albany: State University of New York Press, 1990. [I]
Jung, Carl G. *Synchronicity.* Translated by R. F. C. Hull. Princeton, N.J.: Princeton University Press, 1973. [I]
Koestler, Arthur. *The Roots of Coincidence: An Excursion into Parapsychology.* New York: Random House, 1972. [B]
Skinner, B. F. "The Force of Coincidence." *The Humanist* 37, no. 3 (1977): 10-11. [B]

Computation and Complexity
Balcázar, José L., Josep Daz and Joaquim Gabarr. *Structural Complexity.* 2 vols. Berlin: Springer-Verlag, 1988-90. [A]
Dembski, William A. "Converting Matter into Mind: Alchemy and the Philosopher's Stone in Cognitive Science." *Perspectives on Science and Christian Faith* 42, no. 4 (1990): 202-26. [I]
Garey, M. R., and D. S. Johnson. *Computers and Intractability: A Guide to the Theory of NP-Completeness.* New York: Freeman, 1979. [A]
Haugeland, John. *Artificial Intelligence: The Very Idea.* Cambridge, Mass.: MIT Press, 1985. [B]
Turing, Alan M. "Computing Machinery and Intelligence." *Mind* 59, no. 236 (1950). [I]
Wegener, Ingo. *The Complexity of Boolean Functions.* Stuttgart: Wiley-Teubner, 1987. [A]

Design and Antidesign

Barrow, John D., and Frank J. Tipler. *The Anthropic Cosmological Principle.* Oxford, U.K.: Oxford University Press, 1986. [I]

Bowler, Peter J. *Evolution: The History of an Idea.* Rev. ed. Berkeley: University of California Press, 1989. [I]

Dawkins, Richard. *The Blind Watchmaker.* New York: W. W. Norton, 1987. [B]

Dembski, William A. "Inconvenient Facts: Miracles and the Skeptical Inquirer." *Bulletin of the Evangelical Philosophical Society* 13 (1990): 18-45. [I]

_____ . "Randomness by Design." *Nous* 25, no. 1 (1991): 75-106. [A]

_____ . "Reviving the Argument from Design: Detecting Design Through Small Probabilities." *Proceedings of the Biennial Conference of the Association of Christians in the Mathematical Sciences* 8 (1991): 101-45. [A]

Hume, David. *Dialogues Concerning Natural Religion.* 1779; rpt. Buffalo, N.Y.: Prometheus Books, 1989. [I]

Jaki, Stanley L. *The Road of Science and the Ways to God.* Chicago: University of Chicago Press, 1978. [A]

Jastrow, Robert. *God and the Astronomers.* New York: Warner Books, 1980. [B]

Monod, Jacques. *Chance and Necessity: An Essay on the Natural Philosophy of Modern Biology.* New York: Random House, 1972. [B]

Paley, William. *Natural Theology: Or, Evidences of the Existence and Attributes of the Deity Collected from the Appearances of Nature.* 1802; rpt. London: Farborough, Gregg, 1970. [I]

Probability and Information

Bauer, Heinz. *Probability Theory and Elements of Measure Theory.* London: Academic, 1981. [A]

Borel, Émile. *Probabilities and Life.* Translated by M. Baudin. New York: Dover, 1962. [I]

_____ . *Probability and Certainty.* Translated by D. Scott. New York: Walker, 1963. [B]

Hamming, Richard W. *Coding and Information Theory.* 2nd ed. Englewood Cliffs, N.J.: Prentice-Hall, 1986. [A]

Küppers, Bernd-Olaf. *Information and the Origin of Life.* Cambridge, Mass.: MIT Press, 1990. [I]

Patterson, Wayne. *Mathematical Cryptology for Computer Scientists and Mathematicians.* Totowa, N.J.: Rowman & Littlefield, 1987. [A]

Peirce, Charles S. *Philosophical Writings of Peirce.* Edited by J. Buchler. New

York: Dover, 1955. See the essays on probability theory, esp. "The Red and the Black" and "The General Theory of Probable Inference." [I]

Related Interests

Denton, Michael. *Evolution: A Theory in Crisis.* Bethesda, Md.: Adler & Adler, 1986. [I]

Harris, James F. *Against Relativism: A Philosophical Defense of Method.* LaSalle, Ill.: Open Court, 1992. [I]

Johnson, Phillip E. *Darwin on Trial.* 2nd ed. Downers Grove, Ill.: InterVarsity Press, 1993. [B]

Montgomery, John W., ed. *Evidence for Faith: Deciding the God Question.* Dallas: Probe, 1991. [B]

Moreland, J. P., and Kai Nielsen. *Does God Exist? The Great Debate.* Buffalo, N.Y.: Prometheus, 1990. [B]

PART II

CREATION, DESIGN & SCIENTIFIC EVIDENCE

4
ASTRONOMICAL EVIDENCES FOR A PERSONAL, TRANSCENDENT GOD

Hugh Ross

I̲t really does matter, and matter very much, how we think about the cosmos," says historian and college president George Roche.[1] If the universe is simply uncreated, eternally self-existent or randomly self-assembled, then it has no purpose and consequently we have no purpose. Determinism rules. Morality and religion are ultimately irrelevant, and there is no objective meaning to life. On the other hand, if the Creator is personal, then love, compassion, care, beauty, self-sacrifice, mercy and justice could be real and meaningful.

If there is a personal creator, but this creator is contained within and dependent on the universe, then the universe itself is ultimate reality. The universe itself is supreme, preeminent. By contrast, if there is a personal Creator and this Creator is transcendent, existing beyond the confines of the universe, then the Creator defines ultimate reality and wields authority over it. Extradimensional phenomena such as miracles, heaven and hell, the Trinity all become real and comprehensible possibilities.

Thus the study of cosmology (the origin and development of the universe) is closely related to questions about the meaning and purpose of life. Theistic science postulates that the universe was created by a personal God a finite time ago and that it was intelligently designed with the arrival of human life in mind. Are these two propositions reasonable in light of evidence from astronomy? They are, in fact, the theme of dozens of books and papers produced by world-renowned astronomers in the late 1980s and early 1990s. The following pages review their conclusions and the basis for them. In summary, the research shows that (1) all matter, energy, space and time began simultaneously about 16-18 billion years ago and (2) the characteristics of the beginning event and the subsequent developments within the universe must fit (from a physical and life sciences viewpoint) within certain narrow limits essential for even the possibility of human life.

Agnostic Cosmology

Agnosticism (roughly defined as the belief that God's existence cannot be known) has always had its adherents, but it was the work of Immanuel Kant that really propelled agnosticism to prominence. In his book on physical cosmology, *Universal Natural History and Theory of the Heavens,* Kant concluded that the universe must be infinite: "It is evident that in order to think of it [the universe] as in proportion to the power of the Infinite Being, it must have no limits at all. . . . It would be absurd to represent the Deity as passing into action with an infinitely small part of His potency."[2] From his conclusion that the universe must be infinite, Kant proceeded to work out a strictly mechanistic model of physical reality. For him, everything about and in the universe could be accounted for by Isaac Newton's laws of mechanics. Kant reasoned that an infinite universe yields the possibility of an infinite number of random events. Thus even highly improbable events such as atoms' self-assembling into humans might be possible. Ironically, God, who provided the basis for Kant's assumption that the universe is infinite, becomes unnecessary for explaining life's existence. Though Kant called himself a theist, he provided much of the foundation for nineteenth- and twentieth-century agnosticism.

   Kant's cosmology seemed validated by the leapfrog advances in astronomy during the nineteenth century. Observations through progressively larger telescopes revealed an ever-multiplying number of stars and nebulae. No matter how much farther into deep space the newer telescopes penetrated, the universe appeared the same—no hint of boundary, no hint of change. When many faint nebulae resolved into stars, infinitude seemed certain. Billions of stars and thousands of nebulae stretched imaginations to the breaking point. This mind-boggling universe powerfully suggested countless stars spread throughout limitless space. Thus even the admittedly remote prospect of atoms' self-assembling into living organisms seemed to fall within the realm of possibility.

Early Objections to Agnostic Cosmology

Observations and experiments during the nineteenth century demonstrated again and again the reliability of Newton's laws of mechanics and of James Clerk Maxwell's equations for electromagnetics. Scientists became convinced that these laws and equations described all natural phenomena. Toward the close of the century many physicists voiced the opinion that the only work left for their successors was to "make measurements to the next decimal place." No significant cosmological developments were anticipated; the Newtonian infinite universe model was cast in concrete.

However, this concrete began to crack almost before it dried. Disturbances came from three unexpected developments in physics and astronomy.

1. Discovery of heat transfer by radiation. In the 1880s Josef Stefan and Ludwig Boltzmann demonstrated from the laws of thermodynamics that given enough time, a body will assume the temperature of its surroundings and will radiate away as much energy as it receives (like a cup of coffee left on your table). This finding ruled out the long-accepted answer to an important question about the universe: Why is the night sky dark? Scientists had postulated that some medium among the stars absorbs the light of the stars, keeping that light from filling the universe. Stefan and Boltzmann's work showed that in the process of absorption, this medium would reach a temperature at which it would radiate as much light as it received. The mere fact that the night sky is dark, rather than light, tells us that the universe cannot contain an infinite number of evenly distributed stars for an infinite time.[3]

2. Gravitational potential paradox. Not until 1871 did anyone attempt to calculate the tug of gravity at specific locations within an infinite Newtonian universe. In that year Johann Friedrich Zöllner presented proofs that at any point within an infinite homogeneous universe the tug of gravity becomes infinite (infinite force with no definite direction). Obviously this is not the way things are. However, only when his objection was independently raised by Hugo Seeliger in 1895 and by Carl Neumann in 1896 did astronomers acknowledge a dilemma.[4]

3. Results of the Michelson-Morley experiment. In the 1880s physicists expressed certainty, on the basis of Maxwell's equations, that light travels at a constant velocity relative to an extremely thin, invisible medium (called the aether) contained in absolute space and time and filling the entire universe.[5] In 1887 two American physicists, Albert Michelson and Edward Morley, took up the challenge to determine the absolute velocity of the earth in the "aether" by measuring the speed of light in different directions and at different positions of the earth in its orbit about the sun. To their astonishment, the experiment showed that the velocity of light was the same no matter at what position the earth was in its orbit.

It was immediately obvious that the Michelson-Morley experiment posed a severe threat to any kind of model of the universe, like the Newtonian models, that postulated absolute reference frames of space and time. Still, for almost twenty years physicists attempted to patch up the classical theories. They proposed wild hypotheses such as that all material bodies contract in the direction of motion. Various experiments and astronomical observations, however, forced the rejection of all these desperate stabs. Any one of these three developments was sufficient in itself to throw the infinite Newtonian universe model onto the trash heap. However, so strong was the emotional attachment of most scientists to Kantian philosophy and so confident were all scientists in Newton's gravitational theory that the nineteenth century closed with the infinite Newtonian universe model as firmly entrenched as ever.

Einstein Discovers the Beginning

As the twentieth century dawned, the only conclusions consistent with all observations of the velocity of light were these two:

1. No absolute reference system exists from which absolute motions can be measured.

2. The speed of light with respect to all observers is always the same.

In 1905 Albert Einstein, a German engineer who studied physics in his spare time, formally presented these conclusions in his paper on the theory of special relativity.[6] Further, he derived a dilation, or stretching, factor that revealed by exactly how much two observers moving with respect to one another would disagree on their measurements of length, velocity, mass and time. Applying this dilation factor to the classical expressions for momentum and to Newton's law of force, any high-school student can easily derive the famous equation governing the conversion of matter into energy:[7] $E = mc^2$.

Resistance to Einstein's theory broke when experiments and observations repeatedly confirmed all of its dilation predictions. The success of Einstein's equations in predicting all manner of observations and experiments was overwhelming.[8] In fact, a recent experiment[9] proved the accuracy of the relativistic dilation factor to within one part in 10^{21}.

The triumph of special relativity gave Einstein the boldness to extend his theory beyond velocity effects and on to the acceleration effects between observers.[10] The results were the ten equations of general relativity. Subtracting one set of these equations from another yielded yet another equation, whose solution led to the surprising result that everything in the universe is simultaneously expanding and decelerating. The only physical phenomenon in which expansion and deceleration occur at the same time is an explosion. But if the universe is the aftermath of an explosion, then sometime in the past it must have had a beginning. There must have been a moment at which the explosion began. If it had a beginning, then through the principle of cause and effect this beginning implies the existence of a Beginner.

Einstein's own worldview initially kept him from concluding that there is, in fact, a Beginner. Rather, he proposed a hypothetical force of physics that would perfectly cancel out the deceleration and expansion factors. Astronomer Edwin Hubble soon proved that the galaxies are indeed expanding away from one another in the manner predicted by Einstein's original formulation of general relativity.[11] Confronted with this proof, Einstein gave grudging acceptance to "the necessity for a beginning"[12] and to "the presence of a superior reasoning power."[13]

Search for Loopholes

Others were not so ready to concede either that necessity or that presence. Through the years they have proposed a variety of alternatives.

1. The hesitating universe. While accepting the general expansion of the universe, Georges Lemaître, a Belgian priest trained in astrophysics by British mathematician Sir Arthur Eddington, sought to lengthen the age of the universe by proposing that the general expansion had been interrupted sometime in the past by a near static phase. In Lemaître's model, the universe expands rapidly from a beginning, but the density of the universe is such that gravity slowly brings the expansion to a halt. Then, through a judicious reintroduction of Einstein's hypothetical force of physics (a repulsive force) and a careful choice of its value, Lemaître proposed that just when gravity is taking the steam out of the cosmic explosion, the repulsive force builds up to cancel off the gravitational effects. Expansion is slowed almost to a standstill, yielding a quasi-static period. Eventually, the repulsive force begins to dominate again, producing a second phase of general expansion (the phase that the universe would now be in).

Eddington expressed his irritation that Lemaître's model still required "a sudden and peculiar beginning of things."[14] As he stated in a research paper, "Philosophically, the notion of a beginning of the present order of Nature is repugnant to me. . . . I should like to find a genuine loophole."[15] Eddington tried to create one. He stretched Lemaître's quasi-static period to infinity, putting the "repugnant" beginning point all but out of the picture to "allow evolution an infinite time to get started."[16]

Not until the 1970s was enough evidence marshaled against Lemaître's, Eddington's and others' hesitation models to eliminate them from contention. Iranian physicist Vahé Petrosian theoretically established that if the universe hesitates, the galaxies and quasars must be confined to certain spatial limits.[17] Observations have proved that those limits are exceeded.[18] Further, theoreticians have shown that if the quasi-static period exceeds a trillion years, galaxy formation during that period is guaranteed, but so is a subsequent and relatively immediate collapse back to the initial singularity[19] (an infinitely shrunken space representing the boundary at which space ceases to exist or, in the case of the creation event, comes into existence).

2. The steady state universe. In 1948 three British astrophysicists, Herman Bondi, Thomas Gold and Fred Hoyle, attempted to circumvent the beginning by proposing "continual creation."[20] In their models, the universe, though expanding indefinitely, takes on an unchanging and eternal quality since the voids that result from expansion are filled by the continual, spontaneous creation of new matter. Their proposal made the creation of matter no longer a miracle from the past, but an ongoing law of nature that can be tested by observations.

Right from the beginning the steady state proponents made their intentions clear. Bondi stated that the "problem" with other theories was that creation was "being handed over to metaphysics."[21] Hoyle in his opening paper confessed his "aesthetic objections to the creation of the universe in the remote past."[22] Later he expressed his opinion that the Christian view of creation offers to man "an eternity of frustration."[23] In 1982 he reiterated his dogma: "The attribution of definite age to the Universe, whatever it might be, is to exalt the concept of time above the Universe, and since the Universe is everything this is crackpot in itself."[24]

During the 1960s, 1970s and early 1980s a series of complex observational and theoretical tests were developed to prove or disprove the steady state model. Ironically, the simplest test was applied last of all. It was proposed by Sir James Jeans in the 1920s: A universe that has no beginning and no end should manifest a "steady" population. That is, there should be balanced numbers of infant, middle-aged, elderly and extinct stars and galaxies.[25]

While it is true that stars with ages ranging from just a few days to billions

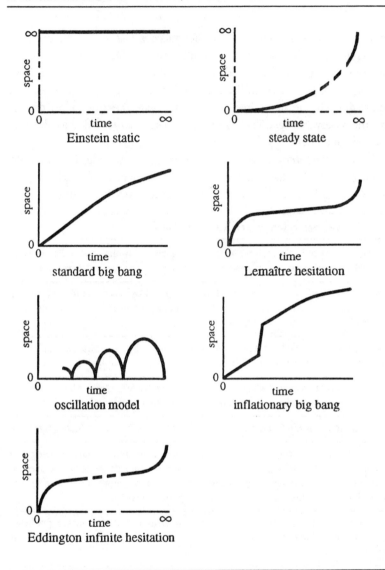

Figure 4.1. Seven types of testable models for the universe. Observations have ruled out all but a certain set of big bang models.

of years can be seen, no star anywhere in the universe has been found to be older than about 16 billion years. As for galaxies, all, or very nearly all, are middle-aged. We see no newly formed galaxies. (A recent report of a newly formed galaxy is considered by most astronomers to be instead the aftermath of a collision between two other galaxies. Galaxies in the universe are so tightly packed together that such collisions and their aftermaths should occur on occasion.) Neither are there any extinct varieties. In fact, in 1985 astronomer Donald Hamilton determined that all the galaxies were formed at approximately the same time.[26] The steady state theories simply do not match the observable data. Table 4.1 presents a summary of evidence disproving this set of models.

3. The oscillating universe. Research that brought about the demise of the hesitating and steady state universe models simultaneously strengthened the case for the big bang and thus the prospect of a relatively recent beginning

---

Table 4.1. Evidence refuting steady state models.

---

1. The lack of very old galaxies near our galaxy negates an infinite age for the universe, while the lack of very young galaxies near our galaxy negates continual creation.

---

2. The paucity of galaxies and quasars (distant celestial objects that radiate far more light than typical galaxies) beyond a certain boundary implies that we are not living in an infinite steady state universe.

---

3. A steady state universe lacks a physical mechanism (such as the primeval explosion) to drive the observed expansion of the universe.

---

4. The observed microwave background radiation (perfectly explained by the cooling off of the primordial fireball) defies explanation in a steady state universe.

---

5. The enormous entropy* of the universe makes no sense in a steady state system.

---

6. In a steady state universe, spontaneously generated matter must come into being with a specified ratio of helium to hydrogen, and that ratio must decrease with respect to time in an entirely ad hoc fashion. Instead, the measured helium abundance for the universe has exactly the value that a hot big bang would predict.

---

7. The observed abundances of deuterium, light helium and lithium are predicted perfectly by some kind of big bang beginning, but cannot be explained in a steady state universe.

---

8. Galaxies and quasars at distances so great that we are viewing them from the remote past appear to differ so substantially in character and distribution from nearby, more contemporary galaxies and quasars as to render steady state models completely implausible.

---

*Entropy is the measure of the energy in a system that is unavailable to perform work. A candle flame, for example, dissipates most of its energy as heat and light, leaving little to perform work. The universe, by comparison, has a specific entropy about 500 million times greater than a candle flame's.

and a Beginner. This turn of research dismayed many cosmologists. In their dismay they resurrected a model first proposed by early Hindu teachers and Roman atheistic philosophers—the oscillating universe.[27]

In the oscillating universe model, the universe is presumed to have sufficient mass that the gravity within it eventually puts the brakes on its expansion. And not only does the expansion halt, but it reverses, bringing about a total collapse. However, rather than crunching itself into a singularity, the imploding universe somehow bounces back and expands again, and so the cycle repeats, according to this model. An infinite number of such cycles is thought to "relieve us of the necessity of understanding the origin of matter at any finite time in the past."[28] Our existence, then, could be attributed to that one lucky bounce (out of an infinite number) that just happened to convert particles into human beings through random, natural processes.

Since 1965, when the oscillation model first received serious consideration, astronomers have engaged in a tireless effort to find sufficient mass in the universe to halt the expansion. Yet all the evidence, both observational and theoretical, still points in the opposite direction.[29]

In 1983 and 1984, Marc Sher, Alan Guth and Sidney Bludman demonstrated that even if the universe did contain enough mass to halt its current expansion, the collapse would yield not a bounce but a thud.[30] Because of the huge entropy of the universe, any ultimate collapse would lack, by many orders of magnitude, the mechanical energy needed to bring about a bounce. This huge entropy was the justification for the title of the paper by Sher and Guth, "The Impossibility of a Bouncing Universe." In other words, the universe would much more closely resemble a wet lump of clay falling on a thick rug than it does a basketball striking a hardwood floor. Apparently the universe either expands continuously or goes through just one cycle of expansion and contraction.

The refutations of oscillation offered by Sher, Guth and Bludman and an earlier one developed by Russian physicists Igor Novikov and Yakob Zel'dovich[31] omitted any discussion of the obscure possibility of black holes merging when the universe is compressed down to the point at which quantum-gravitational effects dominate. Thus there has been a recent attempt to revive the possibility of a bouncing universe based on such speculations. However, as authors Arnold Sikkema and Werner Israel admit, no consistent quantum theory of gravity yet exists (see sidebar), and the revived theory yields an oscillating universe with only a sharply limited, finite number of bounces.[32]

The Quantum Gravity Era

Physicists now are designing theories to cope with conditions before the universe was 10^{-43} seconds old. At 10^{-43} seconds, the force of gravity within the universe becomes comparable to the strong nuclear force (the force that governs the degree to which protons and neutrons stick together in the nuclei of atoms). At such a magnitude, gravity may need to be modified by quantum mechanical effects.

Since the energy densities that exist during the quantum gravity era for the universe far exceed the capabilities of the most powerful particle accelerators, many theoreticians have presumed that they are free to speculate any physical conditions, or for that matter any physical laws, they desire. However, since such physics is "beyond the possibility of observational verification," it would by definition fall outside the realm of science and into the realm of pure speculation. But even though the energies encountered are far beyond current experimental physics, a powerful observational check does exist—the present universe in which we live. If a quantum gravity theory cannot explain how the present universe developed from the initial quantum state, it must be wrong.

Observational checks beyond the universe in which we live are not likely to be forthcoming. As the originator of the inflationary universe model, Alan Guth, once remarked, "We would need a particle accelerator at least 40 trillion miles long . . . and such a machine has little likelihood of funding."

An even stronger statement against this oscillation was established by Russian physicist André Linde at a recent Caltech symposium on the large-scale structure of the universe. Linde demonstrated that for realistic inflationary big bang models (see sidebar)—that is, inflationary models that fit all the current observations—there will exist at least one domain (a volume) within the universe that ultimately will resist being crushed by a collapse.[33] In other words, there exists no possibility for anti-inflation.

Inflation of the universe produces matter (particles) out of space, actually out of space curvature. As the universe expands, the curvature of space is reduced. The loss of space curvature results in a gain of matter and a huge dissipation of energy. Because of this entropy, the process is not reversible: the particles cannot be converted back into space curvature. Thus inflationary models that bear some resemblance to reality do not permit the universe to oscillate. A summary of evidence against oscillation models is given in table 4.2.

The Inflationary Big Bang

A new version of the big bang model, a model called the inflationary universe, answers most of the previously unanswered questions of big bang cosmology. In the standard big bang model, the universe expands smoothly and adiabatically (temperature dropping due to expansion alone without loss of heat from the system) from the beginning onward. In the inflationary model there is a very brief departure from adiabatic expansion. A much faster, quasi-exponential expansion occurs between about 10^{-35} and about 10^{-33} seconds after the beginning.

There is now little doubt among astronomers that some kind of inflation must operate at some point. The discussion currently centers on what kind of inflation model is correct. A recent development of great theological significance is a paper just produced by Alexander Vilenkin establishing that inflationary models with no beginning are impossible.[34]

Table 4.2. Evidence against oscillation models.[35]

---

1. The maximum radius of the universe would increase from cycle to cycle because of irreversible thermodynamic changes. Therefore a backwards look would show a decreasing radius down to zero in the not-far-distant past.

---

2. The observed density of the universe falls just short of what is needed to force a collapse.

---

3. No known physical mechanism can bring about a bounce, a reversal of cosmic contraction.

---

4. Any hypothesized compression becomes violently unstable near the end of the collapse.

---

5. Even if the universe were to collapse, and even if there were some bounce mechanism, the huge entropy in the universe would severely limit the number of bounces.

The New Cosmology and Eastern Religions

Most Eastern religions, old and new, are founded on the belief that the universe oscillates or "reincarnates." In fact, the popularity of these belief systems soared as the popularity of the oscillating universe model grew, especially when it was recognized that the Hindu number for the length of the oscillation period (specifically, 4.32 billion years)[36] came relatively close to the

20- to 30-billion-year period proposed by astronomers working on the model. Some reasoned that for the ancient Hindus to get that close to the "right" number, Hinduism must hold vital truths.

Now that the hesitation, steady state and oscillation models for the universe have evaporated in the face of new measurements, so too has any scientific basis for the cosmology of Eastern religions. The proofs against the oscillating universe model destroys this scientific foundation of Hinduism, Buddhism and their New Age derivatives. The proofs against the eternal existence of the cosmos translate into the impossibility of pantheism and all of its daughter faiths insofar as they include the notion of an eternal past.

The Beginning of Time

All the evidence against an infinitely old universe has become somewhat academic. In 1968 and 1970 three British astrophysicists, Stephen Hawking, George Ellis and Roger Penrose, extended the solution of the equations of general relativity to include space and time.[37]

The theory of special relativity was derived by Albert Einstein from the combined observations that (1) there is no observable absolute motion in the universe, only relative motion, and (2) the velocity of light is constant and independent of the motion of the source. General relativity extends special relativity to include the effects of gravity on matter, energy, space and time.

What Hawking, Ellis and Penrose demonstrated was that if the equations of general relativity are valid for the universe, then under reasonably general conditions, space and time also must have an origin, concurrent with that for matter and energy. In other words, time itself is finite.

In 1970 general relativity had not yet been overwhelmingly established by observations. But by 1980 observations from a NASA rocket experiment removed any doubts.[38] By 1992 twelve separate evidences had been accumulated.[39] Summaries of the observational verifications of general relativity are available.[40]

Given that time has a beginning, and a relatively recent beginning (17 ± 3 billion years), all age-stretching models are eliminated from serious contention. Moreover, the common origin of matter, energy, space and time establishes that the act(s) or cause(s) of creation must take place in dimensions or realms independent of the space-time dimensions and substance of the universe.

The Bible and Modern Cosmology

The Bible has much to say on the origin and characteristics of the universe.

The early chapters of Genesis give some of the story, but other references are found throughout the Old and New Testaments. Table 4.3 provides a partial list of those references.

Most significantly for our skeptical times, the latest discoveries on the frontiers of astronomy and physics support and help to amplify biblical cosmology. Moreover, the Bible among all "holy books" stands uniquely apart in its statements about cosmology. No other "sacred" writings teach an extradimensional (dimensions beyond length, width, height and time) reality independent of our universe where a personal entity creates the space-time dimensions of the universe.

Though Christianity is the only faith that is wholly and only based on the Old and New Testaments, other faiths like Judaism, Islam and Mormonism appropriate at least a portion of these texts. Insofar as the cosmological doctrines of these other faiths are consistent with the teachings of the Old and New Testaments, they find support from the latest discoveries about the origin and development of the universe. However, all non-Christian faiths deny at least some of the extradimensional, biblically described attributes of God.[41]

Table 4.3. Some biblical statements of cosmological significance.

---

1. God existed "before" the universe. God exists totally apart from the universe and yet can be everywhere within it (Genesis 1:1; Colossians 1:16-17).

---

2. Time has a beginning. God's existence and cause-and-effect activities precede time (2 Timothy 1:9; Titus 1:2).

---

3. Jesus Christ created the universe. He has no beginning and was not created (John 1:3; Colossians 1:16-17).

---

4. God created the universe from what cannot be detected with the five senses (Hebrews 11:3).

---

5. After his resurrection Jesus could pass through walls in his physical body, an evidence of his extradimensionality (Luke 24:36-43; John 20:26-28).

---

6. God is very near, yet we cannot see him—a further suggestion of his extradimensionality (Exodus 33:20; Deuteronomy 30:11-14; John 6:46).

---

7. God designed the universe in such a way that it would support human beings (Genesis 1—2; Nehemiah 9:6; Job 38; Psalm 8:3; Isaiah 45:18).

Quantum Mechanics: A Threat to Theism?

The evidences for a transcendent Creator have grown too voluminous and too strong to be ignored by nontheists. However, for those with an aversion to theism, some way of avoiding the theistic implications of a beginning for the cosmos must be found. Many are looking to quantum mechanics for possible loopholes. Famous physicists and others have produced popular books exploiting the esoteric nature of quantum phenomena to undermine a Christian view of origins. Unfortunately, some theologians have been taken in by this esoteric erudition and have heralded quantum mechanics as "the greatest contemporary threat to Christianity."[42]

In their insistence that the Creator-God implied by the solid data of cosmology does not exist, nontheists grope for a replacement. Five "possibilities" have been proposed.

1. Quantum tunneling. British astrophysicist Paul Davies, in his book *God and the New Physics,* locks all cause-and-effect phenomena into the time dimension of the universe. Because the act of creating represents cause and effect, and thus a timebound activity, the evidence for the origin of time, says Davies, argues against God's agency in the creation of the universe.[43]

Apparently Davies is (or was) unaware that the Bible speaks of God's causing effects even before the beginning of time (2 Timothy 1:9; Titus 1:2). As indicated in table 4.3, the Bible also speaks of the existence of dimensions beyond our time and space, extra dimensions in which God exists and operates.

Noting that virtual particles can pop into existence from nothingness through quantum tunneling (the process by which quantum mechanical particles penetrate barriers that would be insurmountable to classical objects), Davies employs the new grand unified theories to suggest likewise that the whole universe popped into existence. Ironically, though, his argument against God's creating can now be turned against his hypothesis. According to quantum mechanics, the larger the time interval, the greater the probability that a specific quantum event will occur. This means that if the time interval is zero, the probability for that quantum event's occurring is also zero. Because the time dimension of our universe began when the universe was created, the time interval for the creation event is zero. (Since we lack thorough understanding about anything that occurs in that instant before the universe was 10^{-43} seconds old, there necessarily exists the *possibility* that the relationship between time and the probability for certain quantum events breaks down in that interval.) This eliminates quantum tunneling as a possible cause of the universe.

To Davies's credit, he has been revising his position. He recently argued that the laws of physics "seem themselves to be the product of exceedingly ingenious design."[44] Still more recently he posed this question: "If new organizational levels just pop into existence for no reason, why do we see such an orderly progression in the universe from featureless origin to rich diversity?"[45] He concludes that we have "powerful evidence that there is 'something going on' behind it all."[46]

2. *Infinite chances.* Astrophysicists have a reasonably good understanding of the universe's development back to when it was only 10^{-34} seconds old. We may see some probing back to 10^{-43} seconds, but that represents the practical limit of research.

American astrophysicist Richard Gott has taken advantage of this infinitesimal period, the quantum gravity era, about which we know nothing. He proposes that there is an infinite loss of information about events before 10^{-43} seconds. With this total loss of information, he says, anything becomes possible, including "the ability to make an infinite number of universes."[47] In this "possibility" for an infinite number of universes some nontheists see an opportunity to replace God with chance or, more specifically, with random fluctuations of a primeval radiation field.

This suggestion by these nontheists is a flagrant abuse of probability theory. It assumes the benefits of an infinite sample size without any evidence that the sample size exceeds one.

Consider the following example. If I flip 10^{301} coins a thousand times each, by random chance one of these coins would be likely to produce a thousand consecutive heads, the other coins different results. But if I had only one coin to flip, then regardless of how many other coins might conceivably exist, should that single coin produce a thousand consecutive heads, I must rationally conclude the coin had been altered to produce nothing but heads when flipped.

Other questions remain. If the universe had zero information before 10^{-43} seconds, how did it acquire its subsequent high information state without the input of an intelligent, personal Creator? A personal Creator seems to be required, too, to explain the existence of the primeval radiation field. Such an effect, like everything else in the universe, requires a cause.

For centuries atheists and agnostics have mocked Christians for their "God of the gaps"—that is, for invoking divine miracles wherever gaps were encountered in human understanding of the physical universe. Now we are seeing the reverse situation, the "Chance of the gaps." It seems that scientists (and others) are relying on gaps, and in this case a very minute one, to give them a way around the obvious theistic implications of scientifically established facts. Surely the burden of proof lies on those who suggest that physical conditions and/or physical laws were totally different in the period before 10^{-43} seconds.

3. No singularity. While evidence for a big bang beginning has gained general acceptance throughout the physical science community, a few have sought to escape it by dodging one of its key components, the singularity.[48] Once again some theoreticians are reaching back into their magician's hat, the quantum gravity era.

As early as 1973, Ed Tryon suggested that a quantum mechanical fluctuation in "the vacuum"—not just a false vacuum of highly curved space where no space curvature has been converted into matter and energy, but a true vacuum where space itself does not yet exist—created the universe.[49] Later he was joined by several well-known peers who proposed similar kinds of hypotheses.[50] While one of this group's members, Alan Guth, concedes that "such ideas are speculation squared," all of their models do circumvent some technical details in the description of the big bang singularity. They do not, however, circumvent the beginning of space-time-matter-energy. Thus agreement with the biblical doctrine of creation still stands.

One of the most elegant quantum vacuum fluctuation models was published in 1984, when Steven Hawking teamed up with American physicist James Hartle.[51] Their notion is that just as a hydrogen atom can be described by a quantum mechanical wave function, so can the universe be described. Thus the singularity as defined in the standard big bang model disappears, yet the entire universe still pops into existence at the beginning of time.

Here is the response of Heinz Pagels, a physicist who, ironically, also fought hard[52] against the notion of a singularity: "This unthinkable void converts itself into the plenum of existence—a necessary consequence of physical laws. Where are these laws written into that void? What 'tells' the void that it is pregnant with a possible universe? It would seem that even the void is subject to law, a logic that exists prior to space and time."[53]

Once again, a conclusion fully consistent with the biblical doctrine of creation is deduced. And as physicist Frank Tipler pointed out, Hawking may simply be substituting, unawares, one kind of singularity for another—specifically the classical singularity of general relativity for one of a family of quantum singularities.[54]

Later, in his popular book *A Brief History of Time* (1988), Hawking himself argued against any real escape for the universe from the singularity and the boundary conditions:

If the universe really is in such a quantum state, there would be no singularities in the history of the universe in imaginary time. . . . [Hawking hypothesizes the splitting of time into what amounts to two dimensions of time, a dimension operating in physical reality and a dimension operating in an imaginary realm.] The universe could be finite in imaginary time but without boundaries or singularities. When one goes back to the real time in which we live, however, there will still appear to be singularities. . . . Only if [we] lived in imaginary time would [we] encounter no singularities. . . . In real time, the universe has a beginning and an end at singularities that form a boundary to space-time and at which the laws of science break down.[55]

If we substitute biblical terminology here, we can say that God transcends "real time" (2 Timothy 1:9; Titus 1:2) and is not confined to boundaries and singularities. Human beings and the physical universe, however, are limited to real time. Hence, they would be confined by boundaries and singularities.

4. Humankind as creator. A case for humankind as the creator has been fabricated from an analogy to delayed-choice experiments in quantum mechanics. In such experiments it appears that the observer can influence the outcome of quantum mechanical events. With every quantum particle there is an associated wave. This wave represents the probability of finding the particle at a specific point in space. Before the particle is detected there is no specific knowledge of its location—only a probability of where it might be. But once the particle has been detected, its exact location is known. In this sense the act of observation is said by some to give reality to the particle. What is true for a quantum particle, they suggest, may be true for the universe.[56]

In other words, the universe produces human beings, but human beings through their observations of the universe bring the universe into reality. Here we find a reflection of the question debated in freshman philosophy classes: If a tree falls in the forest and no one is there to see it or hear it, does it really fall?

Quantum mechanics merely shows us that in the micro-world of particle physics we humans are limited in our ability to measure quantum effects. Since quantum entities at any moment have the potential to behave either as particles or as waves, it is impossible, for example, to accurately measure both the position and the momentum of such an entity (the Heisenberg uncertainty principle). In choosing to determine the position of the entity, the human observer loses information about its momentum.

One can easily get the impression from the physics literature, by the way, that the Copenhagen interpretation of quantum mechanics is the only accepted philosophical explanation of what is going on in the micro-world. According to this school of thought, there is no reality in the absence of observation, and observation creates reality. But physicist Nick Herbert outlines and critiques six additional philosophical models for interpreting quantum events.[57] Physicist-theologian Stanley Jaki presents an eighth model.[58] While a clear philosophical understanding of quantum reality is not yet agreed upon, physicists do agree on the results expected from quantum events.

The observer does not give "reality" to the entity, but rather the observer chooses what aspect of the reality he or she wishes to discern. It is not that the Heisenberg uncertainty principle disproves the principle of causality (that every effect or event has a cause) but simply that causality in this case is hidden from human investigation. The cause of the quantum effect is not lacking, nor is it mysteriously linked to the human observation of the effect after the fact.

This misapplication of Heisenberg's uncertainty principle is but one defect in the "observer-as-creator" propositions arising from quantum physics. Some other flaws include these:

☐ Quantum mechanical limitations apply only to micro, not to macro, systems. The relative uncertainty approaches zero as the number of quantum particles in the system increases. Therefore, what is true for a quantum particle would not be true for the universe as a whole.

☐ The time separation between a quantum event and its observed result is always a relatively short one (at least for the analogies under discussion). The multibillion-year time separation between the beginning of the universe and the beginning of humankind hardly fits the picture.

☐ The arrow of time has never been observed to reverse, nor do we see any trace of evidence that a reversal might have taken place beyond the scope of our observation. Time and causality move inexorably forward. Therefore, to suggest that human activity can somehow affect events billions of years ago is nothing short of absurd.

☐ Intelligence, or personality, is not a key factor in the observation of quantum mechanical events. Photographic plates, for example, are perfectly capable of recording such events.

☐ Both Einstein's theory of relativity and what is called the gauge theory of quantum mechanics, now established beyond reasonable doubt by experimental evidence,[59] affirm that the correct description of nature is that in which the human observer is irrelevant. Science has yet to produce a shred of evidence to support the notion that humankind created its universe.

5. *Universe becoming God.* In *The Anthropic Cosmological Principle and the Structure of the Physical World,* astrophysicists John Barrow and Frank Tipler review many evidences for the design of the universe.[60] They also review standard versions of the anthropic principle such as WAP (weak anthropic principle: conscious beings can only exist in an environment with special characteristics that allow their habitation), SAP (strong anthropic principle: nature must take on those characteristics to admit somewhere, sometime, the existence of conscious beings) and more radical versions including PAP (participatory anthropic principle: observers are necessary to bring the universe into existence, and the universe is necessary to bring observers into existence). They conclude with a discussion of their favorite, FAP (final anthropic principle).

According to FAP, the life that now exists in the universe (and which PAP says created the universe) will continue to evolve until it reaches a state Barrow and Tipler call the Omega Point.[61] In a footnote they declare, "The totality of life at the Omega Point is omnipotent, omnipresent, and omniscient!"[62] In other words, the universe created humankind, humankind created the universe, and together the universe and humankind in the end will become Almighty God.

In *The New York Review of Books* Martin Gardner gave this evaluation of Barrow and Tipler's idea: "What should one make of this quartet of WAP, SAP, PAP, and FAP? In my not so humble opinion I think the last principle is best called CRAP, the Completely Ridiculous Anthropic Principle."[63]

In their persistent rejection of an eternal, transcendent Creator, cosmologists (and others) are resorting to more and more bizarre alternatives. There is a certain logic to it all, however. If for personal reasons the God of the Bible is unacceptable, then given the evidence for transcendence and design, the alternatives are limited to flights of fancy.

Often in such cases the stated basis for rejection of the God of the Bible is a lack of *absolute* proof of his existence. But we humans are limited to the space-time dimensions of the universe, and we lack the means to explore everything within those space-time dimensions. Therefore we are incapable of absolute proof for anything. Nevertheless, that does not mean we cannot draw secure conclusions. For example, we lack absolute proof that the earth is spherical rather than flat. Nevertheless, we accept the sphericity of the earth because the evidences for it have accumulated to such an abundance as to remove reasonable doubt. And as time and research progress, those evidences only increase. A similar state of affairs has developed and is continuing to develop for the existence of the God of the Bible.

*   *   *

So far we have been examining the astronomical evidences for the existence of a transcendent Creator. The transcendence of the Creator is an important component in the Christian conception of God. But equally significant components are his personality and his care for humanity.

Now that many of the limits and characteristics of the universe have come within the measuring capacity of astronomers and physicists, the indications of design in the universe are being examined and acknowledged. Astronomers have discovered that the characteristics of the universe, of our galaxy and of our solar system are so finely tuned to support life that the only reasonable explanation for this is the forethought of a personal, intelligent Creator whose involvement explains the degree of fine-tunedness. It requires power and purpose.

Design Parameters

Scientists have identified over two dozen parameters of the universe that must be carefully fixed in value for any kind of conceivable life (not just life as we know it) to exist at any time in the history of the universe. Some examples of these are given in table 4.4.

Table 4.4. Evidence for the fine-tuning of the universe.[64]

---

1. Strong nuclear force constant
   if larger: no hydrogen; nuclei essential for life would be unstable
   if smaller: no elements other than hydrogen

---

2. Weak nuclear force constant
   if larger: too much hydrogen converted to helium in big bang, hence too much heavy element material made by star burning; no expulsion of heavy elements from stars
   if smaller: too little helium produced from big bang, hence too little heavy element material made by star burning; no expulsion of heavy elements from stars

---

3. Gravitational force constant
   if larger: stars would be too hot and would burn up quickly and unevenly

if smaller: stars would remain so cool that nuclear fusion would never ignite, hence no heavy element production

4. Electromagnetic force constant
   if larger: insufficient chemical bonding; elements more massive than boron would be too unstable to fission
   if smaller: insufficient chemical bonding

5. Ratio of electromagnetic force constant to gravitational force constant
   if larger: no stars less than 1.4 solar masses, hence short and uneven stellar burning
   if smaller: no stars more than 0.8 solar masses, hence no heavy element production

6. Ratio of electron to proton mass
   if larger: insufficient chemical bonding
   if smaller: insufficient chemical bonding

7. Ratio of number of protons to number of electrons
   if larger: electromagnetism would have dominated gravity, preventing galaxy, star and planet formation
   if smaller: electromagnetism would have dominated gravity, preventing galaxy, star and planet formation

8. Expansion rate of the universe
   if larger: no galaxy formation
   if smaller: universe would have collapsed prior to star formation

9. Entropy level of the universe
   if larger: no star condensation within the protogalaxies
   if smaller: no protogalaxy formation

10. Mass density of the universe
    if larger: too much deuterium from big bang, hence stars burn too rapidly
    if smaller: insufficient helium from big bang, hence too few heavy elements forming

11. Velocity of light
    if larger: stars would be too luminous
    if smaller: stars would not be luminous enough

12. Age of the universe
    if older: no solar-type stars in a stable burning phase in the right part of the galaxy

if younger: solar-type stars in a stable burning phase would not yet have formed

13. Initial uniformity of radiation
    if smoother: stars, star clusters and galaxies would not have formed
    if coarser: universe by now would be mostly black holes and empty space

14. Fine structure constant (a number used to describe the fine structure splitting of spectral lines)
    if larger: no stars more than 0.7 solar masses
    if smaller: no stars less than 1.8 solar masses

15. Average distance between stars
    if larger: heavy element density too thin for rocky planets to form
    if smaller: planetary orbits would become destabilized

16. Decay rate of the proton
    if greater: life would be exterminated by the release of radiation
    if smaller: insufficient matter in the universe for life

17. ^{12}C to ^{16}O nuclear energy level ratio
    if larger: insufficient oxygen
    if smaller: insufficient carbon

18. Ground state energy level for ^{4}He
    if larger: insufficient carbon and oxygen
    if smaller: insufficient carbon and oxygen

19. Decay rate of ^{8}Be
    if slower: heavy element fusion would generate catastrophic explosions in all the stars
    if faster: no element production beyond beryllium and hence no life chemistry possible

20. Mass excess of the neutron over the proton
    if greater: neutron decay would leave too few neutrons to form the heavy elements essential for life
    if smaller: proton decay would cause all stars to rapidly collapse into neutron stars or black holes

21. Initial excess of nucleons over antinucleons
    if greater: too much radiation for planets to form

if smaller: not enough matter for galaxies or stars to form

22. Polarity of the water molecule
    if greater: heat of fusion and vaporization would be too great for life to exist
    if smaller: heat of fusion and vaporization would be too small for life's existence; liquid water would become too inferior a solvent for life chemistry to proceed; ice would not float, leading to a runaway freeze-up

23. Supernova eruptions
    if too close: radiation would exterminate life on the planet
    if too far: not enough heavy element ashes for the formation of rocky planets
    if too infrequent: not enough heavy element ashes for the formation of rocky planets
    if too frequent: life on the planet would be exterminated
    if too soon: not enough heavy element ashes for the formation of rocky planets
    if too late: life on the planet would be exterminated by radiation

24. White dwarf binaries
    if too few: insufficient fluorine produced for life chemistry to proceed
    if too many: disruption of planetary orbits from stellar density; life on the planet would be exterminated
    if too soon: not enough heavy elements made for efficient fluorine production
    if too late: fluorine made too late for incorporation in protoplanet

25. Ratio of the mass of exotic matter to ordinary matter
    if smaller: galaxies would not have formed
    if larger: universe would have collapsed before solar-type stars could form

The degree of fine-tunedness for many of these parameters is utterly amazing. For example, if the strong nuclear force were even 0.3 percent stronger or 2 percent weaker, the universe would never be able to support life.[65] More astounding yet, the ground state energies for ^{4}He, ^{8}Be, ^{12}C and ^{16}O cannot be higher or lower with respect to each other by more than 4 percent without yielding a universe with insufficient oxygen and/or carbon for any kind of life.[66] The expansion rate of the universe is even more sensitive.[67] It must be fine-tuned to an accuracy of one part in 10^{55}. Clearly some ingenious Designer must be involved in the physics of the universe.

The discovery of this degree of design in the universe is having a profound theological impact on astronomers. Fred Hoyle concluded in 1982 that "a superintellect has monkeyed with physics, as well as with chemistry and biology."[68] Paul Davies moved from promoting atheism in 1983[69] to conceding in 1984 that "the laws [of physics] . . . seem themselves to be the product of exceedingly ingenious design"[70] to testifying in his 1988 book *The Cosmic Blueprint* that there "is for me powerful evidence that there is something going on behind it all. The impression of design is overwhelming."[71] In 1988 George Greenstein expressed these thoughts: "As we survey all the evidence, the thought insistently arises that some supernatural agency—or, rather, Agency—must be involved. Is it possible that suddenly, without intending to, we have stumbled upon scientific proof of the existence of a Supreme Being? Was it God who stepped in and so providentially crafted the cosmos for our benefit?"[72]

Words and phrases such as *superintellect, monkeyed, exceedingly ingenious, supernatural Agency, Supreme Being* and *providentially crafted* obviously can refer only to a person. But more than just establishing that the Creator is a person, the findings about design provide evidence of what that Person is like. One characteristic that stands out dramatically is his interest and care for living things and particularly for the human race.

For example, the mass density of the universe determines how efficiently nuclear fusion operates in the cosmos. As table 4.4 indicates, if the mass density were too great, too much deuterium (a heavy isotope of hydrogen with one proton and one neutron in the nucleus) would be made in the first few minutes of the universe's existence. This extra deuterium will cause all the stars to burn much too quickly and erratically for any of them to support a planet with life upon it. On the other hand, if the mass density were too small, so little deuterium and helium would be made in the first few minutes that the heavier elements necessary for life would never form in the stars. What this means is that the approximately 100 billion trillion stars we observe in the universe, no more and no fewer, are needed for life to be possible in the universe. Evidently God cared so much for living creatures that he constructed 100 billion trillion stars and carefully crafted them throughout the age of the universe so that at this brief moment in the history of the cosmos humans could exist and have a pleasant place to live. Of all the gods of the various religions of the world, only the God of the Bible is revealed as investing this much (and more) in humanity.

It is not just the universe that bears evidence for design. The sun and the earth also reveal such evidence. Frank Drake, Carl Sagan and Iosef Shklovskii were among the first astronomers to make this point. They attempted to estimate the number of planets (in the universe) with environments favorable for life support. In the early 1960s they recognized that only a certain kind of star with a planet just the right distance from that star would provide the necessary conditions for life.[73] On this basis they made optimistic estimates for the probability of finding life elsewhere in the universe. Shklovskii and Sagan, for example, claimed that 0.001 percent of all stars could have a planet capable of supporting advanced life.[74]

While their analysis was a step in the right direction, it overestimated the range of permissible star types and the range of permissible planetary distances. It also ignored *many* other significant factors. Some sample parameters sensitive for the support of life are listed in table 4.5.

Table 4.5: Evidence for the fine-tuning of the galaxy-sun-earth-moon system for life support.[75]

The following parameters of a planet, its moon, its star and its galaxy must have values falling within narrowly defined ranges for life of any kind to exist. Characteristics 2 and 3 have been repeated from table 4.4 since they apply to both the universe and the galaxy.

---

1. Galaxy type
    if too elliptical: star formation would cease before sufficient heavy element buildup for life chemistry
    if too irregular: radiation exposure on occasion would be too severe, and heavy elements for life chemistry would not be available

---

2. Supernova eruptions
    if too close: life on the planet would be exterminated by radiation
    if too far: not enough heavy element ashes would exist for the formation of rocky planets
    if too infrequent: not enough heavy element ashes present for the formation of rocky planets
    if too frequent: life on the planet would be exterminated
    if too soon: not enough heavy element ashes would exist for the formation of rocky planets
    if too late: life on the planet would be exterminated by radiation

---

3. White dwarf binaries
    if too few: insufficient fluorine would be produced for life chemistry to proceed
    if too many: planetary orbits would be disrupted by stellar density; life on planet would be exterminated

if too soon: not enough heavy elements would be made for efficient fluorine production

if too late: fluorine would be made too late for incorporation in protoplanet

---

4. Parent star distance from center of galaxy
   if farther: quantity of heavy elements would be insufficient to make rocky planets
   if closer: galactic radiation would be too great; stellar density would disturb planetary orbits out of life-support zones

---

5. Number of stars in the planetary system
   if more than one: tidal interactions would disrupt planetary orbits
   if less than one: heat produced would be insufficient for life

---

6. Parent star birth date
   if more recent: star would not yet have reached stable burning phase; stellar system would contain too many heavy elements
   if less recent: stellar system would not contain enough heavy elements

---

7. Parent star age
   if older: luminosity of star would change too quickly
   if younger: luminosity of star would change too quickly

---

8. Parent star mass
   if greater: luminosity of star would change too quickly; star would burn too rapidly
   if less: range of distances appropriate for life would be too narrow; tidal forces would disrupt the rotational period for a planet of the right distance; ultraviolet radiation would be inadequate for plants to make sugars and oxygen

---

9. Parent star color
   if redder: photosynthetic response would be insufficient
   if bluer: photosynthetic response would be insufficient

---

10. Parent star luminosity relative to speciation
    if increases too soon: runaway greenhouse effect would develop
    if increases too late: runaway glaciation would develop

---

11. Surface gravity (escape velocity)
    if stronger: planet's atmosphere would retain too much ammonia and methane
    if weaker: planet's atmosphere would lose too much water

---

12. Distance from parent star

if farther: planet would be too cool for a stable water cycle
if closer: planet would be too warm for a stable water cycle

13. Inclination of orbit
    if too great: temperature differences on the planet would be too extreme

14. Orbital eccentricity
    if too great: seasonal temperature differences would be too extreme

15. Axial tilt
    if greater: surface temperature differences would be too great
    if less: surface temperature differences would be too great

16. Rotation period
    if longer: diurnal temperature differences would be too great
    if shorter: atmospheric wind velocities would be too great

17. Age
    if too young: planet would rotate too rapidly
    if too old: planet would rotate too slowly

18. Magnetic field
    if stronger: electromagnetic storms would be too severe
    if weaker: ozone shield would be inadequately protected from hard stellar and solar radiation

19. Thickness of crust
    if thicker: too much oxygen would be transferred from the atmosphere to the crust
    if thinner: volcanic and tectonic activity would be too great

20. Albedo (ratio of reflected light to total amount falling on surface)
    if greater: runaway glaciation would develop
    if less: runaway greenhouse effect would develop

21. Asteroidal and cometary collision rate
    if greater: too many species would become extinct
    if less: crust would be too depleted of materials essential for life

22. Oxygen to nitrogen ratio in atmosphere
    if larger: advanced life functions would proceed too quickly
    if smaller: advanced life functions would proceed too slowly

23. Carbon dioxide level in atmosphere
   if greater: runaway greenhouse effect would develop
   if less: plants would be unable to maintain efficient photosynthesis

24. Water vapor level in atmosphere
   if greater: runaway greenhouse effect would develop
   if less: rainfall would be too meager for advanced life on the land

25. Atmospheric electric discharge rate
   if greater: too much fire destruction would occur
   if less: too little nitrogen would be fixed in the atmosphere

26. Ozone level in atmosphere
   if greater: surface temperatures would be too low
   if less: surface temperatures would be too high; there would be too much UV radiation at the surface

27. Oxygen quantity in atmosphere
   if greater: plants and hydrocarbons would burn up too easily
   if less: advanced animals would have too little to breathe

28. Seismic activity
   if greater: too many life-forms would be destroyed
   if less: nutrients on ocean floors (from river runoff) would not be recycled to the continents through tectonic uplift

29. Oceans-to-continents ratio
   if greater: diversity and complexity of life-forms would be limited
   if smaller: diversity and complexity of life-forms would be limited

30. Global distribution of continents (for earth)
   if too much in the southern hemisphere: seasonal temperature differences would be too severe for advanced life

31. Soil mineralization
   if too nutrient-poor: diversity and complexity of life-forms would be limited
   if too nutrient-rich: diversity and complexity of life-forms would be limited

32. Gravitational interaction with a moon
   if greater: tidal effects on the oceans, atmosphere and rotational period would be too severe

if less: orbital obliquity changes would cause climatic instabilities; movement of nutrients and life from the oceans to the continents and continents to the oceans would be insufficient; magnetic field would be too weak

Chances for Finding a Life-Support Planet

Each of the thirty-two parameters listed in table 4.5 cannot exceed certain limits without disturbing a planet's capacity to support life. For some, including many of the stellar parameters, the limits have been measured quite precisely. For others, including many of the planetary parameters, the limits are less precisely known. Trillions of stars are available for study, and star formation is quite well understood and observed. On the other hand, only nine planets can be studied, and though a fairly good theory of planetary formation is available, the details have yet to be worked out. Another problem is that planetary formation cannot be fully observed.

Let's look at how confining these limits can be. Among the least confining would be the inclination of a planet's orbit and the distribution of its continents. The limits for these are loose, eliminating only 20 percent of all candidates. More confining would be parameters such as the planet's rotation period and its albedo (see no. 20 in table 4.5), which eliminate about 90 percent of all candidates from contention. Most confining of all would be parameters such as the parent's star mass and the planet's distance from its parent star, which eliminate 99.9 percent of all candidates.

Of course, not all the listed parameters are strictly independent of the others. Dependency factors could reduce the degree of confinement. On the other hand, all these parameters must be kept within specific limits for the total time span needed to support life on a candidate planet. This increases the degree of confinement.

About a dozen more parameters, such as the atmospheric transparency, atmospheric pressure, atmospheric temperature gradient, other greenhouse gases, location of different gases and minerals, and mantle and core constituents and structures, currently are being researched for their sensitivity in the support of life. However, the thirty-two listed in table 4.5 in themselves lead safely to the conclusion that much fewer than a trillionth of a trillionth of a percent of all stars will have a planet capable of sustaining advanced life. Considering that the observable universe contains less than a trillion galaxies, each averaging a hundred billion stars, we can see that not even one planet (see sidebar "How Many Planets?") would be expected, by natural processes alone, to possess the necessary conditions to sustain life. No wonder Robert Rood and James Trefil,[76] among others,[77] have surmised that intelligent physical life exists only on the earth.

How Many Planets?

Only nine planets have been detected in the universe. Perturbations (small disturbances) in the positions of several stars reveal the presence of other planet-sized bodies. Dusty disks have been observed to surround many young stellar objects. Such objects, unlike older stars, can draw on newly available heavy elements. Additional research indicates that only slowly rotating bachelor stars similar to the sun have the possibility of stable planets.

The conclusion? The universe probably contains no more than one planet for every thousand stars. An extreme upper limit would be an average of one planet per star.

It seems abundantly clear that the earth, like the broader universe, has experienced divine design. Evidently personal intervention on the part of the Creator has occurred not just at the origin of the universe but also at much more recent times.

A Senseless Rebuttal

In spite of all this evidence for design, some nontheists claim that our existence is simply testimony to the fact that the extremely unlikely did indeed take place by chance. In other words, we would not be here to report the event unless that highly unlikely event actually took place.

This argument is fundamentally an appeal to infinite chances, which has already been answered in our section on quantum mechanics. Another response has been developed by philosophers Richard Swinburne[78] and William Lane Craig. Craig puts it this way: "Suppose a hundred sharpshooters are sent to execute a prisoner by firing squad and the prisoner survives. The prisoner should not be surprised that he does not observe that he is dead. After all, if he were dead, he could not observe his death. Nonetheless, he should be surprised that he observes that he is alive."[79] To extend Swinburne and Craig's argument, the prisoner could conclude, since he is alive, that all the sharpshooters missed by some extremely unlikely chance. He may wish to attribute his survival to an incredible bit of good luck, but he would be far more rational to conclude that the guns were loaded with blanks or that the sharpshooters all deliberately missed. That is, someone must have purposed that he should live. Likewise, the rational conclusion to draw from the incredible fine-tunedness of the universe and the solar system is that someone purposed that we should live.

Another consideration is the total lack of analogy in the world of observed natural processes. We do not see spontaneous generation of anything highly complex and fine-tuned.

If the God of the Bible may be seen—and seen as essential—in the existence and operation of galaxies and stars and our solar system, the simple systems in the cosmos, how much more clearly should we see him in systems that are orders of magnitude more complex, information-loaded and living? Nothing produced by the ingenuity and technology of humankind can compare with the complexity and efficiency of even the simplest of organisms. Organisms, in fact, are so complex that with all our study of them, we as yet know relatively little of how to build and operate them.

Through time, as we unlock more and more of the secrets of the vast cosmos and of the inner workings of organisms, we will continue to be awed. But where will that awe be aimed, at the created thing or at the Creator? That is each individual's choice.

Conclusion

The more astronomers learn about the origin and development of the universe, the more evidence they accumulate for the existence of God, and for the God of the Bible in particular. Ironically, those who fought hardest against God as the explanation for the cosmos often were the ones whose work provided the most powerful new evidences for him. Today, with the measuring of the creation has come the scientific equipment to make a positive identification of the Creator. Though not many who write about these new measurements acknowledge Jesus Christ as Lord and Savior, they typically confess that the best, perhaps the only, explanation for the universe we observe is the action of an entity beyond the space-time continuum of the universe who/that is capable of design and of carrying out that design. Whether they know it or not, in their confession they have testified of none other than the God who is there, the God of the Bible.

However, this matter of scientific evidence for God need not be confined to factors in astronomy, powerful as they are. The existence of life, along with the precise nature of living systems, provides further evidence for God's existence. To these issues we now turn.

Bibliography

Barrow, John D., and Joseph Silk. *The Left Hand of Creation.* New York: BasicBooks, 1983. [I]

Barrow, John D., and Frank J. Tipler. *The Anthropic Cosmological Principle.* New York: Oxford University Press, 1986. [A]

Block, David. *Starwatching.* Oxford, U.K.: Lion, 1988. [B]

Corey, Michael A. *God and the New Cosmology: The Anthropic Design Argument.* Lanham, Md.: Rowman & Littlefield, 1993. [I]

Craig, William Lane. *The Existence of God and the Beginning of the Universe.* San Bernardino, Calif.: Here's Life, 1979. [I]

Craig, William Lane, and Quentin Smith. *Theism, Atheism and Big Bang Cosmology.* Oxford, U.K.: Clarendon, 1993. [A]

Davies, Paul. *The Cosmic Blueprint: New Discoveries in Nature's Ability to Order the Universe.* New York: Simon and Schuster, 1988. [I]

Greenstein, George. *The Symbiotic Universe: Life and Mind in the Cosmos.* New York: Morrow, 1988. [I]

Jaki, Stanley L. *God and the Cosmologists.* Washington, D.C.: Regnery Gateway, 1989. [I]

Jastrow, Robert. *God and the Astronomers.* New York: Norton, 1978. [B]

Leslie, John, ed. *Physical Cosmology and Philosophy.* New York: Macmillan, 1990. [A]

Ross, Hugh. *The Creator and the Cosmos.* Colorado Springs, Colo.: NavPress, 1993. [B]

———. *The Fingerprint of God: Recent Scientific Discoveries Reveal the Unmistakable Identity of the Creator.* 2nd ed. Orange, Calif.: Promise, 1991. [I]

Trefil, James S. *The Moment of Creation.* New York: Charles Scribner's Sons, 1983. [I]

Yockey, Hubert P. *Information Theory and Molecular Biology.* New York: Cambridge University Press, 1992. [A]

5
INFORMATION
& THE ORIGIN
OF LIFE

Walter L. Bradley & Charles B. Thaxton

I n 1950 Nobel laureate Harold Urey at the University of Chicago gave a course on the origin of the solar system. Taking the course was a twenty-two-year-old graduate student named Stanley Miller. During the course, Urey mentioned that it would be interesting to see what would happen if someone experimentally mimicked the early earth's atmosphere and passed energy through it (alluding to Oparin's hypothesis in 1924 that the development of living systems began with such a scenario[1]). Miller was fascinated by the idea and subsequently became famous for performing a single, simple experiment which at the time seemed to solve what is arguably the greatest mystery ever puzzled over by scientists. Introducing ammonia, methane and hydrogen into a sealed glass apparatus containing boiling water and simulating lightning with a spark-discharge device, he noted within a few days that both the water and the glass were stained with a reddish goo. With subsequent chemical analysis, Miller found to his delight that the goo contained amino acids—the building blocks of protein, the basic stuff of life. The results, which Miller published as a modest two-page article in *Science*,[2] seemed to provide stunning evidence that life could arise out of simple chemical reactions in a "primordial soup."

The response to Miller's experiment within both the scientific community and the general public was extraordinary. For example, Carl Sagan, an astronomer and leader in the search for extraterrestrial life, called Miller's experiment "the single most significant step in convincing many scientists that life is likely to be abundant in the cosmos."[3] Chemist William Day described it as "an experiment that broke the logjam" to show that the first step in the origin of life was not a chance event, but one that had been inevitable.[4] Astronomer Harlow Shapley told a television audience in Chicago in 1959, on the eve of the Darwin Centennial Celebration, that the Miller experiment "assures us of what we had suspected for a long time: that one can bridge the gap between the inanimate and the animate and that the appearance of life is essentially an automatic biochemical development that comes along naturally when physical conditions are right."[5] In fact, it may be said that Miller's experiments spawned a neovitalism, or belief in the power of self-organization inherent in matter.[6] Biochemical predestination even became a subject for textbooks,[7] and evolutionary sequences of the type shown in figure 5.1 were generally taken for granted.

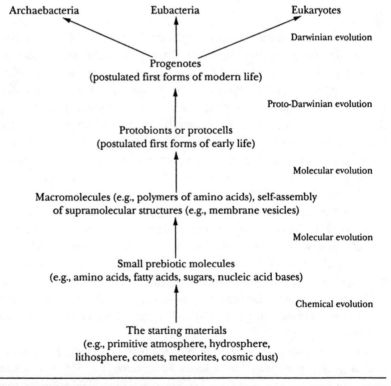

Figure 5.1. Hypothetical scheme of evolutionary steps from the constituents of the primitive atmosphere (as starting materials) to modern (contemporary) cells.

Retrospective Analysis of Origin of Life

Unfortunately, such speculation by pundits has proven to be quite premature. Forty years later, Miller, who had become a professor of chemistry at the University of California at San Diego, was quoted in *Scientific American* as saying, "The problem of the origin of life has turned out to be much more difficult than I, and most other people, envisioned."[8]

This is not to say that there has been no progress since 1953. In the forty years following Miller's original experiments, similar and derivative experiments have been alleged to demonstrate how many of the basic building blocks of DNA (deoxyribonucleic acid) and RNA (ribonucleic acid) as well as those of protein could have been synthesized under prebiotic conditions. These organic compounds might subsequently accumulate in various bodies of water, in some "warm little pond," as Charles Darwin once speculated in a letter. S. W. Fox and K. Dose[9] and others in the 1960s and 1970s showed how such building blocks might be polymerized into biopolymeric precursors to the modern macromolecules of life such as protein and DNA. Experiments in the early 1980s seemed to complete the picture, revealing that RNA might have the ability to make copies of itself without the assistance of enzymes. This important discovery, for which T. R. Cech, a professor at the University of Colorado, received the Nobel Prize, suggested the possibility of first life that consisted of RNA and an early "RNA world" that might provide a bridge from simple chemical building blocks such as amino acids and sugars to the highly complex DNA-based cells found in modern organisms.[10]

While Miller's experiments demonstrating prebiotic formation of building blocks and the "RNA world" as a bridge from simple building blocks to DNA-based cells have been enshrined in textbooks, the veracity of both were seriously challenged by new research findings in the 1980s. RNA has been found to be exceedingly difficult to synthesize under the conditions that likely prevailed when life originated.[11] Furthermore, it has been established that RNA cannot easily generate copies of itself as was first thought.[12] To make matters worse, even Miller's seminal experiments have been found suspect due to atmospheric physicists' newly emerging consensus that the early earth's atmosphere never contained significant amounts of ammonia, methane or hydrogen.[13] Moreover, studies of craters on the moon indicate that the early earth was laid waste repeatedly by huge meteorites and comets. Christopher P. McKay of NASA Ames Research Center was quoted in *Scientific American* as saying, "It looks like life began not in a warm little pond but in a raging tempest."[14]

What then is the nature of the progress of the past forty years? Klaus Dose of the Institute for Biochemistry in Mainz, Germany, suggests that our collective efforts have "led to a better perception of the immensity of the problem of the origin of life on Earth rather than to its solution. At present all discussions on principal theories and experiments in the field either end in stalemate or in a confession of ignorance."[15]

Overview of This Chapter

We have a threefold purpose in this chapter: (1) to review the current scenario of the origin of life based on the Oparin hypothesis of a "prebiotic soup" for the reader who is unfamiliar with this subject, (2) to critique this scenario in light of both actual experimental problems and perceived theoretical problems and (3) to consider alternative hypotheses, including intelligent design, which have surfaced in response to the many seemingly intractable problems of soup theory. We will begin by suggesting what we believe are minimal functional requirements for living systems. Then we will illustrate the relationship between biological function and three-dimensional molecular structure. Subsequently we will show that the three-dimensional molecular structure that controls function in biopolymers depends on the very specific arrangement of various molecular "building blocks" in these biopolymers. This will provide the reader with a conceptual picture of the enigma of the origin of life, which is specified complexity or biological information.

We will then introduce the Oparin hypothesis for the origin of life, which has been the guiding paradigm for most origin-of-life research. We will look at the necessary steps suggested by this paradigm, sometimes called "prebiotic soup theory," as summarized in figure 5.1. Each arrow represents an important step: (1) the formation of the building blocks from an early-earth atmosphere, (2) the combination of these building blocks into various biopolymers and (3) the assembly of these various biopolymers into the first cells, usually called protobionts, protocells or coacervates. We will ignore in this chapter the subsequent development into progenotes (first forms of modern life) and their diversification into archaebacteria, eubacteria and eukaryotes, which are the supposed antecedents of the rest of the plant and animal kingdom.

Finally, we will consider possible alternatives to Oparin's "prebiotic soup" hypothesis, including intelligent design. It is worth noting here that affirming natural causes as the probable source for the origin of life, as most origin-of-life scientists do, does not necessarily mean naturalism. For how does one know from experience that some higher power or intellect (God?) does not stand behind the scenes, guiding the "natural" processes? Indeed, this is precisely what large segments of Christian theists believe. This means we may not infer from experience the metaphysical conclusion of naturalism. According to Ian Barbour, "Naturalism is still a live option, but it is clear that it must be defended as a philosophical viewpoint and not a conclusion of science."[16] Likewise, when one infers by experience an intelligent cause to account for the structure of life, it does not carry the necessary conclusion of supernaturalism. We cannot determine by experience whether the inferred intelligent cause is within the universe (naturalism) or beyond it (supernaturalism). This is a further judgment *not* based on experience.

The Problem of Life's Origin

It is generally agreed that living systems are distinguished from nonliving systems not so much by their unique chemical composition (which in fact consists mainly of very common elements such as carbon, nitrogen, oxygen and hydrogen) as by their complex arrangements leading to unique biological functions. Living systems distinguish themselves from nonliving ones by processing energy, storing information and replicating.[17] Although it is widely agreed that the first living system must have been much simpler than the simplest modern living system, which is bacteria, a certain base level of complexity is necessary to provide these three functions. Also, simple analogies between biological evolution based on natural selection and chemical evolution should be rejected because natural selection in biological evolution presupposes systems that replicate. The problem of the origin of life is to develop just such systems. Bertalanffy cogently makes this point: "Selection, i.e., favored survival of 'better' precursors of life, already presupposes self-maintaining, complex, open systems which may compete; therefore selection cannot account for the origin of such systems."[18]

One may easily illustrate the relationship between biological activity and molecular structure by considering a protein molecule that acts as a catalyst, as seen in figure 5.2. In an aqueous solution, the ATP molecule and glucose (sugar) chemically react at a very slow rate: it is unlikely that the two molecules can be maintained in an optimal position long enough for the chemical reaction to occur. However, in the presence of a protein molecule that functions as a catalyst, the ATP and the glucose are attached to the catalyst in a way that optimizes their position relative to each other; this facilitates a very rapid chemical reaction. The result is a ten-millionfold increase in the chemical reaction rate.

The regulation of chemical reactions by such catalysts is ubiquitous in living systems. Figure 5.2 makes it clear that the three-dimensional topography and the local surface chemistry of the catalyst must be quite exact if meaningful acceleration of the reaction between ATP and glucose is to come about.

AN ENZYME AT WORK

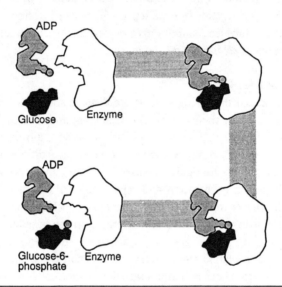

Figure 5.2. Schematic representation of the relationship between topography and function as a catalyst.

Three-dimensional topography is now known to be integrally related to both the sequence of building blocks in the polymer chain (which is the protein) and the nature of the attachments between building blocks via chemical bonding.[19] Figure 5.3 is an example of a protein molecule. It consists of a sequence of L-amino acids, which come in twenty varieties, joined in a very specific way by peptide chemical bonds. Although the three-dimensional structure does not depend on having the correct amino acid at every site along the chain, approximately half of the sites are quite critical. At these so-called active sites, a wrong amino acid can have fatal consequences, as it does in sickle cell anemia, which has only one incorrect active site along the chain of amino acid "links" that make up the hemoglobin molecule.

Furthermore, only certain kinds of bonds allow for the three-dimensional folding that must follow initial polymerization. In particular, all amino acids must be joined by a peptide bond (shown schematically in figure 5.4), an event that occurs only about 50 percent of the time in prebiotic simulation experiments.

Finally, while amino acids come in left- and right-handed versions, as shown in figure 5.5, biologically functional proteins have all L-amino acids. Since L- and D-amino acids are equally abundant in nature and chemically react without distinction, this represents yet another challenge to the formation of enzymatically functional proteins. As with the peptide bonds, polymerizing only L-amino acids into the chain molecule seems to be an essential condition to allow proper folding into three-dimensional topographies to give catalytic activity.

Similar yet more challenging problems surround the formation of biologically functional DNA or RNA molecules. The key concept is that biological function is integrally connected to highly specific arrangements of the molecular building blocks in the biopolymers. It has been demonstrated that this molecular complexity can be quantified using information theory.[20] Thus the

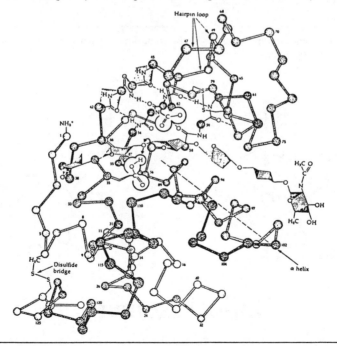

Figure 5.3. Schematic representation of the three-dimensional topography of a chain of amino acids.

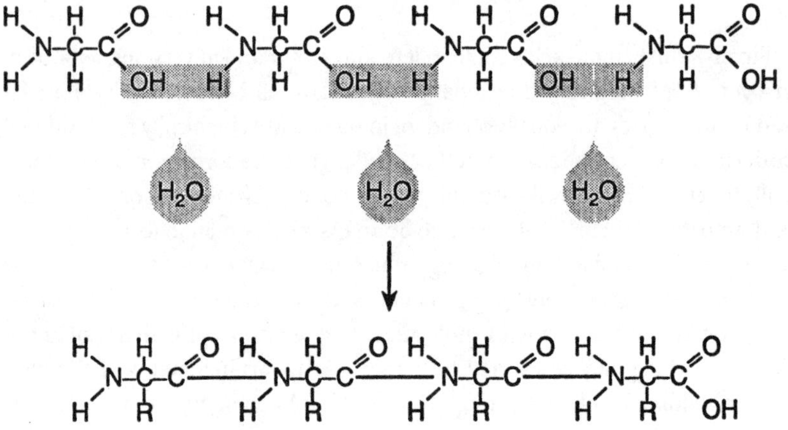

Figure 5.4. Schematic representation of the formation of peptide bonds with water formation as a byproduct.

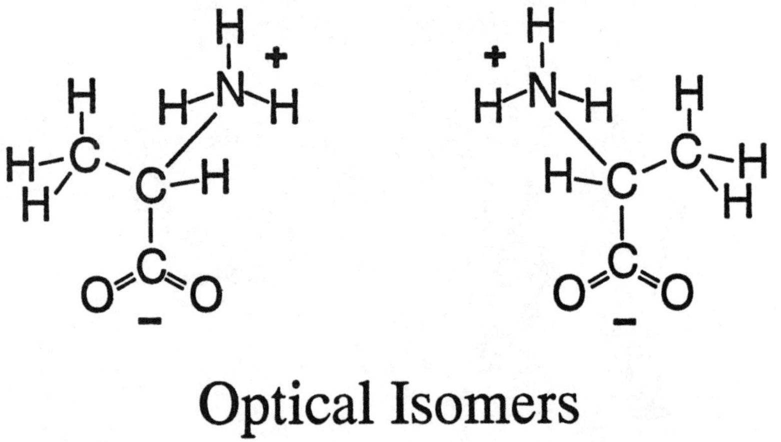

Optical Isomers

Figure 5.5. Schematic representation of L- and D-isomers of an amino acid.

enigma of the origin of life can ultimately be reduced to the question whether information-intensive molecules can be produced from simple building blocks with only the flow of energy through the system and, possibly, the intervention of molecular selection of some sort.

To summarize this section, biological function requires very specific three-dimensional structures that can be realized only with highly specific molecular architecture, which requires information-intensive molecules. The origin of such information-intensive molecules is one of the key challenges in understanding the origin of life.

Oparin's Hypothesis

Louis Pasteur's classic public experiment at the Sorbonne in Paris in 1864 buried the doctrine of spontaneous generation. Pasteur boldly proclaimed, "Never will the doctrine of spontaneous generation recover from the mortal blow of this simple experiment," and confidently added later in the same publication, "No, today there is no circumstance known which one could affirm that microscopical beings have come into the world without germs, without parents resembling themselves."[21] Even then, however, there were reasons to believe that in a general sense his prediction would not stand. Darwin's theory of evolution—published five years earlier, in 1859—was quickly gaining acceptance among academics. If the first cell evolved by natural processes through various kinds of creatures up to humankind, then it was reasonable to assume that there must have been a natural preamble to that evolution. Darwin himself, in an 1871 letter, speculated that in a "warm little pond of chemicals" sunlight might have brought about the reactions necessary to produce the first living thing.[22]

Yet a half-century passed before a detailed hypothesis for life's origin was put forth. In a historic 1924 paper, Russian biochemist A. I. Oparin postulated that the early earth's atmosphere must have been quite different from what we observe today.[23] In particular, he proposed that it consisted of ammonia, methane and hydrogen with some water vapor and no oxygen. He further suggested that under the influence of lightning and ultraviolet light, such an atmosphere would chemically react to form the various organic molecules— including amino acids, bases, sugars and lipids—which are the necessary building blocks of biopolymers. He assumed that such a process would lead over time to a significant concentration of such molecular building blocks in the oceans or lakes, forming the proverbial prebiotic soup. When critical concentrations were reached, these building blocks would have chemically reacted to form polymers (which means many mers or molecular subunits). Over a long period of time, some polymers that formed in the prebiotic soup would likely have had biological activity, or so the story goes. According to Oparin, the agglomeration of polymers into cell-like systems called "coacervates" or "protocells" could eventually lead to cellular behavior.

Oparin's hypothesis circumvented the experimental "proof" against spontaneous genesis provided by Pasteur in 1864 by positing not spontaneous genesis but rather a gradual genesis of life that occurred over many millions of years, one small chemical step at a time. Obviously, such a possibility is in no way precluded by Pasteur's simple but brilliant experiment. The analogy to Darwinian evolution, which was widely accepted by 1924, gave additional credence to Oparin's hypothesis.

In summary, Oparin's hypothesis and similar ideas postulated at about the same time by the British chemist J. B. S. Haldane have provided the intellectual framework, indeed the guiding paradigm, that has shaped much of the origin-of-life research in the twentieth century.[24] Miller's experiments in the early 1950s, with which we began this chapter, were the first experimental efforts to test this paradigm of how life began. Let's look at these experiments in more detail.

The Making of the Molecular Building Blocks of Life

In 1952, Stanley L. Miller, taking up Harold Urey's challenge to test Oparin's hypothesis, put together some glassware and filled it with the early-earth atmosphere proposed by Oparin: ammonia, methane, hydrogen and water vapor. He subsequently sparked the mixture to simulate lightning for several days. Subsequent analysis of the trap used to remove and protect the reaction products revealed, to his and everyone's excitement, that the yield included a small percentage (~ 2 percent) of the molecular building blocks of biopolymer such as amino acids.

A spate of follow-up experiments simulating early-earth conditions have subsequently produced nineteen of the twenty biological amino acids (only lysine remains[25]), all five nucleic acid bases found in RNA and DNA, and various fatty acids found in cell membranes. Earlier claims that the sugars ribose and deoxyribose, critical building blocks of RNA and DNA, had also been synthesized under prebiotic conditions, have recently been found to be false. In a stunning presentation at the International Society for the Study of the Origin of Life (ISSOL) meeting in Berkeley in 1986, Robert Shapiro, a Harvard-educated DNA chemist from New York University, showed that the widespread but second- and thirdhand claims regarding synthesis of ribose and deoxyribose sugar in Miller-type experiments were traceable to one ambiguous paper. He subsequently demonstrated that making ribose sugar under prebiotic conditions was essentially impossible. His work was subsequently published in *Origins of Life and Evolution of the Biosphere*.[26] Similar observations have been offered by Dose, who includes ribose, deoxyribose and replicable oligo or polynucleotides in his list of hard-to-synthesize molecular building blocks.[27] Horgan also notes that RNA and its building blocks are difficult to synthesize in a laboratory under the best of conditions, much less under plausible prebiotic ones.[28]

Despite the fact that Miller's experiment is symbolically hailed as representing a genre of experiments designed to simulate conditions on a prebiotic earth and test the Oparin-Haldane hypothesis, there is a substantial and growing body of criticism that, in several significant respects, shows that these experiments fail to plausibly reproduce conditions on an early earth. First, Miller used methane, but the only energy source used was a spark to simulate lightning. Other energy sources would also have been present. In an early earth's atmosphere subjected to ultraviolet radiation, methane would have been converted to higher-molecular-weight hydrocarbons, forming an oil slick up to ten meters deep.[29]

Miller's response to this difficulty is telling: "If it is assumed that amino acids more complex than glycine were required for the origin of life, then these results indicate a need for methane in the atmosphere."[30] In other words, methane *must* have been present on the early earth, or amino acids would not have been produced (at least naturalistically).

Ammonia, another important ingredient in both Miller's experiment and subsequent imitations, is quickly destroyed under ultraviolet irradiation, which causes it to dissociate into hydrogen and nitrogen gas, with the hydrogen gas escaping into space. The ease with which water vapor is dissociated into hydrogen and oxygen so that the hydrogen escapes into space also raises questions about the assumed oxygen-free condition of the early earth's atmosphere. The strongest argument offered for an early-earth atmosphere void of oxygen comes not from geological arguments regarding the oxidation state of minerals but from the disastrous consequences oxygen has on prebiotic simulation experiments.[31] Again, we find arguments from preconceived conclusions rather than from experimental evidence.

Hydrogen, the third major component in Miller's prebiotic atmosphere along with methane and ammonia, cannot be expected to accumulate in any significant concentrations due to its weak gravitational attraction to the earth. In fact, a consensus has developed since the late 1970s that the early earth's atmosphere never contained significant amounts of ammonia, methane or hydrogen.[32] Rather, it most likely consisted of nitrogen, carbon dioxide and water vapor.

Unfortunately, an attempt to make the building blocks of life from such an atmosphere is like the ancient Egyptians' insistence that their Hebrew slaves make bricks without straw. The reason is simple. A simple mass and energy balance such as is done in freshman chemistry will indicate that making amino acids out of ammonia, methane and hydrogen is an exothermic reaction (energy released) with an enthalpy decrease of approximately 200Kcal/mole. By contrast, making amino acids out of nitrogen, carbon dioxide and water vapor is an endothermic reaction (energy must be added) with an enthalpy increase of +50Kcal/mole. Small wonder that chemists prefer Oparin's hypothetical, but incorrect, atmosphere of ammonia, methane and hydrogen.

Although Oparin had no geological basis for proposing his atmosphere, he had every good reason based on physical chemistry to know that an atmosphere rich in nitrogen, carbon dioxide and water vapor (recognized today as the most likely composition of the early earth's atmosphere) would simply not work. More recent experiments with such an atmosphere have confirmed this to be the case.[33]

Other problems exist with Miller-type experiments. A selective use of energy from a sole source is required to get satisfactory results, but such a condition does not at all mimic the early earth. For example, while short-wavelength ultraviolet light may help convert ammonia, methane and hydrogen into amino acids, the longer wavelengths of light that would have surely also been present in the early atmosphere quickly destroy these amino acids. Similarly, heat can destroy these molecules, as can continued electrical discharge. Only a use of selective energy and quick removal from the energy flux using a trap allows experimenters to produce even small amounts of amino acid reaction products (2 percent or less).

We conclude that the situation has in all respects deteriorated from the optimistic first blush brought on by the Miller experiments. Today there is a more somber recognition that the limited success Miller-type experiments have had in synthesizing amino acids, nucleic acid bases and fatty acids has invariably been achieved under conditions of both chemistry and selective energy sources which have little resemblance to the early earth. Furthermore, the synthesis of key building blocks for DNA and RNA such as ribose sugar have never been successfully done except under highly implausible conditions without any resemblance to those of an early earth.

As will be seen in the next section, the making of the molecular building blocks is actually the easier part of the overall scenario of the origin of life; nevertheless, it is not easy to imagine given our current understanding.

Making DNA, RNA and Protein, the Macromolecules of Life

In this section we will consider the challenging problem of assembling the building blocks into functional biopolymers. We will use thermodynamic analysis to assess the likelihood that functional protein or DNA might be made by combining molecular building blocks with energy flow through the system. We will first quantify the various kinds of work necessary in this assembly and then consider whether the kinds of energy flow available in the early earth might have been suitable to make the biopolymers of life. More comprehensive accounts of this analysis have been published elsewhere[34] and should be consulted by the reader who is interested in the details, especially numerical calculations.

We shall examine in detail the assembly of amino acids to form protein. Similar but more challenging problems are encountered in the production of both DNA and RNA. In terms of classical thermodynamics, polymerization will proceed spontaneously if the Gibbs free energy *(G)* associated with polymerization, or the joining of the building blocks, decreases *(ΔG* is smaller than 0). However, if the assembly of the building blocks results in an increase in the Gibbs free energy in the system *(ΔG* is greater than 0), then work is required to cause this chemical reaction to go forward.

It is analogous to the movement of water on a hill. Water can lower its Gibbs free energy by going downhill, but it increases its Gibbs free energy when it moves uphill. A pump or some source of energy is required to move the water uphill, whereas water will move downhill quite spontaneously on its own.

Getting building blocks to join. The proper assembly of the building blocks using peptide bonds is shown in figure 5.4. Note that two chemical bonds are broken (carbon-hydroxide and hydrogen-nitrogen) and two new ones established (hydrogen-hydroxide and carbon-nitrogen). The Gibbs free energy change $(\Delta G = \Delta H - T\Delta S)$ is physically associated with a change in the chemical bonding energy $(\Delta H = \Delta E + P\Delta V \approx E)$ and a change in the entropy of the system (ΔS). The entropy of the system is associated with the number of ways the mass and energy in the system can be arranged. A system that requires a highly specific arrangement has a higher Gibbs free energy than one that can be arranged in any way. If for the moment we neglect the very specific arrangement necessary for biological function and just consider the change in Gibbs free energy (ΔG) to get two amino acid "building blocks" to chemically react to form the dipeptide bond shown in figure 5.4 (i.e., to become chemically bonded to each other), a 3,000 calorie/mole increase in G is noted, or about 30 calories/gm of amino acids.[35] Thus energy flow through the system must be able to provide enough work to raise the system to the higher energy level associated with the polymerized building blocks. If a typical protein contained approximately one hundred amino acids, then the total work required would be three hundred kilocalories per mole of protein formed to get a "random" assembly of the amino acids.

Fox and Dose have summarized experiments in which this assembly work has been done successfully.[36] By heating dry amino acids and driving off the water that forms as a byproduct of the chemical reaction between two amino acids (see figure 5.4), one is able to successfully get amino acids to polymerize (chemically react to form a chain of the building blocks). Thus the work associated with *random* assembly of the building blocks can be successfully extracted from energy flow through the system if it is in the form of heat.

Getting the right arrangement of building blocks. The difficulty comes in getting these amino acids to join in the very specific ways required to provide functional protein, as described earlier in this chapter. There are at least four specific challenges in this regard.

First, amino acids exist in two forms that are mirror images of each other, as shown previously in figure 5.5, and called L- and D-amino acids. These form in equal numbers in prebiotic simulation experiments and react as rapidly with each other as with amino acids of the same symmetry. Yet all biological proteins found in nature contain only L-amino acids. The additional work required to include only L-amino acids in a chain of one hundred amino acids (a typical number for one protein molecule) is 4.2 cal/gram of protein formed.[37]

Second, the peptide bond (see figure 5.4) to chemically attach two amino acids represents only one of several possible ways that amino acids may be joined together. Analysis of the bonds formed when amino acids are joined in prebiotic simulation experiments indicate that no more than half of the bonds are peptide bonds.[38] Yet functional protein requires 100 percent peptide bonds to be able to fold into the particular three-dimensional structures that give biological function. Again, the additional work required to provide only peptide bonds where otherwise 50 percent nonpeptide bonds would form in the joining of one hundred amino acids can be calculated; it is 4.2 cal/gram of protein formed.[39]

A third challenge in assembling amino acids to give functional protein is the need to get a particular sequence of the various amino acids. Figure 5.6 schematically illustrates five of the twenty amino acids found in protein. The three-dimensional topography that determines biological function depends on the sequencing of these amino acids. While having a particular amino acid at each site along the chain is not required to get the right morphology or topography, at least half of the sites (called active sites) do require a very specific amino acid. The additional work required to get this degree of specificity can be calculated to be 18.2 cal/gm for one hundred active sites or 9.1 cal/gm for fifty active sites in a protein molecule consisting of one hundred amino acids.[40]

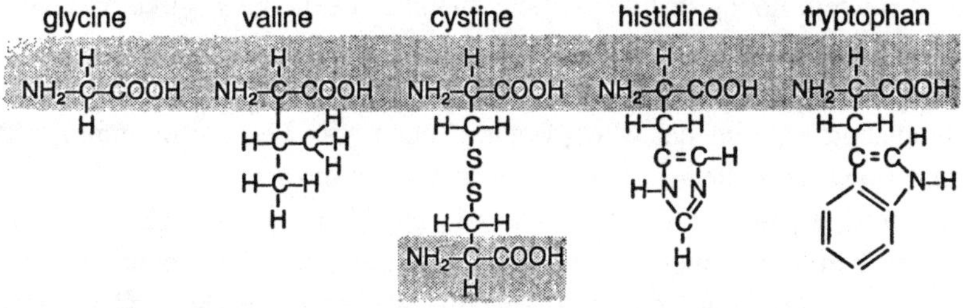

Figure 5.6. Schematic representation of five of the twenty amino acids that are found in living systems.

The fourth and possibly the most difficult problem in assembling amino acids into chains that fold into three-dimensional structures that give biological function is to react the amino acids only with each other and not with the many other chemical substances that would be present in a prebiotic soup. The fact that one has to do work (30 cal/gm) to chemically react amino acids with each other indicates that amino acids do not readily react chemically. However, amino acids *would* chemically react readily with many other substances that would be abundant in a prebiotic soup, with a resultant decrease in the Gibbs free energy. So it is difficult to imagine how amino acids could be either concentrated in solution or selectively adsorbed on surfaces such as clays before they were consumed in chemical reactions with other substances in the prebiotic soup. Since the chemical makeup of the prebiotic soup is not known, it is not possible to quantify the magnitude of work required to prevent such reactions and have only selective reactions between amino acids, but it would certainly be much larger than the three work terms already calculated.

We have calculated the work required to provide the necessary specified complexity in a protein of one hundred amino acids and found it to be similar in magnitude (18.2 + 4.2 + 4.2 cal/gm) to the required work to get random assembly of the building block (30 cal/gm), *if* we neglect the major problem of amino acids' tendency to react with other molecular species in the prebiotic soup. While energy flow is clearly able to do the required work to get assembly, it is doubtful that energy flow is ever coupled to, or capable of, the generation of information.

It is likely the case that biological information, while being mathematically identical to configurational entropy (as we have described elsewhere[41]), has no physical connection whatsoever. Jeffrey S. Wicken has also argued this position very convincingly.[42]

It is worth noting that all prebiotic simulation experiments that have been performed to try to form protein from amino acids have been conducted with pure amino acids rather than the reaction products of Miller-type prebiotic simulation experiments, which would contain only 1-2 percent amino acids and many other chemicals that can react with amino acids quite readily. Thus the necessary work in this area is actually provided by the chemist, as it were, which hardly simulates a true origin-of-life scenario. The chemist may also begin with only L-amino acids to avoid the problem of the chemical reaction's forming a chain of molecules containing both L- and D-amino acids. Even so, the chemist is unable to "fix" the experiment so that only peptide bonds (in L-amino acids) form and a biologically significant sequence of amino acids and functional topography occurs, as illustrated in figure 5.3. The net result is that even "contrived prebiotic" simulation experiments have produced chains of amino acids whose catalytic activity is trivial at best.

In summary, we conclude that energy flow through the system is capable of joining molecular building blocks but appears to be incapable of joining them in the very specific ways necessary to have biological function.

Protein Production Problems as Information Problems

How to get all of the building blocks (amino acids) properly arranged if biological function is to result can be thought of as an information problem. The amount of information required to create any system or subsystem component depends on the number of instructions required. A completely random arrangement of amino acids requires no specific instructions. The making of a crystal requires a few instructions to create a small cell with the symmetry features of the crystal and then the instruction to repeat the previous instructions until a large crystal is formed. The creation of a newspaper involves much more information, since the letters on the page have to be properly sequenced to produce coherent words, sentences, paragraphs and articles. The production of biologically functioning proteins is analogous to the production of a newspaper. Let us illustrate.

Consider the problem of trying to write the sentence "HOW DID LIFE BEGIN?" First, we consider the problem of having a mixture of L- and D-amino acids rather than all L-amino acids. This would be equivalent to rotating some of the letters 180 degrees about an axis that runs horizontally through the sentence. These upside-down letters would represent D-amino acids in the sentence mixed with L-amino acids.

HOᴍ DID ᒥⅬE BEᏟⅠᴧᕒ

The problem that occurs when nonpeptide bonds occur in our assembly of amino acid building blocks is illustrated next (figure 5.4 shows a proper peptide bond). The proper placement of letters adjacent to one another has been altered so that some letters have irregular proximity to each other. The information in the sentence is further compromised.

HOᗒ ᗡIᗡ ᒪIꟻE ᗺƎᏟIᴎᡗ

Finally, the problem of improper sequence is illustrated by taking our original statement and rearranging some of the letters, totally obscuring the original message.

DIF HEG INBW ODIEL?

If all three of these problems were superimposed, the original message would be impossible to decipher—there would be a total loss of function. The same degradation of biological function results when a polymer does not have all L-amino acids, all peptide bonds, and proper sequencing of the amino acids in the polymer chain which is the protein molecule.

The greatest problem, however, is how to draw only English alphabet letters from an "alphabet soup" including many English letters (representing amino acids) but also Chinese, Greek and Hebrew symbols (representing other kinds of organic molecules in the prebiotic soup) and get one each of *H, O, W, L, F, B, G, N;* two *D*'s and *E*'s; and three *I*'s.

We suggested in 1984 that the origin-of-life problem is fundamentally a problem of information,[43] but this perception is not unique to us. In his *Information and the Origin of Life* (1990) Bernd-Olaf Kuppers says, "The problem of the origin of life is clearly basically equivalent to the problem of the origin of biological information."[44] Jeffrey Wicken and Robert Shapiro made similar statements in the late 1980s, as did A. E. Wilder Smith and Hubert B. Yockey in the 1970s.[45]

Protein Production as an Improbability Problem

The problem of assembling the amino acid building blocks into functional protein can also be illustrated using probability and statistics. To simplify the problem, one may assume the probability of getting an L-amino acid (versus a D-amino acid) to be 50 percent and the probability of joining two such amino acids with a peptide bond to also be 50 percent. The probability of getting the right amino acid in a particular position may be assumed to be 5 percent, assuming equal concentration of all twenty amino acids in the prebiotic soup. The first two assumptions are realistic, while the third would be too low for some amino acids and too high for others.

Neglecting the problem of reactions with non-amino acid chemical species, the probability of getting everything right in placing one amino acid would be $0.5 \times 0.5 \times .05 = .0125$. The probability of properly assembling N such amino acids would be $.0125 \times .0125 \times \ldots$ continued for N terms of $.0125$. If a functional protein had one hundred active sights, the probability of getting a proper assembly would be $.0125$ multiplied times itself one hundred times, or 4.9×10^{-191}. Such improbabilities have led essentially all scientists who work in the field to reject random, accidental assembly or fortuitous good luck as an explanation for how life began.

If we assume that all carbon on earth exists in the form of amino acids and that the amino acids are allowed to chemically react at the maximum possible rate of $10^{12}/s$ for one billion years (the greatest possible time between the cooling of the earth and the appearance of life), we must still conclude that it is incredibly improbable ($\sim 10^{-65}$) that even one functional protein would be made, as H. P. Yockey has pointed out.[46] D. Kenyon and G. Steinman and Sir Fredrick Hoyle come to similar conclusions, with the latter commenting, "The current scenario of the origin of life is about as likely as the assemblage of a 747 by a tornado whirling through a junkyard."[47]

Making DNA and RNA

The problems of prebiotic synthesis of DNA and RNA are even greater than for protein. Shapiro has summarized his work in this area as follows: "The evidence that is currently available does not support the availability of ribose on the prebiotic earth, except perhaps for brief periods of time, in low concentration as part of a complex mixture, and under conditions unsuitable for nucleoside synthesis."[48] The paper in which Shapiro made this comment had previously been presented to three hundred scientists from around the world at meetings of the International Society for the Study of the Origin of Life, without any challenge to the basic thesis.

RNA and its components are difficult to synthesize under the best of laboratory conditions; the process would have been even more unlikely under plausible prebiotic conditions. For example, the chemical path used to synthesize the sugar ribose, a key building block in RNA, also yields a host of other sugars that would inhibit RNA synthesis. Another major enigma is how phosphorus became a critical ingredient in RNA and DNA when it is a relatively rare substance in nature.

Leslie Orgel of the Salk Institute for Biological Studies, who has probably done more research exploring the RNA-world scenario than any other scientist, believes that experiments that try to simulate early stages of the RNA world are too complicated to represent plausible scenarios for the origin of life. Orgel was recently quoted in *Scientific American* as saying, "You have to get an awful lot of things right and nothing wrong."[49] Nobel laureate Sir Francis Crick says in his book *Life Itself,* "The origin of life appears to be almost a miracle, so many are the conditions which would have had to be satisfied to get it going."[50] In concluding a review article, Dose (1988) comments regarding the synthesis of biopolymers such as DNA and RNA, "The difficulties that must be overcome are at present beyond our imagination. . . . . The flow sheet shown in Figure 2 [showing how nucleic-acid-coded ribosomal protein synthesis might obtain] is a scheme of ignorance. Without fundamentally new insights in evolutionary processes, perhaps involving new modes of thinking, this ignorance is likely to persist."[51] It is clear that the information/complexity problems associated with the origin of life present challenging, maybe even intractable, problems.

Attempts to Solve the Information Problem

Several attempts have been made recently to salvage Oparin's soup theory.

In the summer of 1990, Julius Rebek Jr., chemist at MIT, created a stir by announcing that he had created a synthetic organic molecule that could replicate itself. The molecule, called amino adenosine triacid ester (AATE), consists of two components that resemble protein and nucleic acid. When placed in chloroform stocked with components, AATE can serve as a template for the formation of new AATE molecules. G. Joyce, an RNA specialist at the Scripps Clinic, commented in *Scientific American* on Rebek's work: "They [AATE] only replicate in highly artificial, unnatural conditions, and even more importantly, they reproduce too accurately. Without mutations, the molecules cannot evolve in the Darwinian sense." In the same article Leslie Orgel says, "I don't see its relevance to the origin of life."[52]

Jeffrey Wicken argues that the second law of thermodynamics actually drives the chemical reactions responsible for the origin of life, rather than presenting in some sense an obstacle. He argues that it is the entropic driving force that is responsible for polymerization reactions that join building blocks into biopolymers such as DNA, RNA and protein.[53] In a recent critique of Wicken's work, Bradley notes that an entropic driving force to join building blocks into polymer chains, while quite potent initially in a polymerization reaction, becomes inconsequential once a small yield of polymers has been produced. Were this not the case, we would have had a much easier time getting polymerization to occur in such systems experimentally.[54] For example, chains of amino acids can polymerize only when the water formed as a byproduct is driven off with heat, preventing depolymerization, as experimentally demonstrated by S. W. Fox.[55]

Wicken further argues that the information requirements of living systems are independent of thermodynamic considerations (and thus cannot be realized through any energy flow through the system)—a contention with which we completely agree. Citing the early work of Steinman and Cole (1967), Wicken goes on to suggest that intrinsic chemical properties of the molecular building blocks such as the inherent tendencies for nonrandom sequencing due to stearic interference might account for the specified sequencing of the molecules in the biopolymers.[56] However, a more recent analysis that looks at 250 proteins, rather than ten as Steinman and Cole did, has proved that no such correlation exists if amino acid sequencing in a large number of proteins is considered.[57]

If energy flow through the system cannot "create" the requisite information implicit in the remarkable specificity required for biopolymers, and if inherent self-ordering tendencies in matter are too weak to account for the observed molecular complexity, what is left? Bernd-Olaf Kuppers argues for selection to circumvent the immense improbabilities inherent in the complexities of even the simplest living systems. He says, "The molecular-Darwinistic approach rests upon the working hypothesis that natural selection in the Darwinian sense appears already in the realm of inanimate matter. . . . [This idea] is only valid if a Darwinian natural selection really does take place in the realm of inanimate matter."[58] Since Darwinian natural selection in the biological realm presupposes replicating systems, a very different kind of selection is being alluded to here. It is difficult to imagine on what basis natural selection might provide sufficient guidance on the molecular level to lead to the remarkable complexity associated with the minimal requirements for life: replication, information storage and energy processing. At this time Kuppers's hypothesis has no flesh of conceptual detail on its bones, nor the slightest shred of experimental support.

The Bankruptcy of Soup Theory and Suggested Alternatives

The conceptual bankruptcy of Oparin's "soup theory" was highlighted in a debate held at the international ISSOL symposium in Berkeley, California, in 1986. The "protein-first" side of the debate argued that making RNA under prebiotic conditions was well-nigh impossible, a criticism that was ignored rather than rebutted by the "RNA-first" side. The latter responded by insisting that proteins are too inept to be the vehicle for the first living system, since they are insufficiently versatile. With the protein-first side providing no rebuttal to this criticism, the debate ended with both positions fatally flawed and no more promising alternatives suggested.

The criticisms previously summarized (and dealt with in more detail by A. G. Cairns-Smith [1982], Thaxton, Bradley and Olsen [1984] and Shapiro [1986]) must be considered nearly (if not actually) fatal to "soup theory." What, then, are the alternatives, and why the slow demise of soup theory? The tardiness of the soup theory's demise despite the theory's many problems tells something about the reasonableness of the alternative hypotheses that have been proposed in the past ten years as potential successors.

A clay-based origin of life. In *Genetic Takeover and the Mineral Origins of Life,* University of Glasgow chemist A. G. Cairns-Smith proposed that life arose on solid substrates, probably crystalline clays with enough complexity to mutate and evolve in a lifelike way. He argued that some clays might have become better breeders by developing the ability to attract or synthesize organic compounds such as nucleic acids or proteins. Eventually the organic compounds might have become sophisticated enough to begin replicating and evolving on their own.[59] Cairns-Smith is quoted in a 1991 article in *Scientific American* as cheerfully admitting the shortcomings in his hypothesis: "No one has been able to coax clay into something resembling evolution in a laboratory; nor has anyone found anything resembling a clay-based organism in nature."[60]

Hydrothermal vents on sea floor. In the late 1970s, scientists discovered several hydrothermal vents on the sea floor near the Galápagos Islands which supported thriving communities of life, including tubeworms, clams and bacteria, whose primary source of energy is not light but sulfur compounds emitted by the vents. Dozens of similar vents have since been located. John Corliss of NASA's Goddard Space Flight Center has proposed that vents may have supplied the energy and nutrients needed to create and sustain life.[61]

Thermal vent theory has not provided any hints regarding how the information problem might be addressed, only that the energy-rich environment might facilitate the production of the organic polymers that would have been important in the origin of life. Thus the work of assembly of building blocks, earlier estimated at 30 cal/gm, might be done in this way, but no solution to the more challenging information work term is afforded by the thermal vent hypothesis.

Stanley Miller and Jeffrey Bada at the University of California at San Diego have done experiments that suggest the superheated water inside vents, which sometimes exceeds 572° F, would destroy rather than create complex organic compounds. As a result, Miller actually considers the vents a hindrance to the origin of life. Based on estimates that all of the water in the ocean passes through the thermal vents each ten million years,[62] Miller has estimated an upper limit for amino acid concentrations in the ocean to be 3×10^{-4} M.[63] Since James Corliss and others agree that current life at the vents probably migrated there, the thermal-vent origin of life remains a vague idea, lacking both conceptual details and experimental support.

Metabolism first hypotheses. Some relatively recent proposals suggest that life might have started as a metabolic process—a cyclic chemical reaction that is driven by some source of energy—taking place on the surface of a solid. Gunter Wachterschauser suggests that pyrite (containing iron and sulfur atoms) offers a positively charged surface to which organic molecules might be attached. Continued formation of the pyrite mineral could supply a source of energy that might drive organic molecules to react with one another and grow in complexity. Note that nothing in this model addresses the problem of how to develop information in organic molecules, only the possibility of assistance in polymerization. To his credit, Wachterschauser himself admits that his theory is for the most part "pure speculation."[64]

Christian de Duve's theory, which is described in *Blueprint for a Cell*, revolves around sulfur-based compounds called thioesters.[65] Again, the approach is to look for creative sources of energy flow via systems of chemical reactions which might facilitate the production of important biopolymers. However, the information question is again ignored; only the 30 cal/gm of enthalpy and thermal entropy change would be accomplished by such a system. Thus this approach would at best only give some assistance in the polymerization (joining) of otherwise hard-to-join molecular building blocks, without regard to the careful assembly and sequencing of these molecules necessary to give biological function.

Self-organization in nature. Nobel laureate I. Prigogine has written extensively on self-organizing tendencies in nature, such as convective heat flow and the formation of vortices such as one observes in the emptying of water from a bathtub.[66] Prigogine's work has developed a framework for understanding the circumstances under which such ordering phenomena occur. In particular he has demonstrated that such phenomena are observed in systems far from equilibrium and are due to the nonlinear behavior that is characteristic of such systems.

It is sometimes claimed that Prigogine's work offers a potential solution to the origin-of-life problem, though Prigogine is more modest in his own assessment.[67] The difficulty in applying his work to the origin-of-life problem is that the spontaneous ordering that is typical of Prigogine's far-from-equilibrium systems bears little resemblance to the information-rich, aperiodic structures of biopolymers. There is little similarity between the ordering associated with crystals, vortices and the like and the specified complexity required in the sequencing of amino acids to give a functional protein. Thus it is difficult to see how these ideas can resolve the information enigma that is at the heart of the origin-of-life mystery.

Eigen and the "hypercycle." M. Eigen has done some of the most complex work in trying to envision how a simple "living" system might develop.[68] His work is sometimes alluded to as having solved the origin-of-life problem. However, Eigen acknowledges that his "simple" system is actually quite complex, requiring as it does a whole assembly of various protein molecules and RNA. He agrees that his work addresses the *development* of a possible early living system rather than its *origin*. Thus it is not significant for helping us understand the origin of life except possibly as it conceptualizes a particular system of minimal complexity to provide basic life functions and with some capacity to develop.

Information: The Holy Grail in Origin-of-Life Research

A variety of ingenious schemes have been developed to get otherwise energetically unfavorable chemical reactions to occur so that the various building blocks can be assembled into biopolymers. However, assembling biopolymers (such as protein) with only the right building blocks (e.g., amino acids in protein) and only the correct isomers (L-amino acids in protein) joined with the correct bonds (peptide bonds for protein) and with the correct sequence of the building blocks (proper sequencing of amino acids for protein) presents a truly formidable problem.

Living systems solve this problem with what amounts to information-rich templates. Thus the production of information-rich biopolymers can be easily understood. But the *origin* of such a sophisticated system that is both information-rich and capable of reproducing itself constitutes the core problem for origin-of-life researchers.

In considering this and other problems, Sir Francis Crick has noted that the "origin of life seems almost to be a miracle, so many are the difficulties in its occurring."[69] Dose concludes his excellent 1988 review by saying that solutions to difficulties in origin-of-life research seem "beyond our imagination."[70] Shapiro argues strongly that all current theories are bankrupt and that we need to find a new and more fruitful paradigm to guide our search for a naturalistic explanation for the origin of life.[71]

We find ourselves in complete agreement. The Oparin-Haldane paradigm seems "dead in the water," with no suitable replacement in sight. However, we believe that the problem is unnecessarily exacerbated by the conventional wisdom that would restrict our considerations to natural causes, explanations based on chemistry and physics alone.

In 1967 the British philosopher and physical chemist Michael Polanyi published a remarkable paper in *Chemical and Engineering News* entitled "Life Transcending Physics and Chemistry." He said that chemistry and physics are adequate to explain everything in nature *except* the machines of people and living systems. While the operation of each part of an automobile can be explained within the usual confines of the laws of nature as elucidated in chemistry and physics, he said, the *existence* of the automobile requires an explanation that transcends chemistry and physics alone. Someone had to fix the highly unusual (information-intensive) boundary conditions under which the laws of chemistry and physics are constrained to operate in an automobile to accomplish a purposeful end result.

Living systems, Polanyi argued, have precisely the same problem. Their operations may be well understood within the confines of chemistry, but their origin seems to defy a simple chemical, physical explanation. The source of the information-intensive initial conditions seems to be outside the realm of chemistry and physics alone.

In the next section we will develop more fully the hypothesis that the existence of living systems may be best explained by acceding to the possibility that some intelligent causal agency is responsible.

The Intelligent Design Hypothesis

In light of the foregoing analysis we consider that it is reasonable to doubt whether prebiological evolution occurred, and we suggest intelligent design as an alternative. Sagan, Miller, Fox, Shapiro and most other origin-of-life scientists have insisted that we continue to look for a natural pathway; they are sure that prebiotic evolution produced life. But surely our doubt agrees with experience. The general persistence in defending prebiotic evolution is based on philosophical commitment quite apart from experience.

Scientists usually dismiss the possibility of an alternative to a natural process if they are thinking in terms of the natural-supernatural dichotomy. Many theists and naturalists in metaphysics[72] are agreed in accepting *methodological naturalism*—that is, commitment to the search for natural processes irrespective of metaphysical commitment. Whether the supernatural exists or not, they say, we must approach science in terms of natural processes, for there is no other way to do science. We agree with the intent of this approach to preserve the integrity of science. However, we believe that the approach itself is in error and that those who promote it place an unnecessary demand on both nature and scientific methodology. It insists, in advance of looking, that a natural-cause, continuous world picture will be forthcoming. We think this demand is contrary to the spirit of science and smacks more of metaphysical commitment—which, if unrecognized, becomes dangerous.[73]

The first step in identifying an alternative is to notice that "natural-supernatural" language is appropriate for metaphysics but not for science, which relies on experience. Within the bounds of experience, we use the notion of cause in a generic sense to cover both natural and intelligent causation. That is, we refer to both natural and intelligent cause without regard to metaphysical categories. Science is blind to metaphysics and neither affirms nor denies the supernatural; also, it neither affirms nor denies *naturalism*—that nature is all there is.

Very often one's individual reservoir of experience is insufficient to identify the cause of an event as natural or intelligent. The prudent course then is to follow the advice that philosopher Ludwig Wittgenstein gave in another context, "Whereof one cannot speak, thereof one must be silent."[74] A curious propensity afflicting many people, however, is to go ahead and name a cause even when they cannot be certain. The "cause" is almost always generated by their philosophy or religion. Sometimes they are later shown to have been correct and are hailed for their sagacity and foresight. However, their statement was only a wish or a guess, even though it may have been made with all the assurance and confidence of an eyewitness. At other times they are wrong. In both cases their foolish assertion without experiential basis serves as an obstacle to knowledge about nature.

Unfortunately, this has not been an uncommon event in the history of science. As Daniel Boorstin noted, "The greatest obstacle to discovering the shape of the earth, the continents and the ocean, was not ignorance, but the illusion of knowledge."[75] In our opinion this phenomenon is what led to exaggerated expectations of finding organics, if not life itself, on Mars and accounts for the current optimism of those who are eager to return to Mars for another sample-gathering expedition.

Arguing from analogy. How would one decide in favor of an intelligent cause of some event in the past? In general, we use the same method to identify an intelligent cause that we use for a natural cause: uniform sensory experience. This is called the analogical method. The philosopher David Hume (1711-76), who wrote extensively on the analogical method, said, "From causes which appear *similar* we expect similar effects." Hume also said, "The same rule holds, whether the cause assigned be brute unconscious matter, or a rational intelligent being."[76] Thus if during an afternoon stroll along a beach we happen upon "John loves Mary" written in the sand, we draw on our reservoir of experience to conclude that someone, possibly even John or Mary, wrote it.

For an illustration of the analogical method, consider the field of archaeology. The principle of analogy is used regularly by archaeologists to determine whether some discovery had an intelligent cause. The reasoning goes like this: In the present we see craftspeople making pottery. Therefore, when we search through the dust in an excavation in Mesopotamia and find a broken clay pot, it is reasonable to infer that its source was likewise a craftsperson.

Sometimes it is difficult to tell, as in the case of eoliths. Eoliths were once presumed to be artifacts made of flint; later it was pointed out that they closely resemble natural flints that had been broken by tumbling in a stream. But noted archaeologist Kenneth Oakley has pointed out, "As a general rule naturally chipped flints are easily distinguishable from the works of man, for they lack logical design, flake-scars occur in uneconomical profusion, the edges have a bruised appearance, and flake surfaces are usually scratched."[77]

In the nineteenth century, the astronomer John F. W. Herschel promoted the analogical method of reasoning from observed causes to unknown causes: "If the analogy of two phenomena be *very close and striking,* while, at the same time, the cause of one is very obvious, it becomes scarcely possible to refuse to admit the action of an analogous cause in the other, though not so obvious in itself."[78] The analogical method of assigning causes was also significant in the landmark work of Charles Lyell, whose core principle became enshrined in geological literature as "The present is a key to the past."[79]

Scientists have relied on the analogical method for more than 150 years. The tremendous success of science is at least a partial attestation of the method. We have learned by experience to associate a particular type of effect with a certain kind of cause; when we see a similar effect, then, we routinely and automatically assume a similar cause. This judgment is based on our accumulated reservoir of experience. The analogical method is quite general and is used for identifying either natural or intelligent causes.

The search for ETI. It was once thought there were canals on Mars. This led to speculation that there was intelligent life on the planet. Although the idea was mistaken, it again illustrates the reasoning we all use: when we see certain kinds of effects, we infer intelligent causes, based on the principle of analogy.

This is also the reasoning employed by astronomers in their search for intelligent life in the cosmos. It is routinely used by NASA imaging teams to evaluate data from planets and their moons. These teams use criteria for evaluating evidence of intelligent life on the planets—they are seeking some distinctive mark of things produced by intelligence.

The current search for extraterrestrial intelligence (acronym SETI) also illustrates that intelligent causes are acceptable in science. This is not to suggest that ETI actually exists, for evidence of it is lacking. The current SETI program, however, is being carried out within the bounds of legitimate science.

If scientists ever receive radio waves from space that were sent by ETI, how will they distinguish them from noise? This question is explored in Carl

Sagan's fictional tale *Contact*. Sagan reminds us that though our planet is bathed continuously with radio emissions, they are all natural. Such emissions are "caused by physical processes, electrons spiralling in the galactic magnetic field, or interstellar molecules colliding with one another, or the remote echoes of the Big Bang red-shifted from gamma rays at the origin of the universe, to the tame and chill radio waves that fill all of space in our epoch." So far "there has never been a real signal from the depths of space, something manufactured, something artificial, something contrived by an alien mind."[80]

As in Sagan's novel, various radio telescopes are scanning the heavens for some artificial electromagnetic signal that is clearly not just random radio noise. A signal representing a series of prime numbers, for example, would betray the existence of some distant civilization (prime numbers are numbers that are divisible only by themselves and 1). The SETI community of scientists consider any natural cause mechanism for the generation of prime numbers to be so improbable that a string of them received from space would be hailed as evidence of ETI.

There have been several SETI programs over the years, beginning with Project Ozma in 1960. More recently is Project Sentinel, the major SETI project of the Planetary Society.[81] In its expanded version, called Project META (Megachannel Extraterrestrial Assay), it has the capacity to survey more than eight million radio channels for possible radio signals from space.[82] In 1992 advocates for SETI convinced the U.S. Congress to appropriate $100 million for a radio survey of the heavens, to listen to millions of radio channels for signals that would show that intelligent life has emerged by evolution elsewhere in the cosmos.[83]

Astronomer Carl Sagan has maintained that even a single message from space would establish the existence of extraterrestrial intelligence: "There are others who believe that our problems are soluble, that humanity is still in its childhood, that one day soon we will grow up. The receipt of *a single message from space* would show that it is possible to live through such technological adolescence; the transmitting civilization, after all, has survived."[84]

If Sagan is right in his supposition, what then might we infer from the large amount of information that is intrinsic to even the simplest living system? Is it appropriate to infer from such observations the existence of an intelligent cause? Should the loss of credibility of similar arguments based on design in the 1800s cause us any concern in such inferences? This critical question of when (if ever) one is justified in inferring an intelligent cause from scientific observations will be taken up at some length in the next section.

When uniform experience is lacking, we are unjustified in positing a cause, whether natural or intelligent, for any phenomenon. To illustrate, suppose we are detectives investigating a person's death. Is this a case of murder, or did the person die of natural causes? We cannot know the answer in advance. We have to look and find out. If a detective announced at the beginning of her investigation that the person's death could only have been natural, we would object that this was an illegitimate restriction of possible causes. Since what we hope to discover through our investigation is precisely whether death resulted from an intelligent cause (murder) or was natural, we need a method of inquiry open to either explanation. In the same way, those genuinely seeking to discover whether an event in nature is the result of intellect or of natural process need a method of inquiry open to either explanation. A method is needed that will enable us to determine with the highest probability which it was.

What Present Observations Are Keys to the Past?

We have seen the legitimacy of analogical reasoning that leads from present observations to the past. Transferring this reasoning to the question of origins, we want to know whether life resulted from natural or intelligent causes. We look for evidence that the phenomenon in question bears the characteristics exhibited by objects we know in our experience. Does this object we are trying to explain fit a pattern that we know by experience to mark products of intelligent manufacture? If so, then we assign an intelligent cause. If it fits the pattern that experience shows results from natural causes, we assign a natural cause. Otherwise, we simply acknowledge there is not enough information to decide.

The principle of analogy requires only that the cause observed in the present be similar in kind to the cause posited for the past. For instance, one does not have to find life arising spontaneously from nonliving materials in the present in order to posit that it did so in the past. All that is necessary for a plausible natural-cause scenario is to identify similar instances where some characteristic feature of life is produced naturally (and this is a major goal of laboratory simulation experiments). Likewise, for a plausible intelligent-cause scenario one does not have to catch red-handed an intellect operating in the present that is identical to the one posited in the past. All that is necessary is to observe similar kinds of intelligent causes that regularly produce some characteristic feature of life.[85] How does one conclude that the cause is similar? By determining whether the effects are "very close and striking."[86]

The intelligent cause observable to us today is obviously human. But other forms of intelligence may be posited. When we work backward from effect to cause, the inferred intelligence is generic: it could theoretically be of this earth or off the earth. Scientists involved in the SETI program are not required to posit a human intelligence beaming radio messages from space. On the basis of analogy, we need only to posit an intelligence *similar to* humans. If we posit an intelligent cause for the origin of life, it cannot be a human intelligence, because humans did not yet exist. Nevertheless, if a plausible case can be constructed for it, we may posit a similar intelligent cause.

What cause-and-effect relationships are observed in the present that lead chemical evolutionists to infer a natural cause for life? What relationships lead us to infer an intelligent cause? As in other areas of science, we rely on the touchstone of accumulated sensory experience.

The essential difference in viewpoint between the chemical evolution hypothesis and the intelligent origin hypothesis is that different selected observations in the present form the basis for making an analogy to the past. Chemical evolution is rooted in laboratory experiments which its adherents suggest are acceptable simulations of events that occurred on the early earth. Though neither life nor relevantly similar essential features of life have been produced in these laboratory experiments, much optimism has been generated about the suggested plausibility of pathways to life (as in Miller's early work; this optimism, however, has been gradually evaporating).

Classical Design Arguments

What observations in the present guide proponents of intelligent design in making analogy to the past? The intelligent design view is rooted in the present observation that human intellect is required to produce the complex arrangements of matter we see in computers, literary works, paintings and bridges. If the present is a key to the past, then an intelligent cause similar to humanity must account for all relevantly similar complex assemblages in the past.

The intelligent design view of origins is the one that dominated educated minds throughout most of Western history, until the end of the nineteenth century. The classical design argument went straight from order in the universe to the existence of an ordering intelligence, or God. From time immemorial the beauty of birds and flowers, the cycle of the seasons and the remarkable adaptations in animals have led people to posit some type of intelligent cause behind it all.

During the scientific revolution of the seventeenth century, the argument from order took on even greater force. Scientists studied the intricate structures in nature in a depth and detail unknown in previous ages. Many became more convinced than ever that such order required an intelligent cause. Isaac Newton expressed a common sentiment when he declared, "This most beautiful system of the sun, planets, and comets, could only proceed from the counsel and dominion of an intelligent and powerful Being."[87] The argument from design has always been the argument for God most widely accepted by scientists. It is the most empirical of the arguments, based as it is on observational premises about the kind of order we discover in nature.[88]

Ironically, however, it was also the scientific revolution that eventually led many to reject the argument from design. Repeatedly scientists discovered natural causes for events that until then had been mysterious. If natural causes can explain these things, they reasoned, perhaps they can explain everything else too. Do we really need an intelligent cause to explain the order of the world?

Take the structure of a snowflake. The snowflake's intricate beauty has led many a believer to exclaim at the wisdom of the Creator. Yet the snowflake's structure is nothing mysterious or supernatural. It arises by the natural process of dendritic growth that accompanies the phase change of H_2O from liquid (water) to solid (snow).

The classical argument from design claims that the order we see around us cannot have arisen by natural causes. The snowflake seems to refute this claim. It demonstrates that at least some kinds of order can arise by natural causes. And if matter alone can give rise to order in some instances, why not in all others as well? Why do we need anymore to appeal to an intelligent Being to explain the origin of life and the world? We need only continue to search for natural causes. The trend away from design culminated in Darwin's argument that natural selection produced "apparent design"; this meant there was no need for an intelligent Designer. So the matter has stood in the scientific community and the world at large for over a century.

Through the application of information theory, it is now realized that there are actually two kinds of order. The first kind (the snowflake's) arises from constraints within the material a thing is made of (in this case water molecules) We cannot infer an intelligent cause from it, except possibly in the remote sense of something behind the natural cause. The second kind, however, is not a result of anything within matter itself. It is in principle opposed to anything we see forming naturally. This kind of order does provide evidence for an intelligent cause.

Modern Design Arguments

Let's explain these two kinds of order in greater detail. As you travel through various parts of the United States, you may come across unusual rock formations. If you consult a tourist guide, you will learn that such shapes result when more than one type of mineral make up the formation. Because of the variable mineral composition, some portions of a formation are softer than others. Rain and wind erode the soft parts of the formation faster than the hard parts, leaving the harder sections protruding. In this way the formation may take on an unlikely shape. It may even come to resemble a familiar object such as a face. In other words, the formation may look as though it was deliberately carved. But on closer inspection, say from a different angle, you notice that the resemblance is only superficial. The shape invariably accords with what erosion can do as it acts on the natural qualities of the rock (soft parts worn away, hard parts protruding). You therefore conclude that the rock formed naturally. Natural forces suffice to account for the shape you see.

Now let's illustrate a different kind of order. Say in your travels you visit Mount Rushmore. Here you find four faces on a granite cliff. The angles of these faces do not follow the natural composition of the rock; the chip marks cut across both hard and soft sections. These shapes do not resemble anything you have seen resulting from erosion. In this case the shape of the rock is not the result of natural processes. Rather, you infer from uniform experience that an artisan has been at work. The four faces were intelligently imposed onto the rock material.

None of us finds it difficult to distinguish between these two kinds of order, the one produced naturally and the other by intelligence. To come back to the argument from design, the question is, Which kind of order do we find in nature? If we find only the first kind, then our conclusion will be that natural causes suffice to explain the universe as we see it today. If, on the other hand, we find any instances of the second kind of order, the kind produced by intelligence, these will be evidence of the activity of an intelligent cause. Science itself would then point beyond the physical world to its origin in an intelligent source.

Is there anything in the present biological world that, according to the criteria worked out above, would have the character of being produced by an intelligent cause? Is there anything we know by experience that could justify the claim that life resulted in the past from intelligent activity?

Modern Design Argument and Information

One of the greatest scientific stories of the twentieth century concerns the elucidation of DNA's structure and the discovery of the genetic code. DNA is the famous molecule of heredity. Each of us began as a tiny ball about the size of a period at the end of a sentence. All our physical characteristics—height, hair color, eye color and so on—were spelled out in our DNA. It guided our development into adulthood.

DNA is quite simple in its basic structure, although it is enormously complex in its functioning. By now most literate people are familiar with the double helix structure of the DNA molecule. It is like a long ladder twisted into a spiral. Sugar and phosphate molecules form the sides of the ladder. Four bases make up its rungs. These are adenine, thymine, guanine and cytosine. These bases act as the "letters" of a genetic alphabet. They combine in various sequences to form words, sentences and paragraphs. These base sequences are all the instructions needed to guide the functioning of the cell.

Proponents of an intelligent origin of life note that molecular biology has uncovered an analogy between DNA and language, giving rise to the *sequence hypothesis*. The sequence hypothesis assumes that an exact order of symbols records information. The base sequences in DNA spell out in coded form the instructions for how a cell makes proteins, for example. It works just the way alphabetical letter sequences do in this article to give information about origins. The genetic code functions exactly like a language code—indeed it *is* a code. It is a molecular communications system: a sequence of chemical "letters" stores and transmits the communication in each living cell.

Communication is possible no matter what symbols are used as an alphabet. The twenty-six letters we use in English, the thirty-two Cyrillic letters used in the Russian language and the four-letter genetic alphabet—all serve comparably in communication.

Information theory is the science of message transmission developed by Claude Shannon and other engineers at Bell Telephone Laboratories in the late 1940s. It provides a mathematical means of measuring information. Information theory applies to any symbol system, regardless of the elements of that system. The so-called Shannon information laws apply equally well to human language, Morse-coded messages and the genetic text.

There exists a structural identity between the base sequences in a DNA message and the alphabetical letter sequences in a written message, and this assures us that the analogy is "very close and striking," as Herschel stipulated. This structural identity is the basis for the application of information theory to biology. As Hubert P. Yockey notes in the *Journal of Theoretical Biology*, "The sequence hypothesis applies directly to the protein and the genetic text as well as to written language and therefore the treatment is mathematically identical."[89]

This development is highly significant for the modern origin-of-life discussion and is an observation in the present that proponents of an intelligent origin of life use as a key to the past. In the case of written messages, we have experience that they have an intelligent cause. We use analogical reasoning to conclude that the remarkable information sequences in DNA also had an intelligent source. On the basis of analogy, then, we infer an agent with an intelligence that is similar to human intelligence. Since DNA is an essential molecular component of every form of life we know, we likewise conclude that life on earth had an intelligent cause.

The discovery that DNA conveys a genetic message gives the argument from design a new twist. Since life is at its core a chemical message system, the origin of life is the origin of information. A genetic message is a very special kind of order. It represents "specified complexity."[90] To understand this term, we need to take a brief excursion into information theory as it applies to biology.

Information theory makes information measurable[91] and thus realizes an important goal of mathematicians. It finds its place in biology through its ability to measure organization and to express it in numbers. Biologists have long recognized the importance of the concept of organization. However, little practical advance was possible until there was a way to measure it. Organization, stated in terms of information, does this. "Roughly speaking," says Leslie Orgel, "the information content of a structure is the minimum number of instructions needed to specify the structure."[92] The more complex a structure is, the more instructions are needed to specify it and the more information it contains.

Random structures require very few instructions at all. If you want to write out a series of nonsense letters, for example, the only instructions necessary are "Write a letter between A and Z," followed by "Now do it again," ad infinitum. A highly ordered structure like a series of constantly repeating letters or numbers also requires few instructions. A book in which the sentence "I love you" is repeated over and over is a highly ordered series of letters. A few instructions specify which letters to choose and in what sequence. Those instructions, followed by "Now do it again" as many times as necessary, allow the book to be completed. By contrast with either random or ordered structures, complex structures require many instructions. If we wanted a computer to write out a poem, for example, we would have to specify each letter. That is, the poem has a high information content.

Specifying a Sequence

Information in this context means the precise determination, or specification, of a sequence of letters. We said above that a message represents "specified complexity." We are now able to understand what *specified* means. The more highly specified a thing is, the fewer choices there are about fulfilling each instruction.

In a random situation, options are unlimited and each option is equally probable. In generating a list of random letters, for instance, there are no constraints on the choice of letters at each step. The letters are unspecified.

On the other hand, an ordered structure like our book full of "I love you" is highly specified but redundant and not complex, though each letter is specified. It has a low information content, as noted before, because the instructions needed to specify it are few. Ordered structures and random structures are similar in that both have a low information content. They differ in that ordered structures are highly specified and random structures are unspecified.

A complex structure like a poem is likewise highly specified. It differs from an ordered structure, however, in that it not only is highly specified but also has a high information content. Writing a poem requires new instructions to specify each letter.

To sum up, information theory has given us tools to distinguish between the two kinds of order we distinguished at the beginning. Lack of order—randomness—is neither specified nor high in information.

The first kind of order is the kind found in a snowflake. Using the terms of information theory, a snowflake is specified but has a low information content. Its order arises from a single structure repeated over and over. It is like the book filled with "I love you." The second kind of order, the kind found in the faces on Mount Rushmore, is both specified and high in information.

Life Has Information

Molecules characterized by specified complexity make up living things. These molecules are, most notably, DNA and protein. By contrast, nonliving natural things fall into one of two categories. They are either unspecified and random (lumps of granite and mixtures of random nucleotides) or specified but simple (snowflakes and crystals). A crystal fails to qualify as living because it lacks complexity. A chain of random nucleotides fails to qualify because it lacks specificity.[93] No nonliving things (except DNA and protein in living things, human artifacts and written language) have specified complexity.

For a long time biologists overlooked the distinction between these two kinds of order (simple, periodic order versus specified complexity). Only recently have they appreciated that the distinguishing feature of living systems is not order but specified complexity.[94] The sequence of nucleotides in DNA or of amino acids in a protein is not a repetitive order like a crystal. Instead it is like the letters in a written message.

A message is not composed of a sequence of letters repeated over and over. It is not, in other words, the first kind of order. Indeed, the letters that make up a message are in a sense random. There is nothing inherent in the letters *g-i-f-t* that tells us the word means "present." In fact, in German the same sequence of letters means "poison." In French the series is meaningless. If you came across a series of letters written in the Greek alphabet and didn't know Greek, you wouldn't be able to read it. Nor would you be able to tell if the letters formed Greek words or were just random groupings of letters. There is no detectable difference.

What distinguishes a message is that certain random groupings of letters have come to symbolize meanings according to a given symbol convention. Nothing distinguishes the sequence *a-n-d* from *n-a-d* or *n-d-a* for a person who doesn't know English. Within the English language, however, the sequence *a-n-d* is very specific and carries a particular meaning. In Henry Quastler's colorful expression, it is an "accidental choice remembered."[95]

We now know there is no connection at all between the origin of order and the origin of specified complexity. There is no connection between orderly repeating patterns and the specified complexity in protein and DNA. We cannot draw an analogy, as many have incorrectly done, between the formation of a crystal and the origin of life. We cannot argue that since natural forces account for the crystal, they account for the structure of living things. The order we find in crystals and snowflakes is not analogous to the specified complexity we find in living things.

Are we not back to a more sophisticated form of the argument from design? With the insights from information theory we need no longer argue from order in a general sense. Order with low information content (the first kind) does arise by natural processes. However, there is no convincing experimental evidence that order with high information content (the second kind or specified complexity) can arise by natural processes. Indeed, the only evidence we have in the present is that it takes intelligence to produce the second kind of order.

Scientists can synthesize proteins suitable for life. Research chemists produce things like insulin for medical problems in great quantities. The question is, How do they do it? Certainly not by means of chance or natural causes. Only by highly constraining their experiments can chemists produce proteins like those found in living things. Placing constraints on the experiment limits the "choices" at each step of the way. That is, it adds information.

If we want to speculate on how the first informational molecules came into being, the most reasonable speculation is there was some form of intelligence around at the time. We cannot identify that source any further from a scientific analysis alone. Science cannot supply a name for that intelligent cause. We cannot be sure from the empirical data on DNA whether the intelligence is within the cosmos but off the earth, as asserted by Hoyle and Wickramasinghe.[96] Note that they do not argue per se for intelligent cause but against natural causes. The agency might be beyond the cosmos, as historic theism maintains. All we can say is that given the information in a DNA molecule, it is certainly reasonable to posit that an intelligent agent made it. Life came from a "who" instead of a "what."

We might be able to identify that agent in greater detail through other arguments. We might, for example, gain insight from historical, philosophical or theological argument or by considering relevant lines of evidence from other areas of science. But scientific investigations of the origin of life have clearly led us to conclude that an intelligent cause may, in the final analysis, be the only rational possibility to explain the enigma of the origin of life: *information.*

When we turn to issues involved in the origin of major taxonomic groups, we see further evidence for an intelligent Designer. In the next chapter, Kurt Wise will pick up the thread and focus on the origin of such groups.

Bibliography

Bradley, Walter L. "Thermodynamics and the Origin of Life." *Perspectives on Science and Christian Faith* 40 (1988): 72. [I]

Cairns-Smith, A. G. *Genetic Takeover and the Mineral Origins of Life.* New York: Cambridge University Press, 1982. [I]

Crick, Francis. *Life Itself: Its Origin and Nature.* New York: Simon and Schuster, 1981. [B]

De Duve, Christian. *Blueprint for a Cell: The Nature and Origin of Life.* Burlington, N.C.: Patterson, 1991. [I]

Dose, Klaus. "The Origin of Life: More Questions Than Answers." *Interdis-*

ciplinary Science Reviews 13 (1988): 348. [A]

Ferre, Frederick. "Design Argument." In *Dictionary of Ideas*, 1:673. New York: Charles Scribner and Sons, 1973. [B]

Horgan, John. "In the Beginning." *Scientific American*, February 1991, p. 117. [B]

Hoyle, Fred. *The Intelligent Universe*. New York: Holt, Rinehart and Winston, 1984. [B]

Hoyle, Fred, and C. Wickramasinghe. *Evolution from Space*. New York: Simon and Schuster, 1981. [B]

Kuppers, Bernd-Olaf. *Information and the Origin of Life*. Cambridge, Mass.: MIT Press, 1990. [A]

Miller, Stanley L. "Which Organic Compounds Could Have Occurred on Prebiotic Earth?" *Cold Spring Harbor Symposia on Quantitative Biology* 52 (1987): 17. [A]

Polanyi, Michael. "Life Transcending Physics and Chemistry." *Chemical and Engineering News*, August 21, 1967, p. 54. [B]

Prigogine, I. *From Being to Becoming*. San Francisco: Freeman, 1980. [A]

Shapiro, Robert. *Origins: A Skeptic's Guide to the Creation of Life in the Universe*. New York: Summit Books, 1986. [B]

_____ . "Prebiotic Ribose Synthesis: A Critical Analysis." *Origins of Life and Evolution of the Biosphere* 18 (1988): 71. [A]

Thaxton, Charles B. "DNA, Design and the Origin of Life" and "In Pursuit of Intelligent Causes: Some Historical Background." Papers presented at Sources of Information Content in DNA: An Interdisciplinary Conference, Tacoma, Washington, June 23-26, 1988. [A]

_____ . "A Word to the Teacher." In *Of Pandas and People*. Edited by Percival Davis and Dean H. Kenyon. Dallas: Haughton, 1989.

Thaxton, Charles B., Walter L. Bradley and Roger L. Olsen. *The Mystery of Life's Origin: Reassessing Current Theories*. 1984; rpt. Dallas: Lewis and Stanley, 1992. [I]

Wicken, J. S. *Evolution, Thermodynamics and Information*. New York: Oxford University Press, 1987. [A]

Yockey, H. P. *Information Theory and Molecular Biology*. Cambridge, U.K.: Cambridge University Press, 1992. [A]

6
THE ORIGIN OF LIFE'S MAJOR GROUPS

Kurt P. Wise

Anyone who reads whodunit mysteries is familiar with most of the basic principles involved in reconstructing the history of life. First of all, mysteries begin with a question or series of questions. What happened, in what order and when? We ask similar questions about living organisms (e.g., "What events occurred in what order and when to produce the incredible variety of organisms we see about us today?"). Second, since the events of interest occurred in the past and cannot now be observed, the sleuth in a mystery must diligently search for anything that might still remain from those events. Historical biologists also diligently search for any clues that might remain from the time when life's diversity came to be. Third, the sleuth and those of us tagging along begin to construct scenarios to explain the discovered clues; based on the new scenarios, the sleuths search for more clues. Likewise, biologists imagine scenarios to explain the evidence they find of the origin of life's diversity, then search for more evidence to evaluate each of these scenarios.

Invariably as we follow a mystery several scenarios are imagined, tested and rejected before the solution presents itself. Ultimately a given scenario is accepted over another because it explains more evidence. In this comparison the strength of any given piece of evidence is not terribly important—the key is how simply and satisfactorily a given scenario explains the *entire* package of evidence.

As scientists have studied the origin of life's diversity, many scenarios have been imagined, tested and rejected over the years. Currently, most of the scientific community has accepted the scenario of *macroevolution*. Under this scenario, life, starting with a single-celled organism, has changed and diverged along the path of an "evolutionary tree." Following nonintelligent natural law and process over many millions of years, life has repeatedly branched to produce new organisms and organismal groups. Today the many terminal twigs of the tree are present about us as living species.

Macroevolution seems to explain many clues thought to relate to the origin of life's diversity. Other scenarios do exist, however. I would like to suggest that at least one of these scenarios—that of an intelligent Designer—can explain more evidence better than macroevolution can.

Similarities

Similarities among brothers and sisters are due to their having inherited similar genetic material from their parents. Greater similarities are generally found between brothers and sisters than between first cousins, and between first cousins than second cousins. Similarities indicate relationship. Degree of similarity indicates degree of genetic relatedness. If carefully measured, similarities could be used to reconstruct trees of genetic relationship.

In like manner, the macroevolutionary claim that all organisms are related explains why all organisms share similarities (e.g., the presence of RNA). The degrees of similarity among organisms can then be used to reconstruct trees of genetic relationship called *phylogenies*. Each tree of similarity can be used to construct a separate and apparently independent phylogeny. In this way one phylogeny can be developed from adult similarities (e.g., skeletal or muscular similarities), another from similarities in embryological development (e.g., similarities in order of organ development) and others from molecular similarities (e.g., similarities in amino acid sequences of cytochrome and blood plasma proteins). The trees produced from these different methods are generally very similar. This remarkable degree of concordance seems to be strong evidence in support of macroevolution. It is often offered as a defense of macroevolutionary theory and a challenge to other models to explain.[1]

On the other hand, similarities don't always denote genetic relatedness. First, even in macroevolutionary theory, some organismal similarities are not thought to be due to common descent. Squid eyes, for example, are often dissected in biology classes to help students understand the very similar eye of humans. Yet squid and human eyes are not thought to have been derived from a common ancestor. The same can be said of the origin of multicellularity in green, red and brown algae; the origin of wings in bats, pteranodons, birds and insects; the origin of the streamlined body form in fishes and whales; and countless other examples. This has led evolutionists to classify similarities into two categories—*homologies* (similarities due to genetic relationship) and *analogies* (similarities independently derived).

Analogies can be identified through the use of trees of similarity. Assuming the organisms in such a tree are related through a common ancestor, each tree then represents a possible phylogeny. From such phylogenies one can determine the order in which various features of the organisms would have come into existence if the groups had followed that evolutionary pathway. In this way it is possible to tell whether any given feature could have evolved just once or must have evolved more than once. With the assistance of computers, an increasing number of trees of similarity are being produced. One of the striking features of such trees is that analogies are being found to be a very common feature of life. Every tree that takes into account at least a couple dozen features and includes several major groups of organisms seems to encounter several noninherited similarities.[2]

Considering the fact that organisms are composed of millions or even billions of features, the true number of analogies is likely to be extremely high. Yet this does not seem to be consistent with evolutionary theory. In an evolutionary scenario, analogies are features formed independently in two different organismal groups. The pathway that evolution takes is thought to be so fraught with unpredictable events that the likelihood that two separate evolutionary pathways will end up at the same place is thought to be very low. This is the major theme of Stephen Jay Gould's book *Wonderful Life*.[3] If the evolutionary process were run over again, one would not expect to get the same organisms again. Only when a feature is extremely advantageous to the organism *and* easy to produce naturalistically can it be considered reasonable that it could have evolved more than once. Most features, however, are so very complex that it is not clear that any of them could be so easily produced as to make even one a probable event. In evolutionary theory analogies would be expected to be a very uncommon feature of life. If, on the other hand, the diversity of life is due to an intelligent Designer's creating a number of distinct organisms, analogies should be common, as is observed, and as will be more commonly recognized with time.

Second, organisms all share atomic and subatomic similarities to each other and to rocks on planetary surfaces and to gases in stellar atmospheres, but this does not indicate genetic relatedness. Nor does the degree of similarity indicate anything about the degree of relatedness.

Third, humans and other intelligences construct objects that possess similarities. The similarities in these cases do not indicate genetic relatedness, and the degree of similarity is not a measure of relatedness. Rather, the similarities are due to a combination of factors—common purpose (e.g., similarities among guns, among cars, among houses, among dishes), common materials (e.g., similarities among the products of glassblowers, among the products of carpenters, among the products of machinists) and common signature (e.g., the Impressionism of Monet, the columns of the Romans, the suspense of Poe).

If an intelligent Designer was responsible for the variety of life, we should expect similarities among organisms. It is also easy enough to see how that the more similar two adult organisms are, the more similar their molecules and embryology will be. If the intelligent Designer has a common purpose—the production of adult organisms—then embryonic forms and molecular structures were designed to produce the adult structures. Similarities in adults would be expected to be tied to similarities in embryology and molecules.

All organisms, for example, develop from a single cell. This means that any two organisms start out looking very similar. Two organisms that have similar adult forms *end* up looking very similar. The purpose of embryonic development is the same in each case—to efficiently produce an adult from an initial egg. Given that the starting points, the ending points, the purpose and producer of the process are similar or identical, one would expect similar development in organisms that are very similar as adults. In fact, one would expect the degree of adult similarity and the degree of developmental similarity to track each other quite well.

In like manner, similar adult forms would most likely involve construction by using similar materials. Thus one would expect degree of similarity of both molecules and development to track the degree of similarity among adults. This would explain the concordances in trees of similarity constructed from different types of data.

Besides the abundance of analogies, a second challenge to macroevolutionary theory are the *discordances* among trees of relationship. Identical methods of calculating similarity on different criteria of similarity produce similar but rarely identical trees of relationship. Since genetic relatedness might be expected to produce higher correspondence than would the actions of an intelligent Designer, the commonness of discordances seems to argue more in favor of a common Designer than in favor of macroevolution.

A third challenge comes from molecular similarities. Although a number of molecules show similarity across groups, other molecules do not. There appears to be evidence of many molecular discontinuities within the life of the earth. Those discontinuities appear to coincide with between-group gaps. If, for example, one looks at the blood serum protein similarities in turtles, one finds evidence of substantial drops in similarity across certain boundaries. Between the two primary types of turtles, cryptodires and pleurodires, for example, there is a substantial drop in serum similarity.[4] Serology studies such as this examine dozens of different proteins at the same time. At least some of the proteins must be very similar across the groups (for reasons considered above). Yet the similarity in some proteins does not cancel out the differences in the other molecules. This would suggest that many molecules are *very* different on opposite sides of the boundary. Many of the serum molecules are thus likely to indicate a molecular discontinuity between cryptodires and pleurodires. This discontinuity corresponds to the substantial gap in form that exists between the side-necked and vertical-necked turtles.

Further molecular studies, especially with individual molecules, are likely to demonstrate many more such discontinuities between major groups of life. A theory of intelligent design would predict that these discontinuities will correspond to gaps in form and reinforce the claim that major groups of life are not related by descent.

Embryological Recapitulation

One evidence of macroevolution popularly heralded in the later part of the nineteenth century was *embryological recapitulation.* According to this hypothesis, as organisms develop from a fertilized egg, they pass through stages very similar to the evolutionary stages of their ancestors. Each human, for example, starts as a single cell—as all life supposedly did—then develops through a wormlike stage, then a fishlike stage (complete with gill slits), then a froglike stage, then a stage in which there is a tail, and finally the stage of a human child.[5] In this way an organism's embryology (development) recapitulates (briefly repictures) its phylogeny (evolutionary history).

But recapitulation theory has fallen on hard times.[6] First, some organisms are thought to be a product of almost the opposite process. Some organisms are thought to have evolved by retaining juvenile characteristics into adulthood (paedomorphosis), such as by slowing down the development of all but the reproductive systems (neoteny). The axolotl, for example, is an example of a paedomorphic amphibian, retaining larval characteristics often to an advanced age. The human being is thought to be an example of neoteny, being an ape with an immature body but a mature reproductive system. The existence of such antirecapitulation transformations would indicate that recapitulation is not a general law of evolutionary development.

Second, if the theory is correct, it would seem to mean that organisms evolve by *adding* developmental stages to their ancestors' developmental process. Yet organisms that are thought to be more evolutionarily derived don't seem to have longer development. This might suggest that previous development was accelerated, but the genetic mechanism for this acceleration is unknown. Also, organisms do not seem to pass through earlier stages any faster than through later stages, and DNA does not seem to be longer or more complicated in evolutionarily more derived forms (such as different vertebrates). Another suggestion might be that earlier stages are selectively lost, but again no genetic mechanism is known to account for this, and it makes the origin of a coherent developmental sequence even more difficult.

Third, although developmental stages appear to be *broadly* similar to earlier evolutionary stages, when examined closely the similarities break down. In human development, for example, the fertilized egg is a diploid eukaryotic cell with twenty-three chromosome pairs—not a haploid, prokaryotic cell with a single strand of DNA from which we supposedly evolved. In like manner, the similarity between human developmental stages and worms and frogs breaks down very quickly upon close examination. The so-called gill slits in human development are not gill slits, and the "tail" in human development is not actually a tail. These things only bear superficial resemblance to those structures.

Fourth, in many cases development runs through stages in "incorrect" order for phylogeny. In sum, embryological recapitulation suffers from too many difficulties to be considered a viable theory. It has been rejected by a number of evolutionary biologists and has even been expunged from textbooks over the years.[7]

Yet embryological recapitulation theory is not dead. The general similarities between embryology and phylogeny are so compelling that they demand an explanation. Some feel that only macroevolutionary theory can provide that explanation.[8] I would suggest that an intelligent Designer hypothesis provides yet another explanation. In this hypothesis, as claimed above, the optimally designed transformation of an organism from a single cell is its *embryology*. Evolutionary biologists have also designed what they feel is the most efficient series of transformations connecting the ancestral cell with a given organism of today. The adult embodiment of the stages in this process makes up the organism's *phylogeny*. The general similarities between embryology and phylogeny are due to similar endpoints demanding similar pathways and broadly similar designs resulting from a higher-order similarity in intelligences. The differences in detail are simply the result of the lower-order differences between the intelligence that designed life and the intelligences that designed evolutionary phylogenies. In this sense intelligent design provides a *better* explanation for embryological recapitulation than does evolutionary theory.

Nested Hierarchy of Form

Given that a set of objects have different degrees of similarity, there are still many ways that such similarities could suggest groupings or classifications of the objects. Let's say we are considering two characteristics of some objects— their length and their color. Each characteristic has a linear spectrum of possibilities, and their combination has an areal "spectrum" of possibilities. We can lay down two axes perpendicular to each other, where the rectangle described by the two axes represents all possible combinations of length and color (figure 6.1a).

Let's now consider a few of many possible ways the objects could be distributed in our length-color character space. First it could be that objects occupy the space randomly (figure 6.1b). In this case no one classification of objects suggests itself—all seem equally arbitrary. Another possibility is that all the objects are evenly spaced in our length-color plane (figure 6.1c). Once again, any classification seems arbitrary. Unlike the random distribution of points, however, the orderly arrangement here leads one to believe that there is cause for the pattern. Yet another possibility is shown in figure 6.1d. As in the previous figure, there appears to be a pattern to be explained, but here a way of classifying the objects appears evident (figure 6.1e).

It seems that the similarities group some objects together, distinct from other objects (groups a through h), yet even some of these lower-level groupings can be grouped, or nested, into distinct higher-level groups (groups 1, 2 and 3). This "nested hierarchy" of form not only allows for a way to classify the objects, but also begs for an explanation. We could imagine that as we considered a third characteristic of the objects, figure 6.1's examples could each be placed into three-dimensional character space. As we added more and more characters, the same could be said about the distribution of objects in n- dimensional character space.

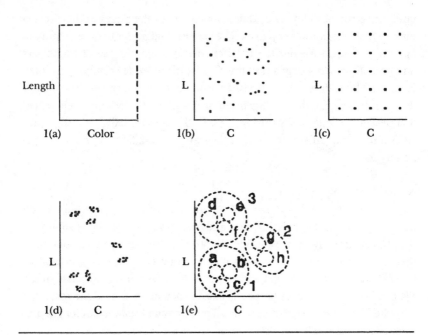

Figure 6.1. (a) 2-dimensional character space; (b) a random scatter of objects; (c) a regular pattern; (d) a nested hierarchy pattern; and (e) the classification of the pattern in d.

When we study organisms, we measure many characteristics. We can then plot our organisms in *n*- dimensional character space (sometimes called *morphospace*) and see how organisms are distributed. When we do, we find that they are distributed as in figure 6.1d—in a nested hierarchy of form. This has permitted the hierarchical classification of organisms—of species within genera, genera within families, families within orders, orders within classes, classes within phyla, and phyla within kingdoms. It also begs for an explanation. Why are organisms in a nested hierarchy of form?

Macroevolutionists maintain that nested hierarchy is the result of macroevolution—and some claim it can *only* be due to that.[9] After all, evolutionary change is to have followed the path of an "evolutionary tree"—a trunk that branched into large limbs, which in turn branched into smaller limbs, which branched into smaller branches, which branched into even smaller branches, which finally branched into twigs. The twigs are species that can be grouped together into genera (small branches) and then into families (larger branches) and so on.

But the analogy of the evolutionary tree as an explanation for the nested hierarchy of biological form meets up with a few difficulties. If it is a "tree," then it is a very unusual tree indeed. First, the twigs of a real tree (analogous to modern species) tend to occupy most of the space available to them. This is because the twigs can proliferate more quickly than the large limbs, and the large limbs cannot diverge more rapidly than one twig at a time. The twigs thus tend to fill in the gaps. As a result, the twigs (when you ignore the branches to which they are connected) tend to fill space more or less randomly (as in figure 6.1b). This is unlike modern species, which are distributed much more like figure 6.1d. Most of morphospace is unfilled.

It would appear that (1) on the average, species do not proliferate as rapidly as larger groups are produced, and/or (2) large groups are produced in larger steps than species-by-species, and/or (3) species have a *much* higher extinction rate than higher groups. The first two possibilities run counter to gradualist theory and would demand an explanation for the rapid and/or huge-step origin of major groups. Although such proposals have been made, no suitable mechanism for such an origin has been found. Although the last possibility has an element of truth in it, it does not seem capable of explaining the distribution of species. Since higher groups become extinct only when every species in the group becomes extinct, species have a higher probability of becoming extinct than higher groups. Studies in the fossil record indicate, however, that most extinctions are more or less indiscriminate or random.[10] If that is the case, then a random extinction among organisms distributed randomly in morphospace would simply produce another random distribution of organisms—just rarer. That in fact happens in a real tree, for twigs are more susceptible to death than larger branches, and still they are distributed more like a random pattern than a nested hierarchical pattern. In order to produce the pattern in figure 6.1d by extinction, one needs to be selective in extinction—selectively preserving species most similar to their ancestors. It is unclear that any currently proposed macroevolutionary process could truly produce a nested hierarchy of form.

Second, in the tree analogy, as one travels from the tree's base to its twigs, one is going forward through time. As one does, the trunk gradually diverges into branches, the large branches diverge into smaller branches and so on. By this we see that trees grow by gradual divergence. If the analogy is to hold, organismal groups should have arisen by gradual divergence. Yet the gaps in form between living groups also exist in the fossil record. As one goes back in time, organismal groups tend not to converge in morphology, but remain distinct. Most major groups remain identifiable by modern characters and distinct from their supposed ancestors all the way back to their oldest fossil representatives. This would seem to imply that the branching event of one major group from another never did occur.

Third, in a real tree the connection between branches and their sub-branches is clearly seen. In the fossil record, on the other hand, transitions between major groups are rarely evidenced. Interspecific transitional forms seem to be rare to absent in the fossil record,[11] and transitional series between major groups are conspicuously rare to absent.

Fourth, in the tree analogy, the number of major branches increases through time. The branches arise due to the proliferation of twigs, so the number of twigs increases faster than numbers of branches. In the fossil record, however, such a "cone of increasing diversity" is not observed. Instead, the number of major groups we have today was achieved early in earth history, when species diversity was low. In fact, the number of classes of arthropods and echinoderms at the time of the first appearance of each of these groups was actually *higher* than it is at present.[12] This would argue—as do the distribution of species, higher group stasis and the paucity of interme-diates—that major groups do not arise due to a proliferation of species. Yet no evolutionary mechanism for how this transformation *did* occur has yet been found.

Another possible explanation for the nested hierarchy of biological form is in an intelligent Designer. Think of it this way: Humans have designed a large number of different types of teaspoons. Some are made of stainless steel, others of silver. Some have monograms on them, others do not. Some have artistic designs engraved on their handles, others do not. Yet they are all classifiable as teaspoons. And though there are many types of tablespoons, many types of soup spoons and many types of serving spoons, all these types of spoons can be classified together as spoons. The wide variety of spoons can be classified with the wide variety of forks and the wide variety of knives as silverware; and the silverware can be classified with plates, bowls and cups as tableware. Tableware can be classified with furniture and appliances as housewares, and so on. Humans, without so intending, create objects that are distributed in character space in a nested hierarchy of form.

If life is the result of an intelligence analogous to humankind's, then a nested hierarchy of life forms would be the expected result. Furthermore, an origin by intelligent design allows the possibility that organisms originated at times and/or places where fossilization did not occur. It also allows for the possibility that no transitional forms were involved at all. Either way, the lack of transitional forms, higher group stasis, and the inverted cone of diversity would be explained. And if the gaps between major groups were so large that speciation has had insufficient time to bridge them, the general stasis of major groups and the marked nested hierarchy of biological form through time would be an expected result. In this sense intelligent design is more successful at explaining the nested hierarchy of biological form than is modern evolutionary theory.

Suboptimal Improvisations

Near-optimum form is often thought to be equally predictable from the always-perfecting process of natural selection and the optimum design of an intelligent Creator. Stephen Jay Gould, on the other hand, has suggested that the theories are distinguishable by *imperfections*.[13] As he reasons, the evolutionary process, being blind to purpose, limited in resources and constrained by history, might be expected to produce less-than-optimal designs. These "suboptimal improvisations" of evolution would be expected in an evolutionary process, but not in the design of an intelligent Creator. Gould's showcase example is the panda, which, because of the constraints of being descended from five-fingered bears, lacks an opposable thumb. Yet the inefficient, blind process of evolution provided the panda with a "second-best" solution: an extension of the radial sesamoid bone in the wrist which can function as an immovable "thumb." This thumb is used by the panda to strip leaves off bamboo shoots for food. Such a less-than-optimal design is evidence, Gould claims, for evolution and not intelligent design.

There are at least two reasons to doubt that suboptimal improvisations are truly suboptimal. First of all, we are far from understanding the complexity of individual organisms, let alone the entire ecosystem in which that organism lives. What appears to be less than optimal design to us with our limited knowledge may actually be an optimal design when the entire system is considered. Consider the thickness of armor plating on the side of a warship. Since the purpose of such plating is to protect the ship from the puncture of an incoming warhead, it is advantageous to make the plating as thick as possible. Yet the plating on actual warships is much thinner than it could be made. The reason is, of course, that an increase in plating thickness makes the ship heavier, and thus slower. A less mobile ship is more likely to get hit more often and less likely to get to where it is needed when it is needed. The actual thickness of the armor on a warship is a tradeoff—not so thin as to make the ship too easily sinkable, and not so thick as to make the ship too slow. We know too little about the complexity of organisms and the environment in which they live to conclude that any one particular feature is actually less than optimal.

In the case of the panda, it's not clear that an opposable thumb would be any better design than its current wrist-bone extension. My sixth-grade career in basketball was cut short by a pass made to me when my wonderfully designed opposable thumb was oriented in such a way so as to receive the full force of the ball along its main axis. At that moment I would have preferred that my thumb had been an extension of a bone in my wrist than a dexterous digit with two well-designed hinge joints. So it's not at all clear that an immovable stub would be any less desirable to a panda than a relatively fragile, hinged, opposable thumb.

Second, all claimed suboptimal improvisations seem to work efficiently enough. The thumb of the panda, for example, seems quite efficient at stripping bamboo leaves. In fact, according to evolutionary history, the panda's thumb has probably provided food for the panda for millions of years. The fact that the panda is now endangered seems to be due to dwindling food reserves and the encroachment of human beings—neither of which is likely to have been prevented if the panda had had an opposable thumb.

Vestigial Organs

According to macroevolutionary theory, not only do species, genera and higher groups of organisms come and go, but so do organismal structures. Species will linger in dwindling populations (e.g., endangered species) for long periods of time before submitting to extinction. In like manner, organismal structures probably linger with reduced function for long periods of time before finally disappearing. These organs with reduced or no function are called *vestigial.*

Although many organs once thought vestigial have been found to have function, others are sure to have at least a reduced function from the past (e.g., hip bones that appear briefly in the embryology of sperm whales and small appendage bones that are found in some snakes). These then are less-than-optimal organs that would seem to be evidence of evolution rather than intelligent design.[14]

A serious problem with this argument for evolution is that whereas vestigial organs are known, nascent organs are not. If evolution were true, one would expect to see not just organs "going out" but also organs "coming in." These new organs would be called *nascent* organs. The absence of such organs would seem to argue that although we have evidence of degeneration from an earlier, more optimal design, we lack evidence of a move toward a new optimal design. It would seem that if an intelligent Designer created optimal designs *in the past* and life's history has been a move away from that optimum, the presence of vestigial organs and the absence of nascent organs would be better explained by intelligent design than by evolutionary theory.

Macrobiogeography

The last major class of evidences in support of evolution from the living world includes those in the field of biogeography. There are two sorts of biogeographical evidences. One type of claim is that very similar species are often found near to one another, as if they evolved from one another. This type of biogeography, which I call *microbiogeography*, has many supporting examples. Microbiogeography is evidence for microevolution (the evolution of populations) and the origin of species, however, *not* for macroevolution and the origin of major groups. What I call *macrobiogeography* is the claim that major types of organisms tend to be associated with one another.

There are very few examples of macrobiogeographical evidences for macroevolution, and none of them is very strong. The best-known claim is the concentration of marsupials in Australia. But there are several reasons that marsupials in Australia are actually a poor example. First, all marsupials are not in Australia. The Virginia opossum of North America, for example, is a marsupial. It is thought to have come from South America, not Australia. Thus not all similar organisms *are* in the same area. Second, in the fossil record marsupials are known from every continent.[15] Third, marsupials are the oldest fossil mammals known from Africa, Antarctica and Australia—in that order.[16] The fossil record seems to show a migration of marsupials from somewhere around the intersection of the Eurasian and African continents and then a survival in only the continents farthest from their point of origin (South America and Australia). The same major groups of marsupials (opossums) are found in both South America and Australia. Macroevolutionists claim that these major groups of marsupials are together because they evolved from a common ancestor, but the evidence can be at least as well explained as similar organisms (fit for similar environments and with similar capabilities) traveling more or less together to similar environments.

Fossil Order

If one were able to see the history of life in accelerated playback, macroevolution should show up as major changes in life on earth. It turns out that we can, in a way, see life in this accelerated mode. It is generally thought that the geologic column of rocks was formed over the course of most of earth history. Every once in a while those rocks preserved a sample of that life—an occasional motion-picture frame in earth history. As a result, a review of the fossils (picture frames) from the deepest (oldest) rocks to the present should provide an accelerated playback of earth history. It's only reasonable that evolutionary theorists should turn to the fossil record for evidence of macroevolutionary theory. Three types of evidences for evolution are found in the *order* of the fossils.

First, if evolution were true, the fossil record "playback" should show an ever-changing set of organisms. This would allow researchers to identify where one is in the geologic column (and time) by the set of fossils known in that section of the column. And truly such a wholesale change in fossils is seen through the fossil record, and an order has been found that allows relative dating by the suites of fossils that are known from particular rocks.

Second, if evolution were an ongoing process, species should be coming and going. At any given time there should be species that have just recently come to be (young species), species that have been around for a long time and are about ready to go extinct (old species), and species in between (middle-aged species). And as one moves above and below that group of fossils, one should see suites of species that gradually show less and less similarity with the original group. This is exactly what is seen in the fossil record. In the Cenozoic (the uppermost deposits), for example, the frequency of species that are known to be alive today gradually drops to zero as one travels lower— or further into the past.

Third, if macroevolution were true and we knew the evolutionary phylogeny of an organism or group of organisms, then one would expect to see the members of that pathway appearing in the order predicted by the phylogeny. Such a correspondence between first-appearance order and phylogeny *is* seen in the fossil record. In the phylogeny of humankind, for example, the following are the steps (with the radiometric time of first appearance of each step in parentheses, in millions of years before the present): bacteria (3500[17]); protists (1500-1800[18]); invertebrate animals (590-570[19]); jawless fish (517-510[20]), jawed fish (424-409[21]), bony lobe-finned fish (408[22]), amphibians (377-363[23]), reptiles (323-311[24]), mammals (210-208[25]), primates (70-

65^{26}), apes (22^{27}), hominid (5.5^{28}), *Homo* ($1.8?-1.6^{29}$), *H. sapiens* (0.1^{30}), art (0.05), civilization (0.01). Within this list is recorded the general correspondence between the first appearance of vertebrate classes and their phylogeny. Similarly, arthropod classes tend to appear in phylogenetic order. Finally, in a most remarkable manner, the plant phyla appear in the order predicted by their phylogeny.[31]

Although at first glance the order of fossils seems to be good evidence for macroevolutionary theory, it does present a couple of difficulties. The first concerns the issue of polarity. Although macroevolutionary theory predicts major changes over the course of time, it is incapable of predicting ahead of time what the direction or nature of change will be. For example, parasites have limited internal complexity, but macroevolutionists generally do not know whether they were derived from simpler animals without internal complexity or whether they were derived from more complex organisms but have since lost internal complexity due in some part to disuse. Green algae are thought to be related to land plants because of similar photosynthetic chemistry, but without the fossil record it might have been impossible to determine whether land plants evolved from algae or algae from plants. Similarly, without the fossil record it might have been difficult to determine whether marine mammals evolved from or into land mammals. As a result, to use the fossil record to verify the "predictions" of phylogeny may in some cases (or all?) be assuming the order of fossils to prove it. The details of this relationship need to be studied in detail to determine how this affects the use of fossil-record order to evidence evolution.

Second, the correspondence between phylogeny and the fossil record is not as strong as it might first seem. When the order of *all* kingdoms, phyla and classes is compared with the most reasonable phylogenies, over 95 percent of all the lines are not consistent with the order in the fossil record.[32] The only statistically significant exceptions are the orders of first appearances of the phyla of plants and the classes of vertebrates and arthropods. Yet these three lineages also order organismal groups from sea-dwellers to land-dwellers. The land-plant phyla, for example, are in a simple sequence from plants that need standing water to survive (e.g., algae and bryophytes) to those that can survive extreme desiccation (e.g., the cacti). The vertebrate classes go from sea-dwellers (fish) to land/sea creatures (amphibians) to land creatures (reptiles, mammals), to flying creatures (birds). The arthropod classes go from sea-dwellers (e.g., trilobites, crustaceans) to land-dwellers (e.g., insects). So it's not clear that macroevolution is truly a good explanation for the order of fossil first appearances of major groups of life. Such a radical idea as a global flood, for example, which gradually overcame first the sea and then the land, actually explains the primary order of major groups in the fossil record (sea to land) better than macroevolutionary theory.[33]

The general features of the fossil record that *are* explained by evolutionary theory are at least as well explained by other theories. The existence of a Creator who introduced organisms on the earth in a particular order could explain the general change in organisms through the record, but so could the effects of a global flood as it successively sampled from a biogeographically zoned distribution of organisms. The general change in organisms through time can be predicted by any one and all of these three theories (macroevolution, progressive creation, global deluge). On the other hand, the rarity or absence of evidence for transitions between major groups and the fact the major groups do not converge on one another as one goes back in the fossil record seem to argue that major groups were introduced in the fossil record only *after* they were fully formed. This is more consistent with creative order and global deluge theories than with macroevolutionary theory. As for the linear relationship of species similarity above and below a particular level in the geologic column, this can be just as well explained by global deluge theory or progressive creation theory as it is by macroevolution. In deluge theory, different species are found in different preflood environments and get mixed with species from adjacent environments, providing the species similarity relationship. Continual introduction of species whether by evolution or creation would produce the same relationship. In short, all fossil-record order can be at least as well explained by order of creation decided by creative fiat or ocean-to-land burial of organisms in a diverse world overcome by global deluge as it is by macroevolution.

Fossil Transitions

If macroevolution is true, then organisms have made many substantial transformations in the course of history. The preservation of these transformations might be expected in the fossil record. Series of fossil species like the horse series, the elephant series, the camel series, the mammal-like reptile series, the early birds and early whales all seem to be strong evidence of evolution. Another class of fossil evidence comes in individual *stratomorphic intermediates*. These are fossils that stand intermediate between the group from which they are descendent and the one to which they are ancestral—both in stratigraphic position and in morphology. They have a structure that stands between the structure of their ancestors and that of their descendants. However, they are also found in the fossil record as younger than the oldest fossils of the ancestral group and older than the oldest fossils of the descendent group.

Stratomorphic intermediate species and organismal groups should be a common feature of the fossil record. And examples of stratomorphic intermediates do exist. Mammal-like reptiles stand between reptiles and mammals, both in the position of their fossils and in the structure of their bones. The same can be said of the anthracosaurs, which stand between amphibians and reptiles, and the phenacodontids, which stand between the horses and their claimed ancestors. In like manner, some fossil genera are stratomorphic intermediates in the group in which they are classified. They are the oldest fossils known in the group and most similar to the group from which they are supposedly descendent. Examples include *Pikaia* among the chordates, *Archaeopteryx* among the birds, *Baragwanathia* among lycopods, *Ichthyostega* among the amphibians, *Purgatorius* among the primates, *Pakicetus* among the whales and *Proconsul* among the hominoids.

Once again, the existence of stratomorphic intermediate groups and species seems to be good evidence for evolution. However, the stratomorphic intermediate evidences are not without difficulty for evolutionary theory. First, none of the stratomorphic intermediates have intermediate structures. Although the entire organism is intermediate in structure, it's the *combination* of structures that is intermediate, not the nature of the structures themselves. Each of these organisms appears to be a fully functional organism full of fully functional structures. *Archaeopteryx*, for example, is thought to be intermediate between reptiles and birds because it has bird structures (e.g., feathers) and reptile structures (e.g., teeth, forelimb claws). Yet the teeth, the claws, the feathers and all other known structures of *Archaeopteryx* appear to be fully functional. The teeth seem fully functional as teeth, the claws as claws, and the feathers as any flight feathers of modern birds. It is merely the *combination* of structures that is intermediate, not the structures themselves. Stephen Jay Gould calls the resultant organisms "mosaic forms"[34] or "chimeras." As such they are really no more intermediate than any other member of their group. In fact, there are *many* such "chimeras" that live today (e.g., the platypus, which lays eggs like a reptile and has hair and produces milk like a mammal). Yet these are not considered transitional forms by evolutionists because they are not found as intermediates in stratigraphic position.

As a result, the total list of claimed transitional forms is very small (the above list is very nearly complete) compared to the total number of mosaic forms. The frequency seems intuitively too low for evolutionary theory. The very low frequency of stratomorphic intermediates may be nothing more than the low percentage of mosaic forms that happen to fall in the correct stratigraphic position by chance—perhaps because of random introduction of species by a Creator or the somewhat randomized burial of organisms in a global deluge.

Second, stratomorphic intermediates tend to be found in groups that we have already seen show a fossil-record order consistent with evolutionary order—that is, vertebrates and plants. They are absent among the groups of invertebrates. In some cases a series of intermediates cannot even be imagined. More often the imagined intermediates cannot have survived. Transitions from one major group of organisms to another are challenges to the ingenuity of even the most capable macroevolutionists.

Just as the more general order may be due to a pattern of a Creator's introduction or of the advance of a global flood, these few stratomorphic intermediates may be explainable in the same way. If, for example, the general order of the fossil record is due to introduction of organisms, then one might occasionally expect stratomorphic intermediates to have been created in the sequence between the two groups. Likewise, on an earth that is zoned biologically, fully functional, structurally intermediate organisms are likely to be geographically located between the two groups they lie between structurally. An advancing global flood would then tend to land structural intermediates between the other two groups in the fossil record. Thus, whereas the mosaic nature of claimed "transitional forms" presents a challenge to evolutionary theory, that and the existence of stratomorphic intermediates *are* consistent with progressive creation and global deluge theories.

Evidence That Evolution Leaves Unexplained

Complexity. Anyone who has taken college biochemistry has been impressed with the extraordinary complexity of replication, transcription, the Krebs cycle and other features of living things. For those who did not take such a course, these are a few of the many chemical processes that occur within any one of your trillions of body cells at any given moment. Photosynthesis, as an example of a subcellular process, is thought to involve as many as five hundred chemical steps—of which we "fully" understand only a few. Yet a number of these kinds of processes occur spontaneously within individual cells.

At a higher level, introductory biology classes often require the biology student to understand the general structure and function of Golgi bodies, smooth and rough endoplasmic reticulum, microbodies, lysosomes, mitochondria, nucleus, chromosomes and the cell membrane. These are some of the fascinating and complex structures found *within* cells of our body. At an even higher level, in advanced biology we learn the classes of cardiac, smooth muscle, striated muscle, epidermal and other tissues. These are special associations of specialized cells that make up larger structures of our body.

At an even higher level, we learn early in our education of human organs—the heart, lungs, liver, gall bladder, kidney, gonads, brain and the like. There are many such complex working elements within each of our bodies. Science education has also told us about systems in our bodies—circulatory, respiratory, urinary, digestive, nervous, skeletal, muscular and so on. Each of these systems challenges our powers of memorization and understanding.

At a higher level still, there are countless fascinating and complex interrelationships between one organism and others. For example, living in our intestines there is a diverse set of microorganisms from which we benefit almost as much as they benefit from us. These organisms break down molecules we cannot break down, providing us with food we would otherwise lack. In return, they are provided with a comfortable home (to them!) and a constant supply of food. Similar cases of mutual symbiosis exist throughout our world (e.g., cellulose-lignin-digesting microorganisms in the guts of termites; sulfur-reducing bacteria in ocean-vent tubeworms; algae and fungi in lichens; photosynthetic microorganisms in corals).

At a higher level again, communities of organisms are made up of a complex arrangement of a large number of organisms—herbivores and carnivores; pollinators and flowering plants; decomposers; under-story and upper-story plants, and so on.

Higher than these, the earth and its living organisms exist together in a great network of complex interactions—oxygen used by animals must be produced by photosynthesizers, and carbon dioxide used by plants must be released by animals. The complex interaction of the earth and its life can be seen in how the earth and its life have responded to the changes that humankind has made (such as the interaction of fossil-fuel burning and global climate, the interaction of aerosol sprays and ozone).

On a level even above this, the earth exists in a complex arrangement of planets, asteroids, moons, stars and galaxies in such a way as to allow life on earth to exist and persist.

Each of these levels features a complexity that is staggering to the human mind—a complexity greater than any that in our experience can be produced by nonintelligent natural cause. If we follow the principle of appealing only to principles that are reasonable in our experience, then the complexity of any one of these levels seems to require an appeal to an intelligent cause. However, the *total* complexity is at least the sum of the complexities of each level. If the complexity of each level suggests an intelligent cause, the total complexity screams for an intelligent cause. Macroevolutionary theory has never successfully explained the acquisition of any level of this complexity, let alone the total complexity.

Integration. As if the basic complexity of things were not enough, the integration of that complexity is truly astounding. Not only do subcellular chemical processes involve a large number of complex molecules and chemical steps, but those items and events are connected in a well-balanced and well-timed series of items and steps to produce a well-integrated process. Similarly, the workings of subcellular organelles, cells in tissues, tissues in organs, organs in systems, systems in bodies, organisms with other organisms, organisms in communities, and communities in the biosphere all show staggering integration. As with the complexity of these items and events on any given level, such a level of integration has never been observed to arise from nonintelligent natural law and process. Integration seems to argue for intelligent cause.

In addition, the integration that is so striking *within* levels is even more striking *between* levels. Not only do subcellular organelle systems and chemical processes show integration, but the chemical and organelle systems are themselves linked together, and must be for the cell to survive. Even more impressive, a similar integration exists between all levels. Once again, this level of integration is unexplained by evolutionary theory but is addressable by intelligent cause theory.

Another interesting point here concerns the observed structure of integration. Chemical processes lie within subcellular organelles, subcellular organelles within cells, cells within tissues. There is a nested hierarchy of complexity and integration of life on earth. This nested hierarchy of complexity might be expected if it came about by means of the same intelligent cause that brought about the nested hierarchy of classification of biological form. It is not expected by macroevolutionary theory.

Aesthetics. One striking characteristic of life unexplained by evolution is its aesthetic nature. Mathematicians often find aesthetic beauty in elegant proofs. The remarkable integration of organismal complexity strikes mathematicians as another example of profound beauty. Artists see beauty in life's symmetry and its vast array of color. The countless pieces of fine and performing art sparked by the symmetry and colors of life testify to the level of beauty perceived by artists worldwide through all of earth history.

This magnificent beauty, observed across a variety of levels among living organisms, cannot be explained by macroevolutionary theory. It is, however, consistent with an intelligent cause for life—a Designer whose tastes and predilections human beings may share.

Table 6.1. Types of data explained by theories of macroevolution and intelligent creator. "?" indicates possible or partial explanation.

Macroevolution	Intelligent Creator
Adult similarities	Adult similarities
Embryological similarities	Embryological similarities
Molecular similarities	Molecular similarities
Correspondence of similarities	Correspondence of similarities
	Abundant analogies
	Discordances in phylogenies
Embryological recapitulation	Embryological recapitulation
Evidences?	Evidences
	Counterevidences
Nested hierarchy of life	Nested hierarchy of life
	Nested hierarchy of complexity
	Large morphological gaps
	Molecular discontinuities
	Higher group stasis
Stratomorphic intermediates	Stratomorphic intermediates?
	Mosaic/chimera nature of
	Rarity of
	Inverted cone of diversity
Suboptimal improvisations	Suboptimal improvisations?
Vestigial organs	Vestigial organs?
	Absence of nascent organs
Macrobiogeographic evidences	Macrobiogeographic evidences?
Water-to-land fossil order	Water-to-land fossil order
	Nonevolutionary order of first appearances
	Organismal complexity
	Integration of complexity
	Aesthetics of life

Conclusion

Macroevolutionary theory explains a large number of seemingly independent categories of evidence (see table 6.1). The many *corresponding similarities* among adults, embryologies and molecules of organisms are explained as characters shared by reason of common descent. The *nested hierarchy of form* is explained as due to the successive branching pattern of evolutionary transformation. *Suboptimal improvisations* are explained as structures that are suboptimal because of the transformation of organisms by purposeless, infinitely myopic process of evolution. *Vestigial organs* are explained as organs that have fallen into disuse because of organic change. The *biogeographic distribution* of Australian marsupials is explained as due to the origin and diversification of Australian marsupials solely in Australia. The *change in fossils* through the fossil record is explained as due to the continuous change of organisms through time. The *orders of first appearance* of plant phyla, vertebrate classes, arthropod classes and organisms in the phylogeny of humankind are explained by major evolutionary transformations being preserved in the fossil record. *Fossil series* and *stratomorphic intermediates* are explained as specially preserved steps in the evolutionary process. Macroevolution is a powerful theory of explanation for a wide variety of physical data.

But macroevolution is not the only theory capable of explaining such a wide variety of data. I would maintain that the claims of Scripture provide us with a model that can give a better explanation of far more of the major features of life than evolution (again, see table 6.1). According to the Bible, God is an all-knowing, intelligent being with immeasurable beauty and glory. According to Scripture, he created all things, including life on the earth, in such a way that they reflect his very nature (including his intelligence and his beauty). We infer from the nature of other things he created that he fashioned all things in a mature form in a hierarchical pattern. In the case of life, we are told that he created a number of distinct kinds of organisms. These organisms have been allowed to change since the time of introduction. And we are told that God created humankind in his own image, to reflect him in unique ways (e.g., to reason in similar ways, to appreciate aesthetics in similar ways and to produce hierarchical pattern in similar ways). We are also told that sometime after the creation God judged the earth with a global deluge.

A single wise Designer creating a variety of organisms to construct a fully integrated biosphere explains the *corresponding similarities* among adults, embryologies and molecules which are traditionally used to evidence evolution. It also explains the high frequency of *analogies,* the *discordances in trees of relationship* and possibly *molecular discontinuities* that evolution cannot explain. A wise Designer might well produce embryologies that are generally similar and specifically different from phylogenies engineered by human minds—thus explaining both *embryological recapitulation evidences* and the *counterevidences* that are challenges to current evolutionary theory. A wise Designer who creates in nested hierarchy of form explains the *nested hierarchy of life* explained by evolutionary theory and the *nested hierarchy of complexity* that is not explained by evolutionary theory. Distinct kinds of organisms' being created in the recent past explains the *large gaps* between major groups of organisms, *higher group stasis,* the *mosaic/chimera nature and rarity of stratomorphic intermediates* and the *inverted cone of diversity,* which are not explained by evolutionary theory. *Suboptimal improvisations,* thought to be confirmations of evolutionary theory, may turn out to be optimal designs when the entire ecosystem is considered. Environmental changes and genetic errors introduced since the creation can explain *vestigial organs,* traditionally explained in the context of evolutionary theory.

If intelligent design were the only source of biological complexity and innovation, then the *absence of nascent organs* would be explained, as it is not in evolutionary theory. Similar organisms' migrating together into similar environments and postcreation diversification within created groups may explain *biogeographic evidences for macroevolution.* A global deluge that gradually buried organisms already filling a well-integrated biosphere explains the *general water-to-land fossil order* as well as *stratomorphic intermediates* among the plants and vertebrates, often used as evidence for evolution. At the same time, it explains the *general nonevolutionary order of higher group appearance,* the *rarity of stratomorphic intermediates* and *higher group stasis,* which are not explained by evolutionary theory. The high level of intelligence of the Creator explains the high level of life's *complexity* and *integration of complexity,* unexplained by evolutionary theory. Finally, the aesthetic nature of the Creator explains the *strong aesthetic components* of life, which again cannot be explained by evolutionary theory.

A hypothesis of divine Designer and Judge based on biblical claims is much more successful at explaining the major features of life than is macroevolutionary theory. However, the matter need not be left here. In the next chapter we will investigate human language and linguistic capacity. We will see that these features of human beings are utterly unlike the various abilities of other species, and that they could not have evolved in the way Darwin and his followers have thought.

Bibliography

Davis, Percival, and Dean H. Kenyon. *Of Pandas and People.* 2nd ed. Dallas: Haughton, 1993. [B]

Denton, Michael. *A Theory in Crisis.* Bethesda, Md.: Adler, 1986. [I]

Frair, Wayne, and Percival Davis. *A Case for Creation.* 3rd ed. Chicago: Moody Press, 1983. [I]

Gould, Stephen Jay. *Wonderful Life: The Burgess Shale and the Nature of History.* New York: Norton, 1989. [I]

Teaching Science in a Climate of Controversy: A View from the American Scientific Affiliation. Ipswich, Mass.: American Scientific Affiliation, 1988. [B]

7
ORIGIN OF THE HUMAN LANGUAGE CAPACITY: IN WHOSE IMAGE?

John W. Oller Jr. & John L. Omdahl

T his chapter explores the undeniable capacity of human beings to express themselves through various representational systems, of which language is the most abstract and the most versatile. Other representational systems include our senses and our abilities to move, touch, point to and otherwise reveal to ourselves and others our reactions to the happenings of our experience. In what follows a linguist teams up with a biochemist to show how the language capacity is unique to human beings and how it reveals a supremely articulated special design.

The human language capacity is rivaled only by another cascading network of representational systems, the unfolding complexities of DNA, which provide the basis for all living things in the biosphere. Of the many unsolved mysteries hidden within the delicately interrelated systems of DNA's biological language, perhaps the most challenging mystery of them all is how the human language capacity is specified in the human genome. Science is still very far from explaining this ultimate biological mystery, but the search for the elusive ghost in the machinery is an adventure that scientists can hardly resist. We pick up the historical thread with Charles Darwin and follow key elements of the discussion up to the present.

The Orthodox Explanation

In the 1874 revised edition of *The Descent of Man,* Darwin wrote, "I cannot doubt that language owes its origin to the imitation and modification of various natural sounds, the voices of other animals, and man's own instinctive cries."[1] He asks if "some wise ape-like animal" might not "have imitated the growl of a beast of prey, and thus told his fellow-monkeys the nature of the expected danger?" In the next clause he supposes that "this would have been a first step in the formation of a language."

In this chapter we ask if it is true that the human language capacity, as it is understood by contemporary linguistic sciences, is an elaborated system of animal cries and calls. Is it merely a short step beyond the communication systems of a chimp or a gorilla, or is it something more and (more importantly) of an entirely different nature? Are human beings just beasts with more flexible and better-developed vocal systems, or are we utterly unique creatures who approximate the divine traits of an invisible, omniscient (all-knowing), omnipresent (always present) and omnipotent (all-powerful) Creator who, according to the Bible, stands both within and outside the space-time continuum?

What can we learn from a close examination of the human language capacity? Are there any other structures known to science that are like the textual forms and conversations that result from the exercise of the human language capacity? What is this language capacity, and where did it come from?

The Essence of Intellect

Darwin was intrigued by the fact that all the higher powers of the human mind seem to be inevitably linked to the language capacity. He said, "A complex train of thought can no more be carried on without the aid of words, whether spoken or silent, than a long calculation without the use of figures or algebra."[2] Darwin insisted on the now-rejected theory of Jean Baptiste Lamarck, "the principle of the inherited effects of use,"[3] which Darwin claimed would help to explain the transition from apelike creatures to humans. This, apparently, by all modern accounts was an error. However, Darwin was correct in asserting a close relation between language abilities and intellect. He supposed that "the mental powers in some early progenitor of man must have been more highly developed than in any existing ape, even before the most imperfect form of speech could have come into use,"[4] but apparently he did not see the full extent to which the whole of mathematics is dependent on the abstract logic underlying natural language systems.

Darwin seems to have identified language closely with speech, though speech is only one of the garments that language wears when it goes out to meet the press. Besides speech, surface forms that language may assume include all the forms of writing, verbal thought, the conventional gestures that accompany speech, and all of the sign systems of the deaf.

According to Darwin, the mental powers in question must have developed little by little in many steps. He proposed an analogy between the acquisition of any sign system—such as the singing of a particular kind of bird or the acquisition of a particular language (English, say, or Mandarin Chinese) by a young child[5]—and the origin of the human language capacity, which he supposed must have taken place over long eons of time. He observed that as the young organism matures, the appropriate expressive system is acquired gradually. Therefore, he concluded, the language capacity in human beings must also have developed gradually. Darwin supposed that there must have been many generations of related but prehuman predecessors that gradually built up elaborated sign systems that would eventually turn into the present-day human language capacity.

He could not have imagined, writing as he did in the latter quarter of the nineteenth century, that by the middle of the very next century an intricate network of representational systems would be found to underlie all the complexity of the biosphere. Nor could he have imagined that the arrangement of biological texts involved in the structure of the least complicated organisms known to science would rival the complexity of the texts produced as the output of the human language capacity. Our primary task here, then, is to see just what that human capacity consists of. Secondarily, we want to show that the products of human language capacity are similar in design to the biological texts that form the basis for living organisms.

To begin with, we may ask just what are the mental powers of present-day modern human beings that would have had to be invented by a long and lucky series of bootstrap operations, according to the Darwinian outlook. What steps would have had to be followed to get from some protozoanlike organism (or perhaps a bacterium or yeast) to a human being? What capacities would the hypothesized manlike ape that supposedly preceded *Homo sapiens* have had to invent in order to become, after many generations, a modern human being?

Darwin Reexamined

The science of linguistics—together with related fields created by crossing with psychology and biology (and genetics) to produce such hybrids as psycholinguistics, biolinguistics, and so on—has done much to clarify the problems that had to be solved by Darwin's apelike, almost-but-not-quite-human being. It turns out that the difficulties to be overcome by this hypothetical creature were not unlike those that confronted the prebiotic molecules in the primordial sea that had to form themselves, according to the neo-Darwinian orthodoxy (that is, the Darwinian view stripped of its commitment to Lamarck's incorrect theory), quite accidentally into the first living organism. The problem of the origin of the human language capacity is not unlike the problem of the origin of life itself.[6]

Readers familiar with the biblical story of creation may recall a line or two from the book of John where the "Word of God" is personified and identified with a certain man, Jesus of Nazareth. John writes: "In the beginning was the Word, and the Word was with God, and the Word was God. He was with God in the beginning. Through him all things were made; without him nothing was made that has been made. In him was life, and that life was the light of men. . . . The Word became flesh and made his dwelling among us" (1:1-4, 14). In Darwin's day, the biblical explanation of God's creation was hardly considered germane to the scientific question of the origin of life; much less was the biblical account relevant to the origin of the language capacity. Even theologians rarely dared to suppose any analogy between representations of any sort (much less the human language capacity) and the biological basis of life. The Bible, after all, was not a science text, so theologians regarded "the Word of God" merely as a metaphor for the spiritual (abstract and immaterial) character of "the invisible God who made the visible world" (as was commonly agreed by them). Few would have imagined that such a statement would actually suggest a basis for the best of twentieth-century theories about life itself.

In fact, the majority of the scientists of Darwin's day (and up to the present as well) tended to see organisms in terms of their physical, chemical and behavioral properties. Only the rarest of minds in Darwin's time gave any scientific credence to the notion that life might be linked to language. But the few who did imagine such a connection could also see that there had to be an intimate relation between language and intelligence. The latter relation was noticed by Darwin himself, who wrote about it extensively. The close analogy between the peculiar ability of human beings to use language and the genetic basis of life, however, escaped the general awareness of most scientists, not to mention the general public, for a very long time even after the partial deciphering of the genetic code, which took place toward the middle of the twentieth century. The main reason for the delay was that human language abilities have typically been seen in terms of language's surface forms, especially the sounds and cadences of speech, rather than in terms of the deeper meanings, categories and inferences underlying those and all other surface forms of language.

Nevertheless, the connection between language and life itself was anticipated by at least two scientists of the nineteenth century. One was Alfred Binet, and the other was Charles Sanders Peirce.

Alfred Binet

Binet (1857-1911) was a biologist who turned psychologist near the beginning of the twentieth century and went on to initiate the intelligence-testing movement worldwide. In 1888 he had published a modest little book on the mental powers of microorganisms. In it he speculated that those mental abilities were somehow bound up in commands that had to originate within the organism— probably, he surmised, in the cell nucleus. He noted that if the nucleus were damaged or removed, the cell would either die or lose most of the mental powers of interest. Three-quarters of a century would pass before it would be discovered that indeed it is in the cell's nucleus that the vast majority of the genetic material is stored.[7]

In the same book Binet detailed the intelligent activities of these so-called protozoans (literally, "preanimals"), which included hunting for a particular prey, remembering the location of a hole in a glass wall, building an encasement for an offspring before its birth, fleeing from a predator or acid dropped into the medium, and playing the game of hard-to-get before engaging in a sexual union. He pointed out that these mental capacities could not have been added to higher organisms by some long-term evolutionary process because they were, in fact, already present in the protozoans themselves.

Not only did Binet see the relation between certain representations (e.g., the internal commands issued to the protoplasm in some manner) and the production of voluntary movements, but he would later be one of the first psychologists to write about the connection between the human language capacity and intelligence. In 1911 he wrote, "One of the clearest signs of awakening intelligence among young children is their understanding of spoken language." And in the same place he told of the "first test" of intelligence, which was designed to show "that the child understands the meaning of ordinary words."[8]

Charles S. Peirce

The anticipation of the relationship between language, intelligence and the whole of the biosphere shines even more brightly through the writings of the American scientist C. S. Peirce, who lived from 1839 to 1914. According to Ernest Nagel, "There is a fair consensus of historians of ideas that Charles Sanders Peirce remains the most original, versatile, and comprehensive philosophical mind this country has yet produced."[9] As has been pointed out more recently by Edward Moore, chief editor of the second volume of more than 650 pages in a planned chronological series of thirty such volumes of Peirce's writings, "It is becoming increasingly clear that the philosophical problems that interested him the most were those of the scientist."[10]

Peirce saw logic, grammar and rhetoric as themes in a single unifying system of thought, which he referred to as *semiotics*—the study of representations. He viewed the study of language as an important branch of semiotics and described it in 1902 as "the vast and splendidly developed science of linguistics."[11] In the last quarter of the twentieth century, the world's leading linguist would acknowledge Peirce as the closest mentor of modern linguistic thought.

By age twenty-eight Peirce already had begun to understand the unique role played by representational systems in science. In his notebook on logic he wrote, "I cannot explain the deep emotion with which I open this book again. . . . Here are the germs of the theory of the categories which is (if anything) the gift I make to the world. That is my child. In it I shall live when oblivion has me—my body."[12] "The categories" Peirce sought to understand were the abstract pillars of all representational systems and the necessary preconditions of thought and logic. Some scholars believe that his approach improved on that of Aristotle and that of Immanuel Kant and surpassed even the later reasoning of Einstein in his search for a "unified field theory." Regardless of what the final verdict may be on the latter, there is no doubt that Peirce's conception of representational systems (of which human language is the most abstract and general) was the linchpin of his own scientific accomplishments.

For example, independently of the Russian Dmitri Mendeleev, Peirce discovered the periodicity of the elements. He was the first astronomer at the Harvard Observatory, and one of the first ever, to show that our own Milky Way (the galaxy in which our solar system resides) is among the spiral galaxies. His achievements in logic and mathematics were such that C. I. Lewis remarked that "the head and front of mathematical logic is found in the calculus of propositional functions, as developed by Peirce and Schröder."[13] Among other mathematical contributions, Peirce proved that any plurality of relations can always be reduced to a complex of triadic (three-way) relations but that they can never be further reduced. Some Peirce scholars would later speculate that his interest in the number 3 and in trichotomies, concepts that pervade his work, was owed to the biblical conception of the Trinity—because Peirce, as was well known and evident in nearly all his writings, was an evangelical Christian.

It is said that Peirce was the first logician since Aristotle to contribute any new material advance to the study of logic. His advance was to amplify deductive (strictly axiomatic reasoning, as in geometry) and inductive logic (the kind we do in science with the aid of statistics and probability) by proving the existence and validity of a third kind of reasoning, which he called *abduction* (the kind of reasoning that inevitably underlies perceptual experience, such as recognizing a familiar object, event or person). Peirce's theory of abduction provided the basis for pragmatism, America's only distinctive brand of philosophy, as represented by William James and John Dewey (though Peirce's own approach differed from theirs). In addition Peirce's thought provided the best philosophical basis for the modern approaches to linguistics as developed by MIT professor Noam Avram Chomsky—indisputably the foremost language scientist of the twentieth century.[14] Chomsky has said that his approach is "almost paraphrasing . . . Charles Sanders Peirce," in particular Peirce's "principle of abduction."[15]

In engineering and physics Peirce was the first to measure the standard yard and meter with light-waves. He singlehandedly overturned decades of research on gravitational measurements (which were aimed at accurately assessing the shape of the earth) and at the same time provided superior measurements based on devices he engineered. In higher education, Peirce's lectures on the history of logic at Johns Hopkins University in 1869 and 1870 were later referred to as "the germ of the graduate school"[16] where the first Ph.D. degrees in the United States were granted.

For our purposes in this book, Peirce's most significant contribution was his development of semiotics, the theory of representations or signs. C. K. Ogden and I. A. Richards said, "By far the most elaborate and determined attempt to give an account of signs and their meanings is that of the American logician C. S. Peirce, from whom William James took the idea and the term Pragmatism, and whose Algebra of Dyadic Relations was developed by Schröder."[17]

The Modern Picture
Nearly four decades after Peirce's death the genetic code would be discovered

(see chapter five, by Bradley and Thaxton). Within a couple of decades after that, a handful of scientific linguists such as Roman Jakobson, Thomas A. Sebeok and the much-celebrated Umberto Eco, together with an occasional microbiologist such as Michael Denton and Dmitri Kouznetsov[18] would have the spine-tingling realization that there really is a profound similarity between the human language capacity and the unfolding series of biological language systems including the genetic code. For this reason, it is nearly impossible to address the question of how the human language capacity came to be without coming eventually to consider the closely related mystery of how life itself came to be. Conversely, biologists today are increasingly aware that insights from linguistics are apt to aid our understanding of molecular biology and biophysics (and vice versa). But to see what the modern conception of language capacity is, it will be useful to follow the historical thread from Peirce to the present through four other major scientists who noted the amazing relation between the language capacity and human intelligence.

Albert Einstein

Many scientists are surprised to find out that the great physicist Albert Einstein chose to write about the logical basis of the human language capacity. He explained why in 1936: "The whole of science is nothing more than a refinement of everyday thinking. It is for this reason that the critical thinking of the physicist cannot possibly be restricted to the examination of the concepts of his own specific field. He cannot proceed without considering critically a much more difficult problem, the problem of analyzing everyday thinking."[19]

Why did Einstein insist that the analysis of everyday thinking was more difficult than physics? Because *all* the sciences are grounded in the sort of ordinary thinking that we normally express in some language or language-related sign system. Einstein noted that the abstract concepts of mathematics would be utterly meaningless and uninterpretable if they could not be connected in some way to sensory impressions grounded in the world of experience. He understood (as Peirce had independently proved) that all the axioms of mathematics and logic must ultimately be invested with meaning through the ordinary thought processes that relate forms of language to sensory impressions grounded in the world of experience. While it is true, as Peirce noted, that mathematical systems may achieve a high degree of independence from the world of experience, if any such system were to achieve a *complete* independence, it would by definition also become utterly meaningless. It was one of the achievements of modern logic (especially of Peirce) to show that there cannot be any such thing as a completely abstract general proposition (or any system of them). The reason that such an abstraction cannot exist, or that at least it cannot exist in our thinking, is that it would by definition be altogether beyond the reach of our comprehension. It could not even be expressed, because the expression of any nonempty proposition requires not only some particular surface-form(s) in which it may be stated but also some particular connection(s) with experience (however remote and convoluted that connection might be) which can provide it with some content or significance.

Like Peirce, Einstein criticized David Hume and Bertrand Russell for their neglect of the necessary connection between abstract ideas and the material world. In fact, Einstein agreed with Peirce so completely that their criticisms of Hume and Russell (though written many years apart and quite independently, by all accounts) sound as if they might have been penned by the same person. From J. P. Moreland's introduction to this volume, the reader may recall that Hume had attempted a general refutation of arguments from design to a Designer. But Hume had tried to go even further. He said that all concepts of a metaphysical character—that is, any that could not be derived directly from objective evidences in experience—should be excluded from scientific thinking altogether. In response to Hume's critique, Peirce wrote, "A careful reader will see that if he proves anything at all by his reasoning, it is that reasoning, as such, is *ipso facto* and essentially illogical, 'illegitimate,' and 'unreasonable.' "[20] Or as Einstein put it, Hume's argument against metaphysical entities in thought—"if only carried through consistently—absolutely excludes thinking of any kind."[21]

Hume had argued that all metaphysical concepts had to be abandoned. The trouble with this recommendation was that there are no concepts at all that do not have a metaphysical (abstract, nonphysical) aspect. Neither can abstract concepts be derived from raw, uninterpreted physical events or objects or relations between them. Peirce proved that facts are known to us exclusively by what he called "abductive" (as contrasted with deductive and inductive) inference. That is, *whatever facts we know can be known only by linking prior knowledge from our innate conceptual capacities with an external world.* This fact is a central theme of modern linguistics, to which we will return in what follows.

Nevertheless, Einstein argued (and Peirce rigorously proved) that Hume and Russell were correct in implying this much: "all thought acquires material content only through its relationship with . . . sensory material."[22] That is, a representation that cannot be linked to sensory experience is a representation devoid of meaning. It has no material content.

Thoughtful readers may object that fantasy and fiction may achieve a great deal of independence from ordinary experience, but a little thought will show that even fantasy and fiction must resemble actual experience in order to be the least bit interpretable. The rattlesnake in our nightmare has to resemble the real rattlesnakes that we or others have encountered in actual experience, or we could not identify the one in the dream for what it is. The pink-and-white-spotted baboon that we imagined floating outside the classroom window as we daydreamed our way through our high-school English class actually resembled the pink, white and spotted things of our experience as well as the baboons we had seen before conjuring up the imaginary one. Remove all such resemblances, and any representation will lose all hope of ever being known as anything meaningful at all.

With this understanding as background, we return to consider Einstein's reflections on the human language capacity. He succinctly stated and extended Darwin's notion that language acquisition by a child sums up the steps that might have been followed in the origin of language:

The first step towards language was to link . . . commutable [i.e., exchangeable] signs to sense impressions. Most likely all sociable animals have arrived at this primitive kind of communication—at least to a certain degree. A higher development is reached when further signs are introduced and understood which establish relations between those other signs designating sense-impression[s]. At this stage it is already possible to report somewhat complex series of impressions; we can say that language has come into existence.[23]

He went on to argue that it was only at a still later stage, "where frequent use is made of so-called abstract concepts," that "language becomes an instrument of reasoning in the true sense of the word." Here language achieves "greater inner coherence" but at the same time becomes less directly dependent on "the background of impressions." As a result, questions of truth and falsehood and of degrees of meaningfulness enter the picture. Einstein says that at this later stage "everything depends on the degree to which words and word-combinations correspond to the world of impression."[24]

Here Einstein gives a succinct and clear definition for what philosophers have called "the correspondence theory of truth." This theory says that a true representation is one that corresponds faithfully to whatever it represents.

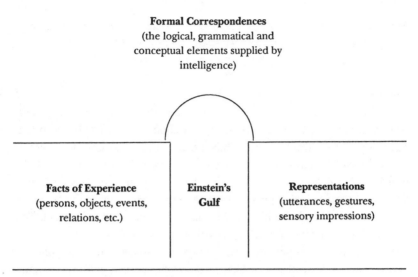

Figure 7.1. The logical form of true representations of particular facts.

The correspondence theory underlies Peirce's theory of abduction[25] and can be pictured in a simple diagram; see figure 7.1.

On the one side of our intellectual understanding of the world, the left side of the diagram, there are the facts of the world that exists outside of ourselves. That world includes our bodies, of course. On the other hand, the right side of the diagram, there are the meaningful representations (utterances, gestures and sensory impressions) that inform us and that constitute our experience of the external world. When the representations correspond faithfully to the facts of the external world, we say that they are true; otherwise not.

In order for representations to have any meaning at all, it is necessary for them to have some correspondence, however tenuous it may be, with the external world. Representations that are deficient with respect to their connection with the external world (other things being held equal) will also be increasingly defective as representations per se. These propositions were assumed to be true by Einstein, but had been extensively developed and proved by Peirce.[26]

Later we will return to Einstein and to figure 7.1. Until then it is important to keep in mind his conclusion that there is "an intimate connection between language and thinking" and the related inference, in the same context, that a child deprived of the normal "verbal guidance of his environment" would come to a "mental shape" that "would be very poor."[27] Subsequently we will show that the products of human language capacity and those of the genetic basis of life are alike in this respect: both linguistic and biological structures reveal an articulate design and thus are supreme evidences of intelligence.

Jean Piaget

In 1947 the Swiss psychologist Jean Piaget (1896-1980) reported a conclusion very similar to Einstein's of six years earlier about the relation between language and the child's developing intellect. Piaget argued that "the system of collective signs" that a child will eventually acquire develops the symbolic function "to a degree that the individual by himself [or herself] would never know."[28] An individual deprived of the opportunity to acquire the language of a community would be hindered in his or her mental development. The sad proof of this claim is found in cases of profoundly deaf children who have been prevented from acquiring sign language systems under the policy of urging them to lip-read and speak.[29] The outcome of such policies is to stunt the intellectual growth of which a deaf child is capable if allowed to acquire a sign language system.

Lev Semenovich Vygotsky

A contemporary rival of Piaget was the Russian psychologist Lev Vygotsky. His brilliance shines all the brighter because of his early death at age thirty-eight (Piaget, born in the same year as Vygotsky, went on living for forty-six more years). Vygotsky's professional work addressed "one of the most complex problems of psychology, the interrelation of thought and language."[30] In exploring that connection, Vygotsky anticipated the thesis of the much later linguist Noam Chomsky that the study of language might provide a fairly clear window through which to view the mind.

Vygotsky also noted that the development of our native language is important to the development of all abstract reasoning skills, including mathematics, and he was one of the first psychologists to see the intrinsic relatedness of "reading and writing, grammar, arithmetic" to the rest of the traditional curriculum.[31] He rejected the compartmentalization of intellectual skills, though the practice remains prevalent in education even today. He wrote, "We found that intellectual development, far from following Thorndike's atomistic model, is not compartmentalized according to topics of instruction," but that "instruction in a given subject influences the development of the higher functions far beyond the confines of that particular subject."[32] He concluded that "the main psychic [mental] functions involved in studying various subjects are interdependent" and thus anticipated the modern resolution of the long-standing controversy over the relation between general and specific factors of intellect. Are there specific measurable capacities that pertain, say, to arithmetic or to reading that are not common to all other representational tasks? It appears that there are such specific components, but they are undergirded (just as Vygotsky and others, notably Charles Spearman,[33] had predicted) by a unifying capacity to represent abstract meanings.[34] Moreover, this unifying capacity can be identified with the universal ability of normal human beings to acquire and use languages. Therefore, the origin of that capacity is bound to intrigue modern scholars all the more.

With a little help from the German author Johann Wolfgang von Goethe (1749-1832), Vygotsky clarified the underlying premise of any Darwin-based perspective on the origin of the human language capacity. He quoted Goethe's fictional character Faust (a man who sold himself to the devil) as saying, "In the beginning was the deed."[35] Reflecting on this proposition will show a crucial scientific difference between the biblical and the Darwinian perspectives.

A *deed*, of course, is an act performed intentionally by some intelligent and animate organism capable of voluntary movement. We cannot call the action of a falling rock a *deed*. If the falling rock were loosened by an earthquake or the spring rains, its falling might be called "an act of God" by a modern insurance company, but strictly speaking, anything that does not involve the deliberate intention of some particular actor ought to be called what it is, an event or an accident, but not a deed. The very idea of *doing* something—that is, performing some *deed* (which comes from an Old English conjugation of the verb *do*)—necessitates a doer.

Analysis will show that any intentional act is invariably a revelation of the intention itself. While in some cases the intention may be found out more or less at the same time as the act is performed (as in an act of passion), logically speaking the intention is presupposed and must exist prior to the act. Therefore a deed cannot logically be the beginning of any intentional act whatsoever. Any deed requires an underlying intention as a prior condition for its existence.

To see the consequence of this conclusion for theories of origins, we need to carry our argument only one step further. Consider the nature of an intention. What is it? Suppose that a jilted lover is angry and wants to harm the rival who has taken away the person he or she loves. What is the nature of this intention? It is not yet a *deed*. It is certainly not a physical *act*. It cannot become an overt deed until the jilted lover performs it. If he or she were to harm or kill the rival, then the intention would become a deed. But what is it beforehand, while it is still in the intentional phase?

Logical analysis shows that any intention to do something is, from the physical point of view, merely a hypothetical possibility, not yet an act. It is just an abstract proposition associating a subject *(a certain jilted lover)* with a predicate *(wants to harm a certain rival)*. The proposition itself describes in its predicate *(to harm a certain rival)* a purely abstract possibility. The disappointed lover may have imagined performing certain acts to harm the rival, but the harming cannot become an overt physical act until the intention is carried out through the swinging of a fist or an ax, the pointing of a gun and the pulling of the trigger, or whatever else the jilted lover may do to harm the rival. Before such events are caused by the person who intends to cause them, they are merely abstract propositions about potential states of affairs in the mind of the person who is considering or willing to do them.

Are they real? According to Vygotsky, Hume, Russell and any consistent Darwinian perspective, the answer ought to be "No. Intentions merely thought of, but not yet physically acted upon, are not yet real." This follows from the claim that only physically material events are real because all metaphysical (abstract) concepts are ruled out of play in any thoroughgoing materialistic outlook.

On the other side, according to the biblical perspective (and according to Peirce and Einstein), the answer must be "Yes. Abstract ideas represented by the mind are real, so intentions are also real regardless of whether they result in overt physical actions." Within a nonmaterialistic realism, mental acts and all representations are accorded real status.

Peirce argued that an intention or any representation whatever is real even if it is not known to us at any particular moment in time. I hold my coffee cup in my hand above the tile floor. I don't drop it. If I did drop it (though I do not intend to and will not), it would fall. Is the fact that it would fall a real fact? Shall I do the experiment? Of course not. No one doubts that if the experiment were done, it would come out just as it always does. The cup would fall to the floor. This fact, Peirce contended, must be accepted as real and general. It is independent of any particular experiment. Intentions, thoughts and the abstract propositions that they truly manifest are all quite real irrespective of any particular physical event.

Recall the Sermon on the Mount, where it is argued that lust (Matthew 5:28) and unwarranted hatred (5:21-22) will be judged in the end as equivalent to acts of sexual immorality and to murder, respectively. Therefore the biblical perspective assigns no more weight of reality to the physical, material world than to the realm of merely abstract representations. On the contrary, according to the biblical perspective it is the representational side of Einstein's definition of truth (the correspondence of abstract representations to material facts) that deserves greater weight than does the material side. The Word is before the creation of the material world and endures eternally after the material world is gone.

Vygotsky's putting the deed ahead of the word attributes greater reality to the physical world than to the abstract world of thought. This is necessary to any Darwinian perspective, or to any purely materialistic philosophy. If we suppose, as Hume did, that the only valid concepts are those that come directly from the material events of experience, anything that is not demonstrably part of that physical world cannot count as real.

Moreover, Darwin assumed (just as Hume did) that abstract ideas (and intellect itself) could be produced directly from material facts. But Peirce and Einstein showed that this is not possible. It is, in fact, impossible in principle; the reverse is true. The material event is entirely incapable, without the aid of an intervening intellect, of creating, suggesting or inferring (all of which are exclusive acts of intelligence) any conceptual abstraction. Any physical event is so completely physical that it reveals only a complete absence of any abstractness whatever.

The biblical statement "In the beginning was the Word" assigns greater reality to the power of representation than to all the material facts of the entire physical universe. This is because the material facts of the space-time continuum, according to the Bible, depend on the representations that underlie and enable them to exist. The writer to the Hebrews says, "The Son is the radiance of God's glory and the exact representation of his being, sustaining all things by his powerful word" (1:3). According to the Bible, in fact, the world of experience is less real (Isaiah 34:4; Revelation 6:14) than its underlying representational basis. Paul says, "What is seen is temporary, but what is unseen is eternal" (2 Corinthians 4:18). In the Psalms, David says that the physical universe will "wear out like a garment" (102:26) and be thrown away. The scientific ideas that follow from the Bible are very different from those of Darwin's philosophy, or any other materialistic philosophy.

Looking back to figure 7.1 above, we may label the void that separates the abstract realm of representations (or more particularly, the invisible realm of their meanings) from the concrete (visible and otherwise sensory) realm of the facts of experience, as "Einstein's gulf." Einstein himself didn't draw the diagram, but he stated the case for it with crystal clarity: "We have the habit of combining certain concepts and conceptual relations (propositions) so definitely with certain sense experiences that we do not become conscious of the gulf—logically unbridgeable—which separates the world of sensory experiences from the world of concepts and propositions."[36] Peirce described the same separation of the abstract realm of meaning from the concrete world more briefly: "Mind [is] quite as little understood as matter, and the relations between the two [are] an enigma."[37]

Comprehensibility—the Product of Intelligence

The surprising thing about the gulf is that human beings, by virtue of intelligence, are miraculously able to cross it. Peirce referred to such acts of connecting abstract representations to the world of experience as "abduction." Some years later, Einstein addressed the same problem:

> The very fact that the totality of our sense experiences is such that by means of thinking (by the use of concepts, and the creation and use of definite functional relations between them, and the coordination of sense experiences to these concepts) it can be put in order, this fact is one which leaves us in awe but which we shall never understand. It . . . is a miracle.
>
> In my opinion, nothing can be said concerning the manner in which the concepts are to be made and connected, and how we are to coordinate them to the experiences. In guiding us in the creation of such an order of sense experiences, success in the result is alone the determining factor.[38]

Modern linguists are duty-bound to be a little more hopeful than Einstein concerning the possibility of explaining something about the nature of concepts (their semantics or abstract meanings), how they can be arranged to form grammatical structures (their syntax) and how they can be linked with experience (their pragmatics). However, the solution that is almost universally accepted by modern linguists (and by researchers in other disciplines who have studied the case) is to suppose that the conceptual basis for human understanding and the language capacity itself is essentially innate. This solution was argued effectively by Kant, was later elaborated greatly by Peirce and has most recently become the adopted brainchild of Noam Chomsky,[39] who will be discussed at greater length below.

The Absolute Necessity of Special Innate Capacities

Kant contended that it would be impossible for us to have any experience whatsoever if we were not preprogrammed with certain innate categories. For instance, consider an apparently simple case: How could we see the visible spectrum of color if we were not designed with a color-sensitive visual system? It's an absolute certainty that we couldn't. Kant's point was a deductive necessity. To have a certain *experience* that is dependent upon a certain conceptual capacity (e.g., the ability to perceive the bright red color of oxygenated blood as distinct from the darker burgundy of deoxygenated blood, or to perceive any color at all), we must first have that specially designed capacity (in this case color vision). Remove the capacity and there is no chance of ever having the experience at all. Without color vision (or something equivalent to it), what could count as seeing the redness of blood?

But Kant, Peirce and Einstein (presaging Chomsky) would go much further. Unlike Hume, who ended up creating a false basis for doubting the existence of any external reality whatever (as Russell would later do by following out Hume's line of thought[40]), Kant, Peirce and Einstein without hesitation *presupposed* the existence of a real, material, physical universe with certain truly representable qualities. Without such a world, no representation could be said to be true in any meaningful sense of the word. For instance, of what use would color terms such as *red, green, blue* and *yellow* be in a world existing only in black and white?

While it was formerly claimed by some (including Benjamin Lee Whorf[41] and certain of his adherents) that linguistic surface forms shape the concepts that they designate, experimental research has shown that this is not the case. The phenomenal colors that we know appear as they appear because of the innate predispositions of our visual system. The sensations that the system produces are hardly susceptible to any influence at all that might be attributed to the acquisition of a certain language. It makes no difference to the color perceptions of English speakers and speakers of Navajo, for instance, that these two languages divide up the color spectrum differently. In Navajo there is no explicit lexical distinction between *green* and *blue,* though there obviously is such a distinction in English. The experimental studies show that Navajo and English speakers, and all the speakers of the rest of the world's more than five thousand languages, see colors very much the same way.

But the question of how we come to have the concepts that we do and how we are able to associate words with them so readily and to connect both with the facts of our experience is a far richer and more intricate problem than the consideration of color terms can even suggest. We do not learn to perceive the color red (or any other) as we do perceive it. It is clear that we are prewired to come to see it exactly as we do.

But a consistent theory will show much more than this. *We must be prewired for essentially every kind of conceptual knowledge that we will ever associate with our experience.* In fact, here the analogy between the origin of the language capacity and that of the genetic system that makes possible the existence of any particular organism in the whole biosphere becomes most evident. To establish this analogy, an excursion into biogenetics is necessary. Afterward we will proceed with our examination of modern linguistic theory.

Biogenesis and the Innateness Issue

In order for any organism to be whatever it is, its genetic program (DNA) must specify what sort of organism it will be and, within surprisingly narrow limits, what specific characteristics it will assume. Such limits, innately determined, apply as much to a human being or to a Rhesus monkey as to a special variety of fruit fly or yeast or bacterium. Such innately specified limits apply to all species, because all of them are genetically defined to be the species that they are. The design features that are allowed for any given species are determined by its inherited DNA, collectively known as its genome. The human genome, for instance, is already known to specify about a billion bits of information, though only about 10 percent of it is known to be used in the various representational processes that are involved.

In humans, as in mammals generally, there are two kinds of DNA. The largest quantity is contained in cell nuclei and is accordingly called "nuclear DNA." This kind of DNA in humans provides for the generation of about ten thousand distinct proteins, which form essential building blocks of the organism. The other kind of DNA common to humans and other mammals is the so-called mitochondrial DNA. This kind is found only in the mitochondria and, unlike nuclear DNA, is exclusively inherited from the mother. It is involved in the production of only thirteen proteins, but these are nonetheless crucial to cells because they enable chemical processes involved in the release of energy vital to life.

No cell, of course, can become anything other than what it is programmed to become by the information coded in its genome. Its character, within certain limits, is fixed by its DNA. However, in a complex organism such as a human being, many cells with radically different shapes, sizes and functions will be constructed to form distinct and highly specialized organs, glands and tissues, all on the basis of information coded in the genome formed from the union of a single sperm and egg. The zygote thus produced will, in humans, develop into an incredibly well-designed organism consisting of billions of well-differentiated cells. Even in the development of a single-celled organism, the cascading network of representational processes that determine the shape of the organism is exceedingly delicate, articulate and complex, but in the development of a human embryo the complexities are multiplied by many orders of magnitude.

The DNA must be faithfully copied to every single cell of an organism that will eventually consist of billions of cells if the organism as a whole is to remain viable throughout the course of its development. The rarity of genetic disorders and deformities is testimony to the accuracy with which the copying of genetic material is nearly always carried out and to the unlikelihood of any sort of genetic error being created in the first place, say, by chemical or ultraviolet damage. Further, there are conservative repair processes whose main function is to restore damaged DNA to its original content.

But the accuracy of the replication process must be linked with an equally difficult feat. In the construction of each particular kind of cell, the DNA must be read in such a manner as to differentiate all the distinct kinds of tissue (bone, skin, the cornea of the eye and so on) and to produce just the right sort of protein structures in the right arrangement so as to form a hand, say, as distinct from an eye. Therefore, in addition to maintaining the accuracy of the storage of information in each cell as it is produced, there is the difficulty of determining just which "sentences" in the DNA are to be read from the many millions that are available in the entire genomic library.

It is important to remember that each cell does not merely contain the portions of the DNA library that it will specifically need to use; each initially contains the whole library. The problem is vaguely analogous to the one faced by a master builder who must select just the right set of tools at just the right time in order to complete each in a long series of intricate and delicately related steps on a complex job. Moreover, for each task the right set of tools must be selected and used in the right sequence from a toolbox containing millions of possibilities.

The information-rich portions of the DNA genome—that is, the genes, which specify the proteins necessary to build the organism—consist of highly organized linear arrays of delicately structured biological texts. Comprehension of these texts by the cell's protein factories (the ribosomes) requires the help of specific DNA binding proteins that find and mark the gene segments. They mark the gene fore and aft so the right position in the text can be found by the RNA polymerase, which will transcribe the DNA information into messenger RNA, which will enable it to be transmitted to the protein factory.

Here we have skipped over a number of steps whereby the information from the gene in question will be converted into one of the necessary protein building blocks of the cell. As the process of translating DNA information into specific proteins proceeds, many steps (resembling a nearly perfectly verbatim copying, transcription, transfer and translation of a lengthy and highly organized text) must be completed. The procedures at each step involve a delicate process of fitting complex molecular structures into strings, much as a human being might fit a particular true and correct interpretation to a certain kind of representation or vice versa. Imagine what goes into producing or interpreting a particular statement, paragraph or text; the problem is like the true and appropriate fitting of a verbal description to a certain factual state of affairs in the world of experience. Like such articulate uses of language, the biological use of DNA is a consummately articulate balancing act that involves the interrelationship of many factors simultaneously. This holistic balancing act defies the imagination.

It is difficult for the linguist to say how any human being can ever arrive at a true representation of any particular fact of experience (even of the simplest kind—say, that today was January 26, 1993, and that it is now about 9:40 p.m. in Albuquerque, New Mexico). In the same way it is difficult for the biochemist to say exactly how even a single protein can be produced at just the right time and location in the development of the life of a particular organism. The problems are, as far as we can tell, exactly analogous. Every time the information from DNA is passed from one stage to another stage in the cascading network of biological processes, Einstein's gulf is miraculously crossed. For instance, the formation of messenger RNA from the original DNA seems to involve such a crossing. The ribosome-dependent transfer of the information to protein involves one or more such crossings. The function of the protein within the cell involves such a crossing—and on and on it goes.

In the final analysis, the biochemist seems to be pointed toward the same surprising conclusion as the linguist. The whole cascading network of relationships must be specified within rather narrowly defined limits in order for any organism whatever to be a viable possibility. Moreover, the problem of biogenesis and the origin of the human language capacity are linked at their basis by more than just a remarkable analogy. It turns out that the human genome must include the essential characteristics of the entire conceptual system that we find manifested in the great variety of languages and their uses, but within rather narrow limits, by human beings throughout the world.

Apparently human beings, and only humans, are specially designed to acquire just the range of language systems that we see manifested in the world's five thousand-plus languages. Therefore the human language capacity must be expressed in the human genome itself.

Noam Chomsky and Modern Linguistic Theory

The case for a rich and largely innate system of concepts underlying the human language capacity was summed up by Chomsky as follows: "The rate of vocabulary acquisition is so high at certain stages of life, and the precision and delicacy of the concepts acquired so remarkable, that it seems necessary to conclude that in some manner the conceptual system with which lexical items are connected is already substantially in place."[42] In other words, the conceptual system is not really constructed in the child's mind as if out of nothing, but must be, in an important sense, known before the fact. *The whole system must be in place before it can be employed to interpret experience.*

This statement will come as a shock to most educated persons, but the logical arguments and empirical evidences in its favor are so strong that Chomsky has been able to win over nearly everyone in the biological sciences who has looked closely at the evidence. Consider, for instance, the positive reception Chomsky received from Nobel laureate biologist Jacques Monod, physicochemical biologist Antoine Danchin and molecular biologist Dieter Dütting, to name only a few of those who participated in the discussion of the debate on the nature of language and learning by Chomsky and Piaget at the Abbaye de Royaumont just outside Paris, France, in 1979.[43]

Even some of Chomsky's most outspoken detractors (such as the world-renowned psychologist David Premack) now admit that there is no escaping the overwhelming evidence in favor of the theory of innate ideas. Later we will see that human beings are uniquely equipped to acquire languages and that our capacity to do so involves a remarkably abstract system of expression that is totally unparalleled in any other species. Premack was the psychologist who engineered the training of a chimp named Sarah to use a primitive sign language. In 1982 he argued against the "ethnocentric limitations," as he called them, of modern linguistics and in favor of the ability of chimpanzees to represent abstract meanings as humans do. Later, in the repeatedly aired 1988 WNET and BBC TV series *The Mind,* Premack plainly admitted that the human language ability is unattainable by the most intelligent of the trained apes.

Chomsky also argues that the human ability to manipulate numbers parallels the character of the language faculty in important respects. Concerning our "capacity to deal with the number system" he writes, "It seems reasonable to suppose that this faculty is an intrinsic component of the human mind" unparalleled in other species.[44] For instance, he points out that birds can be trained to select a certain number of elements out of an array so long as the number is 7 or smaller; this shows that they do not have the number capacity as we know it at all. He says,

> The concept of infinity is not just "more" than seven, just as human language with its discrete infinity of meaningful expressions is not just "more" than some finite system of symbols that can be laboriously imposed on other organisms—nor, by the same token, just "less" than an essentially continuous system of communication, like the dance of bees. The capacity to deal with the number system or with abstract properties of space is surely unlearned in its essentials. Furthermore it is not specifically "selected" through evolution, one must assume—even the existence of the number system could not have been known or the capacity exercised until human evolution had essentially reached its current stage.[45]

Chomsky has opposed the orthodox view concerning the origin of language for many years. In 1972, for instance, he argued against Karl Popper's paraphrase of Darwin's idea that

> the evolution of language passed through several stages, in particular a "lower stage" in which vocal gestures are used for expression of emotional states, for example, and a "higher stage" in which articulated sound is used for expression of thought—in Popper's terms, for description and critical argument . . . but in fact he establishes no relation between the lower and higher stages and does not suggest a mechanism whereby transition can take place from one stage to the next. . . . There is no reason to suppose that the gaps are bridgeable. There is no more of a basis for assuming an evolutionary development of "higher" from "lower" stages, in this case, than there is from breathing to walking; the stages have no significant analogy.[46]

Nor does Chomsky modify his position in later writings (see the Managua lectures published in 1988[47]). He still maintains that the language capacity reveals special design properties that are entirely lacking in the communication systems of other species. (Later we will consider why Chomsky and most other scientists believe that the human language capacity is not shared by other species.) Indeed, Chomsky has been so emphatic in rejecting the standard orthodoxy that he has been accused by Francine (Penny) Patterson and

E. Linden of taking "a creationist view of the universe."[48] Patterson is the well-known Stanford psychologist who trained the gorilla Koko to use a primitive version of American Sign Language, and it is not at all difficult to see why she pegs Chomsky's view as that of a creationist. Even with reference to other species, Chomsky contends that "what is important for the behavior of an organism is its 'special design.' "[49]

In view of this, we might expect Chomsky to draw an inference to a Designer. This, however, he does not do, though he claims that "some intellectual achievements, such as language learning, fall strictly within biologically determined cognitive capacity. For these tasks, we have 'special design,' so that cognitive structures of great complexity and interest develop fairly rapidly and with little if any conscious effort."[50]

Can Apes Acquire Human Language Systems?

A question that is crucial to the whole discussion is whether apes are capable of acquiring human languages. In the 1970s strong opinions were stated both pro and con. For instance, the distinguished Harvard professor emeritus D. L. Bolinger wrote in 1975 that a couple of well-known chimpanzees had "matched the language ability of a four-year-old child and . . . proved that creatures other than humans had the intelligence to transfer meaning and to create syntax."[51] But after reviewing the same evidence Chomsky said,

> It is difficult to imagine that some other species, say the chimpanzee, has the capacity for language but has never thought to put it to use. Nor is there any evidence that this biological miracle has occurred. On the contrary, the interesting investigations of the capacity of the higher apes to acquire symbolic systems seem to me to support the traditional belief that even the most rudimentary properties of language lie well beyond the capacities of an otherwise intelligent ape.[52]

The idea that apes might be taught to speak had almost immediately occurred to researchers hoping to find some conclusive evidence that Darwin's theory of evolution showed the true relation of humans and apes. In 1925 Robert M. Yerkes (the primatologist after whom the Yerkes Regional Primate Research Center of Emory University in Atlanta was named) is said to have "remarked casually" that apes "might at least be capable of communicating in the sign language of the Deaf."[53] The suggestion may have come originally from the long-standing idea that gestures of some sort had been the evolutionary precursors of speech—a notion that was common among the Marxist scholars of the once-great Soviet Union. The idea that apes might learn some form of gestural sign system was also recommended, independently it would seem, by Lev Vygotsky.[54] These recommendations would go unheeded, however, for more than three decades.

Gua and Vicki

In the meanwhile, during the 1930s, Winthrop and Luella Kellogg tried to teach a female chimpanzee they called Gua to speak. They treated her as they did their own infant son, but she never uttered a recognizable word—though she was apparently able to understand about one hundred of them. A little over a decade later, in the 1940s and extending into the 1950s, Keith and Cathy Hayes tried again to teach a chimpanzee to speak. Their chimp was named Vicki. Like the Kelloggs, the Hayeses treated their chimp as if she were their own human child. They reported being able to get her to actually say four distinguishable (if imperfect) utterances that they identified as *mama, papa, cup* and *up*. But this four-word accomplishment of Vicki, who died at the end of the six-year experiment, together with previous attempts, actually tended more to erode hopes than to build them.

After all, a human child over the same six years would normally be expected to learn thousands of distinct words in a language and would have become able to string words together to form (as Chomsky has shown) a "discrete infinity" of significant signs. The child would have been able to participate in essentially limitless amounts of discourse and to construct phrases appropriate to his or her experience. In fact, a normal child's linguistic output by age six would have exceeded the capacity of the experimenters to record and analyze it. Vicki's performance, in the final analysis, held out little hope for the view that apes would one day express thoughts and feelings in the way that *Homo sapiens* has, apparently, always been able to do.

The Chimps and Koko

Then, in 1966, two different husband-and-wife teams of researchers, independently and in separate parts of the United States, set out to teach a couple of chimpanzees to use sign systems. Apparently without any awareness of the recommendations that had been made some thirty years earlier by Yerkes and by Vygotsky, both teams got the idea to use one or another system of visible signs rather than speech as their medium of communication. Beatrice and Allen Gardner taught their chimp, Washoe, to use a radically impoverished version of the American Sign Language (ASL) of the Deaf, while Ann James Premack and her husband, David, invented a language with manipulable tokens that could be stuck to a felt board to form "meaningful utterances."

Over the course of several years each of these chimps acquired about 130 words, which they used with about 80 percent accuracy according to their trainers. The much greater success with sign language systems caused some to suppose that "beyond a doubt . . . a chimpanzee is capable of learning true language."[55]

By the middle of the next decade, another precocious chimp, named Lana,[56] would learn yet another manual system of signs that involved selecting keys on a specially prepared computer keyboard. The system that Lana learned was called Yerkes, after the famous primatologist (the center where the research was done was also named for him). Lana performed at about the same level as her signing predecessors.

While she was undergoing her regimen of training, Herbert S. Terrace of Columbia University acquired funding for an even more extensive project with a chimpanzee he called "Nim Chimpsky" (a whimsical parody on the name of the world's foremost linguist). Terrace said,

> My initial reactions to the achievements of Washoe, Sarah, Lana, and the other apes who followed their trail was mixed. . . . I felt excited by the possibility of a fundamentally new type of communication with another species. If chimpanzees could use symbols to encode relationships, feelings, and different features of the environment, there was the potential for communicating with them in ways never thought possible.[57]

His objective was to see if apes could really acquire the underlying syntax of signs. That is, could they use signs in a way that would show the apes' dependence on the kinds of structural relationships that human children readily acquire? Further, could they use abstract signs somewhat independently of any particular context, as any human child can? Could they achieve the human sort of independence from immediate stimulus contexts (e.g., by asking for a banana when none was present and had not just been brought up by someone else)? As we noted above, even the physicist Einstein had realized long before Chomsky came on the scene that only when language becomes free of the control of immediate external stimuli does it become "an instrument of reasoning in the true sense of the word."

After his extensive research, Terrace summed up his own skepticism somewhat poignantly:

> When Washoe signed *time,* did she do so out of a sense of time, or had she simply learned a gesture to request food, as in the sequence *time eat?* *Time* was never contrasted with other signs, such as *now, later, before, soon,*

and so on. As far as I could tell, if Washoe had a sense of time, she was not expressing it when she signed *time*. Instead, she seemed to be imitating her teacher, who had just signed for her, *time eat?* Adding a meaningless sign to the sign for *eat* is hardly the same as saying, *It is now time to eat.*[58] The problem is a general one for all research aimed at teaching apes to communicate with humans. The question is how to determine what they mean by their signs and likewise how to differentiate between strings of meaningless elements and genuinely structured phrases and sentences. For instance, a child may say (as one of the author's did) something that sounds like "On't-fa-way" meaning something like "outside," because his mother had frequently said "Don't go far away" whenever she let him go outside to play. In such cases it appears that the sequence is a single word to the child, while it may appear to be a complex sequence to the analyst. The only way to sort out the truth is to carefully examine the contexts of use and to see if the string of words is always used as a simplex or if its *apparent* components actually enter into other meaningful combinations.

But the ape trainers were not much hindered by the controversy, and the research went on. In fact, all the accomplishments of the superstar chimps were already being greatly surpassed by a female gorilla.

By 1978, the lovable gorilla named Koko, trained by Stanford psychologist Francine (Penny) Patterson, had easily surpassed all of her chimp predecessors by acquiring approximately 375 signs from American Sign Language over a training period of six and a half years. While Robert Yerkes had speculated that gorillas might be smarter than chimps, until Patterson began to work with Koko no one had attempted to teach a gorilla to sign on account of their strength and size and the presumed danger of domesticating one of them.

By 1981 Patterson and Linden would report that Koko's active repertoire of signs had been expanded to roughly six hundred words (though she tended to forget quickly and had to be reminded frequently of words she was expected to know). She was credited with such speech acts as bantering, cursing, arguing with her trainers, pretending to smoke a stick, lying about poking holes in the screen mesh on her trailer house, holding pretend tea parties, reacting to childhood stories such as "The Three Little Kittens Who Lost Their Mittens," and all kinds of humor. Patterson would report that Koko was also capable of using abstract words pertaining to sequence in time and that she was able to perform feats of reasoning formerly thought to be limited only to humans.

But Was It Really Language?

Not all the skeptics were convinced. The reported successes of the chimps and of Koko were weighed in the balance by Thomas A. Sebeok and Jean Umiker-Sebeok in 1981 and were still found wanting: "That apes can be taught fairly large vocabularies of symbols has been well established. Time and again, however, reports indicate that there is only a faint resemblance between a chimpanzee's or a gorilla's application of these newly acquired tools and that of humans."[59]

David and Ann James Premack reacted to such criticisms by arguing that "man is understandably prejudiced in favor of his own species, and members of other species must perform Herculean feats before they are recognized as having similar abilities." In fact, the Premacks even went so far as to claim that "linguists and others who study the development of language tend to exaggerate the child's understanding of language and to be extremely skeptical about the experimentally demonstrated language abilities of the chimpanzee."[60]

So the controversy was bound to be put to more stringent rational tests. The issue had come down to determining more carefully the properties of human language systems.

What the Apes Could and Could Not Do

There was little doubt that a well-tutored chimpanzee or a gorilla had the intellectual capacity to acquire a surprisingly large number of associations between actual object situations and what could be called sign-tokens (actual tangible tokens in the case of Sarah) or visible signs in the case of apes taught words in ASL or keystrokes on a keyboard. For instance, Lana was trained in a keyboard language, and Koko later became "bilingual" when she learned to operate a keyboard in addition to her ASL skills. What the apes could do was to associate up to several hundred factual contexts with visible gestures, keystrokes or tangible tokens, all of which were immediately present in their experience. This fact clearly reveals that they are highly intelligent creatures.

But it is also important to note what the apes were *unable* to do. It turns out that there are several properties of the linguistic behavior of ordinary human children that no ape has ever been able to approximate. We will see shortly that every one of these properties involves the capacity to use fully abstract representations (that is, to cross Einstein's gulf). The apes are universally incapable of entering the realm of abstract thought. They cannot separate representations from the situations to which they are appropriate.

Therefore they cannot achieve the freedom of choice that comes with the ability to consider purely hypothetical abstractions (e.g., if I were to drop the cup on the tile it would break, so I won't drop it). Freedom of will and moral responsibility as humans know them both depend on this sort of abstract capability.

While the following list of things the apes cannot do is not exhaustive, it shows conclusively that the precocious trained apes have not, contrary to much wishful thinking, acquired the kinds of linguistic abilities that all normal humans display.

No Questions? No Grammar?

One of the most remarkable missing elements in the pseudolinguistic behavior of the trained apes is that they don't ask questions. They simply don't seem to be able to understand what a question is. This is strange in view of the fact that apes are extraordinarily inquisitive creatures and not at all shy about exploring and trying out new approaches to things. Even a dog may seem capable of asking permission to get in the car when the family is going somewhere by cocking its head to one side and raising an ear slightly, but the trained apes never ask questions. When asked why not, the Premacks swept the issue aside by saying, "It was easier to teach Sarah to answer questions."[61] Washoe did not ask questions either, nor did Lana or Nim or Koko.

The absence of questions is paralleled by a complete absence of the sort of dependence on syntactic structure (rule-governed arrangement) that is universal to all human language systems and that is relied upon by all normal children in the process of acquiring their first language. For instance, children begin very early to distinguish subjects (represented by noun phrases, e.g., *the dogs* in *The dogs chased the cat*) and predicates (represented by verb phrases, e.g., *chased the cat*). Children make certain correct guesses about which category is which and where the boundaries are, and they correctly (though subconsciously) parse the structures in the process of comprehending and acquiring them. Moreover, children will very soon begin to mark nouns for number (e.g., one *dog* versus several *dogs*). They also mark verbs for tense and aspect. For instance, the predicate in *The dogs chase the cat all the time* indicates present tense and iterative aspect showing repeated or habitual action. It contrasts with a predicate such as *chased the cat up a tree yesterday*, which is marked for past tense and perfected or completed aspect (by *-ed*). The verb differs significantly in *were chasing the cat all over the neighborhood*, where it is marked for progressive aspect (by *were* and *-ing*).

Structure-Dependence

Noam Chomsky calls this universal syntactic aspect of language systems the "structure-dependence" principle. For example, how does the English-speaking child learn to distinguish the nouns from the verbs? Or, to take a slightly more abstract problem, how does the child learn to correctly form even a very simple question? Suppose a certain dog looks as if it might bite the child. He or she may suppose, *The dog is (or might be) mean.* If an adult or someone who knows the dog well is nearby, the child might want to ask, *Is the dog mean?*

How can a child learn to form such a question? A possible grammatical rule that the child might infer (subconsciously) would involve looking for the first occurrence of *is* (or *can, will, might, could,* etc.) in the underlying supposition that *The dog is (or might be) mean* and then to moving it to a position before the subject noun phrase *The dog.* This rule would result in the right form in the present example: *Is the dog mean?* But it would fail to give the right result if the supposition to be turned into a question were a little more complex. For instance, what if the child notices that *The dog that is chasing the neighbor's husband up a eucalyptus tree is (or looks to be) fairly mean.* The child might then want to ask, *Is the dog that is chasing the neighbor's husband up a eucalyptus tree fairly mean?* Acting by the rule stated earlier, he or she would actually get a wrong form of the question: *Is the dog that chasing the neighbor's husband up a eucalyptus tree is fairly mean?* This turns out to be obviously ungrammatical, but it is a kind of error that children never make!

The child learning English (or any language) clearly does not go through all possible hypotheses about how to form a certain structure, but apparently has some correct notions about how to do so before the fact. Otherwise, as Chomsky has shown, it would be impossible to explain the speed and accuracy with which such problems (many of them enormously more complex than the one just illustrated) are correctly solved by all normal children in the learning of absolutely any human language. It is exactly as if human children were able to limit in advance the possible hypotheses for the formation of the kinds of structures that actually occur in human languages. Moreover, any child can perform this miraculous feat for any of the world's five thousand-plus languages on the basis of thirty-six to sixty months of experience with relatively scant data. Any normal human child can acquire any language to which the child is suitably exposed.

Now the apes do nothing remotely similar to this. They do not follow any sort of structure-dependency principle, and there is no evidence that they make any distinction at all between any grammatical categories of any type (not even nouns and verbs). Herbert Terrace explains just how different the accomplishment of the human child is from the "chained responses" the trained apes learn by rote repetition. Suppose that a pigeon, he suggests, were taught to peck keys of different colors in a certain order: green, then white, then red, then blue. Such training has often been done. Then suppose the words *PLEASE, GIVE, ME, FOOD* were typed on the same keys and the pigeon pecked them out in order. Could this behavior be construed as a linguistic act?

Pragmatic Recursion

Related to the structure-dependency principle, which seems to be entirely lacking from the performance of the trained apes, is the "principle of pragmatic recursion," which may be described as the ability to talk about talk about talk. Every child is capable of this. The childhood dispute over who said what to whom and what they meant by it is not uncommon for five- or six-year-olds. Even younger children can be made to smile at a story about when we were once all sitting around a campfire when someone said, "Let's have a story," and the story began like this, "We were all sitting around the campfire, when someone said . . ." and so forth. The possibility of using linguistic forms to refer to other linguistic forms that also refer to other linguistic forms ad infinitum is one that any normal child can both understand and perform.

But no ape can even so much as comment upon a comment. Koko never says, "Ah, but Penny, why do you say that? Of course, what you should call it is a 'home' and not a 'tree,' for the heart is where the tree is!"

Koko never argues about the meanings of signs or their appropriateness, yet every child is prone to do so. The child can also readily see the possibility of the story about the campfire going on forever. Where does this knowledge come from? It cannot be from experience, because no one has ever told or heard a story that went on forever. Such an idea must be innate. It logically cannot be learned by any number of iterations. Yet any normal child of five or six can understand the formulaic ending "And they all lived happily ever after."

An Infinitely Expandable Vocabulary

There are many other specific differences between the language capacities of apes and human beings, but we will conclude with just one more. The human child rapidly acquires a rich and extensive vocabulary that is so completely expandable, owing to different combinations of words that may be formed, as to cover every imaginable conceptual contingency as well as a great many that are difficult even to imagine (e.g., a square circle, a song that never ends, a magic idea with royal blue iron wings). Moreover, unlike the case of the trained ape, who achieves only about an 80 percent level of accuracy using signs, the child, even at play, rarely applies a sign that is not articulately appropriate to the situation to which it is applied. The child's linguistic performance is so much more delicately fitted to situations than is the "verbal behavior" of the trained ape that it is difficult even to conceive of a common metric by which the one could be compared with the other. It is like comparing the crowing of a rooster at daybreak with the responsible discourse of a man or woman laying out the plans for the day.

To say, then, that some prehuman creature's first primitive cry was the first step toward language is analogous to supposing that the first animal to climb a tree took the first essential step in the exploration of outer space.

Summing Up and Concluding

We have examined the human language capacity from a scientific point of view and have seen how closely it is connected with the distinctive abstract capabilities of human intelligence. We have seen that the intricate and articulate structures of language are mirrored in the delicate arrangements of biological representations in correspondence to information coded in DNA. We have shown logically that the language capacity cannot have originated in any purely materialistic manner. The logical gulf that separates mind from matter really is an uncrossable barrier to any materialistic origin. If the definitions of Peirce and Einstein are accepted, the gulf they described cannot be crossed without the intervention of a truly transcendent Intelligence—a conclusion both of them accepted.

As remarkable as it is, human beings really do have at least a darkling conception of an eternal realm beyond the space-time world. A simple and trivial human choice, such as to drop or not to drop a certain cup, indisputably proves our access to that which is eternally true and yet which is not necessarily realized physically at all. Consider the action that was thought of but not performed and all of the consequences that would have but did not follow from it. We know what would have happened if the cup had been dropped, and this proves our access to an abstract eternal realm that must be at least as real as the one we inhabit—as real as the fact that if I had dropped the cup, it would have fallen to the floor.

We humans through our language capacity not only can describe the material world around us with a surprisingly high degree of accuracy, but we can easily overreach the entire scope of the space-time world in order to express ideas that touch the unseen eternity of abstract ideas. That eternal, unseen realm is accessible to us through the gift of language.

Though we are surely not omniscient, nor omnipresent, nor omnipotent, by the powers released in us through the gift of language we are undeniably able to entertain such concepts, and in doing so we give as clear a proof as ought to be required that our capacity for language cannot have originated within the narrow confines of any finite duration of experience. The language capacity necessary for abstract representations absolutely must precede experience as we know it, and cannot therefore come from it.

All experience is finite and particular (it occurs at a certain point in time and space). Suppose I dropped the cup and it fell. This would be a particular event. Yet our conception of that event, like all conceptions whatever, is completely general. The conception would apply equally well to any event similar to the one at hand and thus reaches out to an infinity of possibilities that have never been experienced.

If all the eons of the space-time world could be multiplied clear to infinity, the material world would still fail to account for the abstract conceptions that any human being can easily conceive of through the gift of language. The amount of time, space, matter and energy that exists and even the exact character of the physical mechanisms that resulted in the states of the space-time continuum that we observe today are tangential and hardly relevant to the question of how the abstract and nonfinite human language capacity came about. The most peculiar property of that capacity, the one that demands explanation, is that it enables us to step outside the bounds of time and space.

We cannot see the eternal realm that we enter through language, but to deny that it exists is tantamount to denying the simplest exercise of choice. For instance, it is to deny all reality to the road not taken (or the cup not dropped). Or it is to assert that any reality attributed to such hypothetical possibilities must be a strictly physical reality, which would be absurd. The cup is still here before me and was not dropped and consequently remains as yet unbroken. If any choice is to be regarded as real, we must accept the fact that the rejected alternative is as real as the one selected, though neither was physically determined before the choice was made. Otherwise there could be no real choice between dropping the cup or not. We could still prove that the choice exists by dropping and breaking the cup even now, but we choose not to because the proof is not needed.

So we reach our final question, the same one with which we began, "In whose image?" Imagine that you are the judge and that your own words by an act of your own free will can decide the case. What will your verdict be?

Bibliography

Binet, Alfred. "New Investigations upon the Measure of the Intellectual Level Among School Children." *L'Année Psychologique* 11 (1911): 145-201. Reprinted in Binet, Alfred, and Theodore Simon. *The Development of Intelligence in Children (the Binet-Simon Scale)*. Translated by Elizabeth Kite. Baltimore, Md.: Williams and Wilkins, 1916. [B]

_____. *The Psychic Life of Micro-organisms*. Chicago: Open Court, 1888. [B]

Bolinger, Dwight L. *Aspects of Language*. New York: Harcourt Brace Jovanovich, 1975. [I]

Chomsky, Noam A. *Cartesian Linguistics: A Chapter in the History of Rationalist Thought*. New York: Harper & Row, 1966. [I]

_____. *Language and Mind*. New York: Harcourt, 1972. [B]

_____. *Language and Problems of Knowledge: The Managua Lectures*. Cambridge, Mass.: MIT Press, 1988. [I]

_____. *Language and Responsibility: Based on Conversations with Mitsou Ronat*. Translated by John Viertel. New York: Pantheon, 1979. [B]

_____. *Rules and Representations*. New York: Columbia University Press, 1978. [I]

Clark, Virginia P., Paul A. Eschholz and Alfred F. Rosa, eds. *Language: Introductory Readings*. 3rd ed. New York: St. Martin's, 1981. [B]

Darwin, Charles. *The Descent of Man*. 2nd ed. New York: D. Appleton, 1874. [B]

Denton, Michael. *Evolution: A Theory in Crisis*. Bethesda, Md.: Adler and Adler, 1986. [B]

Einstein, Albert. "Physics and Reality" (1936) and "The Common Language of Science" (1941). In *Out of My Later Years*. Secaucus, N.J.: Citadel, 1936. Also in *Language and Experience: Classic Pragmatism*. Edited by John W. Oller Jr. Lanham, Md.: University Press of America, 1989. [B]

_____. "Remarks on Russell's theory of knowledge." In *The Philosophy of Bertrand Russell*, ed. Paul Arthur Schilpp. New York: Tudor, 1944. Also in *Language and Experience: Classic Pragmatism* Edited by John W. Oller Jr. Lanham, Md.: University Press of America, 1989. [I]

Horgan, John. "Free Radical: A Word or Two About Linguist Noam

Chomsky." *Scientific American* 262 (May 1990): 40-44. [B]

Kouznetsov, Dmitri A. "Modern Concepts of Species: Do We Come Back to Fixism?" *CENTech Journal* 5, no. 2 (1991). [I]

Nagel, Ernest. "Charles Sanders Peirce: A Prodigious but Little Known American Philosopher." *Scientific American* 200 (1959): 185-92. [B]

Ogden, C. K., and I. A. Richards, eds. *The Meaning of Meaning*. New York: Harcourt Brace, 1949. [B]

Oller, John W., Jr. "Language as Intelligence?" *Language Learning* 31 (1981): 465-92. [B]

────── . "Reasons Why Some Methods Work." In *Methods That Work*. 2nd ed. Edited by John W. Oller Jr. Boston: Heinle and Heinle, 1993. [I]

────── . "Semiotic Theory and Language Acquisition." In *Georgetown University Round Table on Languages and Linguistics 1990*. Edited by James E. Alatis. Washington, D.C.: Georgetown University, 1990. [I]

────── . "Some Working Ideas for Language Teaching." In *Methods That Work: A Smorgasbord of Ideas for Language Teachers*. Edited by John W. Oller Jr. and Patricia Richard-Amato. Rowley, Mass.: Newbury House, 1983. [B]

Oller, John W., Jr., ed. *Language and Experience: Classic Pragmatism*. Lanham, Md.: University Press of America, 1989. [I]

Oller, John W., Jr., Steven Chesarek and J. Robert Scott. *Language and Bilingualism: More Tests of Tests*. Cranbury, N.J.: Associated University Presses, 1991. [I]

Patterson, Francine. "Conversations with a Gorilla." *National Geographic* 154 (1978): 438-65. [B]

Patterson, Francine, and E. Linden. *The Education of Koko*. New York: Holt, 1981. [B]

Peirce, Charles S. *Collected Papers of C. S. Peirce*. Vols. 1-6, edited by Charles Hartshorne and Paul Weiss; vols. 7-8, edited by A. W. Burks. Cambridge, Mass.: Belknap/Harvard University Press, 1935-58. [A]

────── . *Writings of C. S. Peirce: A Chronological Edition*. Vol. 1, edited by Max H. Fisch et al.; vol. 2, edited by Edward C. Moore et al. Indianapolis: Indiana University Press, 1982-84. [I]

Piatelli-Palmarini, Massimo, ed. *Language and Learning: The Debate Between Jean Piaget and Noam Chomsky*. Cambridge, Mass.: Harvard University Press, 1980. [A]

Premack, Ann James, and David Premack. "Teaching Language to an Ape." In *Human Communication: Language and Its Psychobiological Bases*. Edited by William S. Y. Wang. San Francisco: W. H. Freeman, 1982. [B]

Rumbaugh, Duane M. *Language Learning by a Chimpanzee: The Lana Project.* New York: Academic, 1977. [B]

Russell, Bertrand. *Human Knowledge: Its Scope and Limits.* New York: Simon and Schuster, 1948. [B]

Russell, Claire, and W. M. S. Russell. "Language and Animal Signals" (1971). In *Language: Introductory Readings.* 3rd ed. Edited by Virginia P. Clark, Paul A. Eschholz and Alfred F. Rosa. New York: St. Martin's, 1981. [B]

Sebeok, Thomas A., and Jean Umiker-Sebeok, eds. *Speaking of Apes: A Critical Anthology of Two-Way Communication with Man.* New York: Plenum, 1980. [I]

Spearman, Charles E. " 'General Intelligence' Objectively Determined and Measured." *American Journal of Psychology* 15 (1904): 201-93. [I]

Terrace, Herbert S. *Nim: A Chimpanzee Who Learned Sign Language.* New York: Knopf, 1981. [B]

Thaxton, Charles B., Walter L. Bradley and Roger L. Olsen. *The Mystery of Life's Origin.* 1984; rpt. Dallas: Lewis and Stanley, 1992. [B]

Vygotsky, Lev Semenovich. *Thought and Language* (1934). Translated by E. Hanfmann and G. Vakar. Cambridge, Mass.: MIT Press, 1962. [I]

Wang, William S. Y., ed. *Human Communication: Language and Its Psychobiological Bases.* San Francisco: W. H. Freeman, 1982. [B]

Whorf, Benjamin Lee. *Language, Thought and Reality: Selected Writings.* Cambridge, Mass.: MIT Press, 1956. [I]

Wilcox, Sherman, ed. *Academic Acceptance of American Sign Language.* Special issue of *Sign Language Studies* 59 (1988). [B] ·

Appendix
RATIONAL INQUIRY & THE FORCE OF SCIENTIFIC DATA: ARE NEW HORIZONS EMERGING?

John Ankerberg & John Weldon

*I have often thought how little I should
like to prove organic evolution in a court of law.*

E. WHITE, *PRESIDENTIAL ADDRESS
TO THE LINNEAN SOCIETY, 1966*

Suppose for a moment that Darwin's theory of natural selection is a mistaken view about the origin and development of life. If so, wouldn't it be reasonable to conclude that scientists themselves would become increasingly aware of this and publicly state their findings?

After all, how could scientists in different disciplines not say something if they were becoming more aware of the absence of hard evidence in support of Darwin's theory and were face to face with scientific data that pointed to a completely different theory—one that suggests the world was designed and exists for a purpose?

Anyone who reads the private and published reports of evolutionary scientists, especially since the 1980s, cannot help but notice that there are many who admit they doubt the whole paradigm of evolutionary belief.[1] But before we review these conclusions of evolutionary scientists, we offer the following four observations.

First, despite their specific criticisms, most of these scientists are not seeking to discredit what they view as the probable truthfulness of evolution itself.

Second, our citation of those who criticize not just part of evolutionary theory but the entire concept does not imply that these individuals are creationists. In rejecting evolution as a whole, they usually remain agnostic on the subject of origins.

Third, some evolutionists have made controversial statements that were widely circulated and resulted in their embarrassment. Under pressure from their colleagues they "recanted" their views. Nevertheless, for whatever reason those statements were given, the fact is that they were initially made in good faith. When we quote them, all we are saying is that they have made these statements—and we think they have made some astute observations.

Finally, when one considers the great number of scientists who have expressed serious reservations regarding a particular area of evolutionary thought, their collective weight is formidable. Virtually all aspects of evolutionary theory have recently encountered major critique by someone. Thus collectively considered, what now remains factually and scientifically established in evolutionary theory as a whole would appear to be marginal. Therefore we think it is appropriate to consider new paradigms.

The Rising Doubts

Michael Denton, an Australian medical doctor and molecular biologist, is one scientist who has boldly made his views public. His 1986 book *Evolution: A Theory in Crisis* tells how it became apparent to him that the scientific evidence simply did not support the evolutionary model of life's origin. Evolution "is still, as it was in Darwin's time, a highly speculative hypothesis entirely without direct factual support," he says.[2] Consider his comments on the difficulty of cell evolution and the unexpected lack of fossilized evidence in oceanic sediments:

> The first stage on the road to life is presumed to have been the buildup, by purely chemical synthetic processes occurring on the surface of the early Earth, of all the basic organic compounds necessary for the formation of a living cell. These are supposed to have accumulated in the primeval oceans, creating a nutrient broth, the so-called "prebiotic soup." In certain specialized environments, these organic compounds were as-

sembled into large macromolecules, proteins and nucleic acids. Eventually, over millions of years, combinations of these macromolecules occurred which were endowed with the property of self-reproduction. Then driven by natural selection ever more efficient and complex self-reproducing molecular systems evolved until finally the first simple cell system emerged.

The existence of a prebiotic soup is crucial to the whole scheme. Without an abiotic accumulation of the building blocks of the cell no life could ever evolve. If the traditional story is true, therefore, there must have existed for millions of years a rich mixture of organic compounds in the ancient oceans and some of this material would very likely have been trapped in the sedimentary rocks lain down in the seas of those remote times.

Yet rocks of great antiquity have been examined over the past two decades and in none of them has any trace of abiotically produced compounds been found. Most notable of these rocks are the "dawn rocks" of Western Greenland, the earliest dated rocks on Earth, considered to be approaching 3,900 million years old. . . . As on so many occasions, paleontology has again failed to substantiate evolutionary presumptions. Considering the way the prebiotic soup is referred to in so many discussions of the origin of life as an already established reality, it comes as something of a shock to realize that there is absolutely no positive evidence for its existence.[3]

In addition to the problems mentioned by Denton, there are those of a more intractable nature, such as the lack of a reducing atmosphere (the presence of free oxygen), which further complicates the alleged process of abiogenesis. Biochemists generally agree that the presence of free oxygen would, in the words of R. T. Brinkmann of the California Institute of Technology, "preclude biological evolution as presently understood."[4] Yet the evidence for an early oxidized atmosphere is increasingly so compelling that A. Henderson-Sellers, A. Benlow and A. Meadows concede that, despite the implications, it is "becoming the new orthodoxy."[5]

But difficulties such as these pale to insignificance when faced with the heroic difficulty of finally evolving a human being. The noted scientists Francis Crick, L. M. Murkhin and Carl Sagan have estimated that the difficulty of evolving a human by chance processes alone is one in $10^{-2,000,000,000}$—which Borel's law says is no chance at all.[6] Indeed, a number so small is not conceivable. Many other eminent scientists have attempted to grapple with the practical difficulty of the chance origin of life and the magnitude of the problem of explaining the complex information content in living things.[7]

Few would argue that despite its inherent complexities, the discussion of probability theory in reference to evolution is fascinating to contemplate for both layperson and scientist.[8] The weight of factual information underlying such discussions which mitigates against evolution may be why Francis Crick, Nobel Prize-winner, biochemist and codiscoverer of the structure of the DNA molecule, once wrote: "An honest man, armed with all the knowledge available to us now, could only state that in some sense, the origin of life appears at the moment to be almost a miracle, so many are the conditions which would have had to have been satisfied to get it going."[9]

Sir Fred Hoyle, founder of the Cambridge Institute of Theoretical Astronomy and originator of the steady state theory of the origin of the universe, also seems to have problems with evolutionary theory. Citing Hoyle, *Nature* magazine commented, "The chance that higher life forms might have emerged in this way is comparable with the chance that 'a tornado sweeping through a junk-yard might assemble a Boeing 747 from the material therein.' "[10]

Hoyle and his research partner Chandra Wickramasinghe press the point in their book *Evolution from Space*. They argue that the chance of life's evolving randomly is too improbable. Thus they speculate that it had to have arisen from other intelligent life somewhere in space. After outlining the reasons that it is unlikely that life originated by chance, they supply probability calculations to support the idea that life must have been assembled by intelligence:

> Any theory with a probability of being correct that is larger than one part in $10^{40,000}$ must be judged superior to random shuffling. The theory that life was assembled by an intelligence has, we believe, a probability vastly higher than one part in $10^{40,000}$ of being the correct explanation of the many curious facts discussed in preceding chapters. Indeed, such a theory is so obvious that one wonders why it is not widely accepted as being self-evident. The reasons are psychological rather than scientific.[11]

In a chapter called "The Evolutionary Record Leaks like a Sieve," Hoyle and Wickramasinghe even credit the natural theology of William Paley, an eighteenth-century British philosopher: "The speculations of *The Origin of Species* turned out to be wrong, as we have seen in this chapter. It is ironic that the scientific facts throw Darwin out, but leave William Paley, a figure of fun to the scientific world for more than a century, still in the tournament with a chance of being the ultimate winner."[12]

On April 25 and 26, 1962, some of the most distinguished evolutionist scientists of that day gathered for a scientific symposium at the Wistar Institute of Anatomy and Biology in Philadelphia. The symposium was entitled "Mathematical Challenges to the Neo-Darwinian Interpretation of Evolution." Its chair, Sir Peter Medawar of the National Institute for Medical Research in London, launched the symposium with a statement of purpose:

> The immediate cause of this conference is a pretty widespread sense of dissatisfaction about what has come to be thought of as the accepted evolutionary theory in the English-speaking world, the so-called neo-Darwinian theory. . . . These objections to current neo-Darwinian theory are very widely held among biologists generally; and we must on no account, I think, make light of them. The very fact that we are having this conference is evidence that we are not making light of them.[13]

In his symposium paper, "Inadequacies of Neo-Darwinian Evolution as a Scientific Theory," Murray Eden, professor of electrical engineering at MIT, emphasized the following: "It is our contention that if 'random' [chance] is given a serious and crucial interpretation from a probabilistic point of view, the randomness postulate is highly implausible and that an adequate scientific theory of evolution must await the discovery and elucidation of new natural laws, physical, chemical and biological."[14]

In "Algorithms and the Neo-Darwinian Theory of Evolution" Marcel P. Schutzenberger of the University of Paris calculated the probability of evolution based on mutation and natural selection. Along with many other noted scientists, he concluded that it was "not conceivable" because the probability of a chance process accomplishing this is zero: "there is no chance ($< 10^{-1000}$) to see this mechanism appear spontaneously and, if it did, even less for it to remain. . . . Thus, to conclude, we believe there is a considerable gap in the neo-Darwinian theory of evolution, and we believe this gap to be of such a nature that it cannot be bridged within the current conception of biology."[15]

Even Charles Darwin thought his own theory was "grievously hypothetical"[16] and gave emotional content to his doubts when he said, "The eye to this day gives me a cold shudder."[17] To think the eye had evolved by natural selection, Darwin said, "seems, I freely confess, absurd in the highest possible degree."[18] But he thought the same about something as simple as a peacock's feather, which he said, "makes me sick."[19] Of course, anyone who has knowledge of the intricacies of the human eye and other living structures immediately realizes the problem Darwin sensed. How could an organ of such intricate magnificance ever have originated via random chance?

It is easy to sympathize with Darwin. Such feelings have probably occurred to most biologists at times, for to common sense it does indeed appear absurd to propose that chance could have thrown together devices of such complexity and ingenuity that they appear to represent the very epitome of perfection. . . .

Aside from any quantitative considerations, it seems intuitively impossible that such self-evident brilliance in the execution of design could ever have been the result of chance. For, even if we allow that chance might have occasionally hit on a relatively ingenious adaptive end, it seems inconceivable that it could have reached so many ends of such surpassing "perfection."[20]

The eminent biologist L. Harrison Matthews wrote the following in his introduction to Darwin's *Origin of Species*. He noted that biology was in the position of being founded on an unproved theory that nearly placed it in the category of a "religious" faith:

In accepting evolution as a fact, how many biologists pause to reflect that science is built upon theories that have been proved by experiment to be correct, or remember that the theory of animal evolution has never been thus proved? Even "Darwin's bulldog," as Thomas Huxley once called himself, wrote in 1863: "I adopt Mr. Darwin's hypothesis, therefore, subject to the production of proof that physiological species may be produced by selective breeding"—meaning species that are infertile if crossed. That proof has never been produced, though a few not entirely convincing examples are claimed to have been found. The fact of evolution is the backbone of biology, and biology is thus in the peculiar position of being a science founded on an unproved theory—is it then a science or a faith? Belief in the theory of evolution is thus exactly parallel to belief in special creation—both are concepts which believers know to be true but neither, up to the present, has been capable of proof.[21]

Some scientists have suggested that they could find some evidence for life originating from nonlife on some other planet. This would give them circumstantial evidence that life could originate by evolutionary processes someplace else. (They have not found this evidence on earth.) I. S. Shklovskii and Carl Sagan say, "The discovery of life on one other planet—e.g., Mars—can, in the words of the American physicist Philip Morrison, of the Massachusetts Institute of Technology, 'transform the origin of life from a miracle to a statistic.' "[22]

Crick, thoroughly aware of the awesome complexity of cellular life and the extreme difficulty of explaining how such life could evolve in the short time scientists now realize was available on earth for evolution to take place, has advanced a theory he calls "directed panspermia." His theory, outlined in the book *Life Itself*, advances the idea that an extraterrestrial civilization sent primitive life-forms to earth in a spaceship. Because enormous time was required for interstellar travel, the senders chose primitive forms that would be capable of surviving the voyage and the conditions they would meet upon arriving on earth.

Impossible Chances
But this "solution" to the problem of origins only seems to push the issue back a notch. How did the advanced life that sent primitive life to our earth ever originate by chance processes? In fact, research indicates that this scenario cannot resolve the problem. For example, in the October 1969 issue of *Nature*, Frank Salisbury of Utah State University, then on leave at the Division of Biomedical and Environmental Research at the U.S. Atomic Energy Commission, examined the chances of occurrence of one of the most basic chemical reactions for the continuation of life. This reaction involves the formation of a specific DNA molecule. (It is important to realize that Salisbury was assuming that life already existed. His calculations do not refer to the chance of the origin of life from dead matter—something infinitely more improbable—but to the continuance of already-existing life.)

He calculated the chance of this molecule's evolving on 10^{20} hospitable planets (having favorable atmospheric and biologic conditions). These one hundred thousand million billion planets constitute at least one thousand times more hospitable planets than the number many scientists have estimated could exist. Salisbury allows 4 billion years for the chance coming into existence of this molecule on all these planets. Remember, he is not speaking here of life as we know it—developed, intelligent living beings, or even one single cell for that matter. He is only calculating the chance of one appropriate DNA molecule.

Salisbury concluded that the chances of this one tiny DNA molecule's coming into existence over 4 billion years, with conditions just right, on just one of these almost countless number of hospitable planets, including the earth, as one chance in 10^{415}.[23] This figure far exceeds the standard of Borel's law, which says that beyond a certain point improbable events never happen, regardless of the time span involved. Indeed, 10^{50} planets would pack the known universe, yet the chance that life could evolve from dead matter on any one of them is still beyond possibility.[24]

Further, the problems associated with human life's evolving from microbial forms are at least as difficult as those of primitive life's evolving from dead matter. Most scientists assume that the great amounts of time involved will allow highly improbable events to become virtually inevitable and thus solve the problem. But even A. I. Oparin concedes that "no serious quantitative arguments . . . are given in support of such conclusions."[25]

All this may explain why many scientists who have examined this theory critically consider the "directed panspermia" hypothesis untenable and do not think it is a solution to the problems we face.

Gaps in the Record

It is generally admitted that the fossil record contains the most cogent evidence for the evolutionary hypothesis. As the eminent French biologist and zoologist Pierre-P. Grassé says,

> Zoologists and botanists are nearly unanimous in considering evolution as a fact and not a hypothesis. I agree with this position and base it primarily on documents provided by paleontology, i.e., the [fossil] history of the living world. . . .
>
> Naturalists must remember that the process of evolution is revealed only through fossil forms. A knowledge of paleontology is, therefore, a prerequisite; only paleonotology can provide them with the evidence of evolution and reveal its course or mechanisms. Neither the examination of present beings, nor imagination, nor theories can serve as a substitute for paleontological documents. If they ignore them, biologists, the philosophers of nature, indulge in numerous commentaries and can only come up with hypotheses. This is why we constantly have recourse to paleontology, the only true science of evolution. . . . The true course of evolution is and can only be revealed by paleontology.[26]

Huxley also realized the importance of this issue when he wrote, "If it could be shown that this fact [gaps between widely distinct groups] had always existed, the fact would be *fatal* to the doctrine of evolution."[27]

The problem here is how evolutionary theory can ever be demonstrated when it necessarily postulates vast periods of time. Eminent biologist Theodosius Dobzhansky logically points out that no scientist can claim to have lived long enough to observe the evolution of major life forms.

> These evolutionary happenings are unique, unrepeatable, and irreversible. It is as impossible to turn a land vertebrate into a fish as it is to effect

the reverse transformation. The applicability of the experimental method to the study of such unique historical processes *is severely restricted before all else by the time intervals involved, which far exceed the lifetime of any human experimenter.* And yet, it is just such impossibility that is demanded by anti-evolutionists when they ask for "proofs" of evolution which they would magnanimously accept as satisfactory.[28]

But if scientists cannot observe evolution taking place, how can they state that evolution is a fact of science? Again, they attempt to do so by pointing to the fossil record. They believe it provides the critical evidence for evolution: the record of the past that demonstrates gradual evolutionary change between lower and higher life forms.

But even Darwin was concerned here. In thinking the geologic record incomplete, he confessed the following:

[Since] innumerable transitional forms must have existed, why do we not find them imbedded in countless numbers in the crust of the earth? Why is not every geological formation and every stratum full of such intermediate links? Geology assuredly does not reveal any such finely graduated organic chain; and this perhaps is the most obvious and gravest objection which can be urged against my theory.[29]

Again he asked, "Why if species have descended from other species by insensibly fine gradations, do we not everywhere see innumerable transitional forms?"—for "the number of intermediate and transitional links between all living and extinct species must have been inconceivably great."[30]

Yet 130 years later, it has become clear that the fossil record does not confirm Darwin's hope that future research would fill in the extensive gaps in the fossil record. Paleontologist Stephen Jay Gould of Harvard points out, "The fossil record with its abrupt transitions offers no support for gradual change. . . . All paleontologists know that the fossil record contains precious little in the way of intermediate forms; transitions between major groups are characteristically abrupt."[31]

With an estimated 250 million, or ¼ billion cataloged fossils of some 250,000 fossil species, the problem does certainly not appear to be an imperfect record. Many scientists have conceded that the fossil record is sufficiently complete to provide an accurate portrait of the geologic record.[32] University of Chicago professor of geology David Raup says, "Well, we are now about 120 years after Darwin and the knowledge of the fossil records has been greatly expanded. We now have a quarter of a million fossil species but the situation hasn't changed much. The record of evolution is still surprisingly jerky and, ironically, we have even fewer examples of evolutionary transition than we had in Darwin's time."[33]

The gaps remain. Prior to Gould's time, George Gaylord Simpson was one of the world's best-known evolutionists. He was professor of vertebrate paleontology, also at Harvard University, until his retirement. In *The Major Features of Evolution* he admitted, "It remains true, as every paleontologist knows, that *most* new species, genera, and families and that nearly all new categories above the level of families appear in the record suddenly and are not led up to by known, gradual, completely continuous transitional sequences."[34]

Perhaps this explains why Austin Clark, once curator of paleontology at the Smithsonian Institute in Washington, D.C., wrote in 1928, "Thus so far as concerns the major groups of animals, the creationists seem to have the better of the argument."[35] His statement would appear to remain true today. In his *Biology, Zoology and Genetics,* A. Thompson agrees: "Rather than supporting evolution, the breaks in the known fossil record support the creation of major groups with the possibility of some limited variation within each group."[36] Derek V. Ager points out what every informed scientist knows, that "if we examine the fossil record in detail, whether at the level of orders or of species, we find—over and over again—not gradual evolution, but the sudden explosion of one group at the expense of another."[37]

Simpson believed that the fossil record was almost complete for the larger terrestrial forms of North America; yet, he said, "the regular absence of transitional forms is an almost universal phenomenon" among all orders of all classes of animals and analogous categories of plants.[38] If so, it is not surprising to hear E. J. H. Corner of the botany department of Cambridge University say, "But I still think that, to the unprejudiced, the fossil record of plants is in favor of special creation. . . . Can you imagine how an orchid, a duck weed, and a palm have come from the same ancestry, and have we any evidence for this assumption? The evolutionist must be prepared with an answer, but I think that most would break down before an inquisition."[39]

Indeed, if as several evolutionary scientists admit, the fossil record "fails to contain a single example of a significant transition,"[40] and if the fossil record is generally complete, then we are correct in concluding that paleontological histories of the plants and animals simply do not exist. Ichthyologist Donn Rosen, curator of fish at the American Museum of Natural History in New York, noted that evolution has been "unable to provide scientific data about the origin, diversity and similarity of the two million species that inhabit the earth and the estimated eight million others that once thrived."[41]

This complaint has been registered for almost every species of plants, mammals, insects, birds and fish known to humankind.[42] For example, Donald C. Johanson observes, "Modern gorillas, orangutans, and chimpanzees spring out of nowhere, as it were. They are here today; they have no yesterday."[43] Concerning the evolution of reptiles, University of California paleontologist R. A. Stirton points out, "There is no direct proof from the fossil record."[44] Boston University biologist Paul B. Weiss comments, "The first and most important steps of animal evolution remain even more obscure than those of plant evolution."[45] Pierre-P. Grasse is considered an outstanding scientist and the dean of French zoologists. In his *Evolution of Living Organisms* he declares, "We are in the dark concerning the origin of insects."[46] An authority on lungfishes, E. White, reflects, "Whatever ideas authorities may have on the subject, the lungfish, like every other major group of fish that I know, have their origins firmly based on nothing."[47]

Colin Patterson is the senior paleontologist at the British Museum of Natural History in London and author of the museum's general text on evolution. He wrote in a letter to Luther D. Sunderland on April 10, 1979: "I fully agree with your comments on the lack of direct illustration of evolutionary transitions in my book. If I knew of any, fossil or living, I would certainly have included them. . . . I will lay it on the line—there is not one such fossil for which one could make a watertight argument."[48]

Robert Barnes, in his book *Invertebrate Beginnings,* has confessed: "The fossil record tells us almost nothing about the evolutionary origin of phyla and classes. Intermediate forms are non-existent, undiscovered, or not recognized."[49] Similarly, Earl L. Core, then chair of the department of biology at West Virginia University, comments, "We do not actually know the phylogenetic history of any group of plants and animals, since it lies in the indecipherable past."[50]

David Raup, who was previously curator of geology at the Field Museum of Natural History and is now professor of geology at the University of Chicago, has said concerning the mysterious origins of higher plant and animal forms: "Unfortunately, the origins of most higher categories are shrouded in mystery; commonly new higher categories appear abruptly in the fossil record without evidence of transitional forms."[51] Steven M. Stanley is professor of paleobiology at Johns Hopkins University. He was a recipient of the Schuchert Award of the Paleontological Society and has also been awarded a Guggenheim Fellowship. He openly admits, "The known fossil record fails to document a single example of phyletic [gradual] evolution accomplishing a major morphologic transition and hence offers no evidence that the gradualistic model can be valid."[52]

So Stephen J. Gould's remark on Darwin's dilemma remains valid: "New species almost always appeared suddenly in the fossil record with no intermediate links to ancestors in older rocks of the same region."[53] Gould concedes that the lack of fossil evidence is the "trade secret" of paleontology.

The extreme rarity of transitional forms in the fossil record persists as the trade secret of paleontology. The evolutionary trees that adorn our textbooks have data only at the tips and nodes of their branches; the rest is inference, however reasonable, not the evidence of fossils. . . . Most species exhibit no directional change during their tenure on earth. . . . In any local area, a species does not arise gradually by the steady transformation of its ancestors; it appears all at once and "fully formed."[54]

What Are the Alternatives?

Interested readers may wonder if evolutionary scientists have developed any new theories to explain the embarrassing lack of transitional forms in the fossil record. Perhaps it was a statement by Darwin concerning the abrupt appearance of many higher plant and animal forms which has recently sparked a new evolutionary theory. Darwin observed: "Nothing is more extraordinary in the history of the Vegetable Kingdom, as it seems to me, than the apparently very sudden or abrupt development of the higher plants."[55] He felt that this absence of plant and animal transitions was "the gravest objection" that could be raised against his theory.[56]

Niles Eldredge and Stephen J. Gould tentatively proposed that to account for the record as it exists, the major gaps should be viewed as real phenomena of nature, an inevitable result of the mechanism of evolution itself. They see evolution taking place in major creative episodes, occurring at different times and places, interspersed with long periods of stability. They call their theory "punctuated equilibrium"; some others call it "evolutionary saltationism." In part, this theory returns us to geneticist Richard Goldschmidt's "hopeful monsters" theory, which, in Stanley's words, "[engenders] such visions as the first bird hatching from a reptile egg."[57]

In *The Panda's Thumb* Gould explains how punctuated equilibria works. Although elsewhere he confesses that he and Eldredge do not hold to the exclusive validity of this concept, they feel that their theory is not inconsistent with the Darwinian model and that it helps to explain the gaps in the fossil record—which they say adequately expresses evolutionary history: "The fossil record is a faithful rendering of what evolutionary theory predicts, not a pitiful vestige of a once bountiful tale. Eldredge and I refer to this scheme as the model of punctuated equilibria. Lineages change little during most of their history, but events of rapid speciation occasionally punctuate this tranquility."[58]

In part, Gould's concept is an admission that Darwin's theory of gradual evolution is not correct. One might argue that the punctuated equilibrium model, which assumes that the higher categories of plants and animals "suddenly" appeared "fully formed" in the fossil record, is perhaps not really much different from the belief that God created life forms instantaneously.

Even the accomplished Swedish botanist and geneticist Nils Heribert-Nilsson concluded, after forty years of attempting to find evidence for the theory of evolution, that the task was impossible and the theory is even "a serious obstruction to biological research." In his twelve-hundred-page magnum opus *Synthetic Speciation*, he confessed the theory "ought to be entirely abandoned," in part because it "obstructs—as has been repeatedly shown—the attainment of consistent results, even from uniform experimental material. For everything must ultimately be forced to fit this speculative theory. An exact biology cannot, therefore, be built up."[59] Having said that "a close inspection discovers an empirical impossibility to be inherent in the idea of evolution,"[60] he went even further than Gould. He concluded that geologic periods having incredible spurts of biogeneration produced billions of biosyntheses simultaneously. Gametes and other necessary cells and biocatalytic substances literally appeared spontaneously and led immediately to their fully formed end products such as orchids, elephants and eagles. He insisted that the empirical evidence forced him to this conclusion:

> As I have pointed out, there is no discussion among biologists today whether an evolution has taken place or not. The discussion concerns the how, the causation of evolution. No definite answer has been given to this question.
>
> It then becomes necessary to ask: Has there really been an evolution? Are the proofs of its occurrence tenable?
>
> After a detailed and comprehensive review of the facts we have been forced to give the answer: No! Neither a recent nor a palaeohistorical evolution can be empirically demonstrated.
>
> If this is the case, all discussions and problems concerning the causation of an evolution lose all interest. Lamarckism or mutationism, monophyletic or polyphyletic, continuity or discontinuity—the roads of the evolu-

tion are not problems any more. It is rather futile to discuss the digestion or the brain functions of a ghost.

When we have arrived at this standpoint, the evolutionist has the obvious right to ask: What has caused the fundamental differentiation in the world of organisms, the immeasurable variation among animals and plants? That it exists is a fact: you owe us an explanation!

We turn to empirical facts to obtain the answer. They tell us that during the geological history of the earth gigantic revolutions have occurred which at the same time mean *tabula rasa* catastrophes for a whole world of organisms but also the origin of a completely new one. The new one is structurally completely different from the old one. There are no other transitions than hypothetical ones. This origination of biota, which from a geological point of view is sudden as a flaring up I have called *emication.*

During palaeobiological times whole new worlds of biota have been repeatedly synthesized.

I will be asked: Do you seriously want to make such a statement? Do you not see that the consequences of such a theory are more than daring, that they would be nearly insane? Do you really mean to say that an orchid or an elephant should have been instantaneously created out of non-living material?

Yes, I do.[61]

Another scientist whose words can be marshaled in support of Gould's new model of evolution is Steven M. Stanley, who wrote in the preface of his *The New Evolutionary Timetable: Fossils, Genes and the Origin of Species:*

The [fossil] record now reveals that species typically survive for a hundred thousand generations, or even a million or more, without evolving very much. We seem forced to conclude that most evolution takes place rapidly, when species come into being by the evolutionary divergence of small populations from parent species. After their origins, most species undergo little evolution before becoming extinct.[62]

But what do other scientists think about replacing Darwin's theory of "gradualism" with Gould's "punctuated equilibrium"? In essence, not much. For example, Ernst Mayr says the "hopeful monsters" theory "is equivalent to believing in miracles."[63]

Denton succinctly explains the problems faced by this approach:

While Eldredge and Gould's model is a perfectly reasonable explanation of the gaps between species (and, in my view, correct), it is doubtful if it can be extended to explain the larger systematic gaps. The gaps which separate species: dog/fox, rat/mouse, etc., are utterly trivial compared with, say, that between a primitive terrestrial mammal and a whale or a primitive terrestrial reptile and an Ichthyosaur; and even these relatively major discontinuities are trivial alongside those which divide major phyla such as molluscs and arthropods. Such major discontinuities simply could not, unless we are to believe in miracles, have been crossed in geologically short periods of time through one or two transitional species occupying restricted geographical areas. Surely, such transitions must have involved long lineages including many collateral lines of hundreds or probably thousands of transitional species. . . . To suggest that the hundreds, thousands or possibly even millions of transitional species which must have existed in the interval between vastly dissimilar types were all unsuccessful species occupying isolated areas and having very small population numbers is verging on the incredible![64]

In other words, if evolution is to be considered a true scientific fact, it must be able to explain the origin of developed life forms by recourse to proven methods of evolutionary change. Can it do so? It would seem that most scientists who have examined this subject critically are honest enough to say no, even though they continue to believe in evolution. The problems of using natural selection, mutation and newer theories to explain how evolution occurs are, put simply, too expansive to be resolved by current knowledge.[65] Indeed, some scientists have confessed to little hope that any conceivable breakthrough in this area will ever be forthcoming.[66]

Writing in the *Physics Bulletin,* H. S. Lipson of the University of Manchester Institute of Science and Technology observes: "I have always been slightly suspicious of the theory of evolution because of its ability to account for any property of living beings (the long neck of the giraffe, for example). I have therefore tried to see whether biological discoveries over the last thirty years or so fit in with Darwin's theory. I do not think that they do." He further states, "In the last thirty years we have learned a great deal about life processes (still a minute part of what there is to know!) and it seems to me to be only fair to see how the theory of evolution accommodates the new evidence. This is what we should demand of a purely physical theory. To my mind, the theory does not stand up at all. I shall take only one example—breathing." He proceeds to show how one cannot account for breathing on evolutionary assumptions. After further discussion, he asks, "How has living matter originated?" and concludes, "I think, however, that we must go further than this and admit that the only acceptable explanation is creation. I know that this is anathema to physicists, as indeed it is to me, but we must not reject a theory that we do not like if the experimental evidence supports it."[67]

If science cannot explain the evolution of living matter, neither can it explain the origin of the universe itself, which is certainly the grandest mystery of all, one that has preoccupied the greatest minds of history. Here also we are in the dark scientifically speaking, and of course this too has implications for the evolution of life. If we can never know the original conditions of creation and the early earth, it becomes difficult to accept that conditions we think were present actually account for spontaneous generation and the evolution of all life. In 1980 John D. Barrow and Joseph Silk said in *Scientific American,* "What happened at the precise moment of creation is not yet known because unfamiliar physical principles unique to the immense densities and temperatures at that moment mask the initial structure of the universe."[68] Robert Jastrow, eminent astronomer and author of the popular *God and the Astronomers,* agrees: "The world had a beginning under conditions in which the known laws of physics are not valid, and as a product of forces or circumstances we cannot discover."[69]

If evolution is truly a fact of science, it seems reasonable to conclude that science would uncover evidence to explain certain crucial questions concerning the origin and development of the universe. But science cannot answer the most fundamental of all questions, "Where did matter come from in the first place?" Indeed, the more we advance our knowledge, the more we realize how much there is we do not understand and probably never can.

Jastrow candidly admits: "Astronomers now find they have painted themselves into a corner because they have proven, by their own methods, that the world began abruptly in an act of creation to which you can trace the seeds of every star, every planet, every living thing in this cosmos and on the earth. And they have found that all this happened as a product of forces they cannot hope to discover."[70]

One wonders whether Jastrow speaks for many scientists today when he writes:

> No explanation other than the Big Bang has been found for the fireball radiation. The clincher, which has convinced almost the last doubting Thomas, is that the radiation discovered by Penzias and Wilson has exactly the pattern of wavelengths expected for the light and heat produced in a great explosion. Supporters of the Steady State theory have tried desperately to find an alternative explanation, but they have failed.[71]

Unfortunately, it would seem that at least for its critics, the big bang theory isn't all that credible either.[72] Despite the latest advances in our knowledge of this theory, the words of Hoyle will, in all probability, remain true or at least suggestive: "Although the highly complicated theoretical investigations of the past fifteen years have drawn heavily on powerful new knowledge in basic physics, results of worthwhile significance seem to be elusive. . . . I have little hesitation in saying that as a result a sickly pall now hangs over the big bang theory."[73]

A Challenge to Conventional Wisdom

On top of all this, along comes a brilliant law professor at the University of California, Berkeley, specializing in the logic of argument, who boldly states the following: "Evolution is taught in the public schools (and presented in the media) not as a theory but as a fact, the 'fact of evolution.' There are none-theless many dissidents, some with advanced scientific degrees, who deny that evolution is a fact and who insist that an intelligent Creator caused all living things to come into being in furtherance of a purpose."[74]

In *Darwin on Trial,* Phillip E. Johnson tells of a remarkable lecture given by Colin Patterson at the American Museum of Natural History in 1981. As noted earlier, Patterson is the senior paleontologist at the British Museum of Natural History and the author of that museum's general text on evolution. He asked his audience of experts a question that reflected his own doubts about much of what has been thought to be secure knowledge about the process of evolution:

> Can you tell me anything you know about evolution, any one thing . . . that is true? I tried that question on the geology staff at the Field Museum of Natural History and the only answer I got was silence. I tried it on the members of the Evolutionary Morphology seminar in the University of Chicago, a very prestigious body of evolutionists, and all I got there was silence for a long time but eventually one person said, "I do know one thing—it ought not to be taught in high school."[75]

Johnson analyzes this story and concludes the following:

> Patterson suggested that both evolution and creation are forms of pseudo-knowledge, concepts which seem to imply information but do not. One point of comparison was particularly striking. A common objection to crea-tionism in pre-Darwinian times was that no one could say anything about the mechanism of creation. Creationists simply pointed to the "fact" of creation and conceded ignorance of the means. But now, according to Patterson, Darwin's theory of natural selection is under fire and scientists

are no longer sure of its general validity.

Evolutionists increasingly talk like creationists in that they point to a fact but cannot provide an explanation of the means.[76]

Now Johnson does not cite Patterson's lecture to imply that Patterson's highly skeptical views are widely held in the scientific community. Patterson was being provocative on purpose and came "under heavy fire" from Darwinists after a bootleg transcript of the lecture was circulated. This caused him to disavow the entire business. Johnson's point is that whether or not Patterson intended his comments for public distribution, he did make a crucial point— scientists know very little about how complex living beings on our planet came into existence.[77]

Johnson believes that viewed strictly from the point of view of logic and the accepted canons of scientific research, the Darwinian theory is severely lacking in confirmatory evidence. He shows how scientists have put the cart before the horse, prematurely accepting the theory as fact and then scrambling to find evidence for it. In the process, Darwinism itself has become a kind of faith, a pseudoscience embraced by its devotees in spite of, rather than because of, the evidence.[78]

This same kind of evidence has led philosophers such as Karl Popper to say, "I have come to the conclusion that Darwinism is not a testable scientific theory, but a *metaphysical research programme*—a possible framework for testable scientific theories. . . . I do not think that Darwinism can explain the origin of life. I think it quite possible that life is so extremely improbable that nothing can 'explain' why it originated."[79] And so many scientists are increasingly dissatisfied: they think evolution is true, but are increasingly confronted by the necessity of faith.[80]

Louis Bounoure, formerly president of the Biological Society of Strasbourg, is the director of the Zoological Museum and director of research at the Natural Center of Scientific Research in France. Concerning evolution he forthrightly confesses, "Evolution is a fairytale for grown-ups. This theory has helped nothing to the progress of science. It is useless."[81] G. Sermonti, noted genetics professor at the University of Perugia and vice president of the Fourteenth International Congress of Genetics, and R. Fondi, professor of paleontology at the University of Siena, refer to "the narrow straits and *blind alleys* of the evolutionistic myth."[82] Denton refers to the idea of evolution operating by random processes as "simply an affront to reason."[83]

Even the noted entomologist W. R. Thompson, in his introduction to the centenary edition of Darwin's *Origin of Species,* observed that Darwinism has had a wasteful influence in numerous scientific disciplines including genetics, biology, classification and embryology.[84] He argued that because evolution had become an indefensible dogma to be defended at all costs, the cause of science itself had suffered: "This situation, where scientific men rally to the defense of a doctrine they are unable to define scientifically, much less demonstrate with scientific rigour, attempting to maintain its credit with the public by the suppression of criticism and the elimination of difficulties, is abnormal and undesirable in science."[85]

The aforementioned Pierre-P. Grassé is a modern "non-Darwinian" evolutionist who is highly critical of neo-Darwinism.[86] His *Evolution of Living Organisms* was reviewed by Theodosius Dobzhansky, who some believe is the greatest living evolutionist of this century. Here are some of Dobzhansky's comments:

> The book of Pierre P. Grassé is a frontal attack on all kinds of "Darwinism." Its purpose is "to destroy the myth of evolution, as a simple, understood, and explained phenomena," and to show that evolution is a mystery about which little is, and perhaps can be, known. Now, one can disagree with Grasse but not ignore him. He is the most distinguished of French zoologists, the editor of the 28 volumes of *Traité de Zoologie,* author of numerous original investigations, and ex-president of the Academie des Sciences. His knowledge of the living world is encyclopedic.[87]

Grassé makes an important point when he observes that evolutionary theory brings with it problems that are apparently insoluble: "Evolution is so vast as to make one stop and consider that its problems are very far beyond the means of present-day science. Interpretations and explanations advanced by *whomever it may be* can only be partial and tentative."[88]

Indeed, there are many reputable scientists who would now probably echo saltationist Søren Lovtrup's words, "I believe that one day the Darwinian myth will be ranked the greatest deceit in the history of science. When this happens, many people will pose the question: How did this ever happen?"[89]

In fact, some scientists today are almost embarrassed by the theory of evolution. As noted anthropologist Loren Eiseley has written:

> With the failure of these many efforts science was left in the somewhat embarrassing position of having to postulate theories of living origins which it could not demonstrate. After having chided the theologian for his reliance on myth and miracle, science found itself in the unenviable position of having to create a mythology of its own: namely, the assumption that what, after long effort, could not be proved to take place today had,

in truth, taken place in the primeval past.[90]

What Difference Does It Make?

Michael Denton has looked beyond evolution's problems to the implications of accepting or rejecting the Darwinian model of life. He correctly states,

The failure to validate the Darwinian model has implications which reach far beyond biology. . . .

The entire scientific ethos and philosophy of modern western man is based to a large extent upon the central claim of Darwinian theory that humanity was not born by the creative intentions of a deity, but by a completely mindless trial and error selection of random molecular patterns. The cultural importance of evolution theory is therefore immeasurable, forming as it does the centrepiece, the crowning achievement, of the naturalistic view of the world.[91]

If the naturalistic view of the world really is true, what difference does it make?

Unfortunately, despite the optimism of a few exobiologists, many have recognized that the picture of humankind given by modern science is one of cosmic isolation. Human beings live alone within a truly massive but terribly impersonal universe—a universe that endlessly piques our awe and curiosity but that, strange as it seems, cannot provide us with a final justification for the things we seem to value most deeply. As William Provine of Cornell University argues, "The implications of modern science, however, are clearly inconsistent with most religious traditions. . . . No inherent moral or ethical laws exist, nor are there absolute guiding principles for human society. The universe cares nothing for us and we have no ultimate meaning in life."[92]

Not surprisingly, in a universe so large and uncertain, millions of persons ponder the purpose of their existence: when all is said and done, is there any real point to life? Leslie Paul once observed,

No one knows what time, though it will be soon enough by astronomical clocks, the lonely planet will cool, all life will die, all mind will cease, and it will all be as if it had never happened. That, to be honest, is the goal to which evolution is traveling, that is the benevolent end of the furious living and furious dying. . . . All life is no more than a match struck in the dark and blown out again. The final result . . . is to deprive it completely of meaning.[93]

Perhaps the *bon mot* that evolution is "$1/10$ bad science and $9/10$ bad philosophy" isn't so odd after all. In *Darwin and His Critics,* philosophy professor

David L. Hull of the University of Wisconsin observes:

> The leading philosophers contemporary with Darwin, John Herschel, William Whewell, and John Stuart Mill, were equally adamant in their conviction that the *Origin of Species* was just one mass of conjecture. Darwin had proved nothing! From a philosophical point of view, evolutionary theory was sorely deficient. Even today, both Darwin's original efforts and more recent reformulations are repeatedly found philosophically objectionable. Evolutionary theory seems capable of offending almost everyone.[94]

Perhaps evolutionary science is "bad philosophy" because it attempts to address the issue of origins on the basis of an inadequate approach. The issue is argued exclusively at the level of naturalism, while it is forgotten that theology itself is a legitimate discipline of knowledge that should also be considered.

Approaching the issue of origins materialistically leaves too many major problems for explaining the data, data that everyone agrees is there. Meaning or interpretation that is assigned on the premise of naturalism alone will be deficient, because the data is incapable of organizing itself adequately solely on this basis. This is why many scientists are currently unhappy with the case for evolution.

What is needed is a discussion of the issue of origins at the worldview level—which is really what's going on in both camps, whether or not this is recognized. The very components of science—classification, theory, experiment and so on—reflect a framework of concepts that transcend scientific data. All attempts to explain or interpret are to some degree impositions on the data. So are attempts to disprove or disallow alternate explanations. In other words, because the data of science does not automatically organize itself, interpretive structures that themselves transcend the data must be imposed upon it. Again, the question is whether a solely naturalistic structure is adequate.

We believe that an approach that attempts to look at the data without a bias against larger theological implications would be more productive. For example, the data from science indicates a point of origin for the universe. Further, the universe and its laws have not always been around in their present state. The data from science also suggests a high degree of complexity throughout the history of life, and such complexity requires explanations that not only include but also transverse natural processes alone. In addition, the data from science indicates an incredibly high degree of fine-tuning or balance within the structure of the universe at all levels. This also calls for an explanation that transcends natural processes.

Thus we believe the theistic worldview is just as adequate an explanatory framework for the scientific data as is the worldview of naturalism—in fact, *more* adequate. In other words, philosophy, logic and science would all suggest that "natural laws" alone are insufficient to account for the existence of the universe and the complexity of life that inhabits it. This becomes especially true when we consider the distinctive character of humankind, such as our abstract reasoning powers, moral sensibility, complex personality and spiritual notions. Humans are so far removed from the level of the animals that we simply cannot account for ourselves on the basis of purely natural processes.[95]

Both reason and nature indicate the necessity of a transcendent intelligence to account for what we find in the universe: the fact of a beginning, the complexity of life, the fine-tuning of the cosmos, the spiritual nature of humankind and so on. Science is undeniably valuable as a part of the larger picture explaining the world, but it cannot explain the entirety of that picture. Theism—in terms of its ability to explain a much larger range of data, as well as the integration of data in other disciplines—actually offers a more coherent "big picture." When creation is affirmed in the context of theism, it meets the criteria of good science: it is testable, unified and fruitful in a heuristic sense.

In conclusion, no single worldview, not even theism, is complete as a philosophical position in that one can expect it to explain all the data of the universe. Both science and theology are needed. And many scientists recognize this in one fashion or another.

In *Chance and Necessity*, the outstanding French biochemist and Nobel Prizewinner Jacques Monod makes his case that all life evolved by random means, yet he says this:

> When one ponders on the tremendous journey of evolution over the past 3 billion years or so, the prodigious wealth of structures it has engendered, and the extraordinarily effective teleonomic performances of living beings, from bacteria to man, one may well find oneself beginning to doubt again whether all this could conceivably be the product of an enormous lottery presided over by natural selection, blindly picking the rare winners from among numbers drawn at utter random. . . . The miracle stands "explained"; [yet] it does not strike us as any less miraculous. As François Mauriac wrote, "What this professor says is far more incredible than what

we poor Christians believe." This is true, just as it is true that there is no achieving a satisfactory mental image of certain abstractions in modern physics.[96]

Although Monod believes that life arose by chance, he freely admits that the chances of this happening before it occurred were virtually zero.[97] We can only be reminded of the statement by another Nobel Prize-winner, biologist George Wald of Harvard: "One only has to concede the magnitude of the task to concede the possibility of the spontaneous generation of a living organism is 'impossible.' Yet here we are—as a result, I believe, of spontaneous generation."[98] What this boils down to is a personal choice—faith, if you will—to believe in what one freely admits is impossible, rather than to believe in creation by intelligent design.

Thus Fred Hoyle's research partner, Chandra Wickramasinghe, has noted that it is not only creationism that relies on the supernatural. Evolution must also, since the probabilities of random formation of life are so minuscule as to necessitate a "miracle," making belief in spontaneous generation "tantamount to a theological argument."[99]

The God Hypothesis

In light of all this, perhaps it really wouldn't hurt anyone to listen again to some of the greatest scientific minds of both past and present who have confessed their belief that God alone can explain the existence of the universe. As Sir Isaac Newton observed, "This most beautiful system of the sun, planets, and comets could only proceed from the counsel and domain of an intelligent and powerful Being."[100]

Robert Jastrow is the founder and director of NASA's Goddard Institute for Space Studies, an internationally known astronomer and professor at Dartmouth and Columbia universities. His oft-cited statement in *God and the Astronomers* is still relevant:

> A sound explanation may exist for the explosive birth of our Universe; but if it does, science cannot find out what the explanation is. The scientist's pursuit of the past ends in the moment of creation.
>
> This is an exceedingly strange development, unexpected by all but the theologians. They have always accepted the word of the Bible: In the beginning God created heaven and earth. . . . At this moment it seems as though science will never be able to raise the curtain on the mystery of creation. For the scientist who has lived by his faith in the power of reason, the story ends like a bad dream. He has scaled the mountains of igno-

rance; he is about to conquer the highest peak; as he pulls himself over the final rock, he is greeted by a band of theologians who have been sitting there for centuries.[101]

In conclusion, we think there is no legitimate reason why good science cannot begin to consider additional ways of organizing data—to the benefit of both science and theology. We hope this text is evidence of a beginning.

Notes

Introduction/Moreland

¹John Kekes, *The Nature of Philosophy* (Totowa, N.J.: Rowman and Littlefield, 1980), p. 158.

²See John Searle, *The Rediscovery of the Mind* (Cambridge, Mass.: MIT Press, 1992) for more on this point.

³Even if one holds that belief in God is "properly basic," i.e., rationally grounded without the need for evidence, it could still be the case that arguments from natural theology provided confirming evidence for the rationality of belief in God.

⁴For overviews of the kalam cosmological argument, see J. P. Moreland, *Scaling the Secular City* (Grand Rapids, Mich.: Baker Book House, 1987), chap. 1; J. P. Moreland and Kai Nielsen, eds., *Does God Exist? The Debate Between Atheists and Theists* (Buffalo, N.Y.: Prometheus Books, 1993). For a technical discussion, see William Lane Craig and Quentin Smith, *Theism, Atheism and Big Bang Cosmology* (Oxford, U.K.: Clarendon, 1993).

⁵See the objections by Anthony Flew and Keith Parsons in *Does God Exist?*, pp. 163-64, 185-88. See also J. L. Mackie, *The Miracle of Theism* (Oxford, U.K.: Clarendon, 1982), p. 93.

⁶Actually, though my argument does not rely on this insight, a beginningless universe could involve the existence of an event that has receded infinitely far into the past. But since this is absurd (it involves traversing an actual infinite by successive addition), it would be another way to show that the universe had a beginning. In a beginningless universe, the number of events in the past is actually infinite, but the ordinality of the set of these events could easily be $\omega^* + \omega^*$ ($\ldots$, -3, -2, -1, $\ldots$, -3, -2, -1) when we remember that we are dealing with actual events in the real world and not with mere mathematical abstractions. We can number the events of the past any way we wish. But in this case there would be an infinite number of events that have receded infinitely far into the past—an absurd conclusion if there ever was one.

⁷See G. J. Whitrow, "Entropy," in *Encyclopedia of Philosophy*, ed. Paul Edwards (New York: Macmillan, 1967), 2:526-29.

⁸I owe this point to William Lane Craig.

⁹See Reinhardt Grossmann, *The Existence of the World: An Introduction to Ontology* (London: Routledge, 1992), pp. 1-45, for a good treatment of the nature of naturalism; cf. my review of this book in *Mind* 102 (July 1993): 407-10.

¹⁰For more on the difference between state-state and agent causation, see William L. Rowe, "Two Concepts of Freedom," *Proceedings and Addresses of the American Philo-

sophical Association, Supplement to Volume 61 (September 1987): 43-64; William L. Rowe, "Responsibility, Agent-Causation and Freedom: An Eighteenth-Century View," *Ethics* 101 (January 1991): 237-57; Stewart C. Goetz, "A Noncausal Theory of Agency," *Philosophy and Phenomenological Research* 49 (December 1988): 303-16; Roderick Chisholm, *On Metaphysics* (Minneapolis: University of Minnesota Press, 1989), pp. 3-15; Richard Swinburne, *The Existence of God* (Oxford, U.K.: Clarendon, 1979), pp. 22-50.

[11]For more on the design argument, see Moreland, *Scaling the Secular City*, chap. 2; A. C. Ewing, *Value and Reality* (London: George Allen & Unwin, 1973), pp. 165-82; William J. Wainwright, *Philosophy of Religion* (Belmont, Calif.: Wadsworth, 1988), pp. 48-58; John Leslie, *Universes* (New York: Routledge, 1989). For a critique of an evolutionary justification of the reliability of our sensory and cognitive faculties, see Alvin Plantinga, *Warrant and Proper Function* (New York: Oxford University Press, 1993), chaps. 11-12.

[12]A. R. Peacocke, *Creation and the World of Science* (Oxford, U.K.: Clarendon, 1979), pp. 90-92. Cf. Stanley L. Jaki, *God and the Cosmologists* (Washington, D.C.: Regnery Gateway, 1989), pp. 142-69.

[13]For a brief treatment of other aspects of Hume's critique and a bibliography for further study, see Moreland, *Scaling the Secular City*, pp. 62-67.

[14]Mackie, *Miracle of Theism*, p. 141.

[15]For more on the multiple world ensembles view, see Paul Davies, *God and the New Physics* (New York: Simon and Schuster, 1983), pp. 164-76; Leslie, *Universes;* William Lane Craig, "Barrow and Tipler on the Anthropic Principle vs. Divine Design," *British Journal for the Philosophy of Science* 38 (1988): 389-95.

[16]Someone may still be convinced that efficiency is important and go on to point out that some living organisms are not perfectly designed but do, in fact, have certain features that even a human engineer could conceivably improve upon. In addition to what has already been said to address this claim, one more point should be stressed. According to creationists, God is the Creator not only of individual kinds of organisms but of entire ecosystems as well. This may require not perfect efficiency on the part of a given species, but maximal efficiency. That is, an organism's efficiency of survival must be balanced with other organisms and factors in the ecosystem. If a given organism were perfectly efficient, then the rest of the ecosystem would go wildly out of balance. So the various organisms in an ecosystem may have an efficiency that represents a compromise with other factors in that ecosystem so as to obtain an optimal balance. By the way, this does not imply that a kind of organism would never become extinct. A kind of organism could have a purpose and be valuable to God without enduring forever.

[17]For a brief critique of Stephen Hawking's *A Brief History of Time*, see William Lane Craig, "In Defense of Rational Theism," in *Does God Exist?*, pp. 147-48; and his "What Place, Then, for a Creator?" *British Journal for the Philosophy of Science* 49 (1990): 473-91.

Chapter 1: Theistic Science & Methodological Naturalism/Moreland

[1]Michael Ruse, *Darwinism Defended* (Reading, Mass.: Addison-Wesley, 1982), p. 322.

[2]Ibid. Cf. David Hull's review of Phillip Johnson's *Darwin on Trial, Nature* 352 (August 8, 1991): 485-86.

[3]For a recent, lively debate about the scientific status of creationist theories involving Alvin Plantinga, Van Till, Pattle Pun and Ernan McMullin, see *Christian Scholar's Review* 21 (September 1991).

⁴See Howard J. Van Till, Robert E. Snow, John H. Stek and Davis A. Young, *Portraits of Creation* (Grand Rapids, Mich.: Eerdmans, 1990), p. 127.

⁵Cf. David L. Hull, *The Metaphysics of Evolution* (Albany, N.Y.: State University of New York Press, 1989), pp. 62-75.

⁶See Van Till et al., *Portraits of Creation;* Paul de Vries, "Naturalism in the Natural Sciences: A Christian Perspective," *Christian Scholar's Review* 15 (1986): 388-96. All references in the text are to these two sources. See also Howard J. Van Till, Davis A. Young and Clarence Menninga, *Science Held Hostage* (Downers Grove, Ill: InterVarsity Press, 1988).

⁷Howard J. Van Till, *The Fourth Day* (Grand Rapids, Mich.: Eerdmans, 1986), p. 195; cf. Van Till et al., *Portraits of Creation*, p. 127.

⁸Howard J. Van Till, "When Faith and Reason Cooperate," *Christian Scholar's Review* 20 (September 1991): 42.

⁹For more on this see J. P. Moreland, *Christianity and the Nature of Science* (Grand Rapids, Mich.: Baker Book House, 1989), pp. 95-98.

¹⁰Cf. Larry Laudan, *Progress and Its Problems* (Berkeley: University of California Press, 1977); *Science and Values* (Berkeley: University of California Press, 1984); Bas C. van Fraasen, *The Scientific Image* (Oxford, U.K.: Oxford University Press, 1980).

¹¹For an example of this see Eugene Fontinell, *Self, God and Immortality* (Philadelphia: Temple University Press, 1986).

¹²Van Till's claim that MN focuses only on those qualities that are intrinsic (wholly resident within the empirically accessible physical universe) is difficult to sustain because, as a Platonist, I would argue that there is no such thing as a property that is wholly "resident" in the physical universe. Indeed, in my view no property is itself physical, though a property may be "physical" in the sense that it can (or perhaps can only) be exemplified by a physical object. See J. P. Moreland, "How to Be a Nominalist in Realist Clothing," *Grazer Philosophische Studien* 39 (1991): 75-101. Van Till seems oblivious to these problems.

¹³Larry Laudan, "The Demise of the Demarcation Problem," in *Physics, Philosophy and Psychoanalysis*, ed. R. S. Cohen and L. Laudan (Dordrecht, Netherlands: D. Reidel, 1983), p. 119.

¹⁴See Neal C. Gillespie, *Charles Darwin and the Problem of Creation* (Chicago: University of Chicago Press, 1979), especially chaps. 1 and 2; Philip Kitcher, *Abusing Science: The Case Against Creationism* (Cambridge, Mass.: MIT Press, 1982), p. 125.

¹⁵Laudan, "Demise of the Demarcation Problem," p. 125.

¹⁶Saul Kripke, *Naming and Necessity* (Cambridge, Mass.: Harvard University Press, 1972), pp. 93-94.

¹⁷Theology (and philosophy) can also provide a metaphysical picture of what some entity is, and this can serve as part of a model for scientific investigation. Thus both David Wiggins and Richard Connell have shown that philosophical arguments in support of viewing living organisms as genuine substance-things with natures and that fall under natural kinds and maintain unity and sameness through change provide materials for (1) rejecting any scientific or other tendency for reducing living organisms to mere heaps, Lesniewskian sums, space-time worms or property-things and (2) for searching for more specific substance-determining capacities and principles of individuation by biologists or other scientists. See David Wiggins, *Sameness and Substance* (Cambridge, Mass.: Harvard University Press, 1980), pp. 117-19; Richard Connell, *Substance and Modern Science* (Notre Dame, Ind.: University of Notre Dame Press, 1988). Now E. Mayr has argued that Darwinian evolution is hard to square with an

essentialist, substantial view of living organisms. See his *Populations, Species and Evolution* (Cambridge, Mass.: Harvard University Press, 1970), p. 4. Thus if philosophical or theological arguments exist for viewing living organisms as substance-things, these can serve as external conceptual problems for standard evolutionary orthodoxy.

[18]There are some affinities between my picture of theological concepts in science and Nicholas Wolterstorff's notion of a theological control belief. See Nicholas Wolterstorff, *Reason Within the Bounds of Religion* (Grand Rapids, Mich.: Eerdmans, 1984).

[19]See Imre Lakatos, "Methodology of Scientific Research Programmes," in *Criticism and the Growth of Knowledge*, ed. by Imre Lakatos and Alan Musgrave (Cambridge, U.K.: Cambridge University Press, 1970), pp. 132-54.

[20]See Laudan, *Progress and Its Problems*. Laudan combines his analysis of the place of empirical and conceptual problems in science with antirealism. But these two theses are distinct, and one need not embrace antirealism to recognize the fact that empirical and conceptual problems have been a significant part of the business of science throughout its history, although one's interpretation of the precise nature of that role will be informed by one's stand on the realism-antirealism controversy.

[21]Cf. Howard E. Gruber, *Darwin on Man: A Psychological Study of Scientific Creativity* (Chicago: University of Chicago Press, 1974), p. 201-17; D. M. Armstrong, *A Materialist Theory of Mind* (London: Routledge & Kegan Paul, 1968), p. 30; Arthur Peacocke and Grant Gillett, eds., *Persons and Personality* (Oxford, U.K.: Basil Blackwell, 1987), p. 55.

[22]Paul Churchland, *Matter and Consciousness* (Cambridge, Mass.: MIT Press, 1984), p. 21.

[23]Hull, *Metaphysics of Evolution*, pp. 74-75.

[24]I am indebted to Mark D. Hartwig and Stephen C. Meyer for pointing out this example to me.

[25]Cf. Richard DeCharms, "Personal Causation, Agency and the Self," in *The Book of the Self: Person, Pretext and Process*, ed. Polly Young-Eisendrath and James Hill (New York: New York University Press, 1987), pp. 384-403; M. Brewster Smith, "Perspectives on Selfhood," *American Psychologist* 33 (December 1978): 1053-63.

[26]DeCharms, "Personal Causation, Agency and the Self," p. 18.

[27]John Searle, *The Rediscovery of the Mind* (Cambridge, Mass.: MIT Press, 1992), pp. 3-4.

[28]I owe this point to Stephen C. Meyer and Mark D. Hartwig.

[29]Recall Ruse's claim cited earlier that if scientific creationism were successful in making its case, it would not produce a scientific explanation of origins, but rather it would prove that there is no scientific explanation of origins. Even if we grant Ruse this point, it only follows that scientific creationism is not science if we grant the further point that science is exhausted by the practice of explanation (and a specific sort of explanation at that: a covering law model of explanation or a realist causal-model type of explanation that can use only naturalistic concepts as part of its model). But as we have seen, there is no good reason to grant this further point.

[30]For more on agent action, state-state causation and agent causation, see William P. Alston, "God's Action in the World," in *Evolution and Creation*, ed. Ernan McMullin (Notre Dame, Ind.: University of Notre Dame Press, 1985), pp. 197-220; William Rowe, "Two Concepts of Freedom," *Proceedings of the American Philosophical Association* Supplementary Volume 61 (September 1987), pp. 43-64; Stewart C. Goetz, "A Noncausal Theory of Agency," *Philosophy and Phenomenological Research* 49 (December 1988): 303-16; Roderick Chisholm, *On Metaphysics* (Minneapolis: University of Minnesota Press, 1989), pp. 3-15; John Bishop, *Natural Agency* (Cambridge, U.K.: Cambridge University Press, 1989).

[31]I am using *agency* and *agent causation* to stand for two different views: (1) agents as substances cause their own actions; (2) agents as substances simply act by exercising their causal powers, and such acts are uncaused and done for reasons. Either approach leaves room for genuine agency and libertarian freedom and contrasts with state-state causation. Recently Dennis M. Senchuk has argued for wholes with emergent properties that, qua wholes, can feedback causal action to their parts. See his "Consciousness Naturalized: Supervenience Without Physical Determinism," *American Philosophical Quarterly* 28 (January 1991): 37-47. Unfortunately Senchuk's view is still deterministic, because he only allows for state-state causation and not agency as I am using it.

[32]For a dualist rebuttal of this charge, see Robert Larmer, "Mind-Body Interaction and the Conservation of Energy," *International Philosophical Quarterly* 26 (September 1986): 277-85.

[33]This point is made repeatedly by Phillip Johnson, who asks, in a number of different ways, what it is that God actually did to bring the world, life and so on into existence. See his *Darwin on Trial*, 2nd ed. (Downers Grove, Ill.: InterVarsity Press, 1993).

[34]An exception to this rule would be in cases where there are theological or philosophical reasons for thinking that God acts directly and by means of primary agent-causal ways in a regular way—e.g., in regeneration.

[35]Van Till et al., *Portraits of Creation*, p. 128.

[36]It may be thought that creationism has been around a very long time and creationists have had more than enough time to develop their models. But I don't think this is the case. It is certainly true that creationism has been around a "very long time" if we regard it as a research program. But more specific creationist theories get refined and replaced from time to time, and it seems to me that current creationist theories, while sharing important features with creationist theories of, say, the nineteenth century, still have important new features that justify the claim that more time is required for the development of contemporary creationist models.

[37]Nicholas Rescher, *The Limits of Science* (Berkeley: University of California Press, 1984), p. 22.

[38]It should be added that some appeals to fruitfulness actually distort an intellectual issue. For example, William Bechtel argues that of two views regarding the relationship between mental states and brain states—the two are different but correlated (property or substance dualism) and the two are identical (type or token identity physicalism)—the identity thesis can be judged as the superior position based on the fruitfulness of the scientific research program that follows from it. See *Philosophy of Mind* (Hillsdale, N.J.: Lawrence Erlbaum Associates, 1988), p. 101-3. This recommendation distorts the proper order of analysis regarding the mind-body problem (philosophy is more basic and important than is science), and in any case, whatever research program the identity thesis generates, the same research program, perhaps with very minor modifications, could be generated from the dualist correlation position.

[39]R. A. Kok, J. A. Taylor and W. L. Bradley, "A Statistical Examination of Self-Ordering of Amino Acids in Proteins," *Origins of Life and Evolution of the Biosphere* 18 (1988): 135-42.

[40]This conviction could be supported by viewing such organisms as substance-things and not property-things. In the former case organisms, qua substances, are wholes that are ontologically prior to their parts, that give structure to the relationship of those parts and in which the parts undergo a substantial change when incorporated

into larger substantial wholes. In the latter case wholes emerge when parts are placed into a certain structure, the wholes depend upon the nature of those parts, and the parts retain their nature in the emergent wholes. If organisms are substances, then the nature and structure of their parts, it could be argued, are due to the blueprint from God contained in the essence of the substance and not to latent potentialities in the parts prior to their incorporation into those wholes.

[41]Alvin Plantinga, "When Faith and Reason Clash: Evolution and the Bible," *Christian Scholar's Review* 21 (September 1991): 29-31.

Chapter 2: The Methodological Equivalence of Design & Descent/Meyer

[1]John D. Barrow and Frank J. Tipler, *The Anthropic Cosmological Principle* (New York: Oxford University Press, 1986). B. J. Carr and M. J. Rees, "The Anthropic Principle and the Structure of the Physical World," *Nature* 278 (1979): 605-12. J. Gribbin and M. Rees, *Cosmic Coincidences* (London: Black Swan, 1991). John Leslie, "Modern Cosmology and the Creation of Life," in *Evolution and Creation*, ed. Ernan McMullin (Notre Dame, Ind.: University of Notre Dame Press, 1985), pp. 91-120.

[2]Fred Hoyle, "The Universe: Past and Present Reflections," *Annual Review of Astronomy and Astrophysics* 20 (1982): 16.

[3]George Greenstein, *The Symbiotic Universe: Life and Mind in the Cosmos* (New York: Morrow, 1988), pp. 26-27.

[4]Timothy Lenior, *The Strategy of Life* (Chicago: University of Chicago Press, 1982), ix.

[5]Ernst Haeckel, *The Wonders of Life* (London: Watts, 1905), p. 111. T. H. Huxley, "On the Physical Basis of Life," *The Fortnightly Review* 5 (1869): 129-45.

[6]For good summaries of different approaches see especially K. Dose, "The Origin of Life: More Questions Than Answers," *Interdisciplinary Science Review* 13 (1988): 348-56; H. P. Yockey, *Information Theory and Molecular Biology* (Cambridge, U.K.: Cambridge University Press, 1992), pp. 259-93. Also Daniel R. Brooks and E. O. Wiley, *Entropy and Evolution* (Chicago: University of Chicago Press, 1985); A. G. Cairns-Smith, *Genetic Takeover and the Mineral Origins of Life* (Cambridge, U.K.: Cambridge University Press, 1982); A. G. Cairns-Smith, "The First Organisms," *Scientific American*, June 1985, pp. 90-100; A. G. Cairns-Smith, *Seven Clues to the Origin of Life* (Cambridge, U.K.: Cambridge University Press, 1985), pp. 90-100; T. R. Cech, "Ribozyme Self-Replication?" *Nature* 339 (1989): 507-8; F. Crick and L. Orgel, "Directed Panspermia," *Icarus* 19 (1973): 341-46; F. Crick, *Life Itself* (New York: Simon and Schuster, 1981); F. Crick, "The Origin of the Genetic Code," *Journal of Molecular Biology* 38 (1968): 367-79; R. E. Dickerson, "Chemical Evolution and the Origin of Life," *Scientific American* 239 (1978): 70-85; M. Eigen et al., "The Origin of Genetic Information," *Scientific American* 244 (1981): 88-118; S. W. Fox and K. Dose, *Molecular Evolution and the Origin of Life* (San Francisco: W. H. Freeman, 1972); S. W. Fox, "Proteinoid Experiments and Evolutionary Theory," in *Beyond Neo-Darwinism*, ed. M. W. Ho and P. T. Saunders (New York: Academic, 1984), pp. 15-60; S. W. Fox, "Self Organization in Evolution," in *Self-organization*, ed. S. W. Fox (New York: Adenine, 1986), pp. 35-56; F. Hoyle and S. Wickramasinghe, *Evolution from Space* (London: J. M. Dent, 1981); S. Kauffman, *The Origins of Order* (Oxford, U.K.: Oxford University Press, 1992), pp. 287-341; D. Kenyon and A. Nissenbaum, "On the Possible Role of Organic Melanoidin Polymers as Matrices for Prebiotic Activity," *Journal of Molecular Evolution* 7 (1976): 245-51; B. Kuppers, *Information and the Origin of Life* (Cambridge, Mass.: MIT Press, 1990); C. N. Matthews, "Chemical Evolution: Protons to Proteins," *Proceedings of the Royal Institution* 55 (1982): 199-206; S. Miller and J. Bada, "Submarine Hotsprings and the Origin of Life," *Nature*

334 (1988): 609-10; G. Nicolis and L. Prigogine, *Self Organization in Non-equilibrium Systems* (New York: John Wiley and Sons, 1977); C. Thaxton, W. Bradley and R. Olsen, *The Mystery of Life's Origin* (New York: Philosophical Library, 1984); J. C. Walton, "Organization and the Origin of Life," *Origins* 4 (1977): 16-35; J. Wicken, *Evolution, Thermodynamics and Information* (Oxford, U.K.: Oxford University Press, 1987); J. Wicken, "Thermodynamics, Evolution and Emergence: Ingredients for a New Synthesis," in *Entropy, Information and Evolution,* ed. Bruce H. Weber, David J. Depew and James D. Smith (Cambridge, Mass.: MIT Press, 1988), pp. 139-69; A. J. Zaug and T. R. Cech, "The Intervening Sequence RNA of Tetrahymena Is an Enzyme," *Science* 231 (1986): 470-75.

[7]For neo-Darwinism: R. Augros and G. Stanciu, *The New Biology* (Boston: Shambhala, 1987); E. J. Ambrose, *The Nature and Origin of the Biological World* (New York: Halstead, 1982); R. H. Brady, "Dogma and Doubt," *Biological Journal of the Linnean Society* 17 (1982): 79-96; G. de Beer, *Homology: An Unsolved Problem* (London: Oxford University Press, 1971); M. Denton, *Evolution: A Theory in Crisis* (London: Adler and Adler, 1986); P. P. Grasse, *Evolution of Living Organisms* (New York: Academic, 1977); S. J. Gould, "Is a New Theory of Evolution Emerging?" *Paleobiology* 6 (1980): 119-30. W. M. Ho, "Methodological Issues in Evolutionary Theory," D.Phil. thesis, Oxford University, 1965; P. Johnson, *Darwin on Trial,* 2nd ed. (Downers Grove, Ill.: InterVarsity Press, 1993); D. Kenyon and P. W. Davis, *Of Pandas and People: The Central Question of Biological Origins* (Dallas: Haughton, 1993); S. Lovtrup, *Darwinism: The Refutation of Myth* (Beckingham, Kent: Croom Helm, 1987); R. Lewin, "Evolutionary Theory Under Fire," *Science* 210 (1980): 883; R. Macnab, "Bacterial Mobility and Chemotaxis: The Molecular Biology of a Behavioral System," *CRC Critical Reviews in Biochemistry* 5 (1978): 291-341, esp. conclusion; Charles Mann, "Lynn Margulis: Science's Unruly Earth Mother," *Science* 252 (1991): 378-81, esp. 379; P. S. Moorhead and M. M. Kaplan, eds., *Mathematical Challenges to the Neo-Darwinian Interpretation of Evolution* (Philadelphia: Wistar Institute Press, 1967); D. Raup, "Conflicts Between Darwin and Paleontology," *Field Museum of Natural History Bulletin* 50, no. 1 (1979): 24; D. Raup, "Evolution and the Fossil Record," *Science,* July 17, 1981, p. 289; P. T. Saunders and M. W. Ho, "Is Neo-Darwinism Falsifiable—and Does It Matter?" *Nature and System* 4 (1982): 179-96; Andree Tetry, *A General History of the Sciences,* vol. 4 (London: Thames and Hudson, 1966), esp. p. 446; J. Valentine and D. Erwin, "Interpreting Great Developmental Experiments: The Fossil Record," in *Development as an Evolutionary Process,* ed. Rudolf Raff and Elizabeth Raff (New York: Alan R. Liss, 1985), esp. pp. 71, 95-96; G. Webster, "The Relations of Natural Forms," in *Beyond Neo-Darwinism,* ed. M. W. Ho and P. T. Saunders (London: Academic, 1984), pp. 193-217.

For origin of life research: W. L. Bradley, "Thermodynamics and the Origin of Life," *Perspectives on Science and Christian Faith* 40, no. 2 (1988): 72-83; Crick, *Life Itself,* p. 88; Dose, "Origin of Life," pp. 348-56; R. A. Kok, J. A. Taylor and W. L. Bradley, "A Statistical Examination of Self-Ordering of Amino Acids in Proteins," *Origins of Life and Evolution of the Biosphere* 18 (1988): 135-42; Hoyle and Wickramasinghe, *Evolution from Space;* D. Kenyon, "A Comparison of Proteinoid and Aldocyanoin Microsystems as Models of the Primordial Cell," in *Molecular Evolution and Protobiology,* ed. K. Matusuno, K. Dose, K. Harada and D. L. Rohlfing (New York: Plenum, 1984), pp. 163-88; D. Kenyon, "The Creationist View of Biological Origins," *NEXA Journal,* Spring 1984, pp. 28-35; K. Maher and D. Stevenson, "Impact Frustration of the Origin of Life," *Nature* 331 (1988): 612-14; P. T. Mora, "Urge and Molecular Biology, *Nature* 199 (1963): 212-19; P. T. Mora, "The Folly of Probability," in *The Origins of Prebiological*

Systems and of Their Molecular Matrices, ed. S. W. Fox (New York: Academic, 1965), pp. 39-64, 310-15; H. J. Morowitz, *Energy Flow in Biology* (New York: Academic, 1968); H. H. Pattee, "The Problem of Biological Hierarchy," in *Towards a Theoretical Biology,* ed. C. H. Waddington (Edinburgh: Edinburgh University Press, 1970), pp. 117-36; R. Shapiro, *Origins* (London: Heinemann, 1986); R. Shapiro, "Prebiotic Ribose Synthesis: A Critical Analysis," *Origins of Life and Evolution of the Biosphere* 18 (1988): 71-85; J. M. Smith, "Hypercycles and the Origin of Life," *Nature* 280 (1979): 445-46; L. Margulis, J. C. Walker and M. Rambler, "Reassessment of Roles of Oxygen and Ultraviolet Light in Precambrian Evolution," *Nature* 264 (1976): 620-24; Miller and Bada, "Submarine Hotsprings," pp. 609-10; Thaxton, Bradley and Olsen, *Mystery of Life's Origin;* Walton, "Organization and the Origin of Life," 16-35; E. Wigner, "The Probability fo the Existence of a Self-Reproducing Unit," in *The Logic of Personal Knowledge: Essays Presented to Michael Polanyi* (London: Routledge and Kegan Paul, 1961), pp. 231ff.; H. P. Yockey, "A Calculation of the Probability of Spontaneous Biogenesis by Information Theory," *Journal of Theoretical Biology* 67 (1977): 377-98; H. P. Yockey, "Self Organization Origin of Life Scenarios and Information Theory," *Journal of Theoretical Biology* 91 (1981): 13-31; Yockey, *Information Theory and Molecular Biology,* pp. 179-330.

[8]Dose, *Origin of Life,* pp. 348ff. See also quotation from Carl Woese in Shapiro, *Origins,* p. 114. D. Collingridge and M. Earthy, "Science Under Stress: Crisis in Neo-Darwinism," *History and Philosophy of the Life Sciences* 12 (1990): 3-26. See also N. Eldredge, *Time Frames: The Evolution of Punctuated Equilibria* (Princeton, N.J.: Princeton University Press, 1985), p. 14.

[9]D. Kenyon, "Going Beyond the Naturalistic Mindset in Origin-of-Life Research," paper presented to Conference on Christianity and the University, Dallas, February 9-10, 1985.

[10]Crick, *Life Itself,* p. 88.

[11]S. J. Gould, "The Senseless Signs of History," in *The Panda's Thumb* (New York: Norton, 1984), p. 118.

[12]B. Willey, "Darwin's Place in the History of Thought," in *Darwinism and the Study of Society,* ed. M. Banton (Chicago: Quadrangle Books, 1961).

[13]R. Grizzle, "Some Comments on the 'Godless' Nature of Darwinian Evolution, and a Plea to the Philosophers Among Us," *Perspectives on Science and the Christian Faith* 45 (1993): 176.

[14]N. Murphy, "Phillip Johnson on Trial: A Critique of His Critique of Darwin," *Perspectives on Science and Christian Faith* 45, no. 1 (1993): 33.

[15]Ibid.

[16]Grizzle, "Some Comments," p. 175.

[17]M. Ruse, *Darwinism Defended: A Guide to the Evolution Controversies* (London: Addison-Wesley, 1982), pp. 59, 131-40, 322-24; M. Ruse, "Creation Science Is Not Science," *Science, Technology and Human Values* 7, no. 40 (1982): 72-78; M. Ruse, "A Philosopher's Day in Court," in *But Is It Science?* ed. M. Ruse (Buffalo, N.Y.: Prometheus Books, 1988), pp. 13-38; M. Ruse, "Witness Testimony Sheet," in *But Is It Science?* pp. 287-306, esp. 301; M. Ruse, "They're Here!" *Bookwatch Reviews* 2, no. 1 (1989): 4; M. Ruse, "Darwinism: Philosophical Preference, Scientific Inference and Good Research Strategy," paper presented at Darwinism: Scientific Inference or Philosophical Preference? conference, Southern Methodist University, Dallas, March 26-28, 1992; S. J. Gould, "Evolution as Fact and Theory" and "Genesis and Geology," in *Science and Creationism,* ed. A. Montagu (New York: Oxford University Press, 1984); G. S. Stent, "Scientific Crea-

tionism: Nemesis of Sociobiology,·' in *Science and Creationism*, pp. 136-41; R. Root-Bernstein, "On Defining a Scientific Theory: Creationism Considered," in *Science and Creationism*, pp. 64-94; A. D. Kline, "Theories, Facts and Gods: Philosophical Aspects of the Creation-Evolution Controversy," in *Did the Devil Make Darwin Do It?* ed. D. B. Wilson (Ames: Iowa State University Press, 1983), pp. 37-44; D. J. Futuyma, *Science on Trial* (New York: Pantheon Books, 1983), pp. 161-74; G. Skoog, "A View from the Past," *Bookwatch Reviews* 2 (1989): 1-2; P. Kitcher, *Abusing Science* (Cambridge, Mass.: MIT Press, 1982), pp. 45-54, 126-27, 175-76. For critique see P. L. Quinn, "The Philosopher of Science as Expert Witness," and L. Laudan, "Science at the Bar—Causes for Concern," both in *But Is It Science?* ed. M. Ruse (Buffalo, N.Y.: Prometheus Books, 1988), pp. 367-85, 351-55.

[18]James Ebert et al., *Science and Creationism: A View from the National Academy of Science* (Washington, D.C.: National Academy, 1987), pp. 8-10; Ruse, *Darwinism Defended*, p. 182.

[19]Darwin's use of methodological arguments against creationists has been well documented: V. Kavalovski, "The Vera Causa Principle: A Historico-Philosophical Study of a Meta-theoretical Concept from Newton Through Darwin," Ph.D. dissertation, University of Chicago, 1974, pp. 104-29; S. C. Meyer, "Of Clues and Causes: A Methodological Interpretation of Origin of Life Studies," Ph.D. thesis, Cambridge University, 1990, p. 125; D. Recker, "Causal Efficacy: The Structure of Darwin's Argument Strategy in the *Origin of Species,*" *Philosophy of Science* 54 (1987):173; D. Hull, "Darwin and the Nature of Science," in *Evolution from Molecules to Men*, ed. D. Bendall (Cambridge, U.K.: Cambridge University Press, 1985), pp. 63-80; C. Darwin, *The Origin of Species by Means of Natural Selection* (1859; rpt. Harmondsworth, U.K.: Penguin, 1984), pp. 201, 430, 453. Notice, for example, his tacit appeal to a definition of science in the following quotation: "On the ordinary view of each species having been independently created, we gain no *scientific* explanation for any one of these facts. We can only say that it has pleased the Creator to command that past and present inhabitants of the world should appear in certain order and in certain areas; that He has impressed upon them the most extraordinary resemblances, and has classed them in groups subordinate to groups. But by such statements we gain no new knowledge; *we do not connect together facts and laws;* we explain nothing" (quoted in N. C. Gillespie, *Charles Darwin and the Problem with Creation* [Chicago: University of Chicago Press, 1979], p. 76; emphasis mine).

[20]Ruse, *Darwinism Defended*, pp. 59, 131-40, 322-24; Ruse, "Creation Science Is Not Science," pp. 72-78; Ruse, "A Philosopher's Day," pp. 13-38; M. Ruse, "Witness Testimony Sheet: *McLean v. Arkansas,*" in *But Is It Science?* ed. M. Ruse (Buffalo, N.Y.: Prometheus Books, 1988), pp. 287-306, esp. 301; Ruse, "They're Here!" p. 4; Ruse, "Darwinism: Philosophical Preference," pp. 1-6; Gould, "Genesis and Geology"; Stent, "Scientific Creationism," pp. 136-41; Root-Bernstein, "On Defining a Scientific Theory," pp. 64-94; Quinn, "Philosopher of Science as Expert Witness," pp. 367-85; Laudan, "Science at the Bar," pp. 351-55; Kline, "Theories, Facts and Gods," pp. 37-44; Futuyma, *Science on Trial*, pp. 161-74; Skoog, ' View from the Past"; Gould, "Evolution as Fact and Theory," pp. 118-21; Kitcher, *Abusing Science*, pp. 45-54, 126-27, 175-76.

[21]Ruse, *Darwinism Defended*, pp. 322-24.

[22]Stent, "Scientific Creationism," p. 137.

[23]Gould, "Evolution as Fact and Theory," p. 118

[24]Ebert et al., *Science and Creationism*, pp. 8-10.

[25]Ibid., p. 8.

[26]L. Laudan, "The Demise of the Demarcation Problem," in *But Is It Science?* ed. M. Ruse (Buffalo, N.Y.: Prometheus Books, 1988), pp. 337-50.

[27]Ibid.

[28]O. Gingerich, "The Galileo Affair," *Scientific American,* August 1982, pp. 133-43.

[29]Laudan, "Demise of the Demarcation Problem."

[30]Ibid.

[31]Ibid.

[32]I. Lakatos, "Falsification and the Methodology of Scientific Research Programmes," in *Criticism and the Growth of Knowledge,* ed. I. Lakatos and A. Musgrave (Cambridge, U.K.: Cambridge University Press, 1970), pp. 189-95.

[33]Laudan, "Demise of the Demarcation Problem"; Laudan, "Science at the Bar," p. 354.

[34]This excessive reliance on a philosophical definition of science to circumvent the hard work of evaluating specific empirical claims ironically credits the philosophy of science with more power than it possesses. That such appeals to philosophical considerations are typically made by positivist-minded scientists who regard appeals to "philosophy" as anathema only compounds the irony of the demarcationist enterprise. If any demarcating is to be done, it ought to be done by the philosophers of science who specialize in such second-order questions about the definition of science. Yet for reasons specified already, philosophers of science have increasingly spurned this enterprise.

[35]Most who make these demarcation arguments are practicing scientists. Nevertheless, they can be found frequently in the work of the philosopher of science Michael Ruse: *Darwinism Defended,* pp. 59, 131-40, 322-24; "Creation Science Is Not Science," pp. 72-78; "Philosopher's Day in Court," pp. 13-38; "Witness Testimony Sheet," pp. 287-306, esp. 301; "They're Here!" p. 4; "Darwinism: Philosophical Preference," pp. 1-6.

[36]M. Eger, quoted by J. Buell in "Broaden Science Curriculum," *Dallas Morning News,* March 10, 1989.

[37]Laudan, "Demise of the Demarcation Problem," p. 349.

[38]Ruse, "Witness Testimony Sheet," pp. 287-306; W. R. Overton, "United States District Court Opinion: *McLean* v. *Arkansas,*" in *But Is It Science?* ed. M. Ruse (Buffalo, N.Y.: Prometheus Books, 1988), pp. 307-31.

[39]It needs to be acknowledged that creationists such as Duane Gish have also employed demarcation arguments against descent. D. Gish, "Creation, Evolution and the Historical Evidence," in *But Is It Science?* ed. M. Ruse (Buffalo, N.Y.: Prometheus Books, 1988), p. 267.

[40]Ruse, "Witness Testimony Sheet," p. 301; Ruse, "Philosopher's Day in Court," p. 26; Ruse, "Darwinism: Philosophical Preference," pp. 1-6.

[41]Skoog, "View from the Past"; Root-Bernstein, "On Defining a Scientific Theory," p. 74.

[42]Gould, "Genesis and Geology," pp. 129-30; Ruse, "Witness Testimony Sheet," p. 305; Ebert et al., *Science and Creationism,* pp. 8-10.

[43]Root-Bernstein, "On Defining a Scientific Theory," p. 73; Ruse, "Philosopher's Day in Court," p. 28; Ebert et al., *Science and Creationism,* pp. 8-10.

[44]Kline, "Theories, Facts and Gods," p. 42; Gould, "Evolution as Fact and Theory," p. 120; Root-Bernstein, "On Defining a Scientific Theory," p. 72.

[45]Ruse, *Darwinism Defended,* p. 59; Ruse, "Witness Testimony Sheet," p. 305; Gould, "Evolution as Fact and Theory," p. 121; Root-Bernstein, "On Defining a Scientific Theory," p. 74.

[46]A. Kehoe, "Modern Anti-evolutionism: The Scientific Creationists," in *What Darwin*

Began, ed. L. R. Godfrey (Boston: Allyn and Bacon, 1985), pp. 173-80; Ruse, "Witness Testimony Sheet," p. 305; Ruse, "Philosopher's Day in Court," p. 28; Ebert et al., *Science and Creationism,* pp. 8-10.

[47]Kitcher, *Abusing Science,* pp. 126-27, 176-77.

[48]Ruse, "Philosopher's Day in Court," pp. 21, 26.

[49]Ibid. One further word of clarification: I am referring to all of the demarcation criteria used in arguments (a)-(h) as methodological criteria. Some of these criteria specify semantic conditions, as noted in my discussion of Laudan's work above. Nevertheless, even these have implications for how scientific theorizing is to be done. To say, for example, that scientific theories must be falsifiable is also to say that in the process of testing one must, as a matter of method, make a prediction or otherwise state a theory in such a way as to allow its falsification. When I say, therefore, that design and descent are methodologically equivalent, I mean that both approaches to origins are equally capable or incapable of fulfilling the demands of various demarcation criteria, whether strictly methodological, epistemic or semantic.

[50]Ruse, "Philosopher's Day in Court," pp. 21-26.

[51]Ibid., p. 26; Ruse, "Witness Testimony Sheet," p. 301.

[52]Ruse, "Darwinism: Philosophical Preference," pp. 1-6; Quinn, "Philosopher of Science as Expert Witness," pp. 367-85; Laudan, "Science at the Bar," pp. 351-55.

[53]By asserting that science must explain by natural law, Ruse is presupposing something called the "covering law" or the "deductive-nomological" view of scientific explanation. The covering-law model was a very popular conception of science during the 1950s and 60s. It was promulgated primarily by the neopositivist philosopher Carl Hempel. Unfortunately, unsolved problems with the covering-law model of science are legion. C. Hempel, "The Function of General Laws in History," *Journal of Philosophy* 39 (1942): 35-48; G. Graham, *Historical Explanation Reconsidered* (Aberdeen: Aberdeen University Press, 1983), pp. 17-28; Meyer, "Of Clues and Causes," pp. 40-76; W. P. Alston, "The Place of the Explanation of Particular Facts in Science," *Philosophy of Science* 38 (1971): 13-34; M. Scriven, "Explanation and Prediction in Evolutionary Theory," *Science* 130 (1959): 477-82; M. Scriven, "Truisms as the Grounds for Historical Explanations," in *Theories of History,* ed. P. Gardiner (Glencoe, Ill.: Free Press, 1959), pp. 443-75; M. Scriven, "Causes, Connections and Conditions in History," in *Philosophical Analysis and History,* ed. W. Dray (New York: Harper & Row, 1966), pp. 238-64; M. Mandelbaum, "Historical Explanation: The Problem of Covering Laws," *History Theory* 1 (1961): 229-42; P. Lipton, *Inference to the Best Explanation* (London: Routledge, 1991), pp. 43-46.

[54]The Latin text reads "Hypothesis non fingo." I. Newton, *Isaac Newton's Papers and Letters on Natural Philosophy,* ed. I. Bernard Cohen (Cambridge, Mass.: Harvard University Press, 1958), p. 302.

[55]Laudan, "Science at the Bar," p. 354.

[56]Scriven, "Truisms as the Grounds," p. 450; Meyer, "Of Clues and Causes," pp. 40-76.

[57]Alston, "Place of the Explanation"; Meyer, "Of Clues and Causes," pp. 40-75.

[58]Ibid., p. 48.

[59]Ibid., pp. 51-56; M. Scriven, "Causation as Explanation," *Nous* 9 (1975): 14; Lipton, *Inference to the Best Explanation,* pp. 47-81.

[60]Scriven, "Truisms as the Grounds," pp. 446-63, 450. One could, for example, legitimately assert that a particular earthquake caused a bridge to collapse even if all other bridges in the area did not fall and even if all earthquakes do not destroy bridges.

[61]Alston, "Place of the Explanation," pp. 17-24.

[62]Alston makes the same point about laws that state sufficient conditions of a particular outcome as well. Alston (ibid., p. 24) considers the law "Passage of a spark through a mixture of hydrogen and oxygen is sufficient for the formation of water." This, he says, exemplifies a sufficient condition law (hereafter SC). Alston argues that knowing such a law does not alone furnish the scientist with enough information to explain a particular case of water formation, because other sufficient conditions of water formation may have been responsible for the case in question. After all, water forms in a fuel cell without a spark, activating the hydrogen-oxygen combination. Knowing an SC law does not allow one to infer from an instance of the consequent (in this case water formation) that the sufficient condition was antecedently present (in this case a spark in the appropriate gas mixture) unless one *also* knows that the antecedent is the only known sufficient condition of the consequent—that is, unless one knows that the antecedent is both a sufficient and a necessary condition of the consequent. Explaining a case of water formation will require independent evidence that a spark was in fact passed through an appropriate gas mixture (as opposed to some other causal antecedent) prior to the event. As Alston states, we can "not tell from the law itself which of the sufficient conditions is responsible in a particular case." Thus, laws of the SC type do not, without supplementary information, constitute explanations of particular facts. To regard laws and explanations as logically identical is, therefore, again mistaken.

[63]Ibid., p. 17.

[64]Ruse, *Darwinism Defended*, p. 58; Gould, "Evolution as Fact and Theory," pp. 119-21; M. Ridley, *The Problems of Evolution* (Oxford, U.K.: Oxford University Press, 1985), p. 15. For a cogent discussion of the different meanings of evolution and the logical independence of the theory of common descent and the various mechanistic theories about how transmutation might occur, see also K. S. Thomson, "The Meanings of Evolution," *American Scientist* 70 (1982): 529-31. Strictly speaking, common descent is an abductive or historical inference, as Ruse himself acknowledges when he speaks of "inferring historical phylogenies" ("Darwinism: Philosophical Preference," p. 7). As defined by C. S. Peirce, abductive inferences attempt to establish past causes by examining their results or effects. As such, it is more accurate to refer to common descent as a theory about facts—that is, a theory about what in fact happened in the past. Unfortunately, such historical theories, and the inferences used to construct them, can be notoriously inconclusive or "underdetermined." As Gould has stated, "Results rarely specify their causes unambiguously" ("Senseless Signs of History," p. 34). Ho, "Methodological Issues," pp. 8-60; E. Sober, *Reconstructing the Past* (Cambridge, Mass.: MIT Press, 1988), pp. 1-4.

[65]By "evolution" here they mean continuous morphological change over time such that all, or most all, organisms are related by common ancestry.

[66]Ruse and Gould regard the theory of common descent as so well established as to make it virtually indistinguishable from a "fact." Ruse, *Darwinism Defended*, p. 58; Gould, "Evolution as Fact and Theory," pp. 119-21.

[67]From the Greek word *nomos* for law.

[68]Indeed, it is even debatable whether the selection-mutation mechanism of neo-Darwinism can be expressed as a system of laws (i.e., nomologically), though some so-called axiomatists such as Williams and Lloyd have tried. My point here is that whether one regards selection-mutation as a nomological theory or as a mechanistic theory, common descent does not depend on it for its scientific status. The logical and epistemic independence of descent from selection-mutation demonstrates the

ability of some theories to explain in the absence of either laws or mechanisms.

[69]Darwin, *Origin of Species*, p. 195.

[70]The untenable nature of Ruse's position is manifest in his own admission that modern evolutionary theory does not meet the demarcation standards that he promulgates elsewhere as normative for his opponents. See, for example, his discussion of population genetics in *Darwinism Defended*, where he acknowledges that "it is probably a mistake to think of modern evolutionists as seeking universal laws at work in every situation" (p. 86).

[71]Ruse, "Darwinism: Philosophical Preference," pp. 1-6; Ruse, "Witness Testimony Sheet," p. 301; Ruse, "Philosopher's Day in Court," p. 26. As Ruse puts it: "Even if Scientific Creationism were totally successful in making its case as science, it would not yield a 'scientific' explanation of origins. The Creationists believe that the world started miraculously. But miracles lie outside of science, which by definition deals only with the natural, the repeatable, that which is governed by law" (*Darwinism Defended*, p. 182). Richard Lewontin expresses a similar fear in *Scientists Confront Creationism:* "Either the world of phenomena is a consequence of the regular operation of repeatable causes and their repeatable effects, operating roughly along the lines of known physical law, or else at every instant all physical regularities may be ruptured and a totally unforeseeable set of events may occur. . . . We can not live simultaneously in a world of natural causation and of miracles, for if one miracle can occur, there is no limit" ([New York: Norton, 1983], p. xxvi).

[72]This dichotomy between "unbroken law" and the action of agency is merely a species of the same genus of confusion that led Ruse and others to insist that science always explains via laws. In Ruse's case the dichotomy is manifest in his assertion that invoking the action of a divine agent constitutes a "violation of natural law." I disagree. Pitting the action of agents (whether seen or unseen) against natural law creates a false opposition. The reason for this is simple. Agents can change initial and boundary conditions, yet in so doing they do not violate laws. Most scientific laws have the form "If *A*, then *B* will follow, given conditions *X*." If *X* is altered or if *A* did not obtain, then it constitutes no violation of the laws of nature to say that *B* did not occur, even if we expected it to. Agents may alter the course of events or produce novel events that contradict our expectations, without violating the laws of nature. To assert otherwise is merely to misunderstand the distinction between antecedent conditions and laws. C. S. Lewis, *God in the Dock* (London: Collins, 1979), pp. 51-55. See R. Swinburne, *The Concept of Miracle* (London: Macmillan, 1970), pp. 23-32, and G. Colwell, "On Defining Away the Miraculous," *Philosophy* 57 (1982): 327-37, for other defenses of the possibility of miracles that assume and respect the integrity of natural laws.

[73]See also Kavalovski, "Vera-Causa Principle," pp. 104-29, for a discussion of the so-called *vera causa* principle, a nineteenth-century methodological principle invoked by Darwin to eliminate from consideration creationist explanations judged to be unobservable (Darwin, *Origin of Species*, pp. 201, 430, 453).

[74]Skoog, "View from the Past"; Gould, "Genesis and Geology," pp. 129-30; Ruse, "Witness Testimony Sheet," p. 305.

[75]F. Grinnell, "Radical Intersubjectivity: Why Naturalism Is an Assumption Necessary for Doing Science," paper presented at Darwinism: Scientific Inference or Philosophical Preference? conference, Southern Methodist University, Dallas, March 26-28, 1993.

[76]Skoog, "View from the Past."

[77]S. C. Meyer, "A Scopes Trial for the '90s," *The Wall Street Journal*, December 6, 1993,

p. A14; S. C. Meyer, "Open Debate on Life's Origin," *Insight,* February 21, 1994, pp. 27-29.

[78]H. Judson, *The Eighth Day of Creation* (New York: Simon and Schuster, 1979), pp. 157-90.

[79]Meyer, "Of Clues and Causes," p. 120; Darwin, *Origin of Species,* p. 398; D. Hull, *Darwin and His Critics* (Chicago: University of Chicago Press, 1973), p. 45.

[80]C. Darwin, *More Letters of Charles Darwin,* ed. F. Darwin, 2 vols. (London: Murray, 1903), 1:184.

[81]Quoted in S. J. Gould, "Darwinism Defined: The Difference Between Theory and Fact," *Discovery,* January 1987, p. 70.

[82]Darwin's use of ɒoth methodological and empirical arguments against creationism has been well documented: Gillespie, *Charles Darwin and the Problem,* pp. 67-81; Kavalovski, "Vera Causa Principle," pp. 104-29; Meyer, "Of Clues and Causes," pp. 123-25; Recker, "Causal Efficacy," p. 173; Hull, "Darwin and the Nature of Science," pp. 63-80. For examples of Darwin's methodological arguments see Darwin, *Origin of Species,* pp. 201, 430, 453. For examples of his empirical arguments see *Origin of Species,* pp. 223, 386, 417-18.

[83]Skoog, "View from the Past."

[84]Kitcher, *Abusing Science,* p. 125. While Kitcher allows for the possibility of a testable theory of divine creation, he believes creationism was tested and found wanting in the nineteenth century.

[85]I am currently undertaking an exhaustive cataloging and evaluation of evolutionary demarcation arguments. Those arguments not discussed here will be addressed in subsequent work published through the Pascal Centre in Ontario, Canada.

[86]This phrase is actually used by astronomer Carl Sagan (in Carl Sagan and Ann Druyan, *Shadows of Forgotten Ancestors* [New York: Random House, 1992], p. 387) but clearly expresses the posture of many evolutionary gradualists and punctuationalists with respect to the absence of transitional intermediates in the fossil record.

[87]The same could be said of the neo-Darwinian selection-mutation mechanism vis-à-vis the theory of common descent. In both cases, however, issues of warrant and issues of scientific status should not be confused.

[88]For a design argument not based on religious authority (i.e., contra g: "Creationist or design theories are not tentative"), see Denton, *Evolution,* pp. 338-42. For an examination and refutation of demarcation argument h (i.e., "Creationist or design theories have no problem-solving capability"), see J. P. Moreland's forthcoming "Scientific Creationism, Science and Conceptual Problems," in *Perspectives on Science and Christian Faith.*

[89]C. S. Peirce, "Abduction and Induction," in *The Philosophy of Peirce,* ed. J. Buchler (London: Routledge, 1956), pp. 150-56; C. S. Peirce, *Collected Papers,* ed. C. Hartshorne and P. Weiss, 6 vols. (Cambridge, Mass.: Harvard University Press, 1931), 2:375; K. T. Fann, *Peirce's Theory of Abduction* (The Hague: Martinus Nijhoff, 1970), p. 33; Meyer, "Of Clues and Causes," pp. 24-34.

[90]Ibid.

[91]These three features can be used as a set of individually necessary and jointly sufficient conditions for the identification of historical, as opposed to nonhistorical, sciences. Nevertheless, this demarcation or definition is admittedly arbitrary. It does not imply that some sciences do not combine elements of both historical and inductive inquiry, or that many disciplines do not have both inductive and nomological branches—e.g., cosmology and cosmogony. This "demarcation" is also unproblemat-

ic because it makes no c.aim, ...i, licit or explicit, for a privileged epistemological statu for disciplines that manifest historical features. The distinction is not, however, without justification, since each of the individually necessary conditions of a historical science do distinguish real qualitative or logical differences between types of inferences, explanations or questions.

[92]A. C. Doyle, "The Boscome Valley Mystery," in *The Sign of Three: Peirce, Holmes, Poppe* ed. T. Sebeok (Bloomington: Indiana University Press, 1983), p. 145.

[93]S. J. Gould, "Evolution and the Triumph of Homology: Or, Why History Matters," *American Scientist* 74 (1986): 61.

[94]This is not to deny that laws or process theories may play roles in support of causal explanation, as even opponents of the covering-law model such as Scriven admit. Scriven notes that laws and other types of general process theories may play an important role in justifying the causal status of an explanatory antecedent and may provide the means of inferring plausible causal antecedents from observed consequents. Nevertheless, as both Scriven and I have argued elsewhere, laws are not necessary to the explanation of particular events or facts; and even when laws are present, antecedent *events* function as the primary causal or explanatory entity in historical explanations. Scriven, "Truisms as the Grounds," pp. 448-50; Scriven, "Explanation and Prediction," p. 480; Scriven, "Causes, Connections and Conditions," pp. 249-50; Meyer, "Of Clues and Causes," pp. 18-24, 36-72, 84-92.

[95]Ibid., pp. 112-36.

[96]C. Darwin, *The Descent of Man*, 2nd ed. (London: A. L. Burt, 1874), p. 61.

[97]Darwin, *Origin of Species*, p. 434. Darwin's next line on the following page and the very first line of his concluding chapter again suggest the primacy of his concern to establish "descent with modification" and the supportive role that natural selection played in his argument. In his words: "As this whole volume is one long argument, it may be convenient to the reader to have the leading facts and inferences briefly recapitulated. That many grave objections may be advanced against [a] the theory of descent with modification [b] through natural selection, I do not deny."

[98]Ibid., pp. 331-434.

[99]Ibid., p. 432.

[100]Ibid., p. 434.

[101]Gould, "Evolution and the Triumph," p. 61.

[102]Quoted in Gould, "Darwinism Defined," p. 70.

[103]Darwin, *Origin of Species*, p. 399.

[104]Ibid., pp. 195, 399. As Kavalovski has noted, Darwin did not limit his claim of *vera causa* to natural selection but included descent itself under this appellation (Kavalovski, "Vera Causa Principle," pp. 104-5). In chapter 5, on "Laws of Variation," Darwin refers explicitly to "community of descent" as a *vera causa* of homologies among plant species (*Origin of Species*, p. 195). Despite many references to natural selection as a *vera causa* of morphological change in general, Darwin also seemed to recognize the need to postulate an historical cause (i.e., a pattern of past events) to explain the particular facts mentioned above. Darwin makes this relationship between causal postulations about the past and explanations of present phenomena explicit at one point in chapter 13 by stating that "we may thus account even for the distinctness of whole classes from each other . . . by the belief that many ancient forms of life *have been utterly lost*" (ibid., p. 413).

[105]Gould, "Evolution and the Triumph," p. 60.

[106]A. I. Oparin, *The Origin of Life*, trans. S. Morgulis (New York: Macmillan, 1938).

[107]Meyer, "Of Clues and Causes," pp. 237-40.

[108]Quoted in Gould, "Darwinism Defined," p. 70.

[109]F. Darwin, ed., *Life and Letters of Charles Darwin*, 2 vols. (London: D. Appleton, 1896), 1:437.

[110]Denton, *Evolution*, pp. 338-42; Thaxton, Bradley and Olsen, *Mystery of Life's Origin*, pp. 113-65, 201-4, 209-12.

[111]Ibid., pp. 201-12.

[112]Ambrose, *Nature and Origin;* Denton, *Evolution;* Augros and Stanciu, *The New Biology;* Kenyon and Davis, *Of Pandas and People.*

[113]D. Hull, "God of the Galápagos," *Nature* 352 (1991): 485-86.

[114]Such a concern was recently raised, for example, in Nancey Murphy's critique of Phillip Johnson's book *Darwin on Trial* (Murphy, "Phillip Johnson on Trial," p. 34). There Murphy cites concern among theistic scientists about the God-of-the-gaps objection as a reason for the exclusion of creative intelligence as a candidate explanation for the origin of life. As Murphy explains, even many theistic scientists worry that theistic explanations give up on science too soon, thus making the God hypothesis vulnerable to future scientific advance. Yet clearly these scientists accept a definition of science and scientific advance that presupposes the very naturalism already asserted as necessary to science. Why *can't* a theistic explanation constitute a scientific advance? Murphy offers no answer to this question, beyond her reference to the story of Laplace's mathematical model supplanting Newton's interventionist explanation of planetary motion.

[115]Historical theories may use process theories or laws to enhance the plausibility of a postulated causal history. For a more complete discussion of the prevailing positivistic confusion of laws and causes, and the subsidiary role that nomological understanding does play in historical science, see Meyer, "Of Clues and Causes," pp. 11-113.

[116]Ibid., pp. 84-92, 113-14.

[117]Thaxton, Bradley and Olsen, *Mystery of Life's Origin*, pp. 113-65, 201-4, 209-12.

[118]An example of theological plausibility and simplicity functioning to limit design hypotheses can be found by examining some of the reasons Laplace's mathematical model superseded Newton's interventionist explanation of planetary motion. While this episode is often interpreted as an example of why design can never be considered as a scientific explanation, I believe it shows no such thing. Instead, this episode illustrates clearly how design was assumed to be a possible scientific explanation, but also how it was constrained by considerations of theological plausibility.

To many eighteenth-century scientists, Newton's interventionism was ill-formed not because it contradicted an inviolate methodological convention, as has often been asserted (e.g., Murphy, "Phillip Johnson on Trial," p. 33). Newton himself made highly regarded design arguments in other contexts and believed gravitation was caused by constant "Spirit Action." Instead, Newton's argument for angelic action was rejected because it was both *theologically unlikely* (given the nomological context of the inquiry) and *less elegant* than Laplace's explanation (given prevailing background assumptions about how God interacts with nature).

The theistic research program of Newton's day assumed that the regularity and universality of natural laws reflected the ordered mind and sovereign power of the Creator. Kepler and Newton both wanted to use science to demonstrate this. To hypothesize as Newton did that angelic gerrymandering was required to maintain the orbital stability of the outer planets seemed improbable and ad hoc to *theistic* scientists. It did so because it clearly violated not a methodological prohibition against reference to divine action but a fundamental (theological) background assumption of many scientists at the time—namely, that special or discrete divine action was unlikely and unnecessary where God's *potentia ordinata*, his regular orderly power, was sufficient and already at work.

Thus, when Laplace demonstrated the stability of the planetary system by showing that orbital perturbations were periodic within fixed quantifiable limits, he "saved" the very regularity of planetary motion that was the triumph of Newton's theistic research program.

In any case, none of the emphasis on the regularity and constancy of laws prevented either Boyle or Newton from invoking special divine action as an explanation for the *origin* of particular natural features. Both did so in biology; Newton even did so in optics and astronomy. Those (e.g., Murphy, "Phillip Johnson on Trial," p. 33) who cite these two men as the source of the current positivistic prohibition against mixing science and metaphysics are simply incorrect. (Instead they should consult Gillespie, *Charles Darwin and the Problem*, on Darwin's positivism.) Boyle in fact devised an interesting classification scheme that makes explicit the metaphysical nonneutrality of origins questions, which he thought occurred in a region where natural philosophy and religion overlapped. While Newton tended to reserve the term *natural philosophy* for nomological disciplines, he in no sense agreed that empirical evidence was metaphysically neutral, for the reasons already stated.

[119]Following Sober, I regard simplicity as a notion that cannot be formally explicated but that nevertheless plays a role in the evaluation of scientific theories. Like Sober I believe that intuitive notions of simplicity, economy or elegance express or are informed by tacit background assumptions. I see no reason that theistic explanations could not be either commended or disqualified on the basis of such judgments, just as materialistic explanations are. See Sober, *Reconstructing the Past*, pp. 36-69.

[120]Theists who invoke the special assistance or activity of divine agency to explain an origin event or biblical miracle, for example, are not, as is commonly asserted, guilty of semideism. It does not follow that those who infer that God has acted in a discrete, special and perhaps more easily discernible way in one case thereby deny that he is constantly acting to "uphold the universe by the word of his power" (see Heb 1:1) at all other times. The medievals resisted this false dichotomy by affirming two powers of God, or two ways by which he interacts with the world. The ordinary power of God they called his "potentia ordinata," and the special or fiat power they called his "potentia absoluta"; see W. Courtenay, "The Dialectic of Omnipotence in the High and Late Middle Ages," in *Divine Omniscience and Omnipotence in Medieval Philosophy*, ed. T. Ruduvsky (Dordrecht, Netherlands: D. Reidel, 1985), pp. 243-69. Many modern theists who affirm the special action of God at a discrete point in history have this type of distinction in mind and are not guilty of denying God's constant providence over nature. To affirm an instance of potentia absoluta is not to deny potentia ordinata.

[121]It may sound as though I am endorsing a philosophical relativism about science, or the kind of methodological anarchism advocated by the philosopher of science Paul Feyerabend in his book *Against Method* (London: Verso, 1978). Quite the contrary: I am not an antirealist, nor do I deny the importance of methodology to the process of formulating warranted belief. Precisely because I recognize the importance of a great number of quite distinct and well-established methods at work within fields already widely acknowledged to be scientific, I deny the utility of attempts to give *a*

single, universal methodological characterization of science.

[122]For example, theories that offer antecedent conditions that are merely necessary to a given outcome do not succeed logically as explanations of that outcome. The methodological convention extant within most historical sciences requiring postulated antecedents to meet a criterion of etiological plausibility (causal adequacy) expresses this logical requirement. See my discussion of the logical and contextual requirements of causal explanation in Meyer, "Of Clues and Causes," pp. 60-71, 84-92.

[123]The logical and epistemic conditions of successful causal explanation are difficult to make explicit, though they are quite easy to apply apparently via a kind of tacit understanding. For a more comprehensive (explicit) discussion of the logical and contextual requirements of causal explanation, see ibid., pp. 36-76.

[124]G. K. Chesterton, *Orthodoxy* (London: John Lane, 1909).

[125]As Basil Willey put it: "Science must be provisionally atheistic or cease to be itself" ("Darwin's Place," p. 15). See also Ruse, *Darwinism Defended,* p. 59; Ruse, "Witness Testimony Sheet," p. 305; Gould, "Evolution as Fact and Theory," p. 121; Root-Bernstein, "On Defining a Scientific Theory," p. 74; Ruse, "Darwinism: Philosophical Preference," pp. 1-13.

[126]W. A. Dembski, "The Very Possibility of Intelligent Design," paper presented at Science and Belief, First International Conference of the Pascal Centre, Ancaster, Ontario, August 11-15, 1992.

[127]P. Thagard, "The Best Explanation: Criteria for Theory Choice," *Journal of Philosophy* 75 (1978): 79; Meyer, "Of Clues and Causes," pp. 99-109; W. Whewell, *The Philosophy of the Inductive Sciences,* 2 vols. (London: Parker, 1840), 2:109, 242; L. Laudan, "William Whewell on the Consilience of Induction," *The Monist* 55 (1971): 371-79.

[128]Lipton, *Inference to the Best Explanation.*

[129]See Haeckel, *Wonders of Life,* pp. 110-11.

[130]Johnson, *Darwin on Trial.* See also Gillespie, *Charles Darwin and the Problem,* pp. 1-18, 41-66, 146-56, for an interesting discussion of the way Darwin succeeded in redefining science so as to make creationist or idealist dissent impossible from within science.

Chapter 3: On the Very Possibility of Intelligent Design/Dembski
[1]The quotes from Voltaire and Emerson can be found in Stanley L. Jaki, *Miracles and Physics* (Front Royal, Va.: Christendom, 1989), p. 39 and note 36. Compare their quotes with Jesus' comment in John 14:11 (NRSV): "Believe me that I am in the Father and the Father is in me; but if you do not, then believe me because of the works themselves."

[2]Quoted by Lawrence J. Peter in *Peter's Quotations for Our Time* (New York: Bantam, 1979), p. 155.

[3]Quoted in Bruce L. Gordon, "God, Woody Allen and the Moral Structure of the Universe: Some Thoughts on Pain, Suffering and the 'Hiddenness' of God," unpublished typescript, 1992, pp. 78. Hanson's challenge calls to mind Cleanthes's comment in David Hume's *Dialogues Concerning Natural Religion* (1779; rpt. Buffalo, N.Y.: Prometheus Books, 1989), p. 37: "Suppose, therefore, that an articulate voice were heard in the clouds, much louder and more melodious than any which human art could ever reach: Suppose, that this voice were extended in the same instant over all nations, and spoke to each nation in its own language and dialect: Suppose, that the words delivered not only contain a just sense and meaning, but convey some instruction

altogether worthy of a benevolent Being, superior to mankind: Could you possibly hesitate a moment concerning the cause of this voice? and must you not instantly ascribe it to some design or purpose?"

[4]Richard Dawkins certainly thinks so. Consider his comment on the origin of the DNA/protein machine: "[To invoke] a supernatural Designer is to explain precisely nothing, for it leaves unexplained the origin of the Designer. You have to say something like 'God was always there,' and if you allow yourself that kind of lazy way out, you might as well just say 'DNA was always there,' or 'Life was always there,' and be done with it" (*The Blind Watchmaker* [New York: Norton, 1987], p. 141).

[5]Quoted in Phillip E. Johnson, *Darwin on Trial* (Downers Grove, Ill.: InterVarsity Press, 1991), p. 114.

[6]The Einstein-Podolsky-Rosen paradox for quantum mechanics derives from just such a thought experiment. Sometimes, as in this case, breakthroughs in technology enable the thought experiment to be carried out eventually—cf. the research of Alain Aspect, J. Dalibard and G. Roger ("Experimental Test of Bell's Inequalities Using Time-Varying Analyzers," *Physical Review of Letters* 49 [1982]: 1804-7) and its important role in resolving the EPR paradox. In other instances the physical constraints on technology forever bar the thought experiment from becoming an actual experiment.

[7]This example may seem silly, but it captures precisely what is at stake with oracles. There are plenty of serious mathematical examples involving oracles, but I fear that to discuss them here would risk losing the reader in technicalities that are not central to this study. For a formal development of oracles, and in particular oracle Turing machines, see José L. Balcázar, Josep Díaz and Joaquim Gabarró, *Structural Complexity*, 2 vols. (Berlin: Springer-Verlag, 1988-90), 1:28-32.

[8]I owe the idea of a talking pulsar to Charles Chastain. The pulsar is an oracle. Here I am using oracles to investigate the possibility of design. Oracles, however, illuminate a host of philosophical questions. I have, for instance, used oracles to investigate the mind-body problem—see William A. Dembski, "Converting Matter into Mind: Alchemy and the Philosopher's Stone in Cognitive Science," *Perspectives on Science and Christian Faith* 42, no. 4 (1990): 203-5.

[9]Perhaps for this story to be more convincing both the questions and the answers should be in Hebrew. But I'm not sure what Hebrew looks like in Morse code, so I'll stick with English.

[10]This universal bound on computational speed is based on the Planck time—currently the smallest physically meaningful unit of time. See David Halliday and Robert Resnick, *Fundamentals of Physics*, 3rd ed. (New York: John Wiley and Sons, 1988), p. 544. Universal time bounds for electronic computers involve clock speeds between ten and twenty magnitudes slower. See Ingo Wegener, *The Complexity of Boolean Functions* (Stuttgart: Wiley-Teubner, 1987), p. 2.

[11]Even at the atomic level, quantum effects make reliable storage unworkable. Indeed, the smallest scale at which vast, reliable storage is known to be possible is at the next level up—the molecular level. We can thank molecular biologists for this insight.

[12]Throughout this discussion I have assumed a noninflationary big bang cosmology. Note, however, that inflation doesn't alter the numbers I've just presented. In an inflationary universe, what we normally regard as the universe (the sum total of energy that can potentially interact with us causally) is just one of a multitude of causally isolated subuniverses. The totality of these causally isolated subuniverses, if we are to believe Alan Guth and his disciples, contains more than 10^{80} elementary particles (see Alan Guth and Paul Steinhardt, "The Inflationary Universe," in *The New*

Physics, ed. Paul Davies [Cambridge, U.K.: Cambridge University Press, 1989]). But particles in subuniverses causally isolated from us cannot contribute to any computation in the subuniverse we inhabit. As a result, particles in subuniverses causally isolated from us cannot serve as a computational resource within the subuniverse we inhabit.

[13]See Balcázar, Díaz and Gabarró, *Structural Complexity,* vol. 2, chap. 11, for the underlying theory. A simple example of a computational problem that is beyond the computational resources of the universe, yet verifiable by humans, is the following: Imagine a string of 0s and 1s of length a thousand is constructed by flipping a coin. This sequence is encoded on an integrated circuit, which in turn is connected to a computer. A programmer who has no knowledge of which string was encoded on the circuit must now determine the precise string. Unfortunately for her, the only way she can determine the string is to send a test string to the circuit. If the test string matches the string encoded on the circuit, the circuit responds yes; otherwise no. How many test strings are there? 2^{1000}, or approximately 10^{300}, test strings exist. The programmer will therefore have to run through about $\frac{1}{2} \times 10^{300}$ test strings before having an even chance of finding the string encoded on the circuit. Thus no matter how many copies of the circuit and now many computers the programmer has at her disposal (thereby enabling her to check multiple test strings at once), there are not enough computers and circuits that can be packed into the universe to give the programmer a hope of finding a solution. Of course, if the programmer is given the actual string encoded on the circuit, she can just send it to the circuit and immediately verify that she has the correct string. This example lacks aesthetic appeal but makes the point.

[14]Huxley claimed that a huge number of monkeys typing away on typewriters would eventually type the works of Shakespeare (see A. E. Wilder-Smith, *Man's Origin, Man's Destiny: A Critical Survey of the Principles of Evolution and Christianity* [Minneapolis: Bethany House, 1975], p. 63). If one assumes the monkeys are typing randomly, not favoring any keys and not letting one keystroke influence another, Huxley's claim is a simple consequence of a fundamental theorem in probability known as the Strong Law of Large Numbers. Huxley's claim is in principle correct, but in practice it carries no weight: the universe has neither enough monkeys nor enough time to make the typing of even the first line of *Hamlet,* much less the complete works of Shakespeare, likely.

[15]Herein lies the problem with making parapsychology into a genuine science. Phenomena like extrasensory perception (ESP) and psychokinesis (PK), because they do not occur on demand, are convincing only to subjects and experimenters taking part in a successful parapsychological experiment.

[16]William A. Dembski, "Reviving the Argument from Design: Detecting Design Through Small Probabilities," *Proceedings of the Biennial Conference of the Association of Christians in the Mathematical Sciences* 8 (1991): 101-45.

[17]My coauthors are Steve Meyer and Paul Nelson.

[18]C. A. Coulson, *Science and Religion: A Changing Relationship* (Cambridge, U.K.: Cambridge University Press, 1955), p. 2.

[19]Ian Barbour, *Issues in Science and Religion* (London: SCM Press, 1966), p. 390.

[20]Epistemological relativists, social constructivists and people who take a dim view of human rationality and its capacity to know truth will no doubt differ even on this point. They might care to have a look at James F. Harris, *Against Relativism: A Philosophical Defense of Method* (LaSalle, Ill.: Open Court, 1992), as well as Étienne Gilson, *Methodical Realism,* trans. Philip Trower (Front Royal, Va.: Christendom, 1990).

[21]It is worth noting that Christian theology has never required a perfectly perspicuous revelation. A case in point is the parables of Jesus. It is widely held that Jesus employed parables to clarify his message to the common folk. Yet when his disciples asked why he spoke in parables, Jesus responded, "To you it has been given to know the secrets of the kingdom of heaven, but to them [the common folk] it has not been given. . . . The reason I speak to them in parables is that 'seeing they do not perceive, and hearing they do not listen, nor do they understand' " (Mt 13:11, 13). Christian belief in God is not based on God's blocking every avenue of doubt, but rather on God's doing enough—both in our hearts and in the world—to elicit faith.

[22]The translation here is actually my own paraphrase.

Chapter 4: Astronomical Evidences for a Personal, Transcendent God/Ross

[1]George Roche, *A World Without Heroes* (Hillsdale, Mich.: Hillsdale College Press, 1987), p. 120.

[2]Immanuel Kant, "Universal Natural History and Theory of the Heavens," in *Theories of the Universe*, ed. Milton K. Munitz. (Glencoe, Ill.: Free Press, 1957), p. 240.

[3]E. R. Harrison, "The Dark Night-Sky Riddle: A 'Paradox' That Resisted Solution," *Science* 226 (1984): 941-45; Stanley L. Jaki, *The Paradox of Olbers' Paradox* (New York: Herder and Herder, 1969), pp. 72-143.

[4]J. D. North, *The Measure of the Universe: A History of Modern Cosmology* (Oxford, U.K.: Clarendon, 1965), pp. 16-18.

[5]Robert M. Eisberg, *Fundamentals of Modern Physics* (New York: John Wiley and Sons, 1961), pp. 7-9.

[6]Albert Einstein, "Zur Elektrodynamik bewegter Körper," *Annalen der Physik* 17 (1905): 891-921; the English translation is in H. A. Lorentz, A. Einstein, H. Minkowski and H. Weyl, *The Principle of Relativity*, with notes by A. Sommerfeld, trans. W. Perrett and G. B. Jeffrey (London: Methuen, 1923), pp. 35-65. Also see Albert Einstein, "Ist die Trägheit eines Körpers von seinem Energieinhalt abhängig?" *Annalen der Physik* 18 (1905): 639-44; the English translation is also in Lorentz et al., *Principle of Relativity*, pp. 67-71.

[7]Robert M. Eisberg, *Modern Physics* (New York: John Wiley and Sons, 1961), pp. 30-35.

[8]Ibid., pp. 37-38, 75-76, 580-92; John D. Jackson, *Classical Electrodynamics* (New York: John Wiley and Sons, 1962), pp. 352-69.

[9]S. K. Lamoreaux et al., "New Limits on Spatial Anisotropy from Optically Pumped 201Hg and 199Hg," *Physical Review Letters* 57 (1986): 3125-28.

[10]Albert Einstein, "Die Feldgleichungen der Gravitation," in *Sitzungsberichte der Königlich Preussischen Akademie der Wissenschaften*, November 25, 1915, pp. 844-47; this article is reproduced in Albert Einstein, "Die Grundlage der allgemeinen Relativitätstheorie," *Annalen der Physik* 49 (1916): 769-822. The English translation is in Lorentz et al., *Principle of Relativity*, pp. 109-64.

[11]Edwin Hubble, "A Relation Between Distance and Radial Velocity Among Extra galactic Nebulae," *Proceedings of the National Academy of Sciences* 15 (1929): 168-73.

[12]Quoted in A. Vibert Douglas, "Forty Minutes with Einstein," *Journal of the Royal Astronomical Society of Canada* 50 (1956): 100.

[13]Lincoln Barnett, *The Universe and Dr. Einstein* (New York: William Sloane Associates, 1948), p. 106.

[14]Arthur S. Eddington, "On the Instability of Einstein's Spherical World," *Monthly Notices of the Royal Astronomical Society* 90 (1930): 672.

[15]Arthur S. Eddington, "The End of the World from the Standpoint of Mathematical

Physics," *Nature* 127 (1931): 450.

[16]Eddington, "On the Instability," pp. 668-78.

[17]Vahé Petrosian, "Confrontation of Lemaître Models and the Cosmological Constant with Observations," in *Proceedings of the I. A. U. Symposium No. 63: Confrontation of Cosmological Theories with Observational Data*, ed. M. S. Longair (Boston: D. Reidel, 1974), pp. 31-46.

[18]P. J. McCarthy et al., "Serendipitous Discovery of a Redshift 4.4 QSO," *Astrophysical Journal Letters* 328 (1988): L29-L33; S. J. Warren et al., "Quasars of Redshift z = 4.43 and z = 4.07 in the South Galactic Pole Field," *Nature* 330 (1987): 453-55; Donald P. Schneider, Maarten Schmidt and James E. Gunn, "PC 1158+4635: An Optically Selected Quasar with a Redshift of 4.73," *Astronomical Journal* 98 (1989): 1951-58; J. S. Dunlop et al., "Quasar with z = 3.71 and Limits on the Number of More Distant Objects," *Nature* 319 (1986): 564-67; B. A. Peterson, A. Savage, D. L. Jauncey and A. E. Wright, "PKS 2000-330: A Quasi-Stellar Radio Source with a Redshift of 3.78," *Astrophysical Journal Letters*, 260 (1982): L27-L29.

[19]Kenneth Brecher and Joseph Silk, "Lemaître Universe, Galaxy Formation and Observations," *Astrophysical Journal* 158 (1969): 91-102.

[20]Herman Bondi and T. Gold, "The Steady-State Theory of the Expanding Universe," *Monthly Notices of the Royal Astronomical Society* 108 (1948): 252-70; Fred Hoyle, "A New Model for the Expanding Universe," *Monthly Notices of the Royal Astronomical Society* 108 (1948): 372-82.

[21]Herman Bondi, *Cosmology*, 2nd ed. (Cambridge, U.K.: Cambridge University Press, 1960), p. 140.

[22]Hoyle, "New Model for the Expanding Universe," p. 372.

[23]Fred Hoyle, *The Nature of the Universe*, 2nd ed. (Oxford, U.K.: Blackwell, 1952), p. 111.

[24]Fred Hoyle, "The Universe: Past and Present Reflections," *Annual Reviews of Astronomy and Astrophysics* 20 (1982): 3.

[25]James H. Jeans, *Astronomy and Cosmogony*, 2nd ed. (Cambridge, U.K.: Cambridge University Press, 1929), pp. 421-22.

[26]Donald Hamilton, "The Spectral Evolution of Galaxies: Part I, An Observational Approach," *Astrophysical Journal* 297 (1985): 371-89.

[27]John Gribbin, "Oscillating Universe Bounces Back," *Nature* 259 (1976): 15-16.

[28]R. H. Dicke, P. J. E. Peebles, P. G. Roll and D. T. Wilkinson, "Cosmic Black-Body Radiation," *Astrophysical Journal Letters* 142 (1965): 415.

[29]Richard J. Gott III, James E. Gunn, David N. Schramm and Beatrice M. Tinsley, "An Unbound Universe?" *Astrophysical Journal* 194 (1974): 543-53; Hyron Spinrad and S. Djorgovski, "The Status of the Hubble Diagram in 1986," *Observational Cosmology: Proceedings of the 124th Symposium of the International Astronomical Union*, ed. A. Hewitt, G. Burbidge and L. Z. Fang (Boston: D. Reidel, 1987), pp. 129-41; Paul J. Steinhardt, "Inflation and the Ω-Problem," *Nature* 345 (1990): 47-49; P. J. E. Peebles, "The Mean Mass Density of the Universe," *Nature* 321 (1986): 27-32; Hamilton, "Spectral Evolution of Galaxies," pp. 371-89; Allan Sandage and G. A. Tammann, "The Dynamical Parameters of the Universe: H^0, q^0, Ω^0, Λ and K," in *Large-Scale Structure of the Universe, Cosmology and Fundamental Physics: Proceedings of the First ESO-CERN Symposium*, ed. G. Setti and L. van Hove (Geneva: CERN, 1984), pp. 127-49; J. Yang et al., "Primordial Nucleosynthesis: A Critical Comparison of Theory and Observation," *Astrophysical Journal* 281 (1984): 493-511; Juan M. Uson and David T. Wilkinson, "Improved Limits on Small-Scale Anistropy in Cosmic Microwave Background," *Nature* 312 (1984): 427-29; G. F. R. Ellis, "Does Inflation Necessarily Imply $\Omega = 1$?" *Classical and Quantum*

Gravity 5 (1988): 891-901.

[30]Alan H. Guth and Marc Sher, "The Impossibility of a Bouncing Universe," *Nature* 302 (1983): 505-7; Sidney A. Bludman, "Thermodynamics and the End of a Closed Universe," *Nature* 308 (1984): 319-22.

[31]I. D. Novikov and Yakob B. Zel'dovich, "Physical Processes Near Cosmological Singularities," *Annual Review of Astronomy and Astrophysics* 11 (1973): 401.

[32]Arnold E. Sikkema and Werner Israel, "Black-Hole Mergers and Mass Inflation in a Bouncing Universe," *Nature* 349 (1991): 45-47.

[33]André Linde, "Self-Reproducing Universe," paper presented at the Centennial Symposium on Large-Scale Structure, California Institute of Technology, Pasadena, September 27, 1991.

[34]Alexander Vilenkin, "Did the Universe Have a Beginning?" CALT-68-1772 DOE Research and Development Report, California Institute of Technology, Pasadena, November 1992.

[35]From Hugh Ross, *The Fingerprint of God*, 2nd ed. (Orange, Calif.: Promise, 1991), pp. 98-105.

[36]Charles W. Misner, Kip S. Thorne and John Archibald Wheeler, *Gravitation* (San Francisco: W. H. Freeman, 1973), p. 752.

[37]Stephen W. Hawking and George F. R. Ellis, "The Cosmic Black-Body Radiation and the Existence of Singularities in Our Universe," *Astrophysical Journal* 152 (1968): 25-36; Stephen W. Hawking and Roger Penrose, "The Singularities of Gravitational Collapse and Cosmology," *Proceedings of the Royal Society of London*, ser. A, 314 (1970): 529-48.

[38]R. F. C. Vessot et al., "Test of Relativistic Gravitation with a Space-Borne Hydrogen Maser," *Physical Review Letters* 45 (1980): 2081-84.

[39]Steven Weinberg, *Gravitation and Cosmology: Principles and Applications of the General Theory of Relativity* (New York: John Wiley and Sons, 1972), p. 198; G. Van Biesbroeck, "The Relativity Shift at the 1952 February 25 Eclipse of the Sun," *Astronomical Journal* 58 (1953): 87-88; Charles C. Counselman III et al., "Solar Gravitational Deflection of Radio Waves Measured by Very-Long-Baseline Interferometry," *Physical Review Letters* 33 (1974): 1621-23; Irwin I. Shapiro et al., "Mercury's Perihelion Advance: Determination by Radar," *Physical Review Letters* 28 (1972): 1594-97; J. H. Taylor, L. A. Fowler and P. M. McCulloch, "Measurements of General Relativistic Effects in the Binary Pulsar PSR 1913+16," *Nature* 277 (1979): 437-40; J. H. Taylor, "Gravitational Radiation and the Binary Pulsar," *Proceedings of the Second Marcel Grossmann Meeting on General Relativity*, pt. A, ed. Remo Ruffini (Amsterdam: North-Holland, 1982), pp. 15-19; Irwin I. Shapiro, Charles C. Counselman III and Robert W. King, "Verification of the Principle of Equivalence for Massive Bodies," *Physical Review Letters* 36 (1976): 555-58; R. V. Pound and J. L. Snider, "Effect of Gravity on Nuclear Resonance," *Physical Review Letters* 13 (1964): 539-40; R. D. Reasenberg et al., "Viking Relativity Experiment: Verification of Signal Retardation by Solar Gravity," *Astrophysical Journal Letters* 234 (1979): 219-21; R. W. Porcas et al., "VLBI Observations of the Double QSO 0957+561 A, B," *Nature* 282 (1979): 384-86; R. J. Weymann et al., "The Triple QSO PG 1115+08: Another Probable Gravitational Lens," *Nature* 285 (1980): 641-43; J. Patrick Henry and J. N. Heasley, "High-Resolution Imaging from Mauna Kea: The Triple Quasar in 0.3 arc s Seeing," *Nature* 321 (1986): 139-42; G. I. Langston et al., "Galaxy Mass Deduced from the Structure of Einstein Ring MG1654 + 1346," *Nature* 344 (1990): 43-45; J. H. Taylor et al., "Experimental Constraints on Strong-Field Relativistic Gravity," *Nature* 355 (1992): 132-36.

[40]Ross, *Fingerprint of God,* pp. 45-47; Hugh Ross, "Evidence Builds, Loopholes Shrink in the Case for Creation," *Facts & Faith* 6 (Spring 1992): 1-2; Hugh Ross, *The Creator and the Cosmos* (Colorado Springs, Colo.: NavPress, 1993), pp. 67-69.

[41]Ibid., pp. 58-63, 71-78, 147-51.

[42]Allen Emerson, "A Disorienting View of God's Creation," *Christianity Today,* February 1, 1985, p. 19.

[43]Paul Davies, *God and the New Physics* (New York: Simon and Schuster, 1983), pp. 25-43, esp. 38-39.

[44]Paul Davies, *Superforce: The Search for a Grand Unified Theory of Nature* (New York: Simon and Schuster, 1984), p. 243.

[45]Paul Davies, *The Cosmic Blueprint: New Discoveries in Nature's Creative Ability to Order the Universe* (New York: Simon and Schuster, 1988), p. 141.

[46]Ibid., p. 203.

[47]J. Richard Gott III, "Creation of Open Universes from de Sitter Space," *Nature* 295 (1982): 306.

[48]Heinz R. Pagels, *Perfect Symmetry: The Search for the Beginning of Time* (New York: Simon and Schuster, 1985), p. 244.

[49]Edward P. Tryon, "Is the Universe a Vacuum Fluctuation?" *Nature* 246 (1973): 396-97.

[50]David Atkatz and Heinz R. Pagels, "Origin of the Universe as a Quantum Tunneling Event," *Physical Review* D 25 (1982): 2065-73; Alexander Vilenkin, "Creation of Universes from Nothing," *Physical Letters* B 117 (1982): 25-28; Yakob B. Zel'dovich and L. P. Grishchuk, "Structure and Future of the 'New' Universe," *Monthly Notices of the Royal Astronomical Society* 207 (1984): 23P-28P; Alexander Vilenkin, "Birth of Inflationary Universes," *Physical Review* D 27 (1983): 2848-55; Alexander Vilenkin, "Quantum Creation of Universes," *Physical Review* D 30 (1984): 509-11.

[51]James B. Hartle and Stephen W. Hawking, "Wave Function of the Universe," *Physical Review* D 28 (1983): 2960-75; Stephen W. Hawking, "The Quantum State of the Universe," *Nuclear Physics* B 239 (1984): 257-76.

[52]Pagels, *Perfect Symmetry,* p. 244.

[53]Ibid., p. 347.

[54]Frank Tipler, "The Mind of God," *The Times Higher Education Supplement,* October 14, 1988, p. 23.

[55]Stephen W. Hawking, *A Brief History of Time: From the Big Bang to Black Holes* (New York: Bantam Books, 1988), p. 139.

[56]John Archibald Wheeler, "Bohr, Einstein and the Strange Lesson of the Quantum," in *Mind in Nature,* ed. Richard Q. Elvee (New York: Harper & Row, 1981), p. 18; George Greenstein, *The Symbiotic Universe: Life and Mind in the Cosmos* (New York: Morrow, 1988), p. 223.

[57]Nick Herbert, *Quantum Reality: Beyond the New Physics—An Excursion into Metaphysics and the Meaning of Reality* (New York: Doubleday/Anchor, 1987), pp. 16-29.

[58]Stanley L. Jaki, *Cosmos and Creator* (Edinburgh: Scottish Academic, 1980), pp. 96-98.

[59]James S. Trefil, *The Moment of Creation* (New York: Charles Scribner's Sons, 1983), pp. 91-101.

[60]John D. Barrow and Frank J. Tipler, *The Anthropic Cosmological Principle and the Structure of the Physical World* (New York: Oxford University Press, 1986).

[61]Ibid., p. 677.

[62]Ibid., pp. 677, 682.

[63]Martin Gardner, "WAP, SAP, PAP and FAP," *The New York Review of Books* 23 (May 8 1986): 22-25.

[64]Ross, *Fingerprint of God,* pp. 120-28; Barrow and Tipler, *Anthropic Cosmological Principle,* pp. 123-457; Bernard J. Carr and Martin J. Rees, "The Anthropic Principle and the Structure of the Physical World," *Nature* 278 (1979): 605-12; John M. Templeton, "God Reveals Himself in the Astronomical and in the Infinitesimal," *Journal of the American Scientific Affiliation,* December 1984, pp. 194-200; Jim W. Neidhardt, "The Anthropic Principle: A Religious Response," *Journal of the American Scientific Affiliation,* December 1984, pp. 201-7; Brandon Carter, "Large Number Coincidences and the Anthropic Principle in Cosmology," in *Proceedings of the International Astronomical Union Symposium 63: Confrontation of Cosmological Theories with Observational Data,* ed. M. S. Longair (Boston: D. Reidel, 1974), pp. 291-98; John D. Barrow, "The Lore of Large Numbers: Some Historical Background to the Anthropic Principle," *Quarterly Journal of the Royal Astronomical Society* 22 (1981): 404-20; Alan Lightman, "To the Dizzy Edge," *Science* 82 (October 1982): 24-25; Thomas O'Toole, "Will the Universe Die by Fire or Ice?" *Science* 81 (April 1981): 71-72; Fred Hoyle, *Galaxies, Nuclei and Quasars* (New York: Harper & Row, 1965), pp. 147-50; Bernard J. Carr, "On the Origin, Evolution and Purpose of the Physical Universe," in *Physical Cosmology and Philosophy,* ed. John Leslie (New York: Macmillan, 1990), pp. 134-53; Richard Swinburne, "Argument from the Fine-Tuning of the Universe," in *Physical Cosmology and Philosophy,* ed. John Leslie (New York: Macmillan, 1990), pp. 154-73; R. E. Davies and R. H. Koch, "All the Observed Universe Has Contributed to Life," *Philosophical Transactions of the Royal Society of London,* ser. B, 334 (1991): 391-403.

[65]Ross, *Fingerprint of God,* p. 122; Barrow and Tipler, *Anthropic Cosmological Principle,* pp. 318-27, 354-59.

[66]Davies and Koch, "All the Observed Universe."

[67]A. H. Guth, "Inflationary Universe: A Possible Solution to the Horizon and Flatness Problems," *Physical Review* D 23 (1981): 348.

[68]Hoyle "The Universe," p. 16.

[69]Davies, *God and the New Physics,* pp. viii, 3-42, 142-43.

[70]Davies, *Superforce,* p. 243.

[71]Davies, *Cosmic Blueprint,* p. 203.

[72]Greenstein, *Symbiotic Universe,* p. 27.

[73]I. S. Shklovskii and Carl Sagan, *Intelligent Life in the Universe* (San Francisco: Holden-Day, 1966), pp. 343-50.

[74]Ibid., p. 413.

[75]Davies and Koch, "All the Observed Universe"; Robert T. Rood and James S. Trefil, *Are We Alone? The Possibility of Extraterrestrial Civilizations* (New York: Scribner's Sons, 1983); Barrow and Tipler, *Anthropic Cosmological Principle,* pp. 510-75; Don L. Anderson, "The Earth as a Planet: Paradigms and Paradoxes," *Science* 223 (1984): 347-55; I. H. Campbell and S. R. Taylor, "No Water, No Granite—No Oceans, No Continents," *Geophysical Research Letters* 10 (1983): 1061-64; Brandon Carter, "The Anthropic Principle and Its Implications for Biological Evolution," *Philosophical Transactions of the Royal Society of London,* ser. A, 310 (1983): 352-63; Allen H. Hammond, "The Uniqueness of the Earth's Climate," *Science* 187 (1975): 245; Owen B. Toon and Steve Olson, "The Warm Earth," *Science* 85 (October 1985): 50-57; George Gale, "The Anthropic Principle," *Scientific American* 245, no. 6 (1981): 154-71; Hugh Ross, *Genesis One: A Scientific Perspective* (Pasadena, Calif.: Reasons to Believe, 1983), pp. 6-7; Ron Cottrell, *The Remarkable Spaceship Earth* (Denver: Accent Books, 1982); D. Ter Harr, "On the Origin of the Solar System," *Annual Review of Astronomy and Astrophysics* 5 (1967): 267-78; Greenstein, *Symbiotic Universe,* pp. 68-97; Templeton, "God Reveals Himself," pp.

196-98; Michael H. Hart, "The Evolution of the Atmosphere of the Earth," *Icarus* 33 (1978): 23-39; Michael H. Hart, "Habitable Zones About Main Sequence Stars," *Icarus* 37 (1979): 351-57; Tobias Owen, Robert D. Cess and V. Ramanathan, "Enhanced CO^2 Greenhouse to Compensate for Reduced Solar Luminosity on Early Earth," *Nature* 277 (1979): 640-41; William R. Ward, "Comments on the Long-Term Stability of the Earth's Obliquity," *Icarus* 50 (1982): 444-48; John Gribbin, "The Origin of Life: Earth's Lucky Break," *Science Digest*, May 1983, pp. 36-102; Carl D. Murray, "Seasoned Travellers," *Nature* 361 (1993): 586-87; Jacques Laskar and P. Robutel, "The Chaotic Obliquity of the Planets," *Nature* 361 (1993): 608-12; Jacques Laskar, F. Joutel and P. Robutel, "Stabilization of the Earth's Obliquity by the Moon," *Nature* 361 (1993): 615-17; H. E. Newsom and S. R. Taylor, "Geochemical Implications of the Formation of the Moon by a Single Giant Impact," *Nature* 338 (1989): 29-34; W. M. Kaula, "Venus: A Contrast in Evolution to Earth," *Science* 247 (1990): 1191-96; P. J. E. Peebles and Joseph Silk, "A Cosmic Book of Phenomena," *Nature* 346 (1990): 233-39; Michael H. Hart, "Atmospheric Evolution, the Drake Equation and DNA: Sparse Life in an Infinite Universe," in *Philosophical Cosmology and Philosophy*, ed. John Leslie (New York: Macmillan, 1990), pp. 256-66; Stanley L. Jaki, *God and the Cosmologists* (Washington, D.C.: Regnery Gateway, 1989), pp. 177-84.

[76]Rood and Trefil, *Are We Alone?*

[77]Frank J. Tipler, "The Search for Extraterrestrial Life: Recent Developments," *Physics Today* 40 (December 1987): 92.

[78]Swinburne, "Argument from the Fine-Tuning," p. 165.

[79]William Lane Craig, "Barrow and Tipler on the Anthropic Principle vs. Divine Design," *British Journal of Philosophy and Science* 38 (1988): 392.

Chapter 5: Information & the Origin of Life/Bradley & Thaxton

[1]A. I. Oparin, *Origin of Life*, trans. S. Morgulis (New York: Macmillan, 1924).

[2]Stanley L. Miller, "Production of Amino Acids Under Possible Primitive Earth Conditions," *Science* 117 (1953): 528-29.

[3]Quoted in R. Shapiro, *Origins* (New York: Summit Books, 1986), p. 99.

[4]William Day, *Genesis on Planet Earth* (East Lansing, Mich.: House of Talos, 1979), p. 7.

[5]Quoted in S. Tax, ed., *Evolution After Darwin* (Chicago: University of Chicago Press, 1960), 1:57.

[6]K. Dose, "The Origin of Life: More Questions Than Answers," *Interdisciplinary Science Reviews* 13 (1988): 348.

[7]D. Kenyon and G. Steinman, *Biochemical Predestination* (New York: McGraw-Hill, 1969).

[8]J. Horgan, "In the Beginning . . ." *Scientific American*, February 1991, p. 117.

[9]S. W. Fox and K. Dose, *Molecular Evolution and the Origin of Life* (New York: Marcel Dekker, 1977).

[10]B. L. Bass and T. R. Cech, "Specific Interaction Between Self-Splicing of RNA of *Tetrahymena* and Its Guanosine Substrate," *Nature* 308 (1984): 820; T. R. Cech, A. J. Zaug and P. J. Grabowski, "*In Vitro* Splicing of the Ribosomal RNA Precursor of *Tetrahymena*," *Cell* 27 (1981): 487.

[11]R. Shapiro, "Prebiotic Ribose Synthesis: A Critical Analysis," *Origins of Life and Evolution of the Biosphere* 18 (1988): 71.

[12]Horgan, "In the Beginning," p. 117.

[13]J. S. Levine, ed., *The Photochemistry of Atmospheres: Earth, the Other Planets and Comets* (Orlando, Fla.: Academic, 1985).

[14]Horgan, "In the Beginning," p. 117.

[15]Dose, "Origin of Life."

[16]I. Barbour, *Science Ponders Religion* (New York: Appleton-Century-Crofts, 1960), p. 200.

[17]W. L. Bradley, "Thermodynamics and the Origin of Life," *Perspectives on Science and Christian Faith* 40 (1988): 72.

[18]L. von Bertalanffy, *Robots, Men and Minds* (New York: George Braziller, 1967), p. 82.

[19]A. L. Lehninger, *Biochemistry* (New York: Worth, 1970).

[20]C. B. Thaxton, W. L. Bradley and R. L. Olsen, *The Mystery of Life's Origin: Reassessing Current Theories* (Dallas: Lewis and Stanley, 1992).

[21]Quoted in R. Vallery-Radot, *The Life of Pasteur,* trans. R. L. Devonshire (New York: Doubleday, 1920), p. 109.

[22]F. Darwin, *The Life and Letters of Charles Darwin* (New York: Appleton, 1887), 2:202.

[23]Oparin, *Origin of Life.*

[24]J. B. S. Haldane in the *Rationalist Annual* 148 (1929): 3.

[25]J. P. Ferris, "Prebiotic Synthesis: Problems and Challenges," *Cold Spring Harbor Symposia on Quantitative Biology* 52 (1987): 30.

[26]Shapiro, "Prebiotic Ribose Synthesis."

[27]Dose, "Origin of Life."

[28]Horgan, "In the Beginning."

[29]Thaxton, Bradley and Olsen, *Mystery of Life's Origin,* p. 43.

[30]Quoted in Shapiro, *Origins,* p. 112.

[31]Fox and Dose, *Molecular Evolution;* I. Shklovskii and C. Sagan, *Intelligent Life in the Universe* (New York: Dell, 1966), p. 231.

[32]Levine, *Photochemistry of Atmospheres.*

[33]Such experiments were reported in several abstracts and presentations at the Fifth ISSOL Meeting, Berkeley, Calif., 1986.

[34]Bradley, "Thermodynamics"; Thaxton, Bradley and Olsen, *Mystery of Life's Origin.*

[35]H. Borsook and E. H. M. Huffman in *Chemistry of Amino Acids and Proteins,* ed. C. L. A. Schmidt (Springfield, Mass.: Charles C. Thomas, 1944), p. 822.

[36]Fox and Dose, *Molecular Evolution.*

[37]Bradley, "Thermodynamics"; Thaxton, Bradley and Olsen, *Mystery of Life's Origin,* chap. 8.

[38]P. A. Temussi et al., "Structural Characterization of Thermal Prebiotic Polypeptides," *Journal of Molecular Evolution* 7 (1976): 105.

[39]Bradley, "Thermodynamics"; Thaxton, Bradley and Olsen, *Mystery of Life's Origin,* chap. 9.

[40]Ibid.

[41]Ibid.

[42]J. S. Wicken, *Evolution, Thermodynamics and Information: Extending the Darwinian Program* (New York: Oxford University Press, 1987).

[43]Thaxton, Bradley and Olsen, *Mystery of Life's Origin.*

[44]B. O. Kuppers, *Information and the Origin of Life* (Cambridge, Mass.: MIT Press, 1990), pp. 170-72.

[45]Wicken, *Evolution, Thermodynamics;* Shapiro, *Origins;* A. E. Wilder Smith, *The Creation of Life* (Wheaton, Ill.: Harold Shaw, 1970); Hubert P. Yockey, "On the Information Content of Cytochrome C," *Journal of Theoretical Biology* 67 (1977): 345; Hubert P. Yockey, "A Calculation of the Probability of Spontaneous Biogenesis by Information Theory," *Journal of Theoretical Biology* 67 (1977): 377; Hubert P. Yockey, "Self-Organization Origin of Life Scenarios and Information Theory," *Journal of Theoretical*

*Biology*1 91 (1981): 13.

⁴⁶H P. Yockey, "A Calculation of the Probability of Spontaneous Biogenesis by Information Theory," *Journal of Theoretical Biology* 67 (1981): 377.

⁴⁷F. Hoyle, *The Intelligent Universe* (London: Michael Joseph, 1983); Kenyon and Steinman, *Biochemical Predestination.*

⁴⁸Shapiro, "Prebiotic Ribose Synthesis."

⁴⁹Quoted in Horgan, "In the Beginning."

⁵⁰F. Crick, *Life Itself* (New York: Simon and Schuster, 1981).

⁵¹Dose, "Origin of Life."

⁵²From Horgan, "In the Beginning."

⁵³Wicken, *Evolution, Thermodynamics.*

⁵⁴W. L. Bradley, "Thermodynamics and the Origin of Life," typescript.

⁵⁵Fox and Dose, *Molecular Evolution.*

⁵⁶Wicken, *Evolution, Thermodynamics;* G. Steinman and M. N. Cole, "Synthesis of Biologically Pertinent Peptides Under Possible Primordial Conditions," *Proceedings of the National Academy of Science* 58 (1967): 735.

⁵⁷R. A. Kok, J. A. Taylor and W. L. Bradley, "A Statistical Examination of Self-Ordering of Amino Acids in Protein," *Origins of Life and Evolution of the Biosphere* 18 (1988): 135.

⁵⁸Kuppers, *Information and the Origin.*

⁵⁹A. G. Cairns-Smith, *Genetic Takeover and the Mineral Origins of Life* (New York: Cambridge University Press, 1982); Thaxton, Bradley and Olsen, *Mystery of Life's Origin;* Shapiro, *Origins.*

⁶⁰From Horgan, "In the Beginning."

⁶¹Ibid.

⁶²J. M. Edmond, K. L. von Damm, R. E. McDuff and C. I. Measures, "Chemistry of Hot Springs on the East Pacific Rise and Their Effluent Dispersal," *Nature* 297 (1982): 187.

⁶³S. L. Miller, "Which Organic Compound Could Have Occurred on Prebiotic Earth?" *Cold Spring Harbor Symposia on Quantitative Biology* 52 (1987): 17.

⁶⁴From Horgan, "In the Beginning."

⁶⁵C. de Duve, *Blueprint for a Cell* (Burlington, N.C.: Patterson, 1991).

⁶⁶I. Prigogine, *From Being to Becoming* (San Francisco: W. H. Freeman, 1980); G. Nicolis and I. Prigogine, *Self Organization in Non-equilibrium Systems* (New York: John Wiley and Sons, 1977).

⁶⁷G. Nicolis, I. Prigogine and A. Babloyantz, "Thermodynamics of Evolution," *Physics Today*, November 1972, p. 23.

⁶⁸M. Eigen and P. Schuster, "The Hypercycle—A Principle of Natural Self Organization," *Naturiwissenschaften* 65 (1978): 341.

⁶⁹Quoted in Horgan, "In the Beginning."

⁷⁰Dose, "Origin of Life."

⁷¹Shapiro, *Origins.*

⁷²Hilde Hein, *On the Nature and Origin of Life* (New York: McGraw-Hill, 1971), pp. 93, 95; Paul de Vries, "Naturalism in the Natural Sciences: A Christian Perspective," *Christian Scholars Review* 15, no. 4: 388-96.

⁷³See David Bohm, "Some Remarks on the Notion of Order," in *Toward a Theoretical Biology*, ed. C. H. Waddington (Chicago: Aldine, 1969).

⁷⁴Ludwig Wittgenstein, *Tractatus Logico-Philosophicus*, trans. D. F. Pears and B. F. McGuinness (London: Routledge and Kegan Paul, 1974; German original in 1921).

⁷⁵Daniel Boorstin, *The Discoveries* (New York: Random House, 1983), p. 86.

⁷⁶David Hume, *An Inquiry Concerning Human Understanding* (1748; rpt. Chicago: Great

Books of the Western World, 1952), pp. 462, 499.

[77]Quoted in I. J. Hester, *Introduction to Archeology* (New York: Holt, Rinehart and Winston, 1976), p. 29.

[78]J. F. W. Herschel, *Preliminary Discourse on the Study of Natural Philosophy* (London: Longman, Rees, Orme, Brown and Green, 1831), p. 149. Emphasis added.

[79]C. Lyell, *Principles of Geology* (1830; rpt. New York: D. Appleton, 1887), 1:319.

[80]C. Sagan, *Contact* (New York: Simon and Schuster, 1985), p. 51.

[81]F. Drake and D. Sobel, *Is Anyone Out There? The Scientific Search for Extraterrestrial Intelligence* (New York: Delacorte, 1992); T. R. McDonough, "Project Sentinel to Grow," *The Planetary Report* 4 (January/February 1984): 3; P. Horowitz, "A Status Report on the Planetary Society's SETI Project," *The Planetary Report* 7 (July/August 1987): 8-10.

[82]P. Horowitz, "SETI and the Planetary Society," *The Planetary Report* 6 (January/February 1986): 17.

[83]Dava Sobel, "Is Anyone Out There?" *Life,* September 1992, pp. 60-69.

[84]C. Sagan, *Broca's Brain* (New York: Random House, 1979), p. 275.

[85]A. D. Kline, "Theories, Facts and Gods: Philosophical Aspects of the Creation-Evolution Controversy," in *Did the Devil Make Darwin Do It?* ed. D. B. Wilson (Ames: Iowa State University Press, 1983), pp. 37-44.

[86]Herschel, *Preliminary Discourse,* p. 149.

[87]I. Newton, "General Schohum," in *Mathematical Principles of Natural Philosophy* (1687; rpt. Chicago: Great Books of the Western World, 1952), p. 360.

[88]F. Ferre, "Design Argument," in *Dictionary of the History of Ideas* (New York: Charles Scribner's Sons, 1973), 1:673.

[89]Yockey, "Self-Organization Origin of Life Scenarios," p. 13-31.

[90]L. Orgel, *The Origins of Life* (New York: John Wiley and Sons, 1973), p. 189.

[91]G. J. Chaitin, "Algorithmic Information Theory," *IBM Journal of Research* 21 (1977): 350.

[92]Orgel, *Origins of Life,* p. 189.

[93]Ibid.

[94]H. P. Yockey, "A Calculation of the Probability of Spontaneous Biogenesis by Information Theory," *Journal of Theoretical Biology* 67 (1977): 377.

[95]H. Quastler, *The Emergence of Biological Organization* (New Haven, Conn.: Yale University Press, 1964).

[96]F. Hoyle and C. Wickramsinghe, *Evolution from Space* (New York: Simon and Schuster, 1981).

Chapter 6: The Origin of Life's Major Groups/Wise

[1]W. D. Stansfield, *The Science of Evolution* (New York: Macmillan, 1977), pp. 103-29; T. M. Berra, *Evolution and the Myth of Creationism: A Basic Guide to the Facts in the Evolution Debate* (Stanford, Calif.: Stanford University Press, 1990), pp. 18-30.

[2]See, for example, E. S. Gaffney, P. A. Meylan and A. R. Wyss, "Computer Assisted Analysis of the Relationships of the Higher Categories of Turtles," *Cladistics* 7 (1991): 313-35; and other articles in this journal.

[3]S. J. Gould, *Wonderful Life: The Burgess Shale and the Nature of History* (New York: Norton, 1989).

[4]W. Frair, W., "Taxonomic Relations Among Chelydrid and Kinosternid Turtles Elucidated by Serological Tests," *Copeia* 1972, no. 1, pp. 97-108.

[5]C. Sagan and A. Druyan, "Is It Possible to Be Pro-life and Pro-choice?" *Parade Magazine,* April 22, 1990.

[6]See the extended discussion in S. J. Gould, *Ontogeny and Phylogeny* (Cambridge, Mass.:

Belknap, 1977).

[7]Ibid.; Stansfield, *Science of Evolution,* pp. 103-13; R. Milner, *The Encyclopedia of Evolution: Humanity's Search for Its Origins* (New York: Facts on File, 1990), p. 44.

[8]Sagan and Druyan, "Is It Possible"; L. W. Swan, "The Concordance of Ontogeny with Phylogeny," *Bioscience* 40, no. 5 (1990): 376-84.

[9]Stansfield, *Science of Evolution,* pp. 98-103; M. Ruse, *Darwinism Defended: A Guide to the Evolution Controversies* (Reading, Mass.: Addison-Wesley, 1982), p. 40.

[10]D. M. Raup, "Extinction: Bad Luck or Bad Genes?" *Acta Geologica Hispanica* 16 (1981): 25-33.

[11]S. J. Gould and N. Eldredge, "Punctuated Equilibria: The Tempo and Mode of Evolution Reconsidered," *Paleobiology* 3, no. 2 (1977): 115-51.

[12]Gould, *Wonderful Life.*

[13]S. J. Gould, *The Panda's Thumb: More Reflections on Natural History* (New York: Norton, 1980), pp. 19-26.

[14]Berra, *Evolution and the Myth.*

[15]D. E. Savage and D. E. Russell, *Mammalian Paleofaunas of the World* (Reading, Mass.: Addison-Wesley, 1983).

[16]Ibid.

[17]A. H. Knoll and J. H. Lipps, "Evolutionary History of Prokaryotes and Protists," in *Fossil Prokaryotes and Protists,* ed. J. H. Lipps (Boston: Blackwell, 1993).

[18]Ibid.

[19]W. B. Harland et al., *A Geologic Time Scale 1989* (New York: Cambridge University Press, 1989), pp. 28-30.

[20]R. L. Carroll, *Vertebrate Paleontology and Evolution* (New York: Freeman, 1988); Harland et al., *Geologic Time Scale.*

[21]Carroll, *Vertebrate Paleontology;* Harland et al., *Geologic Time Scale.*

[22]Carroll, *Vertebrate Paleontology;* Harland et al., *Geologic Time Scale.*

[23]Carroll, *Vertebrate Paleontology;* Harland et al., *Geologic Time Scale.*

[24]Carroll, *Vertebrate Paleontology;* Harland et al., *Geologic Time Scale.*

[25]J. A. Lillegraven, Z. Kielan-Jaworowska and W. A. Clemens, *Mesozoic Mammals: The First Two-Thirds of Mammalian History* (Berkeley: University of California Press, 1977); Harland et al., *Geologic Time Scale.*

[26]Lillegraven, Kielan-Jaworoska and Clemens, *Mesozoic Mammals;* Harland et al., *Geologic Time Scale.*

[27]Savage and Russell, *Mammalian Paleofaunas;* Harland et al., *Geologic Time Scale.*

[28]T. W. Phenice and N. J. Sauer, *Hominid Fossils: An Illustrated Key,* 2nd ed. (Dubuque, Iowa: Brown, 1977); F. H. Smith and F. Spencer, *The Origins of Modern Humans: A World Survey of the Fossil Evidence* (New York: Liss, 1984).

[29]Phenice and Sauer, *Hominid Fossils;* Smith and Spencer, *Origins of Modern Humans.*

[30]Phenice and Sauer, *Hominid Fossils;* Smith and Spencer, *Origins of Modern Humans.*

[31]K. P. Wise, "First Fossil Appearances of Higher Taxa: A Preliminary Study of Order in the Fossil Record," unpublished paper.

[32]Ibid.

[33]K. P. Wise, "Ecological Zonation and the First Appearances of Higher Taxa," unpublished paper.

[34]Gould and Eldredge, "Punctuated Equilibria."

Chapter 7: Origin of the Human Language Capacity/Oller & Omdahl

[1]Charles Darwin, *The Descent of Man,* 2nd ed. (New York: D. Appleton, 1874), p. 87.

²Ibid., p. 88.

³Ibid., p. 87.

⁴Ibid., p. 88.

⁵Ibid., p. 86.

⁶See Bradley and Thaxton in chapter five in this volume; and Charles B. Thaxton, Walter L. Bradley and Roger L. Olsen, *The Mystery of Life's Origin: Reassessing Current Theories* (Dallas: Lewis and Stanley, 1992).

⁷See Michael Denton, *Evolution: A Theory in Crisis* (Bethesda, Md.: Adler and Adler, 1986).

⁸Alfred Binet, "New Investigations upon the Measure of the Intellectual Level Among School Children," *L'Année Psychologique* 11 (1911): 186; reprinted in Alfred Binet and Theodore Simon, *The Development of Intelligence in Children (the Binet-Simon Scale),* trans. Elizabeth Kite (Baltimore, Md.: Williams and Wilkins, 1916).

⁹Ernest Nagel, "Charles Sanders Peirce: A Prodigious but Little Known American Philosopher," *Scientific American* 200 (1959): 185.

¹⁰Edward C. Moore, introduction to Charles S. Peirce, *Writings of Charles S. Peirce: A Chronological Edition,* vol. 2, ed. Edward C. Moore et al. (Indianapolis: Indiana University Press, 1984), p. xi.

¹¹Charles S. Peirce, *Collected Papers of C. S. Peirce,* ed. Charles Hartshorne and Paul Weiss, 8 vols. (Cambridge, Mass.: Belknap/Harvard University Press, 1931-1958), 1:128.

¹²Peirce, *Writings of Charles S. Peirce,* 2:1.

¹³C. I. Lewis, as quoted by Nathan Houser, introduction to Peirce, *Writings of Charles S. Peirce: A Chronological Edition,* vol. 4, ed. Christian J. W. Kloesel et al. (Indianapolis: Indiana University Press, 1986), p. 21.

¹⁴John Horgan, "Free Radical: A Word or Two About Linguist Noam Chomsky," *Scientific American* 262 (May 1990): 40-44.

¹⁵Noam A. Chomsky, *Language and Responsibility: Based on Conversations with Mitsou Ronat,* trans. John Viertel (New York: Pantheon, 1979), p. 71.

¹⁶Moore, introduction to *Writings of Charles S. Peirce,* 2:xxv.

¹⁷C. K. Ogden and I. A. Richards, eds., *The Meaning of Meaning* (New York: Harcourt, Brace, 1949), p. 279.

¹⁸Denton, *Evolution;* Dmitri Kouznetsov, "Modern Concepts of Species: Do We Come Back to Fixism?" *CENTech Journal* 5, no. 2 (1990).

¹⁹Albert Einstein, "Physics and Reality," in *Out of My Later Years* (Secaucus, N.J.: Citadel, 1936), p. 60.

²⁰*Collected Papers,* 6:344.

²¹Albert Einstein, "Remarks on Russell's Theory of Knowledge," in *The Philosophy of Bertrand Russell,* ed. Paul Arthur Schilpp (New York: Tudor, 1944), p. 289.

²²Ibid.

²³Albert Einstein, "The Common Language of Science," in *Out of My Later Years* (Secacus, N.J.: Citadel, 1956), p. 111

²⁴Ibid., pp. 111-12.

²⁵John W. Oller Jr., "Semiotic Theory and Language Acquisition," in *Georgetown University Round Table on Languages and Linguistics 1990,* ed. James E. Alatis (Washington, D.C.: Georgetown University Press, 1990).

²⁶See especially *Writings of C. S. Peirce: A Chronological Edition,* vol. 1, ed. Max H. Fisch et al. (Indianapolis: Indiana University Press, 1982), and vol. 2, ed. Edward C. Moore et al. (1984). Also see *Collected Papers of C. S. Peirce,* vols. 1-6, ed. Charles Hartshorne

and Paul Weiss (Cambridge, Mass.: Belknap/Harvard University Press, 1931-35), and vols. 7-8, ed. A. W. Burks (1958); and John W. Oller Jr., "Reasons Why Some Methods Work," in *Methods That Work: Ideas for Literacy and Language Teachers* (Boston, Mass.: Heinle and Heinle, 1993).

[27]Einstein, "Common Language," p. 112.

[28]Jean Piaget, *The Psychology of Intelligence* (London: Routledge and Paul, 1950), pp. 158-59.

[29]See Sherman Wilcox, ed., *Academic Acceptance of American Sign Language*, special edition of *Sign Language Studies* 59 (1988).

[30]Jean Piaget, "Comments on Vygotsky's Critical Remarks," in L. S. Vygotsky, *Thought and Language*, trans. E. Hanfmann and G. Vakar (Cambridge, Mass.: MIT Press, 1962), p. xix. Vygotsky's original version was published in Russian in 1934.

[31]Vygotsky, *Thought and Language*, p. 97.

[32]Ibid., p. 102.

[33]Charles E. Spearman, " 'General Intelligence' Objectively Determined and Measured," *American Journal of Psychology* 15 (1904): 201-93.

[34]See John W. Oller Jr., "Language as Intelligence?" *Language Learning* 31 (1981): 465-92; John W. Oller Jr., "Some Working Ideas for Language Teachers," in *Methods That Work: A Smorgasbord of Ideas for Language Teachers*, ed. John W. Oller Jr. and Patricia Richard-Amato (Rowley, Mass.: Newbury House, 1983); and John W. Oller Jr., Steven Chesarek and J. Robert Scott, *Language and Bilingualism: More Tests of Tests* (Cranbury, N.J.: Associated University Presses, 1991).

[35]Vygotsky, *Thought and Language*, p. 153.

[36]Einstein, "Remarks on Russell's Theory," p. 287.

[37]*Collected Papers of C. S. Peirce*, 1:47.

[38]Einstein, "Physics and Reality," pp. 61-62.

[39]See especially Noam A. Chomsky, *Cartesian Linguistics: A Chapter in the History of Rationalist Thought* (New York: Harper & Row, 1966).

[40]Bertrand Russell, *Human Knowledge: Its Scope and Limits* (New York: Simon and Schuster, 1948).

[41]Benjamin Lee Whorf, *Language, Thought and Reality: Selected Writings* (Cambridge, Mass.: MIT Press, 1956).

[42]Noam A. Chomsky, *Rules and Representations* (New York: Columbia University Press, 1978), p. 139.

[43]See Massimo Piatelli-Palmarini, ed., *Language and Learning: The Debate Between Jean Piaget and Noam Chomsky* (Cambridge, Mass.: Harvard University Press, 1980).

[44]Chomsky, *Rules and Representations*, p. 38.

[45]Ibid., pp. 38-39.

[46]Noam A. Chomsky, *Language and Mind* (New York: Harcourt, 1972), p. 68.

[47]Noam A. Chomsky, *Language and Problems of Knowledge: The Managua Lectures* (Cambridge, Mass.: MIT Press, 1988).

[48]Francine Patterson and E. Linden, *The Education of Koko* (New York: Holt, 1981), p. 204.

[49]Chomsky, *Language and Problems*, p. 149.

[50]Noam A. Chomsky, *Reflections on Language* (New York: Pantheon, 1975), p. 27.

[51]Dwight L. Bolinger, *Aspects of Language* (New York: Harcourt Brace Jovanovich, 1975). The reference is to the same work as reprinted in *Language: Introductory Readings*, ed. Virginia P. Clark, Paul A. Eschholz and Alfred F. Rosa, 3rd ed. (New York: St. Martin's, 1981), p. 29.

[52]Chomsky, *Rules and Representations*, p. 239.

[53]Quoted in Duane M. Rumbaugh, *Language Learning by a Chimpanzee: The Lana Project* (New York: Academic, 1977), p. 29.

[54]Vygotsky, *Thought and Language*, p. 38.

[55]Claire Russell and W. M. S. Russell, "Language and Animals Signals" (1971) in *Language: Introductory Readings*, ed. Virginia P. Clark, Paul A. Eschholz and Alfred F. Rosa, 3rd ed. (New York: St. Martin's, 1981), p. 233.

[56]Rumbaugh, *Language Learning by a Chimpanzee*.

[57]Herbert S. Terrace, *Nim: A Chimpanzee Who Learned Sign Language* (New York: Knopf, 1981), pp. 247-48.

[58]Ibid., p. 248.

[59]Thomas A. Sebeok and Jean Umiker-Sebeok, eds., *Speaking of Apes: A Critical Anthology of Two-Way Communication with Man* (New York: Plenum, 1981), p. 272.

[60]Ann James Premack and David Premack, "Teaching Language to an Ape," in *Human Communication: Language and Its Psychobiological Bases*, ed. William S. Y. Wang (San Francisco: W. H. Freeman, 1982), p. 33.

[61]Ibid., p. 27.

Appendix/Ankerberg and Weldon

[1]W. R. Bird is a summa cum laude graduate of Vanderbilt University and the Yale Law School who argued the major case on origins before the U.S. Supreme Court in 1981 (*Aguillard et al. v. Edwards et al.*, civil action 81-4787, section H, U.S. District Court for the Eastern District of Louisiana, *Brief of the State in Opposition to ACLU Motion for Summary Judgment;* copyright 1984 by W. R. Bird). In *The Origin of Species Revisited*, 2nd ed., 2 vols. (New York: Philosophical Library, 1993), he documents how evolutionary scientists are increasingly questioning the validity of standard evolutionary theory. The book draws on the research he carried out for the 1981 Supreme Court case, summarized in a 625-page brief that has more than two thousand footnotes. Attorneys for the defendant gathered thousands of pages of depositions from scores of evolutionary scientists, across the spectrum of scientific disciplines. These scientists, along with hundreds of others cited in his book, collectively expressed reservations regarding most areas of evolutionary thinking.

[2]Michael Denton, *Evolution: A Theory in Crisis* (Bethesda, Md.: Adler and Adler, 1986), p. 77.

[3]Ibid., pp. 260-61.

[4]"Theoretical Blow to the Origin of Life," *New Scientist* 19 (February 1970): 344; cf. Bird, *Origin of Species Revisited*, 1:328-29.

[5]A. Henderson-Sellers, A. Benlow and A. Meadows, "The Early Atmosphere of the Terrestrial Planets," *Quarterly Journal of the Royal Astronomical Society* 21 (1980): 74, 81 (quoted in Bird, *Origin of Species Revisited*, 1:329).

[6]Carl Sagan, F. H. C. Crick and L. M. Mukhin, "Extraterrestrial Life," in *Communication with Extraterrestrial Intelligence (CETI)*, ed. Carl Sagan (Cambridge, Mass.: MIT Press, 1973), pp. 45-46; cf. Émile Borel, *Probabilities and Life* (New York: Dover, 1962), chaps. 1, 3.

[7]For example, cf. Denton, *Evolution*, pp. 308-44; Fred Hoyle and Chandra Wickramasinghe, "Where Microbes Boldly Went," *New Scientist* 13 (August 1991): 412-15.

In his survey of the evidence, R. L. Wysong observes that evolution itself requires faith, and he lists some of the problems: "Evolution requires plenty of faith: A faith in L-proteins that defy chance formation; a faith in the formation of DNA codes which, if generated spontaneously, would spell only pandemonium; a faith in a primitive environment that in reality would fiendishly devour any chemical precursors to life; a faith in experiments that prove nothing but the need for intelligence in the beginning; a faith in a primitive ocean that would not thicken but would only hopelessly dilute chemicals; a faith in natural laws including the laws of thermodynamics and biogenesis that actually deny the possibility for the spontaneous generation of life; a faith in future scientific revelations that when realized always seem to present more dilemmas . . . faith in probabilities that treasonously tell two stories— one denying evolution, the other confirming the creator; faith in transformations that remain fixed; faith in mutations and natural selection that add to a double negative for evolution; faith in fossils that embarrassingly show fixity through time, [and the] regular absence of transitional forms" (*The Creation-Evolution Controversy: Implications, Methodology and Surveys of Evidence* [East Lansing, Mich.: Inquiry, 1976], p. 139).

[8]Cf. James Coppedge, *Evolution—Possible or Impossible? Molecular Biology and the Laws of Chance in Nontechnical Language* (Grand Rapids, Mich.: Zondervan, 1973).

[9]Francis Crick, *Life Itself: Its Origin and Nature* (New York: Simon and Schuster, 1981), p. 88. Crick proceeds to state his belief that it was possible for evolution to occur, given the right conditions.

[10]"Hoyle on Evolution," *Nature* 294 (November 12, 1981): 105.

[11]Fred Hoyle and Chandra Wickramasinghe, *Evolution from Space* (London: J. M. Dent & Sons, 1981), p. 130.

[12]Ibid., pp. 96-97.

[13]Paul S. Moorehead and Martin M. Kaplan, eds., *Mathematical Challenges to the Neo-Darwinian Interpretation of Evolution*, Wistar Institute Symposium 5 (Philadelphia: Wistar Institute Press, 1967), p. xi.

[14]Murray Eden, "Inadequacies of Neo-Darwinian Evolution as a Scientific Theory," in *Mathematical Challenges to the Neo-Darwinian Interpretation*, p. 109.

[15]Marcel P. Schutzenberger, "Algorithms and the Neo-Darwinian Theory of Evolution," in *Mathematical Challenges to the Neo-Darwinian Interpretation*, p. 75; cf. Bird, *Origin of Species Revisited*, 1:79-80. For reasons that natural selection would not modify randomness and decrease these probabilities, see Bird, *Origin of Species Revisited*, 1:158-65.

[16]Charles Darwin, letter of November 29, 1859, quoted in David L. Hull, *Darwin and His Critics: The Reception of Darwin's Theory of Evolution by the Scientific Community* (Cambridge, Mass.: Harvard University Press, 1973), p. 9.

[17]Quoted in Bird, *Origin of Species Revisited*, 1:73.

[18]J. W. Burrow, introduction to Charles Darwin, *The Origin of Species by Means of Natural Selection* (Baltimore, Md.: Penguin, 1974), p. 217.

[19]From Francis Darwin, *The Life and Letters of Charles Darwin* (New York: Appleton, 1887), 2:296.

[20]Denton, *Evolution*, pp. 326-27.

[21]L. Harrison Matthews, introduction to Charles Darwin, *The Origin of Species by Means of Natural Selection* (London: J. M. Dent & Sons 1976), pp. x, xi.

[22]I. S. Shklovskii and Carl Sagan, *Intelligent Life in the Universe* (San Francisco: Holden-Day, 1966), p. 358.

[23]Frank B. Salisbury, "Natural Selection and the Complexity of the Gene," *Nature* 224 (October 25, 1969): 342-43.

[24]Personal communication from James Coppedge (director of the Center for Probability Research in Biology, Northridge, Calif.); cf. Coppedge, *Evolution—Possible or Impossible?*

[25]A. I. Oparin, *Life: Its Nature, Origin and Development* (Edinburgh: Oliver and Boyd, 1961), p. 31.

[26]Pierre-P. Grassé, *Evolution of Living Organisms* (New York: Academic, 1977), pp. 3-4, 204.

[27]T. H. Huxley, *Three Lectures on Evolution* (1882), quoted in Bird, *Origin of Species Revisited*, 1:59.

[28]Quoted in Stephen Jay Gould, *Wonderful Life: The Burgess Shale and the Nature of History* (New York: Norton, 1985), p. 3; emphasis added.

[29]Charles Darwin, *The Origin of Species by Means of Natural Selection*, ed. J. W. Burrow (Baltimore, Md.: Penguin, 1974), pp. 206, 292; cf. pp. 313-16.

[30]Quoted in Phillip E. Johnson, *Darwin on Trial*, 2nd ed. (Downers Grove, Ill.: Inter-Varsity Press, 1993), p. 46.

[31]Stephen Jay Gould, "The Return of Hopeful Monsters," *Natural History*, June/July 1977, pp. 22, 24.

[32]See Bird, *Origin of Species Revisited*, 1:48, 59, citing Steven M. Stanley, Stephen Jay Gould, Niles Eldredge, David B. Kitts and Ian Tattersall. See Steven M. Stanley, *Macroevolution: Pattern and Process* (San Francisco: W. H. Freeman, 1979), pp. 1, 4-9, 23, 74, 85, 88-98.

[33]David Raup, "Conflicts Between Darwin and Paleontology, *Field Museum of Natural History Bulletin*, January 1979, pp. 22, 25.

[34]George Gaylord Simpson, *The Major Features of Evolution* (New York: Columbia University Press, 1965), p. 360. Simpson went on to state that these discontinuities did not require a belief in special creation.

[35]Austin Clark, "Animal Evolution," *Triquarterly Review of Biology* 539; quoted in Bird, *Origin of Species Revisited*, 1:50.

[36]A. Thompson, *Biology, Zoology and Genetics: Evolution Model vs. Creation Model* (1983), quoted in Bird, *Origin of Species Revisited*, 1:49. Thompson does not regard the creation theory as scientific.

[37]Derek V. Ager, "The Nature of the Fossil Record," *Proceedings of the Geological Association* 87 (1976): 133.

[38]Simpson, *Major Features of Evolution*, p. 143; and George Gaylord Simpson, *Tempo and Mode in Evolution*, quoted in Bird, *Origin of Species Revisited*, 1:49, 57.

[39]E. J. H. Corner, "Evolution," in *Contemporary Botanical Thought*, ed. Anna M. MacLeod and L. S. Cobley (Chicago: Quadrangle Books, 1961), p. 97.

[40]See Bird, *Origin of Species Revisited*, 1:58-59.

[41]Quoted in James E. Adams, "Evolution: An Old Debate with a New Twist," *St. Louis Post-Dispatch*, May 17, 1981; cf. Bird, *Origin of Species Revisited*, 1:536.

[42]For examples, see Bird, *Origin of Species Revisited*, vol. 1; Bolton Davidheiser, *Evolution and Christian Faith* (Nutley, N.J.: Presbyterian and Reformed, 1969), pp. 302-9.

[43]Donald C. Johanson and Maitland A. Edey, *Lucy: The Beginnings of Humankind* (New York: Simon and Schuster, 1983), p. 363; cf. quote from Niles Eldredge and Ian Tattersall, *The Myths of Human Evolution* (1982) in Bird, *Origin of Species Revisited*, 1:55

[44]R. A. Stirton, *Time, Life and Man* (New York: John Wiley and Sons, 1957), p. 416.

[45]Paul B. Weiss, *The Science of Biology* (New York: McGraw-Hill, 1963), p. 732.

[46]Grassé, *Evolution of Living Organisms*, p. 30.

[47]E. White, "Presidential Address: A Little on Lungfishes," *Proceedings of the Linnean Society* 177 (1966): 8.

[48]Quoted in Bird, *Origin of Species Revisited*, 1:59.

[49]Robert Barnes, review of *Invertebrate Beginnings* in *Paleobiology* 6, no. 3 (1980): 365

[50]Earl L. Core et al., *General Biology,* 4th ed. (New York: John Wiley and Sons, 1961), p. 299.

[51]David Raup and Steven M. Stanley, *Principles of Paleontology* (San Francisco: W. H. Freeman, 1978), p. 372.

[52]Stanley, *Macroevolution,* p. 39; cf. pp. 47, 62.

[53]Stephen Jay Gould, "Evolution's Erratic Pace," *Natural History,* May 1977, p. 12.

[54]Ibid., p. 14.

[55]From Francis Darwin, *The Life and Letters of Charles Darwin* (1887; rpt. New York Johnson, 1969), 3:248.

[56]Darwin, *Origin of Species,* ed. Burrow, p. 292.

[57]Stanley, *Macroevolution,* p. 35.

[58]Stephen Jay Gould, *The Panda's Thumb: More Reflections on Natural History* (New York Norton, 1980), pp. 184-85. Also see note 28, above.

[59]Nils Heribert-Nilsson, *Synthetische Artbildung* (Lund, Sweden: CWK Glerups, 1953), p. 11.

[60]Ibid., pp. 1142-43. (This quote is from the hundred-page English summary, which appears in the German edition on pp. 1141-1246.)

[61]Ibid., pp. 1239-40.

[62]Steven M. Stanley, *The New Evolutionary Timetable: Fossils, Genes and the Origin of Species* (New York: Basic Books, 1981), p. xv.

[63]Ernst Mayr, *Populations, Species and Evolution* (Cambridge, Mass.: Harvard University Press, 1970), p. 253. Cf. Bird, *Origin of Species Revisited,* 1:168-77.

[64]Denton, *Evolution,* pp. 193-94. See also Stanley, *Macroevolution,* pp. 122-23.

[65]For example, see the quotations in Bird, *Origin of Species Revisited,* 1:155-290 (cf. 1:134-55).

[66]Cf. Coppedge, *Evolution—Possible or Impossible?* p. 113.

[67]H. S. Lipton, "A Physicist Looks at Evolution," *Physics Bulletin* 31 (May 1980): 138.

[68]John D. Barrow and Joseph Silk, "The Structure of the Early Universe," *Scientific American,* April 1980, p. 118.

[69]Robert Jastrow, *God and the Astronomers* (New York: Norton, 1978), pp. 113-14.

[70]From an interview by Bill Durbin, "A Scientist Caught Between Two Faiths," *Christianity Today,* August 6, 1982, p. 15.

[71]Jastrow, *God and the Astronomers,* pp. 15-16.

[72]See Bird, *Origin of Species Revisited,* 1:437-64.

[73]Fred Hoyle, *The Intelligent Universe: A New View of Creation and Evolution* (New York: Holt, Rinehart and Winston, 1983) p. 186.

[74]Johnson, *Darwin on Trial,* p. 3.

[75]Quoted in ibid., p. 10.

[76]Ibid., pp. 9-10.

[77]Ibid., p. 10.

[78]Dean H. Kenyon (Ph.D. in biophysics, Stanford) is professor of biology and coordinator of the general biology program at San Francisco State University. He is coauthor of *Biochemical Predestination,* a standard work on the origin of life, and a former evolutionist. He has extensively reviewed the scientific case for creation and accepts it as legitimate, as do hundreds of other established scientists (see H. M. Morris and G. E. Parker, *What Is Creation Science?* [San Francisco: Creation Life, 1982], pp. iii-v; cf. Bird, *Origin of Species Revisited,* 1:xv-xvi).

The religious and/or unscientific nature of evolutionary theory has been pointed out in the following articles by creationists in *The Creation Research Society Quarterly.* Arthur Jones, "The Nature of Evolutionary Thought," vol. 8, no. 1; William J. Ouweneel, "The Scientific Character of the Evolution Doctrine," vol. 8, no. 2; Gary L. Schoephlin, "On Assumptions and Their Relation to Science," vol. 9, no. 2; Raymond C. Telfar II, "Should Macroevolution Be Taught as Fact?" vol. 10, no. 1; John N. Moore, "Retrieval System Problems with Articles in *Evolution*," vol. 10, no. 2; Glenn W. Wolfram, "Evolution, Science and Religion," vol. 12, no. 2; John N. Moore, "An Estimate of the Current Status of Evolutionary Thinking," vol. 18, no. 4; Randall Hedtke, "The Divine Essence in Evolutionary Theorizing: An Analysis of the Rise and Fall of Evolutionary Natural Selection, Mutation and Punctuated Equilibria as Mechanisms of Megaevolution," vol. 21, no. 1; Ralph E. Ancil, "On the Importance of Philosophy in the Origins Debate," vol. 22, no. 3; Robert E. Kofahl, "Correctly Redefining Distorted Science: A Most Essential Task," vol. 23, no. 3; John N. Moore, "Properly Defining 'Evolution,' " vol. 23, no. 3; W. R. Bird, "Expostulated Evidence for Macroevolution and Darwinism: Darwinian Arguments and the Disintegrating Neo-Darwinian Synthesis, Part 2," vol. 25, no. 2.

[79]Karl Popper, *Unended Quest: An Intellectual Autobiography*, rev. ed. (London: Fontana/ Collins, 1976), pp. 168-69.

[80]See notes 7 and 78 above.

[81]Louis Bouroune, quoted in Wysong, *Creation-Evolution Controversy*, p. 418.

[82]G. Sermonti and R. Fondi, *Dopo Darwin: Critica all' Evoluzionismo* (1980), English translation quoted in Bird, *Origin of Species Revisited*, 1:21.

[83]Denton, *Evolution*, p. 351.

[84]W. R. Thompson, introduction to Charles Darwin, *The Origin of Species by Means of Natural Selection*, Everyman's Library 811 (New York: Dutton, 1967), pp. xx-xxiii.

[85]Ibid., p. xxii.

[86]Grasse, *Evolution of Living Organisms*, e.g., pp. 3, 6-7, 104-7, 210-11, 244-46.

[87]*Evolution* 29 (1975): 376.

[88]Grasse, *Evolution of Living Organisms*, p. 243.

[89]Søren Lovtrup, *Darwinism: The Refutation of a Myth* (New York: Routledge, Chapman & Hall, 1987), p. 422.

[90]Loren Eiseley, *The Immense Journey* (New York: Time, 1962), p. 144.

[91]Denton, *Evolution*, p. 357.

[92]William Provine, "Scientists, Face It! Science and Religion Are Incompatible," *The Scientist*, September 5, 1988, p. 10.

[93]Leslie Paul, *The Annihilation of Man* (New York: Harcourt Brace, 1945), p. 154.

[94]Hull, *Darwin and His Critics*, p. 7.

[95]See Mortimer Adler, *The Difference of Man and the Difference It Makes* (Bronx, N.Y.: Fordham University Press, 1993).

[96]Jacques Monod, *Chance and Necessity: An Essay on the Natural Philosophy of Modern Biology* (New York: Vintage, 1971), pp. 138-39. Grasse comments, "Directed by all-powerful selection, chance becomes a sort of providence, which, under the cover of atheism, is not named but which is secretly worshipped" (*Evolution of Living Organisms*, p. 107).

[97]Monod, *Chance and Necessity*, pp. 138-39.

[98]George Wald, "The Origin of Life," in *The Physics and Chemistry of Life*, ed. the editors of *Scientific American* (New York: Simon and Schuster, 1955), p. 9. Wald, of course, does believe in spontaneous generation and proceeds to argue that "time itself performs the miracles" necessary to evolution.

[99]Quoted in Norman L. Geisler, *Creator in the Classroom: "Scopes 2," the 1981 Arkansas Creation-Evolution Trial* (Mieford, Mich.: Mott Media, 1982), p. 151.

[100]Isaac Newton, *Mathematical Principles of Natural Philosophy*, Great Books of the

Western World 34 (Chicago: Encyclopaedia Britannica, 1952), p. 369.

[101]Jastrow, *God and the Astronomers*, pp. 115-16.

List of Contributors

John Ankerberg is a graduate of the University of Illinois (B.A.) and Trinity Evangelical Divinity School (M.A. in church history and the history of Christian thought; M.Div.), in each case with high academic honors. He also holds the D.Min. from Luther Rice Seminary in Atlanta, Georgia, and is host of the nationally seen, award-winning *The John Ankerberg Show*. Ankerberg speaks internationally and is the author or coauthor of over thirty books.

Walter L. Bradley received his B.S. degree in engineering science (physics) and his Ph.D. in materials science, both from the University of Texas at Austin. He is currently professor and head of the department of mechanical engineering, Texas A&M University. He has been the principal investigator on research grants and contracts adding up to more than $3 million for various government agencies such as NSF, NASA, the Air Force and the Department of Energy and such companies as DuPont, Dow Chemical, 3M, Exxon and Shell. He has published over one hundred refereed technical papers and coauthored one book, *The Mystery of Life's Origin: Reassessing Current Theories*. He has received five college-level research awards and one national award. He has been elected a fellow of the American Society of Materials and the American Scientific Affiliation.

William A. Dembski (Pascal Centre) holds a Ph.D. in mathematics from the University of Chicago and a Ph.D. in philosophy from the University of Illinois, Chicago. He has conducted doctoral and postdoctoral research at Cornell (math), MIT (math), the University of Chicago (math and physics), Princeton (computer science) and Northwestern (math and philosophy of science). He has been a National Science Foundation doctoral and postdoctoral fellow. Topics of his publications range from mathematics (e.g., *Journal of Theoretical Probability*) to philosophy (e.g., *Nous*) to theology (e.g. *Epiphany Journal*). He has made fundamental contributions to the foundations of probability theory (for example, exploring randomness and small probabilities). The mathematical and philosophical foundations of design/teleology as well as their implications for natural theology constitute his primary research interest.

Stephen C. Meyer took his B.S. in physics and geology from Whitworth College in Spokane, Washington, and his M.Phil. and Ph.D. from Cambridge University in the history and philosophy of science. His Cambridge dissertation was entitled "Of Clues and Causes: A Methodological Interpretation of Origin of Life Studies." Meyer is currently a professor of philosophy at Whitworth College. His area of specialty is the structure of evolutionary arguments and the methodological character of the historical sciences. He has published technical articles as well as popular ones in the *Los Angeles Times* and the *Wall Street Journal.* Meyer is a fellow of the Pascal Centre and is currently working on a book that will offer a rigorous reformulation of the design argument for a scientific audience.

J. P. Moreland is professor of philosophy at Talbot School of Theology, Biola University, and serves as director of Talbot's M.A. program in philosophy and ethics. He also serves as a bioethicist for PersonaCare Nursing Homes, headquartered in Baltimore, Maryland. He has a B.S. in physical chemistry from the University of Missouri, a Th.M. in theology from Dallas Seminary, an M.A. in philosophy from the University of California at Riverside and a Ph.D. in philosophy from the University of Southern California. He is the author or coauthor of nine books, including *Scaling the Secular City* (Baker), *Christianity and the Nature of Science* (Baker), *Christian Perspectives on Being Human* (Baker), *Does God Exist?* (with Kai Nielsen, Prometheus Books) and *The Life and Death Debate* (with Norman Geisler, Praeger Books). He has published a number of articles in such journals as *Philosophy and Phenomenological Research, The Australasian Journal of Philosophy, The American Philosophical Quarterly, Perspectives on Science and Christian Faith* and *Grazer Philosophische Studien.*

John W. Oller Jr. was an NDEA Fellow from 1966 to 1969, and he earned an M.A. and a Ph.D. in general linguistics from the University of Rochester in New York. In the summer of 1969 he accepted an assistant professorship at UCLA, where he was promoted to tenure and an associate professorship in 1971. In the fall of 1972 he became chair of the department of linguistics at the University of New Mexico. From 1971 to 1976 he served on the Examiner's Committee for the Test of English as a Foreign Language, produced by Educational Testing Service in Princeton. He is author or coauthor of twelve professional books and over 170 articles in linguistics and allied areas. In 1984 he won the Mildenberger Medal, an international prize offered annually by the Modern Language Association. Invited lecture tours have taken him to Europe, the Middle East, Japan, Taiwan, Thailand, Singapore, Mexico, Canada and throughout the United States. He is best known for his technical studies on the relation between language and intelligence; his latest books include *Language and Experience: Classic Pragmatism, Language and Bilingualism: More Tests of Tests, Methods That Work: Ideas for Language Teachers* and *Cloze and Coherence.* At present Oller is full professor of linguistics and educational foundations at the University of New Mexico. He is a charter member of the editorial board of the journal *Language Testing* and serves as consulting editor for several other professional journals in his field.

John Omdahl received his B.S. in chemistry from Colorado State and his Ph.D. in physiology and biophysics from the University of Kentucky. He was awarded an NIH postdoctoral fellowship to study biochemistry at the University of New Mexico School of Medicine in 1972 and is currently a full professor there. He has been a visiting research scientist at Los Alamos National Laboratory, a visiting associate professor in biochemistry at Southwestern Medical School, Dallas, and the University of Adelaide, South Australia. He is a member of the American Society for Biochemistry and Molecular Biology and has research and scholarly interests that include biochemica¹ anal ysis of the abiogenesis theory of evolution and the cellular expression and biochemical characterization of cytochrome P450 enzymes.

Hugh Ross took his B.S. in physics from the University of British Columbia and his M.S. and Ph.D. in astronomy from the University of Toronto. He served as a postdoctoral fellow at the California Institute of Technology for five years, working in radio astronomy. He has lectured at universities throughout the United States. In 1986 he founded Reasons to Believe, headquartered in Pasadena, California, where he continues to do his research, writing and speaking. He has authored a number of journal articles as well as the bestselling book *The Fingerprint of God* and the recently released *The Cosmos and the Creator* (NavPress).

Charles Thaxton received his B.S. in chemistry from Texas Tech and his Ph.D. in chemistry from Iowa State University. For two years he was a postdoctoral fellow at Harvard, where he studied the history and philosophy of science. He had a postdoctoral appointment for three years in the molecular biology laboratory at Brandeis University. He has served as director of curriculum for the Foundation for Thought and Ethics, where he was academic editor for the high-school biology book *Of Pandas and People*. He is current present of Konos Connection and lives in the Czech Republic, where he writes and speaks on Christianity and science. He is a member of the American Chemical Society, the American Association for the Advancement of Science and the International Society for the Study of the Origin of Life (ISSOL); he has been elected a fellow of the American Institute of Chemists and the American Scientific Affiliation. He coauthored *The Mystery of Life's Origin: Reassessing Current Theories* and is coauthor, with Nancy Pearcey, of *The Soul of Science* (Crossway, 1994).

John Weldon is the senior researcher for the Ankerberg Theological Research Institute. He holds five graduate degrees in the field of religion, comparative religion and biblical studies, and he is the author or coauthor of over fifty books on a wide range of topics addressing the rationality of the Christian faith and the interface between Christianity and contemporary issues.

Kurt P. Wise holds a B.A. in geophysical science from the University of Chicago and an M.A. and Ph.D. in paleontology from Harvard University. His Harvard dissertation focused on the stratigraphic distribution of fossils. Wise currently teaches science at Bryan College in Tennessee, where he also serves as the director of origins research. He is working on a number of articles and projects that are in various stages of publication.